The True Wealth of Nations

The True Wealth of Nations

Catholic Social Thought and Economic Life

EDITED BY DANIEL K. FINN

OXFORD
UNIVERSITY PRESS
2010

OXFORD
UNIVERSITY PRESS

Oxford University Press, Inc., publishes works that further
Oxford University's objective of excellence
in research, scholarship, and education.

Oxford   New York
Auckland   Cape Town   Dar es Salaam   Hong Kong   Karachi
Kuala Lumpur   Madrid   Melbourne   Mexico City   Nairobi
New Delhi   Shanghai   Taipei   Toronto

With offices in
Argentina   Austria   Brazil   Chile   Czech Republic   France   Greece
Guatemala   Hungary   Italy   Japan   Poland   Portugal   Singapore
South Korea   Switzerland   Thailand   Turkey   Ukraine   Vietnam

Published by Oxford University Press, Inc.
198 Madison Avenue, New York, New York 10016

www.oup.com

Oxford is a registered trademark of Oxford University Press

Library of Congress Cataloging-in-Publication Data
The true wealth of nations : catholic social thought and economic life/
edited by Daniel K. Finn.
    p. cm.
Includes bibliographical references and index.
ISBN 978-0-19-973981-3; 978-0-19-973982-0 (pbk.)
1. Economics—Religious aspects—Catholic Church.   2. Christian
sociology—Catholic Church   I. Finn, Daniel K., 1947–
BX1795.E27T78 2010
261.8'5—dc22   2009045414

9 8 7 6 5 4 3 2 1

Printed in the United States of America
on acid-free paper

Preface

*The True Wealth of Nations: The Ethics and
Economics of Prosperity*

The detailed demands of a modern economy and the transcendental
concerns of people of faith can no longer be regarded as separate
realities. Economic development presents ethical challenges that
must be addressed. But further than that, religious faith asks: what is
the ultimate purpose of life and how does economic activity best
serve that purpose? What can faith say to economics, about the
nature of creation, about the value of work, about the purposes of
prosperity and the creation of wealth? To say any of those things
intelligibly, those speaking for faith must have an understanding of
the world of economics and be willing to engage in profound
dialogue with the relevant disciplines.

For a long time thinkers in the mainstream Christian traditions
have viewed economic activity, especially that left to private initiative,
with suspicion or even antagonism. Since the Industrial Revolution,
the economic system known as capitalism has been blamed for the
poverty of the poor and for injustices committed toward them. It was
not seen by most Christian theologians as an effective means for
dealing with poverty.

A significant shift in that approach was signaled within the
Catholic tradition by several encyclicals of the late Pope John Paul II,
notably *Centesimus Annus* published in 1991. It argued that the
creation of wealth in a market-driven economic system could, in the
right conditions, promote the common good. It offered general
criteria drawn from Catholic social thought for judging whether

it actually did so. To be morally acceptable, a social and economic system had to place human solidarity at its heart, recognizing that despite difference of role, human beings could never stop being mutually responsible and interdependent. The ordering of society had to respect the principle of subsidiarity; and society's priority had to be the protection of the most vulnerable. Economic processes were not to be regarded as autonomous, but because they were human actions with human consequences, they were subject to these moral criteria. Working on this basis, however, market-driven economic growth could offer the whole of humanity the prospect of shared prosperity and an opportunity, unique in human history, to redress poverty in its many forms.

Prosperity thus understood means access not merely to material goods but to all the conditions necessary for true human prospering; and poverty means their lack. The statement *Economic Justice for All,* issued by the U.S. Catholic bishops in 1986, was a harbinger of *Centesimus Annus* in its more nuanced appraisal of economic systems, evaluating them by their results. It declared:

> We judge any economic system by what it does for and to people and
> by how it permits all to participate in it. The economy should serve
> people, not the other way around.... We have many partial ways to
> measure and debate the health of our economy: Gross National
> Product, per capita income, stock market prices, and so forth. The
> Christian vision of economic life looks beyond them all and asks:
> Does economic life enhance or threaten our life together as a
> community?

One way of defining this new and richer meaning of prosperity is as the very reverse of how Thomas Hobbes described "life in an unregulated state of nature"—as "solitary, poor, nasty, brutish, and short." Prosperity is the opposite of all of those, not just the second of them. It includes participation in community, sufficiency of wealth, pleasure and happiness, civilization and culture, and longevity including good health. The creation of wealth is only part of prosperity, and academic disciplines that focus narrowly on wealth do not grasp the larger aims that economic actors truly seek.

In most countries of the West this fundamental development in Catholic social thought under Pope John Paul II toward a more positive appraisal of a market economy was neglected. One of the most positive responses came from the Catholic bishops of England and Wales, who in 1996 published a document, *The Common Good and the Catholic Churches' Social Teaching,* which drew on the 1986 American bishops' statement and explored the implications of a change in the theological evaluation of wealth creation. In 2005, as a direct sequel, the major ecumenical body Churches Together in Britain and Ireland published *Prosperity with a Purpose,* which adopted the approach described by Pope John Paul II and sanctioned it as a correct application of Christian social ethics in the name of all the major Christian denominations that CTBI represented. The document stated its conclusion thus:

> Under the right conditions, economic growth can serve God's purposes. The conditions are: that humanity is seen as one human family, with a universal bond of solidarity; that wealth creation and the pursuit of social justice are inextricably linked; that market forces encourage economic growth but are regulated in the interests of the community; that the environment is safeguarded by substantial efforts to mitigate the harm caused by pollution; that advancing prosperity leaves no-one behind, not children, retired people, those who care for families, disabled people, nor any other section that is vulnerable or liable to neglect; that globally, priority is given to those whose economies are burdened by unmanageable international debt or are victims of unfair international trading conditions; and that the structures of civil society are renewed so that local communities can shape their own future.

The current project, under the auspices of the Institute for Advanced Catholic Studies (IACS), does not seek to cover again the ground of the British studies mentioned above, nor of other studies produced elsewhere that have reached similar conclusions, but accepts them as its own starting point. However, two areas in particular call for intensive further research and investigation.

First, what is the relationship between this more favorable Christian analysis of market-driven wealth creation and modern secular economic theory? Is its purpose merely to restrain economic development in the name of the common good? Can it also demonstrate that the conditions most favorable to that development are consistent with that teaching's insights into human dignity, the role of work, and the right ordering of society? Can Christian ethics point economists in the right direction—right, from the point of view of ethics, but also from the point of view of economic progress and efficiency?

This is a new area for Christian ethics to explore. More and more emerging national economies are using competitive markets as their dynamic force but find themselves apparently faced with an invidious choice between morality and efficiency, ethics versus economics. This study raises the explosive question: is this choice necessary, or can these apparent opposites be reconciled? Is the neglect of human, social, and ethical issues in the operation of economic systems actually wasteful, and therefore inefficient? Would an alignment of ethics and economics make not just for better ethics but for better economics—efficiency with equity, even efficiency because of equity? Few things would more dramatically lead to a better world.

In the secular sphere, a number of economists and social philosophers since the 1940s have described both from theory and from statistical evidence some of the social, cultural, and ethical conditions that foster economic development. Without them or the Church noticing it, many of their conclusions have parallels within the social teachings of the Church.

What would these two bodies of thought have to say to each once they were in dialogue, and how would each need to be adjusted in order to accommodate the other? Can they develop a common conceptual language? This study will require intense engagement among Christian social ethicists and economists and political philosophers of all persuasions as they engage in a mutual critique. Many secular economists would welcome an opportunity to address ethical issues that are normally seen as outside their remit. Christian social ethicists, while having no economic blueprint of their own, would welcome the opportunity to examine which economic systems and policies have most closely fulfilled their ethical criteria. Policy makers of all sorts should find the fruits of this dialogue of great relevance to their own concerns.

The IACS is therefore proposing a dialogue that should include a series of studies into the relationship between the principles of Christian social ethics, as outlined in the tradition of Catholic social thought, and the conditions necessary for a vibrant and creative economy. The basic proposition to be evaluated would be that the economic and cultural criteria identified in the tradition of Catholic social thought provide an effective path to sustainable prosperity for all.

There is no claim here that these criteria are unique to Catholic social thought, nor that only people of faith could understand or implement them. But the advantage of attending to this fundamental proposition is that it will call for theologians and economists to move toward one another in real dialogue. This approach will require theologians to specify more concretely the economic and cultural conditions that Catholic social thought calls for and will require economists to broaden their focus from GDP as the measure of economic welfare to full human prosperity, broadly defined as in this document, as the goal for which people are striving in economic life. Ethical factors are at work in defining both the means employed in economic processes in accordance with Catholic social thought and the end toward which the means are directed. The fundamental proposition is nonetheless an empirical statement rather than a tautology, as it asserts that the means will generate the ends.

Catholic social thought is the collective intellectual enterprise of Catholic theologians and others, past and present, engaged in the development of social ethics within the context of official Catholic social teaching. One of its concerns is to explore the insights and limitations of mainstream economic theory, which emphasize what is measurable and which presuppose a deterministic account of human economic behavior governed by self-interest and rational choice. The evaluation of the proposition above would include traditional empirical econometric analysis but would not be limited to it, leaving room for judgments based on broader ethical criteria and other approaches to the science of economic measurement. These broader ethical and econometric considerations would seek to give a true account of the role of women in economic life and in the conservation of natural resources.

The development of new ethical and economic insights under conditions of dialogue would have profound implications for the relief of poverty and would provide those trying to counter underdevelopment by economic growth with clear and practical principles and guidelines. It should be possible to begin to identify what conditions need to exist to maximize wealth creation and the resulting economic, social, and ethical benefits and what conditions are most inimical to those goals. This raises profound questions about "what it means to be human," including a positive anthropology of work (such as that set forward by Pope John Paul II in 1981 in *Laborem Exercens*) and an analysis of human rights and dignity. The hypothesis offered by faith is that conditions likely to be the most propitious for human thriving are also most advantageous for economic development, overall and in the long term—that economic growth is not necessarily at odds with human prospering in the broadest sense, but that in the right conditions, they reinforce each other.

Second, the IACS wishes to go beyond the theoretical approach, which needs to be balanced by a practical recognition of specific and often local obstacles to human prosperity, and facilitate the search for concrete solutions. Many of the factors conducive or hostile to economic progress are likely to be cultural, legal, and historical—or even religious—as well as economic and ethical.

A preliminary question is: why should the IACS and this project concentrate on any of these topics? Might one not say, "It's already been done"? There is available, in every case, at least some relevant academic research and empirical evidence. Yet the research is piecemeal and the evidence widely scattered. What is lacking is the "architecture" necessary for accumulating the research and the evidence, distinguishing points of weakness, commissioning work as needed, and providing the framework for a synthesis that is intellectually coherent and pragmatically grounded. Objective certainty is beyond human reach, but such an architecture, developed within the Institute, can sustain in the larger world a well-founded assurance about the conditions for authentic prosperity that engenders the will to take action.

In all these respects, human economic activity works best when working with the grain of human nature and not against it. There is a lot of research required in order to identify what that means in particular circumstances. But following the lead of *Prosperity with a Purpose*, Christians may bless economically productive activities on the grounds that human creativity is nothing less than a continuation of and participation in God's own creativity. One key purpose of this project is to promote that insight at all levels, wherever it is applicable.

This interaction, investigation, and research will result in a flow of articles, learned papers, and books and will provide the themes for many scholarly conferences, both virtual and real. Under the general heading, new topics would be identified as in need of further exploration, so that one body of interdisciplinary research would generate another, in what amounts to an ongoing global conversation. The project would also entail the maintenance of a database of contributions that could be accessed all over the world through the Internet, by which means others engaged in similar studies all over the world could be kept in touch. This specific aspect is being done in conjunction with the Centesimus Annus Foundation.

The approach proposed by the IACS involves several stages. The steering committee for the True Wealth of Nations project organized an advisory meeting of academics in Chicago in the spring of 2007 to discuss the validity of the approach and held a major conference in Los Angeles in the summer of 2008. The IACS believes that it will be able to fund this first step through its own resources and several current donors. Approaches would be made to several foundations requesting grants for the funding of specific research projects and for the infrastructure necessary, including IT, for the distribution of the scholarly output, disseminated as broadly as possible.

Although most of the people involved in this initiative are likely, initially at least, to be based in the United States of America, it is the intention to draw contributions from as widely as possible and in particular to develop a firm base in Europe and elsewhere. The sponsoring body, the IACS, is an academically independent Catholic lay institution located at the University of Southern California.

Contents

Contributors

Albino Barrera, O.P., is a native of the Philippines. He is professor of economics and humanities (theology) at Providence College. His publications include *Globalization and Economic Ethics: Distributive Justice in the Knowledge Economy*, *Economic Compulsion and Christian Ethics*, *God and the Evil of Scarcity: Moral Foundations of Economic Agency*, and *Modern Catholic Social Documents and Political Economy*. In addition to his teaching responsibilities, he helps out on the weekends at local parishes in the diocese of Providence and occasionally preaches out-of-town parish retreats and missions. He has a licentiate in theology (STL) from the Dominican House of Studies in Washington D.C., and a PhD in economics from Yale University.

Simona Beretta is Professor of International Economic Policies at the Catholic University of the Sacred Heart, Milan, and Program Coordinator at ASERI, Postgraduate School of Economics and International Relations. She is a graduate in economics from the Catholic University of Milan and earned the MSc in economics at the London School of Economics and Political Science. She is a member of the editorial board of the *Rivista Internazionale di Scienze Sociali*. Her research includes issues of international monetary theory and policy, financial globalization, the political economy of international relations, European integration, and development.

Maylin Biggadike is an economist, theologian, and priest in the Episcopal Church. She received her doctorate in Christian ethics from Union Theological Seminary in New York. Her dissertation is entitled "A Christian Social Ethical Response to Poverty: Economic Development through the Eyes of Poor Women in Developing Countries." Prior to receiving her doctorate, she was granted the Master of Arts in theology from General Theological Seminary, the Master of Arts in economics from Boston College, and the Bachelor of Arts in economics from the University of Massachusetts. She presently serves as priest associate at St. Elizabeth's Church in Ridgewood, New Jersey, and is a delegate of the Episcopal Church to the United Nations Commission on the Status of Women. Her work involves preparing Anglican delegates from all over the world on the economic aspects and faith basis of the UN theme for 2008, "Financing for Gender Equality and the Empowerment of Women." Her current research project investigates the economic and moral dimensions of the sex trafficking of young girls.

John Carr is Executive Director of the Department of Justice, Peace and Human Development at the United States Conference of Catholic Bishops, coordinating the bishops' policy development and advocacy efforts on a wide range of national and global issues, including poverty, hunger, health care, human rights, religious freedom, debt, development, trade, and war and peace. He has represented the U.S. Bishops at the Vatican and in the Middle East, Central America, Southern Africa, Southeast Asia, and Russia. He has served as Executive Director of the White House Conference on Family and as Director of the National Committee for Full Employment. He currently serves on the board of Bread for the World, the National Religious Partnership for the Environment, the Catholic Health Association, and the Law School of the University of St. Thomas. He is a graduate of St. John Vianney Seminary and the University of St. Thomas in Minnesota.

John A. Coleman, S.J., is associate pastor of St. Ignatius Church in San Francisco and was, prior to his retirement, Charles Casassa Professor of Social Values at Loyola Marymount University. He has published widely on issues related to the sociology of religion, Catholic social thought, social theory, and theories of justice. His publications include *Globalization and Catholic Social Thought* and *Christian Political Ethics*. He has been a research fellow at The Woodstock Center, The Woodrow Wilson Center for International Scholars, the University of Chicago's Institute for Advanced Studies in Religion, and elsewhere. He has taught at the University of Louvain and the University of Santa Clara. He received the BA from St. Louis University, the MA, Licentiate in Philosophy, from St. Louis University, the STM, Licentiate in Theology from Santa Clara University, and the PhD in sociology from the University of California, Berkeley.

Daniel K. Finn teaches at St. John's University in Collegeville, Minnesota, where he is Professor of Theology and holds the William E. and Virginia Clemens Chair in Economics and the Liberal Arts. He is a past president of the Society of Christian Ethics, the Catholic Theological Society of America, and the Association for Social Economics. He has provided leadership on afford- able housing in Central Minnesota and is chair of the steering committee of a project to engage the Catholic Church in Latin America to work with civil society organizations to confront government corruption. His most recent books are *Just Trading: On the Ethics and Economics of International Trade* and *The Moral Ecology of Markets: Assessing Claims about Markets and Justice.* He earned the BS from St. John Fisher College and the MA and PhD from the University of Chicago. He is a member of the steering committee of the True Wealth of Nations research project.

Jon P. Gunnemann is Professor of Social Ethics, Emeritus, at the Candler School of Theology and the Graduate Division of Religion at Emory University. He had previous appointments at The Pennsylvania State University and Yale University, and has been a visiting professor at Uppsala University (Sweden). He taught business ethics at the School of Organization and Management at Yale and at the Goizueta School of Business at Emory. He was a founding fac- ulty member of the Emory Center for Ethics and of the Law and Religion Program at the Emory School of Law and continues to serve on the advisory boards of each. He has taught and written extensively in the areas of Christian ethics and the economy, contemporary theories of justice, and other political and social issues. His publications include *The Moral Meaning of Revolution* and (as coauthor with John Simon and Charles Powers) *The Ethical Investor: Universities and Corporate Responsibility.* He earned the AB from Harvard University, the BD from United Theological Seminary, and the MA and PhD from Yale University.

Mary L. Hirschfeld earned her PhD in economics from Harvard University in 1989, specializing in the fields of macroeconomics and economic history. She was a professor of economics at Occidental College from 1988 to 2003, where she explored interests in feminist economics and heterodox approaches to economic theory. Her work has been published in the *Review of Economics and Statistics,* the *Journal of Economic Education, History of Political Economy,* and the *Journal of the Society of Christian Ethics*. After an unexpected conversion to Catholicism, she left her position to study theology at Notre Dame, earning her MTS in 2005. She is currently a PhD candidate in the field of moral theology at Notre Dame.

Paulinus I. Odozor, C.S.Sp., a native of Nigeria, is Associate Professor of Christian Ethics at the University of Notre Dame. His research and writing include foundational issues in moral theology, contextual theological issues and inculturation, theology and society, African Christian theology, and the theology of marriage. His articles have appeared in journals in Africa, Asia, Europe, and North America. His major publications include: *Moral Theology in an Age of Renewal: A Study of the Catholic Tradition since Vatican II*; *Richard A. McCormick and the Renewal of Moral Theology*; and two edited volumes, *Sexuality, Marriage and Family: Readings in the Catholic Tradition* and *Africa: Towards Priorities of Mission*. He is currently working on a book that will explore the question of morality and tradition from an African Christian theological perspective. He has held numerous academic, administrative, and pastoral positions in Nigeria and Canada. He is currently president of the Governing Council of Spiritan International School of Theology in Enugu, Nigeria. He earned the ThD at the University of Toronto and the STD at Regis College, Toronto.

Vincent D. Rougeau is an associate professor at the Notre Dame University Law School. His current teaching interests focus on contract and real estate law, as well as law and religion, specializing in Catholic social thought. His most recent research has explored the philosophical and theological underpinnings of Catholic social teaching as they relate to various areas of American law. In particular, he has explored how key assumptions underlying Catholic thinking diverge from many of the ideas animating American law and policy in areas such as poverty relief, immigration, and redress for racial discrimination. His book *Christians in the American Empire: Faith and Citizenship in the New World Order* (Oxford University Press) examines these issues in more detail. He spent 2008–2009 as a Senior Fellow of the Martin Marty Institute at the University of Chicago, and currently serves as Senior Fellow of the Contextual Theology Centre in London. He received his AB from Brown University and his JD from Harvard.

Andrew M. Yuengert is a Professor of Economics at Seaver College, Pepperdine University. He has taught economics at Pepperdine for fourteen years, prior to which he taught at Bates College in Maine and was a research economist at the Federal Reserve Bank of New York. He has made research contributions in several fields: economic philosophy, Catholic social teaching, the empirical study of religion, labor economics, and finance. He is a former president of the Association of Christian Economists and currently serves as editor of its journal, *Faith and Economics*. Recent books include The *Boundaries of Technique: Ordering Positive and Normative Concerns in Economic Research* and *Inhabiting the Land: The Case for the Right to Migrate*. He holds a BA in Economics from the University of Virginia and a PhD in economics from Yale University.

Stefano Zamagni is Professor of Economics at the University of Bologna as well as Senior Adjunct Professor of International Economics and Vice Director of the Bologna Center of the Johns Hopkins University. He is a member of the Academy of Sciences, Bologna, Modena, and Milan, and a member of the several editorial boards: the Journal of International and Comparative Economics, the Brock Review, Economics and Philosophy, International Review of Economics, and the Journal of Economic Methodology. He has published widely on issues related to capital theory, theory of consumer behavior, social choice theory, economic epistemology, and ethics and economics. His publications include *An Outline of the History of Economic Thought* (Oxford University Press) with E. Screpanti, *Economia, democrazia, istituzioni in una società in trasformazione, Verso una nuova teoria economica della cooperazione* with E. Mazzoli, *Civil Economy* (Oxford University Press) with L. Bruni, *L'economia del bene comune, Cooperative Enterprise: Facing the Challenge of Globalization* with V. Zamagni, and *Avarizia*. He did his studies in economics at the University of Milan and Oxford University.

Vera Negri Zamagni is Professor of Economic History at the University of Bologna and visiting professor at the Bologna Center of the Johns Hopkins University. She has taught at the Universities of Trieste, Florence, and Cassino. Her research and publications address issues related to Italian and European economic development, regional economic integration, business history, the role of government in the economy, welfare problems, and the history of the cooperative movement. She has been the founder and coeditor of *European Review of Economic History*; she is a member of the editorial board of *Rivista di storia economica* and *Revista de historia economica*. Her books include *Dalla periferia al centro: la seconda rinascita economica dell'Italia: 1861–1990* (English ed. *Economic History of Italy 1860–1990*, Oxford), *Dalla rivoluzione industriale all'integrazione europea* (Spanish ed. *Historia Economica de la Europa Contemporanea*), and *La cooperazione di consumo in Italia. Centocinquant'anni della Coop consumatori: dal primo spaccio a leader della moderna distribuzione* with P. Battilani e A. Casali. A graduate of the Catholic University of Milan, she earned the D.Phil. at Oxford University.

The True Wealth of Nations

Introduction

Developing an Architecture for Relating Catholic Social Thought and Economic Life

The international financial crisis that broke into the headlines in late 2008 demonstrated a number of weaknesses in the world economic system, but among the most important conclusions that most people have drawn from these events is that we suffer from a lack of moral values in the marketplace. This moral vacuum is best exemplified in the personal malfeasance of individuals such as Bernard Madoff and represented by the quest for ever-higher incomes by the largely unnamed hedge fund traders who took greater and greater risks in the derivatives market. Ordinary citizens around the world have come to understand that both our economic system and the prevailing philosophy behind it need to incorporate stronger moral commitments to justice, fair play, and concern for the systemic effects of innumerable individual choices.

Just this sort of concern for the common good has been characteristic of Roman Catholic social thought and its engagement with economic life. Rooted in a long history from the ancient Hebrew Scriptures, through the New Testament, the writings of the fathers of the early church, the economic analysis of medieval theologians, right up to the modern social teaching of the Catholic Church, this tradition has argued both for the well-being of each individual person and for a comprehensive understanding of social life that sees all individuals as intimately related, even in large social, economic, and political institutions.

Most of what has been written about the implications of Christian theology for economic life has been deeply shaped by one of two conflicting prior commitments: to "free markets" or to a liberationist critique of free markets. In both cases, authors have too frequently chosen to employ only those portions of Catholic social thought that support the arguments they want to make about a proper structure for the economy.

It was in this intellectual context that the Institute for Advanced Catholic Studies began its "True Wealth of Nations" research project. This effort is dedicated to discerning the implications of Catholic social thought for economic life today, attempting to minimize the effects of preconceived ideological commitments. That is, the task at hand is to delve into what the Christian tradition, and in particular Catholic social thought, has had to say about economic life and to discern its most important implications for the context of the twenty-first century. In order to do so, the project brings together a diverse group of economists and other social scientists along with theologians and others, the majority of whom have professional experience and academic credentials in more than one discipline, allowing them to move back and forth across disciplinary boundaries that have in the past often stunted efforts at interdisciplinary dialogue.

This volume is the result of an international conference sponsored by the Institute for Advanced Catholic Studies, held at the University of Southern California in June 2008. The conference focused on a fundamental assertion of the True Wealth of Nations research project, chosen both for its clarity and for its capacity to elicit lively conversation from economists, theologians, and many other scholars. This basic proposition is that the economic and cultural criteria identified in the tradition of Catholic social thought provide an effective path to sustainable prosperity for all.

There is no claim here that the criteria identified in this tradition are somehow unique or that only people of faith could understand or implement them. However, the proposition does make an important claim that much of the scholarship on Catholic social thought has not. That is, it makes a causal assertion that if we were to implement the standards identified in this tradition, we would be on a path toward a goal of prosperity for everyone, both in this generation and in the future.

The advantage of attending to such an empirical assertion is that it better allows both theologians and economists to engage in dialogue about the substance of Catholic social thought. This body of literature is not simply a set of moral teachings, something that economists are professionally unequipped to deal with. Nor is it simply a technical economic assertion of cause and effect, since both the criteria the proposition recommends and the character of prosperity it aims for cannot be defined in purely technical economic terms but require the kind of moral judgments that the Christian tradition can provide.

Having annually attended the professional meetings in both economics and Christian ethics in the United States over the past thirty years—and having been president of national professional societies in both fields—I am vividly aware of the difficulties in structuring conversation across boundaries between social scientists and humanists. Disciplinary mind-sets are often so fundamentally different and personal histories often so isolated within a single discipline that many well-meaning attempts at dialogue in the past have brought about confusion and frustration rather than real insight that can be passed on to others. The hope behind the True Wealth of Nations research project is that bringing together social scientists and humanists who are willing and able to stretch to understand one another's points of view promises a fruitful result that can indeed be helpful to others. Thus, beginning with this basic proposition allows us to understand better where we have come from, both within economics and within theology, and offers us a way forward in dialogue together.

Where We Have Been Economically

Fifty years ago, this basic proposition might have been scorned by the vast majority of economists and other experts involved in the work of economic development (the subdiscipline within economics dedicated to understanding how national economics can best be structured to encourage economic prosperity). This was true at international institutions such as the World Bank and the International Monetary Fund and at research universities across the industrialized world.

Today, however, after decades of unfulfilled expectations about economic growth in many of the poorest nations of the world, the intellectual climate has been shifting, even prior to the recent financial crisis. The heads of the World Bank and the IMF, along with their staff economists, have met with bishops and lay leaders in the Church over such issues as third-world debt. The World Bank has worked with the Archbishop of Canterbury to sponsor international gatherings of religious leaders to discuss development issues. Within economics, scores of secular economists have done theoretical and empirical work on previously "noneconomic" issues such as cooperation, trust, moral conviction, and the effects of religious faith on economic growth. Nobel laureate Amartya Sen has, for example, proposed to understand economic development as most fundamentally a development of freedom and of those capacities in people necessary for supporting self and family. Kenneth Arrow, another Nobel Prize–winning economist, has argued for the importance of trust and other moral relations for economic growth. In sum, we see today a greater openness in discussions of economic science and policy to the importance of moral, cultural, and religious factors in economic growth. And as already noted, the international financial crisis has led many economic experts to understand now what they may had missed before: that moral conviction in economic life is just as important as defining market structures in the best way possible.

Where We Have Been Theologically

Not only are we in a new situation regarding economic thought, the same is true regarding theological reflection. The three millennia of the Judeo-Christian tradition are rich with commentaries and analyses of economic life, a vast storehouse of wisdom that remains authoritative. But because ours is a living tradition, teachings sometimes change when new problems arise. When traditional moral commitments conflict, more fundamental insights from earlier eras win out over less fundamental ones. This is why Christian teaching on such issues as usury and slavery has changed. It has now become clear that traditional attitudes toward three aspects of economic life are no longer sustainable: suspicion of the role of incentives in the creation of wealth, doubts about the ethos of trade and business, and disdain for the role of self-interest in economic life.

First, for many centuries, Christian thinkers—as well as their secular counterparts—did little reflection on the creation of wealth. As St. Augustine put it in addressing his wealthy listeners, "You found your wealth here." This ancient view is understandable in its context, since in the premodern world, the wealthy were almost exclusively those who owned large tracts of land, typically used for agriculture and mining. Since the land and minerals had been created by God, and since nearly all the labor was done by others, little attention was paid to the question of incentives for the creation of wealth. The wealthy rarely seemed to work hard. Similarly, little attention was paid to the possible disincentives that can be created in the lives of the poor if they become dependent on the charity of the wealthy instead of moving to sustain themselves. The widespread concern for the origin of wealth and the role of incentives in economic life arose only in the last three centuries.

Second, Christian thinkers—and most secular scholars as well—were deeply suspicious of the "businessmen" of their day, merchants: people whose work involved buying goods in one place to sell them in another, to make money so they can buy more goods to sell. As Thomas Aquinas described it, "trading, considered in itself, has a certain debasement attached to it." Many in business seem to succumb to avarice, which has led thinkers from Plato and Aristotle onward to advise against taking up the trade. Economic activity was regarded as a "zero sum" game: with only a finite pool of wealth available, those who possessed it were regarded as doing so at the expense of others. Much more recently, economic thinkers such as Adam Smith taught that there are discernable reasons why some nations are wealthier than others—reasons that rest on the daily economic productivity of ordinary people—and that wealth is not fixed. If the economy is properly structured, the economic pie can grow and all can benefit without injustice. Not everyone has in fact benefited and injustice still occurs in too many places, but the possibility is there and this is a critically important shift in our moral context.

The third traditional presumption that cannot be sustained is the time-honored Christian view of self-interest. Related to the suspicion of merchants just noted, any exertion of self-interest was often interpreted to be morally wrong, with real altruism in service to God and neighbor the only morally respectable stance. Yet from the time of Bernard Mandeville three centuries ago, the primary moral defense of economic freedom has been that the self-interested choices made by ordinary people in the market can conduce to the economic well-being of the community. This claim is frequently overstated by advocates of free markets (who have too glibly presumed that self-interest, unguided by law or custom, will automatically generate prosperity for all), but Christians have come to realize that a blanket condemnation of self-interest is not ethically warranted. The exercise of initiative, self-reliance, and a concern to provide economic security and even some improvement in economic well-being for self and family is a natural and moral dimension of life. As Bernard Lonergan taught concerning the vitality of the market system, what is needed is not a dam to block the stream, but control of the riverbed through which the stream must flow.

Where We Are Now: The Work to Be Done

A significant shift in the approach of the Catholic Church began in the teaching of Pope John Paul II, especially with his encyclical *Centesimus Annus*. It argued that the creation of wealth in a market-driven economic system could, in the right conditions, promote the common good. Business firms could be structured to serve this greater good, with profit playing a constructive role. And the entrepreneur, who was earlier seen as the epitome of the greedy businessman, was cast in a better light by John Paul: "It is precisely the ability to foresee both the needs of others and the combinations of productive factors most adapted to satisfying those needs that constitutes another important source of wealth in modern society."[1] None of this should be interpreted as altering the ultimate goal of humanity—unending life in God—but it does recognize the importance of economic life, the substratum for all of human life on this earth.

It is interesting to note that prior to writing *Centesimus Annus*, John Paul invited to his personal residence a group of internationally distinguished economists, only a few of whom were Catholic, to give him advice on what they thought he should stress in his upcoming letter. In a similar spirit of cooperation, the True Wealth of Nations project undertakes to sustain ongoing conversations between social science and theology in better discerning the concrete implications of Catholic social thought for economic life today.

Catholics claim no monopoly on insight here. In fact, the natural law tradition understands that insights into the prudential conduct of life are available to all reasonable persons, not just to people of faith. Thus one would expect to find large areas of overlap of Catholic social thought with other religious traditions and secular science.

Thus today, Christian intellectuals have at their disposal a more subtle and realistic approach to economic life—at the same time that economic specialists exhibit more openness to the importance of culture, morality, and religion than at any other time in the last century.

An Overview of the Volume

Because all the essays in this volume take our basic proposition about Catholic social thought and economic life as their starting point, the first two chapters of the book take a careful look at what that basic proposition means. The Preface contains the basic rationale for the broader True Wealth of Nations research project, and the claim is that we would be on the path to sustainable prosperity for all if Catholic social thought were implemented, and so there are two questions to begin with. First, what is it that Catholic social thought recommends for the economy? Second, how would we know if we had achieved sustainable prosperity for all? (That is, what are the descriptors of the economic goal we have set for ourselves?)

Albino Barrera, O.P. takes on the first of these two tasks. He helpfully employs the Scriptural principle of *sedeq* (biblical justice) and modern Catholic social thought to identify the recommendations for contemporary life that the tradition of Catholic social thought proposes. A wide range of evidence will be needed to test our basic proposition, including everything from statistical data to "softer" but more robust evidence from various sciences and the humanities, to a general awareness of the operations of daily economic life. However because this process should in principle be able to be approached from a statistical point of view, Barrera's chapter also proposes for each concrete recommendation one or more empirically specifiable proxies that could be part of an econometric test of the proposition. Barrera understands that an econometric test would include some distortion of morally complex realities, but some attempt in this direction could be worthwhile.

Andrew Yuengert takes on the second question entailed in the investigation of our fundamental proposition, as he employs modern Catholic social teaching to specify the goal toward which Catholic social thought directs human life. The ultimate goal, of course, is life with God, but moving toward that, Catholic social thought also requires a number of economic and cultural goals that would constitute this tradition's understanding of prosperity. Here, too, although a wide range of evidence will be needed to test the fundamental proposition, Yuengert also proposes for each concrete goal one or more empirically specifiable proxies that could be part of an econometric test of the proposition.

The second section of this volume comprises a number of historical views of issues related to the fundamental interaction of faith and economic life.

Stefano Zamagni takes a long historical look at the development of the institutions of capitalism, beginning in the Middle Ages. Importantly, he identifies the creation of fundamental economic institutions such as banks and corporations with the work of Franciscan friars in the thirteenth, fourteenth, and fifteenth centuries. Zamagni argues that the "civil economy" of those days kept in check the worst abuses that would otherwise arise and that the task for us today is to find ways to reinstate a version of a civil economy in the twenty-first century.

Vera Negri Zamagni looks at a more recent historical period and identifies the impact of Catholic social thought in Europe over the last 150 years. Focusing on the development of Christian democracy and the growth of labor unions in Europe, Zamagni identifies the concrete historical impact that Catholics and Catholic social thought have had on both political life and economic structures in Europe.

Vincent D. Rougeau and Daniel K. Finn each present an essay that looks at legal contracts, focusing particularly on the character of contracts that Catholic social thought would understand as unjust. Rougeau gives a brief legal history of contract law in the United States and identifies multiple ways in which it includes a bias toward market decisions and often excludes fundamental concerns of justice. Finn provides a moral evaluation of unjust contracts, identifying those criteria in the history of Christian views of economic life that have been employed to judge a contract unjust and therefore in need of alteration or abrogation.

Mary L. Hirschfeld takes on the task of identifying the change in religious context since the time of Thomas Aquinas. Much of Catholic social thought is rooted in Thomistic natural law analysis, and this inheritance provides great richness to the Catholic view of economic life. However, the world in which Thomas lived was a thoroughly religious one, not characterized by the secularization that has occurred in our world today. Thus, Hirschfeld identifies strains and difficulties in any "translation" of ideas from Aquinas to our own context, something critically important for Catholics today who hope to persuade a secular world of a better way to organize the economy.

The third section of this volume brings together a number of economic issues related to our fundamental hypothesis and examines them in light of the Christian faith.

John A. Coleman investigates the notion of "social capital," beginning with its development among sociologists and its eventual employment by economists and others. Coleman urges a conversation between Catholic social thought and theorists of social capital. On the one hand, the sociological notion of social capital includes elements (such as the claim that social capital is essential for wealth creation) that would be helpful to make more visible within Catholic social thought and, on the other hand, Catholic social thought includes insight into communal life and the common good that could enrich the notions of social capital as employed within social science.

Simona Berreta has taken on the task of examining the economic situation of women and what that would imply for any movement to a more just economic system. Depending on economic research from a number of public sources, Beretta outlines the difficult situation of so many women around the globe in their attempts to engage in economic life to provide for their families. Berreta argues that Catholic social thought has much to contribute in devising better economic policies to improve the status of women worldwide.

Paulinus I. Odozor, C.S.Sp. brings our attention to the questions of economic life and poverty in Africa. He looks carefully at patterns of life and economic interaction in Africa and argues that Catholic social teaching has important contributions to make (such as its deep concern for each individual and a commitment to the common good that transcends traditional tribal loyalties) in assisting Africans to bring about a sustainable economic prosperity.

Jon P. Gunnemann presents an analysis of capital as Spirit, an engaging and creative investigation that invites us to rethink the connection between economic life and Christian faith. Gunnemann argues that a proper understanding of capital will require important changes both in the accountability of corporations and in our daily economic responsibilities as individuals.

Maylin Biggadike provides an ecofeminist analysis of economic life. She employs the work of the Brazilian theologian Ivone Gebara to broaden the usual concerns of economic science to include both a feminist and an ecological critique of existing patterns of analysis and practice. An Episcopal priest herself, Biggadike provides a Christian critique of some of the most fundamental presumptions that economists and others often have about daily economic life.

The final section of the book is provided by John Carr, who addresses a number of the difficulties that must be faced in moving from the scholarly analysis of the other essays in the book toward concrete action in public policy. Carr's long history as head of peace and of justice efforts of the U.S. Conference of Catholic Bishops provides an abundance of experience for analyzing the difficulties and hopes for the transition from thought to action.

As editor of this volume I am aware of debts to a number of important contributors to this work beyond the authors of the essays. Most important here is Paul Caron, who has codirected the True Wealth research project with me and has been a constant source of creative insight and dogged perseverance in both the creation of the project—the conference from which these papers arose—and of the long-term research project itself. I am also grateful for the work of two other members of the steering committee of the True Wealth project in this era: Clifford Longley and Father James Heft, S.M. Their careful thinking, clear planning, and insightful analysis of the process have greatly enriched this book. I'm also grateful to Sheila Garrison for the wonderful logistical support she gave to make the conference possible. To Judy Shank, who has faithfully attended to draft after draft of the essays in this volume, to Tylor Klein and James Foley, for research assistance, to Donald Wigal for creating the index (and Catherine O'Reilly for her assistance there), and to the editors at Oxford University Press, J. D. Daniels, Cynthia Read, Gwen Colvin, Charlotte Steinhardt, Justin Tackett, and others, I am deeply in debt. We are also indebted to the intellectual, moral, and financial support for this project provided by Ernesto Rossi di Montelera and Anthony Brenninkmeyer.

In sum, this volume represents an effort to integrate Christian faith and social scientific analysis. Preliminary reactions to the True Wealth of Nations project have been quite encouraging. Parts of the research to date have been presented at the Association of Christian Economics in January 2009, where reactions were universally positive and where several Protestant economists reported finding the heavily Catholic analysis very valuable. A similar reaction came from World Bank staff at a workshop sponsored at Georgetown University by the Berkley Center for Religion, Peace, and World Affairs and the Woodstock Theological Center.

The participants in this project remain convinced that the prosperity of all peoples and sustainability of our planet depend on a more careful and creative interplay of faith and wealth creation. We have made a beginning, but much work remains, challenging, hopeful, and exciting work.

NOTES

1. John Paul II, *Centesimus Annus*, para. 32.

I

What Does Catholic Social Thought Recommend for the Economy?

The Economic Common Good as a Path to True Prosperity

Albino Barrera, O.P.

It is remarkable that during the long history of Catholic social thought (CST) no one seems to have attempted to list all its recommendations for how economic life should be conducted. Because the True Wealth of Nations project sets out to investigate the claim that implementing Catholic social thought would put us on a path to sustainable prosperity for all, this chapter attempts to set out what it is that Catholic social thought recommends for the economy, and the next chapter, by Andrew Yuengert, sets out to describe how we would know whether we had achieved "sustainable prosperity for all." This chapter will begin with the notion of the economic common good as the way into understanding what CST recommends, will review the scriptural foundations for the Catholic view of economic life, and will then move to more concrete identification of those recommendations.

Economic Common Good as Point of Entry

Although urgently needed today, identifying exactly what Catholic social thought recommends for the economy is not a straightforward exercise because of several methodological problems. First, the tradition is extremely broad and ranges from official Church documents to scholarly monographs to commentaries geared for a general audience.[1] Second, the tradition does not have a single overarching conceptual framework.[2] Third, in those infrequent instances in which modern Catholic social documents advance concrete proposals for the economy, there is the problem of context dependence. Fourth, related to this problem, it is difficult to deal with the shifts and the clashing emphases within this tradition.[3] Fifth, not all concrete or general proposals carry equal weight.[4] Finally, modern Catholic social teachings tend to avoid making concrete recommendations for the economy and stay at a high level of generality.[5] Because they are directed to people in widely differing circumstances across the globe, these social documents offer prudential guidelines in the form of principles.

> In the face of such widely varying situations it is difficult for us to
> utter a unified message and to put forward a solution which has
> universal validity. Such is not our ambition, nor is it our mission. It
> is up to the Christian communities to analyze with objectivity the
> situation which is proper to their own country, to shed on it the light
> of the Gospel's unalterable words and to draw principles of reflection,
> norms of judgment and directives for action from the social teaching
> of the Church.[6]

Yet in spite of the wide diversity of views within this tradition, there is consensus on the central importance of promoting the common good. The common good is acknowledged to be the overarching concern within which competing social claims must be adjudicated, including the inevitable clashes and hard trade-offs that communities will have to make in working toward the four goods that Yuengert has argued are constitutive of "sustainable prosperity for all" in his essay in this volume. The centrality of the common good in CST cannot be overemphasized.[7] Thus, in any summary of what CST recommends for the economy, we should expect a wide array of social principles stemming from the notion of the common good.

Unfortunately, there are significant limitations in the tradition's explanation of the common good as it currently stands. These deficiencies come to the fore whenever we apply CST to concrete issues, as in the case of the economy in the True Wealth project. The most recent official synthesis of CST defined the common good as "the sum total of social conditions which allow people, either as groups or as individuals, to reach their fulfillment more fully and more easily."[8] It was the same definition adopted by Vatican Council II in *Gaudium et Spes*[9] and by the *Catechism*.[10] This definition, first proposed by John

XXIII in *Mater et Magistra* (#65),[11] has yet to be expanded despite major developments in theological social ethics in the last half century.

The shortcomings of this definition are apparent: it is abstract and open to ambiguity in its implementation. In particular, what are these social conditions? How does one define human fulfillment, and what does it mean in practice on the ground? Papal teaching is silent on these questions, thereby making it much more difficult to come to an agreement on the specifics of what CST actually recommends for social life and the economy.

Of course, there is also an advantage, to such an open-ended specification of the common good, because locking in this central concept to any particular view of social life goes against the very nature of CST—an extremely rich, living tradition that continues to grow and develop over time. Nonetheless, we cannot avoid a more precise understanding of the common good if we are to apply it in practice. Fortunately, we can strike a balance between greater specificity and an open-ended architecture of analysis. The tradition itself provides enough insights and teachings that permit a more nuanced and workable understanding of the common good without having to subscribe exclusively to any single definition of the common good. A conceptual middle ground is possible.

The Minimum Conditions of the Economic Common Good

Because of the immense richness, complexity, and dynamism of the human community, it is daunting if not impossible to list all the characteristics of the common good. However, we can make real progress on this effort if we focus our discourse on the minimum conditions that must be present for human flourishing. Both secular and theological literatures analyze many of the characteristics of the common good, and specifying these minimum conditions for the existence of the common good allows us to say something concrete and substantive on what CST recommends for the economy.

Given the focus of the True Wealth project and the limitations of space here, we will further limit the scope of this inquiry to the common good in the economic realm. We must recognize, of course, that this limitation means we are taking only a first step. After all, the common good encompasses all spheres of social life, not just the economic; it must balance claims of both current and future generations; and it deals with a wide range of goods, not simply economic ones. However, we can also note that many of the economic common good's minimum conditions we identify in this study will most likely apply just as well to the common good in noneconomic spheres.

Scriptural Foundations for the Economic Common Good

It is clear that "*the* Common Good," used in its proper sense, is God, our Final End. However, the ordinary use of this term is analogical and pertains to the functional integrity of the person and community. Because modern Catholic social documents give only a general statement of the common good, it is helpful to look to earlier periods in this tradition of social thought for important insights into the common good. Here Sacred Scripture is extremely helpful, since compared to patristic and scholastic social thought it provides a more sustained, focused, and comprehensive treatment of economic life. In addition, its economic norms and insights are more easily grasped, as they are embedded in vivid narratives in history.

In Scripture, we discover some of the minimum conditions that must be satisfied in any economy that aims to promote the common good. After all, it is the narrative of peoples of faith struggling mightily to create the social conditions essential for building a nation (in the case of Israel) and a community of love (in the case of the early church). Not surprisingly, Scripture's economic precepts are about the promotion of a corporate good. We can learn much from the Hebrews and the early church, as we in our own turn seek to advance our common good.

Biblical *sedeq* is an essential backdrop for the common good. In modern terms, *sedeq* is translated as "righteousness" or, more commonly, "justice." Besides providing scriptural warrants for the common good, *sedeq* highlights the fundamentally relational nature of the common good. Scholars agree that *sedeq* is a central theme of biblical theology.[12] God's activity and attributes are its prime analog. Note the following four dimensions of divine righteousness:[13]

- *Sedeq* as an innate quality of God (e.g., YHWH's Covenant fidelity, loving-kindness, and justice).
- *Sedeq* as the due order in God's plans (e.g., creation; the Law).
- *Sedeq* as God's saving act (e.g., Exodus liberation; postexilic restoration; Calvary).
- *Sedeq* as an empowering divine gift to humans to continue the work of God and as a divine invitation for people to be righteous themselves (e.g., Covenant election; Kingdom discipleship).

All four dimensions of divine righteousness are descriptive of elements of the common good. All four point to the natural and moral order in human life and existence.

As we see in the accounts of creation in Genesis, the Lord of creation acts with purpose. The creative activity of God is not arbitrary or whimsical but follows a divine plan, one that is all encompassing, for nothing lies outside the purview of divine sovereignty.[14] Moreover, God, as the Lord of creation, sustains creatures in continued existence and provides for them by working through creatures themselves. For example, God could have provided directly for humanity's needs without involvement of any creature. Instead, God chose to provide for humanity's needs through the gifts of the earth and through mutual solicitude of persons in community. In the same way, the Lord of creation could have directly cared for the earth. Instead, God entrusted the earth and its creatures to humanity's stewardship.

Furthermore, the Lord of creation is also the Lord of history. God is not going to stand idly by while evil wreaks havoc on the order of divine creation. God confronts that evil, holds back the ensuing chaos, and maintains that order. We have repeatedly seen this in the account of the flood in Genesis, in the Exodus liberation, in the release from Babylonian captivity and the resulting postexilic restoration, and most of all, in the incarnation, death, and resurrection of Jesus Christ. God has repeatedly broken into human history to restore and sustain the order of the divine plan.

But there is much more to divine righteousness. The Lord of history has gone even further by eliciting human participation both in confronting the evil and the chaos that continually mar this divine order and in restoring and maintaining such order. Thus, it was not sufficient for YHWH simply to liberate the Hebrews from enslavement. YHWH put them in a land flowing with milk and honey, and as the Chosen People of God, they were to be instrumental in bringing all the nations to the mountain of the Lord in the New Jerusalem (Isa. 2:2-4). They were to be a nation different from all the other nations in the way they cared for one another and in the way they lived their religion in their economics and politics.[15] And so it was with the Christian disciples. They were to partake in building the kingdom of God inaugurated by Jesus in the manner they loved one another both in word and in deed (Luke 10:25-37). Indeed, Scripture's concrete economic moral norms were intended to bring about social conditions consistent with the divine order of creation.

In both the Old and the New Testament, we see the promise of a material sufficiency that is contingent on people's fidelity to their divine election. In the case of the nation Israel, we repeatedly see that prosperity and tenure in the Promised Land were dependent on how well they lived up to the terms of the Covenant. There was supposed to be no poor among them, if only they lived up to YHWH's plans (Deut. 15:4–8). In Matthew (6:25-34) and Luke (12:22–31), we have the promise that there is no need for economic anxiety as long as we genuinely pursue the kingdom of God. From these, we get a glimpse of what human fulfillment is about: it includes the divine gift of material sufficiency for all, a gift that can only be actualized with moral economic behavior.[16] Human fulfillment has both economic and moral dimensions.

Biblical *sedeq* affirms the existence of a natural and moral order that serves as the larger conceptual backdrop of the common good. This natural and moral order provides the terrain on which the common good is actualized. Thus, at a minimum, we can ascribe the following characteristics to the common good:

- The common good is merely part of and serves a divinely created order that is specific in its natural and moral requirements. Thus, the common good is subject to objective standards.[17]
- The pursuit of the common good is an avenue by which humans partake of divine activity in sustaining this order of creation. Hence, far from being an imposition, work for the common good is an unmerited divine gift of human participation in divine governance and in God's righteousness and holiness.
- Just like *sedeq*, the common good is about having everything in its proper place, with all the requirements of relationships duly fulfilled.[18] Simona Beretta, in her essay in this volume, employs a wonderful phrase borrowed from von Baltazar to describe this characteristic when she says that Catholic social thought has "a symphonic nature."

In sum, the biblical theme of *sedeq* (righteousness or justice) provides an excellent scriptural foundation for the notion of the common good.

A Terrain for Sustainable Prosperity for All

Fundamental Commitments in an Enduring Prosperity

In his essay in this volume, Andrew Yuengert argues that sustainable prosperity for all entails the simultaneous attainment of "goods of a personal character, goods of personal initiative, social goods, and material goods." This is not an easy task. However, Sacred Scripture provides eye-opening narratives of the essential commitments and the spirit with which we ought to pursue these requisite goods of enduring prosperity.

Scripture provides several vivid glimpses of various dimensions of the economic common good: Micah's (4:1–5) eschatological description of every man sitting under his own vine and his own fig tree, the promised abundance and tenure on the land flowing with milk and honey in the prophetic literature and the law codes, the Deuteronomist's (15:4–8) claim that there would be no poor among the Hebrews if only they would follow the Law, and the anxiety-free discipleship of Matthew (6:25–34) and Luke (12:22–31). Note the following similarities in these biblical images.

First, the road to true prosperity necessarily includes material sufficiency, at the very least. People should be able to satisfy their basic needs without having to exert themselves in unduly long and hard work. They enjoy peace of mind in knowing that they have ready access to the material requirements of continued existence and secure growth. Norbert Lohfink[19] is emphatic that we should not romanticize material poverty, because this is not God's intention for us. God's gift is one of plenitude, not a hard life of precarious subsistence. God is keenly interested in our material well-being. The Genesis accounts of abundance in creation, the dominion mandate, and the Hebrews' description of the Promised Land as one flowing with milk and honey all corroborate Lohfink's claim, that whether as the Lord of creation or the Lord of history, God is always provident in looking after human needs. The material abundance that contributes to the economic common good is consistent with the goodness God saw after each act of creation (Gen. 1).

Second, moral agency plays a pivotal role in bringing about this genuine prosperity. Human agency cuts both ways. It can ruin the economic order, debase human life, and inflict much harm; or it can ennoble life and be instrumental in God's unfolding providence. In contrast to the erroneous view that economic life is determined by immutable "mechanical" laws of nature,[20] CST contends that the gift of material sufficiency in God's order of creation is contingent on human choices. A virtuous, morally upright life is essential to seeking true prosperity.

Third, material sufficiency is not the ultimate end. It is simply a means to the more important goal of resting in the Lord. Plus, it has been said that the suspension of work and rest in the Lord on the Sabbath day is proleptic, a foretaste of the greater goal that we await.[21] Our earthly state and accomplishments, while important, are means to the greater transcendent end we have in God. Paul VI[22] was emphatic that "development" is neither principally nor primarily an economic phenomenon but moral in nature. This is likewise true for economic development because its end lies not in providing people with a much larger choice set but in affording everyone the socioeconomic conditions for a flourishing life.

Fourth, true prosperity must include everyone. A community that is on the road to achieving its common good is necessarily imbued with the highest of human values of love, truth, freedom, and justice. It is a community of caring, compassion, and sharing.

In sum, true prosperity requires a ceaseless effort to promote the economic common good. It has both material and spiritual requirements and outcomes. It involves the actualization of integral human development, that is, the development of the whole person (body, mind, and spirit), with no one excluded. It is a divine gift whose fruits are contingent on the proper exercise of moral agency. The economic common good has an eschatological dimension in the foretaste of that which is yet to come as we rest in God with peace, joy, and security, even in the here and now.

Constitutive Means to Enduring Prosperity

Figure I.I presents a schematic overview of what the economic common good requires in practice. A fundamental commitment to work for the human fulfillment of all is a necessary condition. Such human flourishing necessarily reveals the beauty and the nature of human dignity. The principle of integral human development defines such human fulfillment more concretely. It is to flourish in God's gifts to humanity, as seen in the Genesis accounts of creation (Gen. I–2): the gift of the self, the gift of each other, and the gift of the earth. We cannot claim to be working toward the common good if we do not discharge our responsibilities in light of these three gifts.[23] At a minimum, human fulfillment is about living up to the full potential afforded by each of these three gifts; to flourish in human life is to blossom in all three gifts.

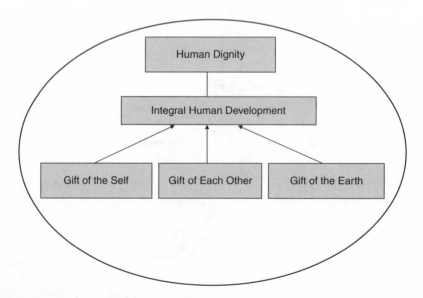

FIGURE I.I. Elements of the Economic Common Good

It is also essential to view human life and experience through the prism of gifts, a theme that Simona Beretta emphasizes in her essay in this volume. First, the language of gift reminds us of the unearned nature of all that we have. We have nothing to boast about that is genuinely ours. Human accomplishments are not and can never be in competition with God's. Second, an appreciation for life as a gift leads us to use the language of obligations, not simply of rights. Our duties are more basic than our claims. Such a focus flows directly from an understanding that everything we have is a trust received from God. Moreover, we are privileged to be instrumental in making these gifts bloom in their fullness as part of the order of creation.

People reach the heights of human fulfillment to the degree that they bring out the best in these gifts of the self, each other, and the earth. Such accomplishment leads us to a better understanding of the profound possibilities latent in human dignity. More important for this paper's thesis, bringing out the fullness of these gifts, to the extent that is humanly possible, is a necessary condition for sustainable prosperity for all.

Thus, in practice, attaining true wealth requires a fundamental commitment to the following essential intermediate means:

- Pursuit of an overarching common good
- Integral human development for self
- Integral human development for others
- Care of the earth

Pursuit of an *overarching common good*: This involves working to attain biblical *sedeq*, with everything in its proper place and the demands of all relationships satisfied accordingly. This entails a union of hearts and minds and an overall level of satisfaction among members of the community. People have a shared vision of the good or at least a shared conception of what justice is.[24] In concrete terms, this entails promoting harmony within community, with strife and violence kept to a minimum. Stefano Zamagni's notion of the civil economy, articulated in this volume, is an example of this. Such harmony manifests itself in the various elements of Yuengert's four constitutive goods and in Finn's *The Moral Ecology of Markets* (p. 45), that is, in the provision of essential goods and services; in the vibrancy of civil society; and in the probity and integrity of individuals, groups, and governments.

Integral human development for the self: Development is human and integral only to the degree that people flourish across the entire range of their personal gifts—body, mind, and spirit.[25] This requires maintaining balance in both one's temporal and spiritual activities. The Hebrew regimen of work, the study of

Scripture, and worship and rest in the Lord are fine examples of such a path toward human fulfillment. In concrete terms, this means that people live in the heights of the human values of truth, freedom, justice, love, and friendship. They enjoy culture and a vibrant spiritual life, avoiding the pitfalls of consumerism and materialism.

Integral human development for others: In its social dimension, the principle of integral human development calls for the authentic personal development of everyone, no one excluded.[26] In concrete terms, this means that socioeconomic life should bring about mutual advantage for all, by how well integral human development is attained by members of the community. Every person is treated as an equal, deserving of respect as a person. The integral development of the self and others requires enormous effort and constant renewal given their incessant and often sacrificial demands.

Care for the earth: It is impossible for humans, whether as individuals or a community, to be truly fulfilled unless they have discharged their obligations implicit in the dominion mandate of Genesis 1. The Hebrews appreciated the centrality of this dominion mandate to human life. Work, collaborative sharing, and the care of the earth are not bothersome impositions or peripheral concerns; like the creating of wealth, they are at the heart of what it is to be human and are constitutive of the order of divine creation. In concrete terms, the functional integrity of the ecology must be maintained. At a minimum this requires balance between the demands of economic development and the preservation of the ecology and balance in satisfying the needs of current versus future generations. Both of these require economic and technical efficiency in the judicious use of the earth's gifts.

Social Principles

Catholic social thought proposes a set of social principles that identifies the means to attaining enduring prosperity. Given the need to keep this exposition short and in order to give readers an overview of the entire framework, figure 1.2 shows the modern social principles in relation to one another and to the economic common good. These principles reflect many of the socioeconomic norms of Sacred Scripture.

GIFT OF THE SELF. The principle of subsidiarity states that people should not depend on others or higher bodies for what they can and should be doing for themselves, for others, and for the community.[27] We find this exemplified well in Scripture in the manner by which neither the Hebrews nor the early church expected the state to provide direct relief to those in need. They themselves

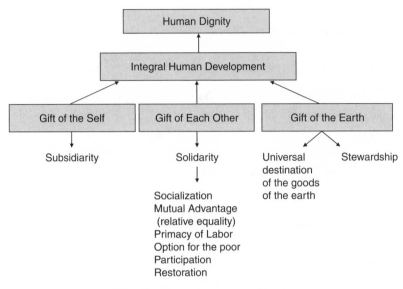

FIGURE I.2. Framework for the Economic Common Good

provided such assistance out of their own substance. Moreover, they were not supposed to be a burden on the community but were obligated to provide for themselves, to the extent possible, through gainful work (2 Thess. 3:6–15). This is also evident in the great care with which the nation Israel ensured that every family had a plot of land for their livelihood. Thus, recall the land division in Jonah, and the laws on land redemption and land return.[28] The same sentiment is operative in Paul's work ethic and teachings (1 Cor. 9; 1 Thess. 2:6–10).

In concrete terms for the economy today, a thriving private sector is a necessary condition for the satisfaction of the principle of subsidiarity. People take responsibility for their own integral human development. Moreover, they attend to social ills themselves, to the extent they have the necessary resources, without having to rely on or wait for governmental action. Thus, it is not surprising that Yuengert identifies goods of personal initiative as constitutive of enduring prosperity for all.

GIFT OF EACH OTHER. Solidarity is an active and genuine concern for the welfare of others because we see them as brothers and sisters, children of God like us.[29] In practical terms for the modern marketplace, this translates to empathy and supererogatory acts for others. There is a vibrant civic sprit, with people and groups contributing their share in building and sustaining the community. The principle of solidarity finds further concrete expression in the following allied principles:

- Socialization
- Participation, relative equality, and mutual advantage
- Primacy of labor
- Preferential option for the poor
- Restoration

Socialization is the obligation incumbent on those who possess the resources to be proactive in intervening and providing assistance to those who are no longer able to function for their own good or for that of the community. This is the spirit that undergirded many of the Scripture's precepts calling on the Hebrews to assist the widows, orphans, aliens, and those who had fallen on hard times. In our economy today, socialization is best seen in the extent to which personal, governmental, and NGO assistance is readily available for those who are in distress.

The principle of participation calls for mutual advantage for all in our shared socioeconomic life. Every person is given the opportunity and the means to partake in the community's socioeconomic life. Again, we find this illustrated in the land distribution after the conquest and in the land-return provision of the Jubilee Law. Besides the theological import of land as the tangible sign of the Hebrews' Covenant election as the Chosen People of God, land was also the principal source of livelihood and the means by which households maintained their independence and participated as equals in the community. Thus, land return and land redemption kept inequalities within limits. In practical terms today, such a principle of participation and mutual advantage means nonexclusion and the meaningful incorporation of all in socioeconomic life (e.g., affirmative action programs). Excessive inequalities are prima facie evidence of a failure to live up to the requirements of the principle of participation and mutual advantage.

The primacy of labor principle requires treating workers with respect, as human beings and not as things or mere factors of production. The dignity and obligation of work are affirmed in the Genesis dominion mandate, in the Jubilee return of land, and in the Pauline work ethic. In contemporary terms, this principle calls on the community to provide living wages, meaningful employment opportunities, and humane working conditions. It also calls on individuals to have a Pauline work ethic in assiduously contributing their share to the common productive effort and in embracing work as a divine gift, a privilege, rather than an imposition or toil. This principle also affirms the right of workers to form unions and engage in responsible collective action.

The preferential option for the poor calls people to look after the vulnerable and the marginalized with even greater care in light of their more pressing needs. This is a principle that can be traced directly back to Scripture. Far from

taking advantage of the vulnerable and the defenseless, there is a duty to provide actively for their needs. A practical application of this principle today would
be along the lines of a progressive incidence in the distribution of the benefits
and burdens of fiscal policy. Taxes are levied according to people's ability to
pay, and benefits are dispensed according to people's needs. Special attention
is devoted to setting up a social safety net that attends to the needs of the
poor.

According to the principle of restoration, the community has an obligation to attend to the adverse unintended consequences of market operations.[30]
Debt forgiveness, slave manumission, land return, redemption of a kin from
bondage, and interest-free loans were means by which the Hebrews sought to
restore those who had fallen on hard times as independent land-holding
households. In contemporary terms, this calls for the establishment of mechanisms and institutions (both governmental and private) that ameliorate the
severe ripple effects of market operations, particularly on those least able to
bear them. For instance, in the case of globalization, this would include
trade-adjustment assistance and job-retraining programs.[31] Bankruptcy and
credit-assistance programs are similar examples of morally important restor-
ative mechanisms.

GIFT OF THE EARTH. In the principle of the universal destination of the goods
of the earth, it is understood that the gifts of the earth are meant for the benefit
of all regardless of how titles of ownership are assigned.[32] We find this principle
operative in the Genesis dominion mandate, in the gleaning law, in almsgiving
and tithing, in the division of the Promised Land, in land redemption, and in
the land-return provision of the Jubilee Law. For us today, this principle requires
an array of public policies. There must be respect for private property ownership,
balanced by provisions that enforce just-use obligations or impose restrictions
on such private ownership (e.g., zoning, capital gains tax, estate tax). Superfluous
income or wealth should be used for the benefit of the propertyless.[33]
Furthermore, this principle calls for the satisfaction of basic needs for all. In
the contemporary global economy of abundance, the large swaths of the global
population that lack food, basic health care, safe drinking water, sanitation
facilities, and education are an indictment of us all in failing to live up to this
principle.

The principle of stewardship calls for an appreciation for both the earth
and our personal gifts as trusts we have received from God. The dominion
mandate in the creation accounts of Genesis illustrates this principle. For our
generation, this entails minimizing our ecological footprint and improving
our environmental bequest to future generations. Moreover, it calls for a non-
idolatrous and nonproprietary attitude toward wealth and possessions.

Consequently, the principle of stewardship overlaps the principle of integral human development in condemning avarice and wasteful, conspicuous consumption.

In sum, modern Catholic social documents were written in response to the burning social questions of their day, and, consequently, they present a network of social principles without an overriding unity. Sacred Scripture partly addresses this deficiency by providing a vivid narrative—a story of human longing and struggle that people of any generation can identify with. For their part, the modern social principles provide both a conceptual structure and a venue that make the biblical narratives relevant and applicable for our own day. *Scripture provides the narrative with its compelling power, while the modern social principles supply the language with which to translate it for contemporary economic life and policy.* This essay has used both of these resources to propose an architecture of analysis with which to frame CST's recommendations for the economy.

CST as It Might Look in Practice

The overarching model summarized in figures 1.1 and 1.2 should be used only as a single framework. The tradition's social principles and teachings cannot be used piecemeal. Thus, unlike Marxism or libertarian capitalism, CST pursues a more difficult path of balancing twofold objectives in a mixed economy.[34] It has an appreciation for the beneficial services provided by market operations even as it calls for extra-market interventions to mitigate the market's unintended consequences and excesses. Contrary to the claims of commentators from both ends of the political spectrum, CST neither dismisses nor fully embraces the market economy. We see this in the manner by which CST:

- affirms both the right to private property ownership and its attendant just-use obligation.
- relies on both the private sector and government as agents of development.[35]
- encourages freedom of enterprise and private initiative, even while calling for more safeguards to protect labor's interests.
- lauds both market and nonmarket allocative mechanisms.
- accepts both efficiency and equity as essential goals in political economy and is attentive to both the allocative and distributive dimensions of the price mechanism.

- sees the need for government's role in guaranteeing economic rights even as it views integral human development as primarily the obligation of the individual.

These six "double" objectives should not come as a surprise, because they flow from the multidimensional nature of CST. Each part of this vision balances the claims of another part. For example, the principles of subsidiarity and socialization provide a delicate balance between private initiative and state action. Integral human development calls for the human person to flourish in body, mind, and spirit. The principles of stewardship, universal destination of the goods of the earth, and primacy of labor affirm both private property rights and their concomitant just-use obligation. Attaining proper balance between these objectives is what makes political economy more art than exact science. It is also what makes prudential judgment extremely important in the Catholic social tradition.

The importance of such a balanced, broad-based approach is well illustrated in the 2008 global financial meltdown. There were many contributory factors that led to this economic crisis. A widely acknowledged lead cause was the failure of regulatory oversight. The public swing toward dismantling government regulations in the wake of the "Reagan revolution" and its fundamental belief in unfettered markets led to a greater reliance on the private sector to police itself. Not only did the U.S. and EU governments remove proven, long-standing safeguards that had been instituted in the aftermath of the Great Depression, but also they refused to exercise even minimal oversight of ever more complex and nontransparent investment instruments and practices (e.g., derivatives and hedge funds) as part of global financial integration. With the benefit of hindsight, we now know that markets are not self-healing and are in fact prone to being abused in the absence of a regulatory framework.

In contrast to such a philosophical commitment to a minimal "night watchman" view of government, CST calls for balance between government and the private sector. Both are necessary agents of development and economic activity. This social tradition has long been critical of the extremes of both laissez-faire capitalism (in its aversion to governmental supervision) and Marxism (in being enamored of collectivism and heavy-handed state intervention). CST's balanced approach is consistent with what has long been known in the literature: truly functional markets are undergirded by extramarket institutions that require deliberate design and maintenance. Both the principles of subsidiarity and socialization (solidarity) are indispensable in maintaining a stable political economy. Twentieth-century economic history is replete with lessons (e.g., the Great Depression, failed Soviet states) that neither principle can be sacrificed in pursuit of the other.

But there is an even deeper and more sobering cause of the 2008 economic crisis that truly highlights the distinctive contribution of CST to what constitutes true wealth. The near total collapse of the global financial system revealed a widespread malaise of avarice and greed, of seeking quick gains that were legal but not necessarily moral, much less virtuous. This was true across the board, from the people who were buying their dream houses that they knew were beyond their means; to the unscrupulous loan brokers and lenders who enticed borrowers with low "teaser" rates while hiding the true interest charges in fine print; to the financial-banking institutions, hedge funds, and insurance companies that highly leveraged their lending and borrowing; down to the ordinary investors demanding ever-higher but riskier returns. There was failure all around and blame to share across a broad spectrum of the global society. The 2008 financial crisis stands as an indictment of that society for having forgotten what economic life was truly about.

This malaise of avarice and greed highlights the value of CST's starting point, that the true prosperity is not about easy gains or wanton accumulation. The end (telos) of economic life is the development of every person and the whole person: mind, body, and spirit. Anything else is fleeting. The dotcom and the housing bubbles of the last decade are proof indeed that the real metric of wealth is whether or not it ennobles and affirms life and virtue. Thus, CST has been adamant that development is not merely, or solely, or even primarily economic in nature. It is a moral phenomenon.[36] Human progress is authentic and enduring only if it flows from and contributes to a development that is integral and human.

So what does CST recommend for the economy? In concrete terms, this social tradition recommends what we would call in economic parlance a "mixed economy." But it is an economy that is attained only through a vigorous commitment to the common good and its constitutive social principles. It is only in this spirit that enduring prosperity for all is attained.

Table 1 provides an outline of how Catholic social teachings on the economy might look in practice for developed countries like the United States and the EU. This is neither an exhaustive list nor the only set of policies consistent with CST. Since CST stays at the level of generalities and principles, many policy postures are consistent with this tradition. Table 1 illustrates the manifold ways of attaining enduring prosperity. After all, CST is an open-ended, harmonic living tradition subject to both continuity and change. Nonetheless, we can say that at a minimum, what Catholic social thought recommends for the economy is the notion of the common good together with its accompanying social principles. These are necessary building blocks in the True Wealth project's goal of developing an architecture for the analysis of economic life.

TABLE I CST on the Economy As It Might Look in Practice

Part I: Economic Agents
A. Government

Concrete Obligations	Measurement
Progressive Taxation	Composition of government revenues (income tax, estate tax, capital gains tax) Tax structure, loopholes and exemptions Tax incidence Sumptuary laws (e.g., luxury-goods tax)
Economic Rights (food, clothing, shelter, medical care, employment, education)	Codification of economic rights in the constitution or in legislation Unemployment insurance, food stamps Housing assistance Energy assistance Trade adjustment assistance Percentage of population without health care insurance Job-training and placement programs Universal primary and secondary education Subsidized college education
Mitigating Consequential Adverse Pecuniary Externalities	Trade adjustment assistance Unemployment insurance, food stamps Housing assistance Energy assistance Bankruptcy protection (e.g., chapter 11 laws)
Labor Protection	Minimum and living wage mandates Work safety oversight
Consumer Protection	Product safety oversight Truth-in-advertising oversight
Private Sector Promotion	Property rights enforcement Bankruptcy assistance and protection Small and medium scale industry assistance Affirmative action in awarding of government contracts Freedom index Size and vibrancy of private sector Size and vibrancy of NGOs
Ecological Responsibility	Carbon tax Emissions caps Energy use efficiency mandates/incentives (e.g., for homes, factories, towns, etc.)
Relative Equality	Affirmative action Poverty alleviation programs UN Millennium Development Goals Measures of relative inequality Gini coefficient of social measures

(continued)

TABLE I Continued

A. Government	
Concrete Obligations	Measurement
	Absolute and relative poverty measures
	Progressive taxation
	Sumptuary laws (e.g., luxury-goods tax)
	Size and vibrancy of middle class
Intergenerational Equity	Size of fiscal deficits and debt
	Unfunded Medicare and social security liabilities
Promotion of Family Life	Pro-family legislation (e.g., family leave)
	Tax structure (e.g., child deduction, "marriage penalty," etc.)
	Educational assistance
	Fiscal incentives and subsidies (e.g., IRA, etc.)
International Relations	Socioeconomic assistance to emerging nations
	Proportion of socioeconomic and military foreign assistance
	International cooperation on economic and security goals

B. Households	
Concrete Obligations	Measurement
Responsible Consumption (as indirect employers)	Recycling rates and patterns
	Consumption patterns
	Household budget survey (census)
	Boycott of unethical firms
	Carbon-footprint offset initiatives
Obligation to Save	Savings rate
Investment in Children	Household time-use surveys
	Expenditure on children
Philanthropy	Rate of charitable giving
	Volunteerism
Self-Investment and Self-Help	Measures of human capital development
Social Responsibility	Active socially responsible investing
	Passive socially responsible investing

C. Business	
Concrete Obligations	Measurement
Labor Protection	Humane working conditions
	Living wage
	Ongoing worker skills development
	Equal employment practices

Consumer Protection	Safe products and services (e.g., product safety recalls)
	Useful products and services (e.g., truth in advertising)
Shareholder Protection	Transparency and accountability
	Executive pay and perks
Environmental Protection	Expenditure on ecological protection
	Product and production-process impact on ecology
Social Responsibility	Stakeholder rather than shareholder orientation
	Active socially responsible investing
	Passive socially responsible investing
	Alternative working arrangements (co-ownership, co-management, profit-sharing)
	Affirmative action
Philanthropy	Rate of charitable giving, volunteerism

Part II Markets Input Markets (Domestic and Foreign)
A. Labor

Concrete Obligations	Measurement
Ban on Human Trafficking	International and national efforts at stemming human trafficking
	International and domestic assistance to victims.
Strict Restrictions on Child Labor	International and national efforts at minimizing and eventually eliminating child labor
	International and domestic assistance to child laborers and their families
	Worldwide harmonized legislation on child labor
Responsible Unionism	Measures of transparency in internal union affairs
	Disruptive union action (e.g., wildcat strikes, public utilities strikes, etc.)
	Anecdotal accounts of union corruption
Labor Protection and Promotion	Humane working conditions
	Living wage
	Ongoing worker skills development
	Equal employment practices
	Harmonized worldwide labor standards
	Labor strife, activism, and complaints
	Anecdotal accounts of sweatshops
	Unemployment and underemployment rates
	Costs incidence of labor protection
Immigration as a Vehicle for Mutual Advantage and Poverty Alleviation	Immigrant protection
	Cross-border remittance
	Immigrant wages and working conditions
	Social services and safety net for immigrants
	Anecdotal accounts of discrimination
Offshore Outsourcing as a Vehicle for Poverty Alleviation	Poverty-related preferential trade arrangements

(continued)

TABLE I Continued

B. Capital	
Concrete Obligations	Measurement
Foreign Direct Investment as a Vehicle for Poverty Alleviation (non-exploitative investing)	Technology and skills transfer
	Repatriated profits
	Extent of domestic forward and backward linkages
	Extent of domestic spillover effects
	Anecdotal accounts of one-sided contracts and bribes for corrupt local governments
Nonspeculative Investing	Short-term portfolio flows
	Capital market restrictions
	Foreign exchange market turnover
Passive Socially Responsible Investing	Investment prohibitions
	Governmental and corporate policies linking commercial policy and human rights
	Boycotts of odious governments and unethical firms
Active Socially Responsible Investing	Microfinance initiative
	Social entrepreneurship
Environmental Protection	Harmonized worldwide environmental standards
	Empirical studies of "pollution haven" phenomenon

Output Markets (Domestic and Foreign)	
Concrete	Measurement
Fair Trade	Cost incidence and ripple effects of trade restrictions (e.g., agricultural subsidies, quotas)
	Anecdotal accounts of bribery and local-government corruption
	Corruption index (e.g., Transparency International)
	Cost-benefit analysis of international, regional and bilateral trade agreements
Trade as Vehicle for Poverty Alleviation	Poverty-related preferential trade arrangements
	Compulsory licensing of life-saving drugs
	Price discrimination of essential goods/services (e.g., price breaks)
Consumer Protection	Safe products and services (e.g., product safety recalls)
	Useful products and services (e.g., truth in advertising)
	Protection against price-gouging
	Anti-trust legislation and enforcement

Environmental Protection	Expenditure on ecological protection
	Product and production-process impact on ecology
	Carbon-footprint offset initiatives
Non-Exploitative or Dishonest Trade	Dirty industries exported to desperately poor countries
	Unsafe, rejected, or recalled products sold to poor countries
Strict Restrictions on Trade in Arms	Linkage between commercial trade in arms and human rights

Notes and Limitations

1. I used the circular flow analysis of standard introductory economics courses as my conceptual framework.
2. Based on the circular flow analysis, the exposition is divided into two parts: the economic agents and the markets.
3. Because of the interrelated nature of the elements of the circular flow analysis, there are occasional overlaps.
4. This is a non-exhaustive list and is a speculative exercise in examining how CST might be applied in practice.
5. This list is time and culturally conditioned. Its contextual reference point is a contemporary developed nation.

NOTES

1. Not surprisingly, there is a cacophony of voices that claim to speak for the tradition ranging from the extreme right that call for relatively unfettered markets to the extreme left that condemn the market economy altogether. We are thus faced with the methodological problem of justifying how we reconcile these disparate views. To get over this quandary, I limit my coverage of the modern period only to the official documents of the Church and exclude the secondary literature.

2. Recall that most of the modern Catholic social documents were written either in response to the crises of their day or to commemorate earlier papal encyclicals. They were not meant to be treatises and, consequently, do not provide a ready-made unifying theoretical account. Thus, it is not possible to assess the economy in a systematic and comprehensive fashion on the basis of these social documents alone, not even with the syntheses provided by Vatican Council II, *Gaudium et Spes*, and the recent *Compendium of the Social Doctrine of the Church* by the Pontifical Council for Justice and Peace.

3. For example, the Paul VI-era social documents were more egalitarian and quite critical of the market economy while John Paul II was more positive toward the market. Compare Paul VI's *Populorum Progressio, Justice in the World*, and *Octogesima Adveniens* with John Paul II's *Centesimus Annus*.

4. For example, most people would agree that the long-standing teaching on the provision of a living wage is more important than the proposals in *Laborem Exercens* for co-ownership of the means of production, co-management, and profit-sharing as alternatives to wage-labor contractual arrangements (John Paul II, *Laborem Exercens*, chap. 3, sec. #14).

5. An example of a specific proposal is *Quadragesimo Anno's call* for industry-level vocational groupings (Pius XI, *Quadragesima Anno*, #81–98).

6. Paul VI, *Octogesima Adveniens*, #4.

7. See, for example, the common good's prominent place in the *Compendium of the Social Doctrine of the Church* and in the Catholic Bishops' Conference of England and Wales' (*The Common Good and the Catholic Church's Social Teaching*) reflection on the U.K.'s political economy.

8. Pontifical Council for Justice and Peace, *Compendium*, #164.

9. Vatican Council II, *Gaudium et Spes*, #26, #74.

10. Catholic Church, *Catechism*, #1906.

11. John XXII, *Mater et Magistra*, #65.

12. John Donohue, "Biblical Perspectives on Justice."

13. P. J. Achtemeier, "Righteousness in the NT."

14. After all, as Thomas Aquinas notes, God is the source of all of existence. See Mary L. Hirschfeld in this volume for a concise exposition.

15. Bruce Birch, *Let Justice Roll Down*, 178–82.

16. See Albino Barrera, *God and the Evil of Scarcity*, for a more extended exposition of this claim using Thomistic metaphysics and Sacred Scripture.

17. This is in sharp contrast to the claims of neoclassical economics and the completely open-ended nature of consumer preferences and sovereignty.

18. Thus, it is not surprising that a common feature of all the essays in this volume is their extended discussion of the various relational features of a truly moral economy. See especially Stefano Zamagni's essay in this volume.

19. Norbert Lohfink, *Option for the Poor*.

20. See, for example, Philip Mirowski, *More Heat than Light*, for an exposition on the much-criticized "physics envy" of neoclassical economics.

21. Richard Lowery, *Sabbath and Jubilee*, 101–2; Patrick Miller, "The Human Sabbath," 81, 88.

22. Paul IV, *Populorum Progressio*.

23. See Stefano Zamagni's essay in this volume.

24. David Hollenbach, "The Common Good Revisited," 79–82.

25. Paul VI, *Populorum Progressio*, #14. Thus, note the importance of personal virtues as a constitutive good of sustainable prosperity. See Yuengert's essay in this volume.

26. The great care with which the Hebrews safeguarded one another's well-being (at least in theory) is illustrative of the inclusive nature of the principle of integral human development. This pivotal importance of integral human development is consistent with Beretta's and Biggadike's points on the generative nature of a truly moral economy (see their essays in this volume); it has to be life-giving and ennobling.

27. Pius XI, *Quadragesima Anno*, #79.

28. Christopher Wright, *God's People in God's Land*.

29. John Paul II, *Sollicitudo Rei Socialis*, #38f.

30. Barrera, *Economic Compulsion and Christian Ethics*, 111–38.

31. See Grant Aldonas, Robert Lawrence, and Matthew Slaughter, *Succeeding in the Global Economy*, for examples of such assistance.

32. Vatican Council II, *Gaudium et Spes*, #69.

33. Leo XIII, *Rerum Novarum*, #36.

34. See Vera Zamagni's essay in this volume for an illustration of how this has been implemented in practice through the Christian Social Democrats' seminal contributions to the formation of an integrated Europe's socioeconomic ethos.

35. See Vera Zamagni's essay in this volume on how a paradoxical unintended consequence of an over-bureaucratized solidarity is greater individualism.

36. Paul VI, *Populorum Progressio*.

REFERENCES

Achtemeier, P. J. "Righteousness in the NT." In *The Interpreter's Dictionary of the Bible*, edited by George Arthur Buttrick. 4 vols. New York: Abingdon Press, 1962.

———. "Righteousness in the OT." In *The Interpreter's Dictionary of the Bible*, edited by George Arthur Buttrick. 4 vols. New York: Abingdon Press.

Aldonas, Grant, Robert Lawrence, and Matthew Slaughter. *Succeeding in the Global Economy: A New Policy Agenda for the American Worker*. Washington DC: Financial Services Forum Policy Research, 2007.

Barrera, Albino. *Economic Compulsion and Christian Ethics*. Cambridge, UK: Cambridge University Press, 2005.

———. *God and the Evil of Scarcity: Moral Foundations of Economic Agency*. Notre Dame, IN: University of Notre Dame Press, 2005.

Birch, Bruce. *Let Justice Roll Down: The Old Testament, Ethics, and Christian Life*. Louisville, KY: Westminster/John Knox Press, 1991.

Catholic Bishops' Conference of England and Wales. *The Common Good and the Catholic Church's Social Teaching*. London: The Catholic Bishops' Conference of England and Wales, 1996.

Catholic Church. *Catechism of the Catholic Church*. Washington, DC: United States Catholic Conference, 1994.

Childs, Brevard. *Biblical Theology of the Old and New Testaments: Theological Reflection on the Christian Bible*. Minneapolis, MN: Fortress, 1993.

Colander, David. "The Lost Art of Economics." *Journal of Economic Perspectives* (1992): 6:91–98.

Congregation for Catholic Education. *Guidelines for the Study and Teaching of the Church's Social Doctrine in the Formation of Priests*. Washington, DC: United States Catholic Conference. Reprinted in *Origins* 19, no. 11 (1989): 169–92.

Cosgrove, Charles. *Appealing to Scripture in Moral Debate: Five Hermeneutical Rules*. Grand Rapids, MI: Wm Eerdmans, 2002.

Curran, Charles. *Catholic Social Teaching 1891–Present: A Historical, Theological and Ethical Analysis*. Washington, DC: Georgetown University Press, 2002.

Donahue, John. "Biblical Perspectives on Justice." In *The Faith That Does Justice: Examining the Christian Sources for Social Change*, edited by John Haughey. New York: Paulist Press, 1977.

Finn, Daniel. *The Moral Ecology of Markets*. Cambridge, UK, and NY: Cambridge University Press, 2006.

Hollenbach, David. "The Common Good Revisited." *Theological Studies* 50, no. 1 (1989): 70–94.

———. *The Common Good and Christian Ethics.* Cambridge, UK: Cambridge University Press, 2002.

John XXIII. *Mater et Magistra.* Boston: Daughters of St. Paul, 1961.

John Paul II. *Laborem Exercens.* Boston: Daughters of St. Paul, 1981.

———. *Sollicitudo Rei Socialis.* Boston: Daughters of St. Paul, 1987.

———. *Centesimus Annus.* Boston: Daughters of St. Paul, 1991.

Lay Commission on Catholic Social Teaching and the US Economy. *Toward the Future: Catholic Social Thought and the US Economy: A Lay Letter.* New York: Lay Commission, 1984.

Leo XIII. *Rerum Novarum.* Boston: Daughters of St. Paul, 1891.

Lohfink, Norbert. *Option for the Poor: The Basic Principle of Liberation Theology in Light of the Bible.* Berkeley, CA: BIBAL Press, 1987.

Lowery, Richard. *Sabbath and Jubilee.* St. Louis, MO: Chalice Press, 2000.

McGoldrick, Terence. "Episcopal Conferences Worldwide on Catholic Social Teaching." *Theological Studies* 59, no. 1 (1998): 22–50.

Miller, Patrick. "The Human Sabbath: A Study in Deuteronomic Theology." *Princeton Seminary Bulletin* 6 (1985): 81–97.

Mirowski, Philip. *More Heat than Light: Economics as Social Physics, Physics as Nature's Economics.* New York: Cambridge University Press, 1989.

National Conference of Catholic Bishops. *Economic Justice for All: Pastoral Letter on Catholic Social Teaching and the US Economy.* Washington, DC: NCCB, 1986.

Nell-Breuning, Oswald von. "The Drafting of *Quadragesimo Anno*." In *Readings in Moral Theology, No 5: Official Catholic Social Teaching*, edited by C. Curran and R. McCormick. New York: Paulist, 1986.

Paul VI. *Populorum Progressio.* Boston: Daughters of St. Paul, 1967.

———. *Octogesima Adveniens.* Boston: Daughters of St. Paul, 1971.

Phan, Peter. *Social Thought.* Message of the Fathers of the Church series. Wilmington, DE: Michael Glazier, 1984.

Pius XI. *Quadragesimo Anno.* Boston: Daughters of St. Paul, 1931.

Pontifical Council for Justice and Peace. *Compendium of the Social Doctrine of the Church.* Vatican, 2004.

Synod of Bishops. *Justice in the World.* Boston: Daughters of St. Paul, 1971.

Vatican Council II. *Dogmatic Constitution on Divine Revelation.* Boston: Daughters of St. Paul, 1965.

———. *Gaudium et Spes.* Boston: Daughters of St. Paul, 1965.

Wright, Christopher. *God's People in God's Land: Family, Land, and Property in the Old Testament.* Grand Rapids, MI: W.B. Eerdmans Pub. Co., 1990.

2

What Is "Sustainable Prosperity for All" in the Catholic Social Tradition?

Andrew M. Yuengert

The economic and cultural criteria identified in the tradition of Catholic social thought provide an effective path to "sustainable prosperity for all."[1]

Imagine taking the place of low-income parents who are both terminally ill, with a very young child. In anticipation of their deaths, they must decide to whom they will entrust their child for upbringing. One option is with a sister's family, back in the home country from which they immigrated to the United States many years ago. Most of their relatives live in that country, so there is a rich family network there. It is a developing country, with a weak educational system and few avenues by which a lower-class but entrepreneurial young person might advance except through emigration. The other option is a second sister who lives in the United States. She lives a stable, very comfortable upper-middle-class existence in a large city hundreds of miles away. No family members live nearby, and her family has a much weaker set of social networks than the family back home.

In this admittedly artificial scenario, where should the couple place their child? There are competing goods in each option: a rich social network in the home country, material goods, and access to education in the United States. As a parent, they of course want to place their child where he or she is most likely to be happy, but what exactly does that mean?

Public conversations about the nature of true prosperity—like those under-taken in the True Wealth of Nations project—are similar to the deliberation of the parents in this example. What is the relative importance of social networks, income, and opportunities for initiative in evaluating which social arrange-ments are most desirable? Is any one social good (income or social goods, for example) paramount or more important than the others?

Where the private conversation of the unfortunate parents and the public conversation about the good society differ is that the public conversation is broader; it includes the question, "What policies and institutions will pro-mote true prosperity"—will allow people " . . . either as groups or as individ-uals, to reach their fulfillment more fully and more easily"?[2] Because Albino Barrera, in the previous chapter, clarifies the nature and constituents of the means that lead to prosperity (the common good), my task in this chapter is easier. It is more like the parents' challenge in the example above: what does a truly prosperous community look like? The purpose of this essay, in the language of the True Wealth project, is to discuss the character of "sustain-able prosperity for all." Although the Catholic social tradition is reluctant to give unqualified practical advice about how to achieve prosperity (making the discussion of means more difficult), it is more confident in its discussion of human fulfillment, in its expertise about what is good for human beings living in community.

The motivation for this paper is the question, "What is true prosperity?" The word "true" here cautions us to avoid easy but incomplete answers to this question. The Catholic Church claims to be "an expert in humanity: she is able to understand man in his vocation and aspirations, in his limits and misgiv-ings, in his rights and duties, and to speak a word of life that reverberates in the historical and social circumstances of human existence."[3] Catholic social teaching is replete with qualifiers that warn against simplistic views of human well-being, and it claims a more complete social worldview: "the whole person,"[4] "the true good of humanity,"[5] "authentic human happiness."[6]

A second question is directly relevant to the first: "How can we know the extent to which a society has achieved true prosperity?" Because we are ulti-mately in pursuit of answers to both questions, the tension between them cannot be ignored here. On the one hand, simplistic answers to the first question make the second one easier to answer, but then the answers are less satisfying. On the other hand, overly complex answers to the first question can render the second question impossible to address. Although I will focus on the first question, "What is true prosperity?" in this chapter, the second question cannot be kept completely offstage. The tensions between the two questions cannot be avoided, even at this early phase of analysis.

In answering the first question ("What is true prosperity?"), I must take a stand on a third crucial question: "How should we distinguish means from ends?" Most important, ought we to define the end of development in terms of the quality of institutions or in terms of the quality of the lived experience of persons? For example, can we say that a community with legally mandated universal access to health care is by definition flourishing? Or should we instead define human flourishing in terms of health outcomes of individuals? Even though universal health care systems in the industrialized world have generally provided very good care, a universal system could be so riddled with problems that people's health was hurt, not helped, by it. Thus, a strong case can be made for classifying the institutional framework (universal access to health care) as a means, and the health outcomes as ends. This accords well with the common good tradition, which stresses that the ultimate purpose of the common good— the end of the social order—is the person. Jacques Maritain puts the matter succinctly: "The common good is common because it is received in persons."[7]

Thus, in this chapter, the nature of prosperity will be specified primarily with reference to the individual person's fulfillment. In contrast, the characteristics of economic and social institutions belong to the specification of the means of prosperity. Of course, the distinction is not airtight; because humans are social beings, human prosperity cannot be defined solely in individualistic terms, without reference to the quality of social life lived in institutions. Nevertheless, the struggle to make the lives of persons the nexus of our discussion can help keep ends and means separate insofar as it is possible.

Catholic social thought is not alone in asking these questions: Plato, Aristotle, Aquinas, Adam Smith, and a host of others are part of a long history of reflection on the nature of true prosperity and the role of wealth, freedom, and community in the generation of human benefits. Modern sources of reflection on this question can be found in the work of the United Nations Human Development Program,[8] in the economics of happiness literature,[9] in work on the distribution of spiritual goods,[10] and in the social capital literature.[11] Although none of these literatures shares fully in the Catholic vision of the human person in society, there is significant overlap. The True Wealth project cannot ignore their reflection on the nature and measurement of human flourishing. Accordingly, the conclusion of this chapter will include a brief comparison of the Catholic vision of true prosperity with the visions of these other literatures.

We will begin our reflections on true prosperity in the same way Catholic social teaching begins: with the nature of the human person, in section 2. Human beings are made in the image of God, personalist subjects, naturally social, created to live in the material world but with an orientation toward the transcendent. Sin, with its attendant alienation of the person from self, from God, and from others, makes the achievement of prosperity arduous and necessitates a set of contingent goods—certain institutions and the virtues—which must be present for human fulfillment. Because of sin, descriptions of prosperity in a fallen world cannot be identical to descriptions of prosperity in the world to come. Institutions such as private property and virtues such as fortitude are crucial to development in this world but will not be needed in the eschaton.

With this understanding in hand, section 3 outlines the place of income and material wealth in the Catholic vision of true prosperity. Command over goods and services cannot be left out of the evaluation of human well-being, of course, but income by itself is a radically incomplete measure of human flourishing. As Barrera notes in the previous chapter, there are other dimensions of human well-being, and growth in income does not guarantee, and cannot substitute for, growth along other dimensions. Section 4 outlines a description of true prosperity in four parts: the personal and social virtues, the quality of social relations, personal initiative, and material wealth. Section 5 compares the Catholic vision of prosperity to alternative theories. Section 6 offers some concluding thoughts on the value of this approach and its empirical implementation.

The Nature of the Human Person

The end of development cannot be described simply as a good community, without reference to how the goods of a community redound to its members. Families and many other institutions are good in ways that go beyond what individuals can extract from them; as we will see in more detail later, every good of a community must in some way be the good of some human person or persons in that community, who experience it as good. The purpose of community is the human person, who is an end and never a means.[12] This focus on the human person as end meets the requirement, discussed by Albino Barrera in the previous chapter, that our conceptual frameworks be morally compelling. This will also avoid the mistake of identifying prosperity with institutions that can become obsolete when historical context evolves, as Vera Zamagni's essay in this volume demonstrates in her discussion of Christian democracy in Italy. All Catholic institutions evolve, even though human nature does not.

In order to know what it means to be a fulfilled, prosperous human being, we must know something about human nature. What are God's purposes in creating us? What is our created nature? How does sin affect our prospects for happiness? Answers to these questions set the stage for the Catholic vision of the person in society.

At the foundation of the Catholic vision is the creation of the human person in the image of God: "God created man in his own image, in the image of God he created him; male and female he created them" (Gen. 1:27). Both the dignity and nature of the person are rooted in the imago Dei (that is, the image of God): "…being in the image of God the human individual possesses the dignity of a person, who is not just something, but someone. He is capable of self-knowledge, of self-possession, and of freely giving himself and entering into commitments with other persons."[13]   *IMAyo DEI*

Being a "someone" and not simply a "something" has five important implications for Catholic social thought. First, it implies the personalist principle: the human person is the subject, the protagonist, of society.[14] All social life is rooted in human agency, and the end of social life is the good of human beings as subjects, not as passive objects. Accordingly, the evaluation of the social order must not focus on what happens to its individual persons, but on what persons are able to do, individually and in community.

The second implication of imago Dei is freedom, "which God has given to him [man] as one of the highest signs of his image."[15] This is closely related to the personalist principle. By freely willing his individual good and society's good, the human person lives out the image of God in himself. This liberty is a condition for effective human agency—for the person to become an agent of his own development. Through the proper exercise of this freedom, the world is ordered toward God, and, more important, the acting person orients himself more completely toward God. A proper regard for this freedom engenders a corollary awareness of the "economic, social, juridic, political, and cultural" conditions that make such freedom possible.[16]

This freedom is not a libertarian, absolute autonomy of action; human beings have a real nature and act within a moral order that is not of their invention. The fullness of human freedom, and of freedom's benefits for society, is only fully realized in obedience to a set of truths whose truth the person cannot change: "in the exercise of their freedom, men and women perform morally good acts that are constructive for the person and for society when they are obedient to truth, that is, when they do not presume to be the creators and absolute masters of truth or of ethical norms."[17]

When the truth about the human person and human society is rejected in the name of a false autonomy, the human person becomes less free; he is easily enslaved to his own passions and vulnerable to manipulation by others.[18]

Catholic social teaching safeguards the free exercise of subjectivity via the principle of subsidiarity: "a community of a higher order should not interfere in the internal life of a community of a lower order, depriving the latter of its functions, but rather should support it in case of need and help to coordinate its activities with the activities of the rest of society, always with a view to the common good."[19]

A community at any level is responsible for developing the goods natural to it, but these goods include both the goods of lower-order communities, which should be protected and nurtured by this higher-level community, as well as the goods of higher-order communities, which seek common goods only possible with the cooperation of communities like this one further down.

The third implication of imago Dei is the dignity of each human person. Although no human person can be understood apart from community, each individual person is unique and unrepeatable and is willed by God for his own sake.[20] Since each person is made in the image of God, each person is a protagonist of society, and each person's free action for the good is crucial for the healthy ordering of society. A human being should never "be manipulated for ends which are foreign to his development."[21] Human dignity is offended when persons are denied the opportunity to participate in their own development, when development "takes place over their heads."[22] To use another person without regard for that person's free agency is a violation of human dignity. True prosperity in a society cannot be brought about without the cooperation and participation of the persons in that society. Moreover, true development must be for each and for all. For this reason the distribution of prosperity is of great consequence.

A fourth implication of imago Dei is the human person's inescapably social nature. The triune Christian God is a community of persons. For this reason, community is natural to human beings made in God's image. Each person is given life and nurtured in community, and a person's social relationships are a crucial component of his happiness. Because the person "can fully discover his true self only in a sincere giving of himself," a communion of persons is crucial to human flourishing.[23] Accordingly, to evaluate the quality of human prosperity, we must take into account the quality of human relationships in community.

The Church's teaching on the social orientation of the person is captured by two related concepts, the common good and solidarity: "It is out of love for one's own good and for that of others that people come together in stable groups with the purpose of attaining a common good."[24] The common good is the purpose of a stable social group; it is a good that can only be attained in groups and includes a wide range of goods: character, friendship, commerce, and education, for example. Solidarity, or social charity, is "a firm and persevering determination to commit oneself to the common good."[25] Society cannot rely solely on individual self-interest to guarantee healthy social groups and the common goods that are generated in groups. Solidarity is needed, as both a means and an end of development; it impels persons to overcome common challenges and is itself a crucial component of mature personality.

A fifth implication of our creation comes from the combination of the imago Dei and our constitution as matter and spirit. God creates man from the dust of the earth but breathes spirit into him (Gen. 2:7). Human life bridges material, bodily existence and the life of the Spirit, which calls the person to transcend the merely material aspects of life and to find fullness of being in relation to others and to God. The dual nature of the human person has important consequences for our attitude toward the material aspects of human life. Although human well-being does not consist simply of material goods, it cannot be completely spiritualized. Humans are not spirits trapped in bodies; what happens to their bodies happens to them. Consequently, the material deprivations of the poor are an affront to human dignity, regardless of the spiritual state of the poor. In creating humans as body-spirit composites, God intended material blessings for them; even after the Fall, the material dimension of our existence is an important medium in which the drama of sin and redemption unfolds. Human material existence partakes of the effects of sin, in hunger and poverty, and in the idolization of riches that blinds man to heavenly wealth. This material existence also should bear the marks of redemption: the promise of the fully realized kingdom of heaven should be reflected in the life of the Christian community and in the salutary work of Christians who leaven the secular order.

The first two chapters of Genesis, which introduce us to the person's place in the created order, leave us with the five principles of prosperity just explored: human persons are subjects, who are supposed to play the central role in their own development as persons; they need the conditions of freedom to act fully as agents; each has great dignity and should not be treated as a means to social ends or left out of development; they are naturally social; and neither the material nor spiritual aspects of their well-being can be ignored. By themselves, these principles guide us toward certain measures of human prosperity. Human beings should be free to exercise initiative toward their own and society's good through work both inside and outside of commercial markets. Their material standard of living is highly relevant, though not supremely so. The quality of social life and relations is crucial to any evaluation of human welfare. Widespread access to knowledge—not only technical but also human knowledge—is also important.

Although the creation accounts teach us much about what counts as prosperity, the Fall (Gen. 3) complicates the analysis of human nature and of man's fulfillment in community. The entrance of sin into the world is not simply a negation of the material goods that human beings seek, making them harder to attain. Since sin is at its heart a rebellion, its consequences touch human character itself. The human person is the protagonist of sin as well as the protagonist of his own development. By denying his created nature, the sinner alienates himself from God, from his neighbor, from the natural world, and even from himself.[26] It is the presence of sin and its effects that make the True Wealth project necessary.

The remedies for the effects of sin are relevant to the means of social development and are thus not directly of interest in this essay, which addresses the nature of development as an outcome. Nevertheless, the Fall must affect our characterization of prosperity in this world. Those who focus on the original created order to the exclusion of the Fall risk taking the eschatological vision of humanity as an earthly end and treating human development as a process that converges to beatitude in its earthly limit. The corruptions of sin will not go to zero in this life, however, even in the lives of saints and the saintly community.

As a result of the Fall and its effects, there is a set of individual and social goods that promote earthly prosperity, but that will be unnecessary in heaven. They are a sort of second-best compromise on earth; they are in fact the best we can do in this life. At the community level these include sound legal institutions, property rights, and safety nets; these will be unnecessary in the world to come (or at least be so changed as to be unrecognizable as their earthly counterparts), but they are crucial constituents of prosperity now. At the individual level, the moral virtues help the individual cope with the internal struggles that block true freedom. These virtues will remain in the life to come, but the worldly impediment to them—concupiscence—will no longer be present. For example, earthly fortitude is directed on the whole to the management of the inner rebellion against difficult and unpleasant tasks. This rebellion is not present in heaven.[27] However unnecessary virtues and institutions will be in heaven, they must factor into our evaluation of prosperity in this fallen world.

Why True Prosperity Is Not Identical to High Income

How should we evaluate human prosperity? A useful starting point is to examine the usefulness and shortcomings of income as a measure of true prosperity.

Income, often measured as gross domestic product per capita, is the most popular measure of well-being, for both theoretical and pragmatic reasons. The pragmatic reasons are clear: income is easy to measure (at least in developed economies where government statistics are reliable), and everyone seems to want more of it (at least we do not observe many people seeking to have less of it). The theoretical reasons for income are more subtle but are no less influential. The simplistic assumptions of economic models of the person give rise to an exaggerated role for income in human happiness. To put income into its proper perspective—at the service of well-being—we must turn our attention to the realism of the assumptions of mainstream economic modeling, which reflect and undergird reductionist accounts that equate material prosperity and true prosperity.

In economic theory, there are markets for nearly everything that human beings want, from groceries, to marriage and children,[28] to spiritual goods.[29] In economics, income is assumed to be a comprehensive measure of command over everything that could possibly matter in life because everything that matters is assumed to be for sale in markets. If we further assume away all internal difficulties in choosing—no concupiscence or internal inconsistency of choice—income becomes the sufficient measure of well-being. More income generates a wider range of choices over the set of all things that matter to humans, which means greater well-being.

The western philosophical and religious traditions have long rejected income as a sufficient measure of well-being. Both Aristotle and Aquinas noted that income is good only to the extent it promotes happiness and that it sometimes leads to great unhappiness.[30] The Old Testament and New Testament warn that material wealth can easily become a trap. Those who have great wealth often end up idolizing their goods, making wealth into an ultimate end, to the neglect of duties to God and neighbor, especially to the poor. This inversion of means and ends—the displacement of happiness by wealth as the ultimate end in life—leads to great injustice and unhappiness, both for the oppressed and the wealthy.

A strand of recent economic research explores the limits of income in generating human well-being. The capabilities approach of Amartya Sen, which takes as its measure of well-being what human beings are able to do, highlights the limits of approaches that consider income in isolation from other resources needed to effect human flourishing.[31] The work of Richard Easterlin seeks explanations for why higher incomes are not always associated with higher levels of subjectively reported well-being.[32] Robert Frank models the social consequences of status goods, which generate well-being only in comparison to the consumption of others.[33]

Catholic social teaching has long been part of this Western skepticism about employing income as a metric of human well-being. The theoretical world in which income and happiness are perfectly correlated does not exist; there are important human goods that are not available to individuals in markets, and inequalities in the distribution of income may limit the opportunities and active participation of the poor.

Goods not attainable by money purchased in markets fall into three categories: character, social relationships, and public goods. Each of these is, in a different way, a component of the common good.[34] Character goods include both the spiritual orientation that makes the authentic enjoyment of material prosperity possible and the virtues that make the production of material prosperity possible. The goods of social relationships focus our attention on those social goods that material prosperity is supposed to make possible: participation and gift-giving. Public goods are those that are not fully available through markets to each individual: public health, infrastructure, and access to education for the poor, for example.

It is possible to be rich and not to have gained wealth through virtuous agency; it is equally possible to gain wealth and not enjoy it because it is too important. Both of these possibilities impress upon us the importance of our spiritual orientation toward material goods. A certain poverty of spirit is necessary to put material goods at the service of the good life. Wealth that is gained too easily or because of personal vices ultimately does its recipient little good. Both the wisdom and prophetic literatures of the Old Testament testify to the futility of easily or ill-gotten gain:

> An inheritance gotten hastily in the beginning will in the end not be blessed (Prov. 20:21).

> The getting of treasures by a lying tongue is a fleeting vapor and a snare of death (Prov. 21:6).

> You have sowed much, and brought in little: you have eaten, but have not had enough: you have drunk, but have not been filled with drink: you have clothed yourselves, but have not been warmed: and he that hath earned wages, put them into a bag with holes (Hag. 1:6).

John Paul II points out an additional reason why wealth may lead, not to happiness, but to slavery. In his discussion of the problems of underdevelopment, he points out an equally serious problem, that of "super-development":

> This super-development, which consists in an *excessive* availability of every kind of material goods for the benefit of certain social groups,

easily makes people slaves of "possession" and of immediate gratifi-
cation, with no other horizon than the multiplication or continual
replacement of the things already owned with others still better. This
is the so-called civilization of "consumption" or "consumerism,"
which involves so much "throwing away" and "waste."[35]

Those who invert the correct order of goods—who place material wealth
above spiritual goods—end up slaves of possessions. The attainment of goods
leads to the desire for more and to dissatisfaction with what has been achieved.
As a result, personal agency itself is compromised; man becomes less free and
more at the mercy of social forces and of those who would manipulate material
desires for their own ends. All the while, "deeper aspirations remain unsatisfied or even stifled."[36]

A crucial component of human fulfillment is the quality of relationships. If
income is generated in ways that damage human community, or if it is spent in
ways that do the same, then it is a poor measure of human well-being. Catholic
social teaching emphasizes the social, noneconomic aspects of production and
consumption. A business is not simply a "society of capital goods"; it is a "society
of persons,"[37] and its good cannot be measured simply in terms of output and
income. John Paul II, in *Centesimus Annus*, notes that "…it is possible for the
financial accounts to be in order, yet for the people—who make up the firm's
most valuable asset—to be humiliated and their dignity offended."[38]

Just as the value of income must depend on the quality of the commercial
institutions in which it is earned, its value depends on the uses to which it is
put. The proper attitude toward wealth includes a lively awareness of the
universal destination of goods: "Riches fulfill their function of service to man
when they are destined to produce benefits for others and for society."[39] The
universal destination of goods is a clear requirement of charity and of justice,
but its scope should not be needlessly narrowed; the sharing of goods within
family and local community, the support of local government initiatives, and
national and international charity are all included within its broad scope.

In addition to goods of character and social goods, a third sort of good is not
available for money purchase and is thus left out of income-based measures of
well-being: public goods. A public good is one that, because of its nature,[40] is not
efficiently provided by individually oriented markets.[41] Examples include a well-
functioning police and legal system, access to education and public health, and
infrastructure. A country or community with poorly functioning governmental
or community institutions may lack these goods; this deprivation may not show
up in individual income statistics. The United Nations Development Program
critique of income-based measures of development centers on the importance

of these public goods; its Human Development Index includes life expectancy (as a measure of public health) and literacy (as a measure of access to education), in addition to per capita income.[42]

In addition to the goods that are not available for money purchase, there are two additional concerns that reduce the usefulness of income as a metric of well-being. First, how income is earned affects its evaluation. Income that results from the agency of a free person is more desirable than income that is received passively or at the cost of forced labor. Amartya Sen offers the example of slavery: slaves would rather be free, even if freedom comes at the cost of material comforts.[43] Moreover, a meager income that is earned is better than the same income that comes without effort, from others or from the government. The same is true for larger incomes.

The second additional concern about income is inequality: the Catholic tradition evaluates the distribution as well as the level of national income. Aggregate or per capita income is not a sufficient measure of prosperity: "The economic well-being of a country is not measured exclusively by the quantity of goods it produces but also by taking into account the manner in which they are produced and the level of equity in the distribution of income, which should allow everyone access to what is necessary for their personal development and perfection."[44]

Inequality of income is not per se troubling; it becomes troubling when it results in a denial of development opportunities to those at the bottom of the economic ladder. The evaluation of inequality hinges crucially on the analysis of the conditions that generate it and on its social and political effects.[45]

In sum, income is not by itself a comprehensive measure of prosperity; certain human goods crucial to prosperity can be absent even when incomes are high, and inequalities in the distribution of income can undermine prosperity by denying opportunity to the poor. But if income is not a perfect measure, neither is it useless. After all, human beings have a material existence, and material prosperity is fitting for them. Other things being equal, countries with greater income are more prosperous than countries with less. Researchers are correct to include it in any index of prosperity, and households are very often justified in seeking to improve their material circumstances. There are other goods that constitute prosperity, however. To these we now turn.

True Prosperity in Catholic Social Thought

As we saw in section 2, Catholic social teaching delineates five principles that provide a framework for thinking about true prosperity. Any comprehensive approach to prosperity must address them and trace out their practical expressions in society. The last section argued that the most common measure of prosperity, income, is a necessary but insufficient measure of true prosperity. This section goes on to suggest four kinds of goods that should be present in a truly prosperous community: (1) goods of personal character, (2) goods of personal initiative, (3) social goods, and (4) material goods. These are four distinct categories of human goods: none of them is unimportant. It is difficult to make value comparisons across categories, and deprivations of any are a threat to human prosperity. They are the raw material for an index of prosperity, discussed at the end of this chapter.

The Virtues

Character is both a means to prosperity and a principal component of it. A prosperous community bears fruit in the virtuous character of its people. If material prosperity is gained through institutions that erode the character of a people, it will not be enjoyed and will probably not be sustainable.

The more virtuous a person is, the more fully human. The virtues are the characteristic excellences of human beings, and they represent a sort of ideal fulfillment in this world of our created nature amid the challenges of the Fall. The cardinal virtues—temperance, fortitude, prudence, justice—make the person more able to deliberate about and successfully pursue both his own good and the good of the communities to which he belongs.[46]

At the center of the cardinal virtues is prudence, "the virtue that makes it possible to discern the true good in every circumstance and to choose the right means of achieving it."[47] It is through prudence that we live up to our vocation as persons, acting in the created world according to our created nature, ordering it toward our own good and the good of society. Temperance and fortitude give prudence a space in which to deliberate and act, free from inordinate attraction to pleasure and inordinate aversion to danger and difficulty.

The virtues of justice and solidarity orient the person to others. Justice is the "constant and firm will to give their due to God and neighbor."[48] Justice has four component parts. Commutative justice governs exchange, assuring that equal value is given in return for equal value, without fraud or exploitation. Distributive justice governs the allocation of the goods of a community (a business or a local government, for example) to its members in an equitable way. Legal justice governs the obligations of a member of a community to obey its laws, for the good of the community. Social justice, which is a development of the concept of legal justice, governs the obligation to seek institutional changes that make communities more prosperous and just.[49]

The virtue of solidarity goes beyond social justice to social charity. It is "a firm and persevering determination to commit oneself to the common good. That is to say the good of all and each individual, because we are all really responsible for all."[50] Solidarity and justice are closely bound together. Justice is presupposed in solidarity, and solidarity overcomes the limitations of justice, which can degenerate into a network of legalistic obligations that can be barriers to social progress: "No legislation, no system of rules or negotiation will ever succeed in persuading men and peoples to live in unity, brotherhood, and peace; no line of reasoning will ever be able to surpass the appeal of love."[51] Solidarity is creative in a way that justice cannot be, "capable of inspiring new ways of approaching the problems of today's world, of profoundly renewing structures, social organizations, legal systems from within."[52]

It is impossible to imagine a truly prosperous country whose people are not virtuous. How might we measure the virtues of a community's people? I know of no systematic attempt to construct indices of virtue, but there exist data that, used creatively, might provide material for such a project. As is often the case, most of the existing data capture deficiencies in virtue: addiction rates to everything from alcohol to gambling to videogames offer a window into temperance or its lack. Varieties of justice can be measured by data on tax evasion, charitable giving, the treatment of workers by employers, and the treatment of employers and workplace property by employees. Solidarity can be measured by data on social commitment and participation, both within the family and in local and national communities.

Personal Initiative

The life and vigor of a prosperous community spring from the initiative of its members, made in the image of God. Human beings are only fulfilled to the extent that they participate in their own development. The principle of subsidiarity embodies this solicitude for the person as subject. Given effective responsibility for himself and others through appropriate social and material space, each person is expected to bring about his own good and the good of the communities to which he belongs. Communist experiments failed to respect personal initiative in the economic, political, and cultural spheres, resulting in the rejection of those experiments by the Catholic social tradition.[53]

The measure of prosperity in the area of initiative must capture more than the opportunity for creative initiative. The opportunities for initiative given by the means—property, education, effective subsidiarity—should give rise to actual initiative for the good. It is the initiative itself, and the fruits of initiative, that are integral to prosperity.

What should creative initiative yield as observable fruit? A population of actively engaged subjects should, first of all, be producing a steady stream of new ventures at every level of society. New families are the ultimate new ventures and become centers of further social and personal growth. New businesses likewise are evidence of creative initiative in the economic sphere; their establishment requires the effective exercise of personal as well as social virtues.[54] Community initiatives, embodied in the establishment of new organizations to meet evolving community needs and in the renewal of old organizations, are crucial to the establishment and maintenance of prosperity. Government itself should be characterized by creative energy at each level (particularly at the local level) in those things appropriate to it.

The establishment of new family, economic, social, and governmental ventures is only a sign of prosperity to the extent that each group is characterized by widespread participation. Just as a local community group is less healthy when one or two people do all of the work, a community network of organizations will be less energetic, will contribute less to the community's common good, if few participate in them. Measures of personal initiative must thus contain information on how widespread participation is in social groups. Rates of volunteering can offer some insight into how many have taken up the opportunity to be active agents.

Social Relations

Because human beings need society and are naturally oriented toward it, it is not surprising that personal initiative most often gives rise to social groups. Consequently, a prosperous society will be characterized by a rich network of social relations, within which a true communion of people can emerge. Any attempt to evaluate the prosperity of a people must take into account the existence and quality of these networks and the amount of activity that takes place within them. Both libertarian and collectivist ideologies ignore the importance of what the *Compendium of the Social Doctrine of the Church* calls the "sphere of civil friendship."[55]

The vital importance of social life and institutions pushes to the limit an important but difficult-to-maintain distinction introduced at the beginning of this chapter: between the social means of prosperity (realized in community and political institutions) and the ends of prosperity (realized in the lives of individual persons). It is impossible to rely entirely on individually based measures of social engagement, for both practical and theoretical reasons. Empirically, individually based measures may be unavailable. For example, we may have to be content with measures of the number and legal status of unions when measures of individual participation in workplace governance are not collected; we may have to be content with measures of the independence of the judicial system when information on the just treatment of various classes within society are unavailable. Even when individually based measures are available, however, the nature of social goods requires us to treat social entities as ends because they are humanly good. People establish families and other social, economic, and political institutions in part because they are themselves good for persons, and not just for what they can extract from those institutions as individuals. Keeping in mind these considerations, let us turn to the Catholic tradition's discussion of social relations.

At the heart of any network of social relations is the family. The *Compendium* calls the family the "vital cell of society" and gives it pride of place in its application section, before work, economic life, politics, the international community, the environment, and peace.[56] No other social network can replace the family, which trains the person in responsibility, in virtue, in solidarity, and in mutual self-giving: "In the climate of natural affection which unites the members of a family unit, persons are recognized and learn responsibility in the wholeness of their personhood." The family is crucial to sustainable prosperity, as well: "A society built on a family scale is the best guarantee against drifting off course into individualism or collectivism, because within the family the person is always at the center of attention as an end and never as a means."[57]

Beyond the family are other social groups, which together provide an arena within which humans can reach their fulfillment—a fulfillment impossible without them: the complete fulfillment of the human person, achieved by Christ through the gift of the Spirit, develops in history and is mediated by personal relationships with other people, relationships that in turn reach perfection thanks to the commitment made to improve the world, in justice and peace.[58]

The social groups that constitute civil society are only signs of prosperity to the extent that everyone has access to them. Participation in economic enterprises, in the political arena, and in the social groups that shape the culture should not be limited to a few elites. Each person should be connected in some way to the institutions that make up civil society, so that each can exercise responsible agency in society, to the extent he is able.

There is a wealth of data on the quality of social life. Most governments collect data that can be used to evaluate the health and stability of the family. Recent research on social capital and civil society leaves us with an excellent body of thought on how to measure the presence and effects of social networks in society.[59] Although in the social capital literature social relations are treated as means to other things (usually economic growth),[60] in this section they are of interest primarily as ends, as humanly good in themselves. The number and size of intermediary groups, their autonomy and scope, and the degree of participation within them, all must be evaluated to determine the quality of social relations in a community.

One might measure the importance of social groups by collecting data on the number of groups to which the average person belongs or by how many people belong to no social group. Another intriguing approach would be to measure the volume of social "transactions" that occur in such groups. Everything from the material sacrifices parents make for their children, to the value of volunteer work and material donations to and from organizations, to the exchange of gifts within organizations is an indicator that important segments of life are characterized by reciprocity and self-giving in community.

Material Goods

Although material goods appear last in this outline of true prosperity, they are nonetheless important. A country rich in the virtues and social networks but suffering from severe material deprivation should not be counted among the prosperous. Section 3 discussed the insufficiency of income as a measure of prosperity. This section emphasizes the necessity of material prosperity to true prosperity.

The material world is good; God's creation is intended by him to be a gift to his children. It meets human needs, at the same time providing the medium in which human persons express their agency and identity. An individual's personal or family income represents control over material goods, intended for individual use and for the good of others. When the other material goods—public goods, available through the agency of governments and intermediary groups—are included, we get a clear sense of a person's material prosperity; the Human Development Index of the United Nations Development Program (UNDP) is an attempt to capture a range of material provision needed for prosperity; it includes money income and measures of access to health care and education.

Because the distribution of income matters in the evaluation of material prosperity, income must be supplemented by measures of deprivation and inequality. Rates of poverty, illiteracy, and morbidity focus our attention on the poor and their plight. Societies in which some suffer from inadequate incomes and inadequate access to public goods are not prosperous, no matter how high the incomes of the middle class and rich.

Measures of inequality in the income distribution are also informative, although they are easily misinterpreted, largely because poverty almost always accompanies inequality. Inequality is not in itself morally offensive, as long as those at the bottom of the distribution have a dignified standard of living. Inequality becomes socially destructive when it affects participation, when the poor are shut out from social groups and from the legal and democratic process by their poverty.[61] Consequently, the ill effects of income inequality will show up in measures of participation among the poor.

Mutual Necessity and Sustainability

Each of the four aspects of true prosperity—the virtues, personal initiative, social relations, and material goods—is crucial to true prosperity. None can be left out. A society rich in three of the aspects but poor in one is conceivable but would not be called truly prosperous. Consider, for example, a society with a dense, rich network of social groups, opportunities for the exercise of free initiative, and which is materially prosperous, but whose members were not virtuous. Such a situation might come about because of the failure of one generation, itself virtuous, to pass on to its progeny the virtues by which it built up true prosperity. We would not call such a society truly prosperous, since its corrupt populace would be unable to enjoy the riches it has and would be unlikely to sustain the compromised prosperity it has been bequeathed.

Similarly, a society with virtuous people, rich community life, and abundant reservoirs of personal initiative, but which is denied material blessings, but would not be called truly prosperous. Although some might fear the loss of the other human goods that such a materially poor community might lose through economic development, no one would wish to see the community remain materially impoverished.

Implicit in the notion of true prosperity is sustainability. The common good includes the conditions that maintain prosperity into the future.[62] Sustainability requires that a society contain sources that renew the constituents of prosperity. Since prosperity is not solely material, the sources of renewal of prosperity cannot be simply material.

The virtues—the cardinal virtues plus solidarity—are indicative of current prosperity and are the wellsprings of future prosperity. Prudence, which makes a person most truly a subject of development, is itself developed through the experience of deliberating and acting. The exercise of prudence at the individual or household level safeguards the personal virtues; its exercise in the political arena is oriented toward future prosperity. Solidarity is the resource that generates social relations; when it is present, it provides the energy for new institutions and social groups.

Sustainability in material goods depends on physical capital and natural resources as well as on spiritual capital and, as John Coleman argues in an essay in this volume, social capital. The depletion of physical and environmental capital is a sign that sustainability is threatened. Kenneth Arrow et al. calculate sustainability by measuring the evolution of capital and environmental investment across time for a sample of countries.[63] Measures of resource and environmental depletion can help us to evaluate whether current prosperity comes at the cost of future generations.

Secular Resources for the Evaluation of True Prosperity

As we have seen, sustainable prosperity for all must be evaluated along four dimensions: personal and social virtues, personal initiative, social relations, and material goods. Each person, made in the image of God, must share in prosperity. Any attempt to test the basic hypothesis of the True Wealth project—that implementing the principles of Catholic social thought will lead to true prosperity for all—should take into account the efforts of ongoing research into the various constituents of human well-being just enumerated.

Chief among these research programs is the capabilities approach of Amartya Sen, which has born empirical fruit in the work of the United Nations Development Program (UNDP).[64] This work defines development as an expansion of the capabilities of people to lead lives that they have reason to value. The capabilities approach values freedom and human agency highly; its principal concern is to give people effective choice over a range of life options and does not concern itself with the choices actually made. Although the UNDP's Human Development Index and the complementary Human Poverty Index focus primarily on access to private and social material goods, the theory of capabilities is broader, and much can be learned about empirical implementation in this literature.

Another intriguing recent literature offers a comprehensive measure of human well-being.[65] Survey data on subjective evaluation of happiness, going back fifty years across a wide range of countries, has given rise to the field of happiness economics. Although some of this research has taken a decidedly utilitarian direction, measuring momentary affect instead of subjective evaluation of overall well-being,[66] research in this area has called into question the primacy of income as a measure of well-being. Any research into human well-being must take those findings seriously.

The social capital literature, although limited by a narrower focus than that taken here, offers great insight into the measurement of the extent, quality, and effects of social networks. Robert Putnam has documented the decline and recovery of community in the United States.[67] Charles Lindblom explores the connections between market organization and the quality of social relations.[68] This literature offers a wealth of data and reflection on social relations.

There are other research programs whose reflections are worthy of attention. Robert Fogel has clearly documented the striking improvements in material welfare in developed and developing economies over the last several centuries.[69] Improvements in material wealth have turned his attention to spiritual goods. The field of development ethics, exemplified best in the work of Denis Goulet, is a rich resource for reflection on the nature of human development.[70] Catholic social teaching should draw on these various disciplines, both to understand the differences between the visions they promote and Catholic thought, and the True Wealth project should make use of the empirical resources they can provide.

Conclusions: Implementation

In constructing a four-part framework for the evaluation of True Prosperity, this essay draws on a part of the Catholic social tradition in which the Church expresses great confidence. The Church claims to be "an expert in humanity;"[71] John Paul II offered Catholic social teaching as an "ideal and indispensible orientation...."[72] This confidence is well-founded. The Catholic tradition, based in its reflection on Christian revelation and the experience of life in community, offers a reflection of the nature of the human person that is at once comprehensive and accessible to non-Catholic Christians and to non-Christians. In Catholic reflections on human nature and purpose, the extremes of Marxian materialist determinism and libertarian rationalistic autonomy are avoided. The human person is both spirit and matter: a nexus of agency, creativity, and dignity, at the same time acting in a world that both constrains action and expresses the goods achieved by that action. Any description of human flourishing must take into account the dignity of human beings as agents in society, at the same time recognizing the need for human virtues, the quality and extent of social relations, and material abundance.

This essay addresses the empirical implementation of its framework only indirectly, pointing the way to possible measures of the goods of prosperity and to lines of research that offer resources for empirical implementation. Thus, a final note on the limitations and possibilities of empirical measurement is in order.

Even in the event that researchers develop excellent empirical measures of the four kinds of goods (the virtues, personal initiative, social goods, and material goods), there are limits to what can be done with them to capture what the Catholic tradition means by "true prosperity." These limits are a result of the inherent arbitrariness in constructing indices that combine goods for which there are no clear metrics of comparability.

To see this difficulty more clearly, consider the following questions: why measure prosperity along four dimensions? Why four kinds of goods? Why not one? Are we offering an account of prosperity that is unnecessarily complicated? The answer is simple: we cannot collapse the four kinds of good enumerated here into one kind of good, because they are not the same sort of good. Both material goods and the human virtues are good, but they are not the same kind of good; both social goods and human agency are good, but they are not the same kind of good. In technical terms, the four are incommensurable.

Each of the four goods is crucially important to human flourishing—as noted in section 4, we would not call a human community fully prosperous if it were deficient in any one of them. At the same time, there are no clear criteria by which to compare deficiencies or abundance across the goods. Imagine two countries like those the unfortunate parents in the introductory example had to evaluate. In the first, the scope for human initiative is relatively constricted, and its material standard of living is low, but it boasts rich social networks and social participation. In the second, incomes are high and human initiative is given free rein, but social networks are relatively thin. Which is more prosperous?

There is no consistent, technical way to make these comparisons. This is not the same as saying that we cannot determine that one country is more prosperous than another. We can talk (and argue) about the relative importance of the various goods in each country's context, about whether our choices are consistent with God's plans for us and our human nature. In whatever way we make the comparison, it is not something that can be captured in an index formula, unless we make the mistake of anointing one good (income, for example) as paramount or of arbitrarily assigning weights to the four goods. Choosing one good as primary denies the independent importance of the other three, and arbitrarily choosing a weighting scheme (even equal weights on all four goods) is by definition unsystematic and unwarranted.

The independent importance of the four kinds of good, along with a certain incomparability among them, makes the construction of a single index of prosperity—a weighted average of the four kinds of good—inescapably arbitrary. This arbitrariness gave rise to some internal institutional resistance to the construction of the United Nations' index of human development, which gives one-third weight to income, literacy, and longevity. The decision to construct and release the index can be justified by the way it has focused attention on human development across countries, but this is a political, not a theoretical, justification.[73]

By pointing out the difficulties of index construction, I do not mean to derail empirical implementation. The True Wealth project need not develop a single-valued "index of true prosperity" to make valuable contributions to the ongoing conversation about what it means to be prosperous. Even if the project satisfied itself with the difficult task of developing measures of the four kinds of goods (indices of the virtues, of personal initiative, of social relations, and of material abundance), and did not take the next step of combining the indices into an overall measure of prosperity, it could shed light on two important questions:

1. How are the means of development (discussed by Barrera) related to each of the four kinds of goods individually? Are they affected similarly by the same economic and cultural institutions?
2. How are the four kinds of goods related to each other? Do they increase and decrease together? For example, does an improved quality of social relations always generate greater material abundance, as is implied in the social capital literature?

Knowing that there are four kinds of goods at stake in development, and not one, and how these four goods are related to the means of development and to one another, would be a substantial contribution to the Catholic understanding of true prosperity and its relation to the common good.

NOTES

1. From the Preface to this volume, "The True Wealth of Nations."
2. Vatican Council II, The Church in the Modern World, *Gaudium et Spes*.
3. Pontifical Council for Justice and Peace, *Compendium of the Social Doctrine of the Church*, para. 61. In general, I will cite the *Compendium*, and not the documents it cites.
4. Ibid., para. 5.
5. Ibid., para. 6.
6. Ibid., para. 334.
7. Jacques Maritain, *The Person and the Common Good*, 49. Maritain elegantly negotiates difficult territory in this work, avoiding the extremes of individualism, in which the common good is nothing more than an aggregation of individual goods, and totalitarianism, in which the person exists for the sake of the collective.
8. Sakiko Fukuda-Parr and A.K. Shiva Kumar, eds., *Readings in Human Development: Concepts, Measures, and Policies for a Development Paradigm*.
9. Bruno Frey and Alois Stutzer, "What Can Economists Learn from Happiness Research?"
10. Robert W. Fogel, "Catching Up with the Economy."
11. Robert D. Putnam, *Bowling Alone*; see also Charles E. Lindblom, *The Market System*. See also the essay by John A. Coleman in this volume.

12. This claim that the person must be the end of society is not the libertarian claim that individual judgments and choices are the metric of all good and that the social good can be defined only as the sum of individual goods. See Ludwig von Mises, *Human Action*, and Friedrich A. Hayek, *Mirage of Social Justice*. The error of libertarian approaches lies in their rejection of the social nature of human beings, in granting an absolute autonomy of moral judgment to the individual, and in downplaying the communal origins of human preferences and character. (See Daniel Rush Finn, "The Economic Personalism of John Paul II.")

13. Pontifical Council for Justice and Peace, *Compendium*, para. 108.

14. Ibid., para. 106.

15. Ibid., para. 135.

16. Ibid., para. 137.

17. Ibid., para. 138.

18. Ibid., para. 143.

19. *Catechism of the Catholic Church*, para. 1883.

20. Pontifical Council for Justice and Peace, *Compendium*, para. 133.

21. Ibid.

22. John Paul II, *Centesimus Annus*, para. 33.

23. Pontifical Council for Justice and Peace, *Compendium*, para. 34.

24. Ibid., para. 150.

25. John Paul II, *Solicitudo Rei Socialis*, para. 38.

26. Pontifical Council for Justice and Peace, *Compendium*, paras. 115–19.

27. Thomas Aquinas, *Summa Theologica*, I–II, 67.1.

28. Gary S. Becker, *A Treatise on the Family*.

29. Laurence R. Iannaccone, "Introduction to the Economics of Religion."

30. Aristotle, "Nicomachean Ethics," 1.5.

31. Amartya Sen, *Development as Freedom*.

32. Richard Easterlin, "Building a Better Theory of Well-Being."

33. Robert Frank, *Luxury Fever*.

34. Andrew Yuengert, "The Common Good for Economists."

35. John Paul II, *Solicitudo Rei Socialis*, para. 28.2.

36. Ibid., para. 28.3.

37. Pontifical Council for Justice and Peace, *Compendium*, para. 338.

38. John Paul II, *Centesimus Annus*, para. 43.

39. Pontifical Council for Justice and Peace, *Compendium*, para. 329.

40. A public good is both nonexcludable (those who do not pay cannot be excluded from enjoying it) and nonrival (one person's consumption does not lessen its value to others). Both of these characteristics make it difficult for private providers to charge for the good; as a result, private markets have few incentives to provide public goods.

41. If individuals are not completely self-interested, but are motivated to some degree by a sense of reciprocity (outlined in the essay by Stefano Zamagni in this volume), the public goods problem may be somewhat mitigated, but not eliminated.

42. Mahbub ul Haq, "The Birth of the Human Development Index," 127–37.

43. Sen, *Development as Freedom*, 28–29.

44. Pontifical Council for Justice and Peace, *Compendium*, para. 303.

45. See Dennis P. McCann, "Inequality in Income and Wealth," 189–208.

46. I have chosen not to include the theological virtues in the list of virtues enumerated here, since they are not available to non-Christians in the same way that they are present through grace in the Christian community. It may perhaps be possible to examine the secular counterparts to the theological virtues: something along these lines is attempted in Deirdre N. McCloskey, *The Bourgeois Virtues*.

47. Pontifical Council for Justice and Peace, *Compendium*, para. 547.

48. Ibid., para. 201.

49. Ibid.

50. Ibid., para. 193.

51. Ibid., para. 206.

52. Ibid., para. 207.

53. Leo XIII, *Rerum Novarum*, para. 13.

54. Pontifical Council for Justice and Peace, *Compendium*, para. 343.

55. Ibid., para. 390.

56. Ibid., para. 95.

57. Ibid., para. 213. At this point it is worth noting that the aspects of prosperity discussed so far have not taken into account sex and gender. This is of course a crucial oversight, which is most glaring in the discussion of the family's crucial role in true prosperity. The origin and purpose of sexual differences in the social and moral orders are sources of tremendous contention within the Catholic and Christian communities, however. The visions of Beretta and Biggadike, in their essays in this volume, agree in important ways but reveal important differences. I will not attempt to negotiate this contested ground in this essay but simply note the hard work that will be needed to negotiate the differences in vision on offer within the Catholic and Christian communities.

58. Pontifical Council for Justice and Peace, *Compendium*, para. 58.

59. Putnam, *Bowling Alone*; Lindblom, *Market System*; John Coleman's essay in this volume.

60. See Coleman's essay in this volume.

61. See McCann, "Inequality in Income and Wealth"; and Michael Walzer, *Spheres of Justice*. The thresholds at which inequality affects participation are crucially underresearched, given the importance of the topic.

62. Pontifical Council for Justice and Peace, *Compendium*, para.164.

63. Kenneth Arrow et al., "Are We Consuming Too Much?" 147–72.

64. Sen, *Development as Freedom*.

65. Frey and Stutzer, "What Can Economists Learn from Happiness Research?"

66. Daniel Kahneman et al., "Toward National Well-Being Accounts," 429–34.

67. Putnam, *Bowling Alone*.

68. Lindblom, *Market System*.

69. Robert W. Fogel, *The Escape from Hunger and Premature Death*.

70. Denis Goulet, *Development Ethics*.

71. Pontifical Council for Justice and Peace, *Compendium*, para. 61.

72. John Paul II, *Centesimus Annus*, para. 43.

73. Amartya Sen, in the foreword to Fukuda-Paar and Kumar, *Readings in Human Development*, makes this very point: "There were plenty of grumbles that the diverse concerns on which Mahbub concentrated did not automatically yield one 'operational metric.' Of course it didn't; it could not—and indeed should not—have. The domain of social valuation cannot be taken over by some kind of a value-neutral engineering" (p. ix).

REFERENCES

Aquinas, Thomas. *Summa Theologica*. Translated by Fathers of the English Dominican Province. New York: Benziger Brothers, 1948.

Aristotle. "Nicomachean Ethics." In *The Basic Works of Aristotle*, translated by David Ross; edited by Richard McKeon. New York: Random House, 1941.

Arrow, Kenneth, Partha Dasgupta, Lawrence Goulder, Gretchen Daily, Paul Ehrlich, Geoffrey Heal, Simon Levin, Karl-Göran Mäler, Stephen Schneider, David Starrett, and Brian Walker. "Are We Consuming Too Much?" *Journal of Economic Perspectives* 18, no. 3 (Summer 2004): 147–72.

Becker, Gary S. *A Treatise on the Family*. Cambridge, MA: Harvard University Press, 1981.

Catechism of the Catholic Church. Washington, DC: U.S. Catholic Conference, 1994.

Easterlin, Richard. "Building a Better Theory of Well-Being." In *Economics and Happiness: Framing the Analysis*, edited by Luigino Bruni and Pier Luigi Porta, 29–64. New York: Oxford University Press, 2006.

Finn, Daniel Rush. "The Economic Personalism of John Paul II: Neither Right nor Left." *Journal of Markets and Morality* 2 (Spring 1999): 74–87.

Fogel, Robert W. "Catching Up with the Economy." *American Economic Review* 89, no. 1 (March 1999): 1–21.

———. *The Escape from Hunger and Premature Death, 1700–2100: Europe, America, and the Third World*. Cambridge: Cambridge University Press, 2004.

Frank, Robert. *Luxury Fever: Why Money Fails to Satisfy in an Era of Excess*. New York: Free Press, 1999.

Frey, Bruno, and Alois Stutzer. "What Can Economists Learn from Happiness Research?" *Journal of Economic Literature* 40, no. 2 (June 2002): 402–35.

Fukuda-Parr, Sakiko, and A.K. Shiva Kumar, eds. *Readings in Human Development: Concepts, Measures, and Policies for a Development Paradigm*. Oxford: Oxford University Press, 2003.

Goulet, Denis. *Development Ethics: A Guide to Theory and Practice*. New York: The Apex Press, 1995.

Haq, Mahbub ul. "The Birth of the Human Development Index." In Fukuda-Parr and Kumar (eds.), *Readings in Human Development*, 127–37.

Hayek, Friedrich A. *Law, Legislation, and Liberty*. Vol. 2, *The Mirage of Social Justice*. Chicago: University of Chicago Press, 1978.

Iannaccone, Laurence R. "Introduction to the Economics of Religion." *Journal of Economic Literature* 36, no. 3 (September 1998): 1465–95.

John Paul II. *Solicitudo Rei Socialis*. December 30, 1987.

———. *Centesimus Annus*. May 1, 1991.

Kahneman, Daniel, Alan B. Krueger, David Schkade, Norbert Schwarz, and Arthur Stone. "Toward National Well-Being Accounts." *American Economic Review* 94, no. 2 (May 2004): 429–34.

Leo XIII. *Rerum Novarum*. Para. 13. May 15, 1891.

Lindblom, Charles E. *The Market System: What It Is, How It Works, and What to Make of It*. New Haven, CT: Yale University Press, 2002.

Maritain, Jacques. *The Person and the Common Good*. South Bend, IN: University of Notre Dame Press, 1966.

McCann, Dennis P. "Inequality in Income and Wealth: When Does It Become Immoral, and Why?" In *Rediscovering Abundance: Interdisciplinary Essays on Wealth, Income, and Their Distribution in the Catholic Social Tradition*, edited by Helen Alford, O.P., Charles M.A. Clark, S.A. Cortright, and Michael J. Naughton. Notre Dame, IN: University of Notre Dame Press, 2006.

McCloskey, Deirdre N. *The Bourgeois Virtues: Ethics for an Age of Commerce*. Chicago: University of Chicago Press, 2006.

Mises, Ludwig von. *Human Action: A Treatise on Economics*. Auburn, AL: von Mises Institute, 1998.

Pontifical Council for Justice and Peace. *Compendium of the Social Doctrine of the Church*. Washington, DC: United States Conference of Catholic Bishops, 2004.

Putnam, Robert D. *Bowling Alone: The Collapse and Revival of American Community*. New York: Simon and Schuster, 2000.

Sen, Amartya. *Development as Freedom*. New York: Anchor Books, 1999.

———. "Foreword." In Fukuda-Parr and Kumar (eds.), *Readings in Human Development*: iii–xii.

Vatican Council II. Pastoral Constitution on the Church in the Modern World: *Gaudium et Spes*. December 7, 1965.

Walzer, Michael. *Spheres of Justice: A Defense of Pluralism and Equality*. New York: Basic Books, 1984.

Wilber, Charles, and Amitava Dutt, eds. *New Directions in Development Ethics: Essays in Honor of Denis Goulet*. Notre Dame, IN: University of Notre Dame Press, forthcoming.

Yuengert, Andrew. "The Common Good for Economists." *Faith and Economics* 38 (Fall 2001): 1–9.

3

Catholic Social Thought, Civil Economy, and the Spirit of Capitalism

Stefano Zamagni

Modern economic development did not occur due to the adoption of stronger incentives or better institutional arrangements, but mainly because of the creation of a new culture. The idea that incentives or efficient institutions will generate positive economic results regardless of the prevailing culture is simply baseless, since what makes the difference is not the incentives themselves but the way agents perceive and respond to them. And reactions depend precisely on the particular cultural matrix, which in turn is crucially influenced by religion as a set of organized beliefs.[1] It is well established that values and attitudes (such as the propensity for risk, the practice of granting credit, the attitude toward work, and the willingness to trust others) are intimately related to the prevailing religious beliefs in a given time and place. For its continual reproduction, capitalism, like all other social orders, requires a series of cultural inputs and a sophisticated moral code that capitalism is not itself capable of generating, although it certainly does play a part in modifying social, cultural, and moral circumstances over time. This is why we can today reflect on the relationship between an ethics founded upon religion, such as Catholic social thought, and the capitalist economic system.

This essay is a preliminary test of the fundamental hypothesis of the True Wealth of Nations project: "The economic and cultural criteria identified in the tradition of Catholic social thought (CST) provide an effective path to sustainable prosperity for all." By adopting a history of ideas approach, I will endeavour to show that in the era of civil humanism during the thirteenth through fifteenth centuries, the principles of CST were able to inspire and shape an institutional order, a civil economy, aimed at the common good. While I refer the reader to Andrew Yuengert's paper in this volume for a definition of what one should mean by sustainable prosperity in the sense of human flourishing, this essay will address three questions. First, in what sense can it be argued that Catholic ethics served to nourish and inform the spirit of capitalism? Second, was Max Weber correct in his claim that the Protestant ethic encouraged the spirit of capitalism? Third, what explains the recent revival of interest in both historical and economic research aimed at assessing the impact of culture on economic outcomes and, more specifically, the impact of religious beliefs on civic life and economic progress?[2]

The Catholic Social Thought and the Civil Market

Did Catholic ethics serve to nourish and inform the spirit of capitalism? From the beginning, the relationship between Catholicism and capitalism has been characterized by structural ambivalence. On the one hand, Catholic thought, especially the Franciscan school of the thirteenth to the fifteenth centuries, provided the formulation of most of the analytical categories and a number of the economic institutions that would later serve the full flowering of the spirit of capitalism. On the other hand, the Catholic ethic essentially rejects the very mind-set of capitalism, what Max Weber called its *Geist*, its spirit.

How can we account for this? The ambivalence—which has provoked countless, often inconclusive, debates—stems from the inconsistent use of the term "capitalism" to denote diverse phenomena, in particular both the civil market economy and the capitalistic market economy. This ambivalence is eliminated once the Catholic ethic is causally linked to the birth and establishment of the civil market economy, the economy that predated the capitalist market economy. The modern world was born in the socioeconomic form of capitalism, and Catholicism cannot seek compromise with it if compromise is taken to mean the capacity of two powers to "promise" themselves to the same end. Why? According to Catholic ethics the goal of economic action is the common good, whereas the goal of capitalism is the total good (defined as the sum total of individual "goods").

Clearly, the defence of a thesis like this requires us to define "civil market economy" and "capitalist market economy." Before proceeding, a note on the origin of the term "capitalism" is in order. The word "capital" came into general use in the fourteenth century to denote funds, monetary or not, that could produce an income, that is, a surplus. But the word "capitalism" was first brought into scientific and theoretical discussion by Werner Sombart at the beginning of the twentieth century to designate the economic system that issued from the Industrial Revolution.[3] To be exact, "capitalism" in the English language was coined in 1853 by the satirist William Thackeray, as is demonstrated by the anthropologist Jack Goody, who also shows that such derivative words as "capitalism" and "capitalist" began to enter into European culture in France as early as the first half of the eighteenth century.[4] One of the scholars who has inquired most deeply into the origins and evolution of the concept of capitalism was Fernand Braudel, though he did give up the idea of an unequivocal definition.[5] At least one point is firmly established, however: at first, in the twelfth century, as the civilization of the medieval city was being formed, "capital" and "capitalist behaviour" were terms referring to the particular human occupation of using wealth (monetary or other) to produce additional wealth by means of a productive activity. The fact is extremely important for any understanding of markets. A capitalist is not someone who appropriates a surplus thanks to *de jure* power (such as a sovereign or a rentier) or *de facto* power (such as a brigand or a usurer) but someone who, taking a risk, generates new wealth.

Oreste Bazzichi has shown that a decisive contribution to this doctrine was made in the thirteenth century by the Francisan friar Giovanni Olivi, who saw capital as a sum of money that, being assigned to business, already contains a "seed of gain."[6] Olivi's concept of capital as seed money—expanded upon by Alexander of Alessandria, the author of *De Usuris* (1303), made known throughout Europe by Bernardino of Siena and Bernardino of Feltre—is the postulate that permitted the subsequent justification of the additional value that the borrower must pay back over and above the amount lent to him. Leo X's bull *Inter multiplices* (1515) finally cleared away all doubt as to the legitimacy of charging interest on the loans of the *Monte di Pietà* pledge banks.

What, then, were the characteristics of the civil market economy as it developed beginning in the thirteenth century? The late twelfth century saw the beginnings of a profound transformation of European society and economy, a process that lasted into the mid-sixteenth century. It began in Italy, in Umbria and Tuscany in particular, but even by the end of the thirteenth century, it extended to other parts of the continent: Flanders, northern Germany, southern France. This was the period during which the mercantile reawakening of the previous centuries, in connection with the invention of machines that greatly increased productivity, came to full maturity. The new social order that was forming is known as "urban civilization," a model that owes much to the theoretical work of "civil humanists," as they have been called by Eugenio Garin and J. G. A. Pocock.[7] These medieval scholars were diverse in background and in training, but they shared the desire to interpret events of their own times in the light of the thought of the past.[8]

Monastic culture was the source of the first economic lexicon, which gained currency throughout Europe in the late Middle Ages. Europe's first complex economic institutes were the monasteries, where the need for proper forms of management and accounting emerged. Saint Benedict's *ora et labora* (pray and work) was not just the path to individual holiness, but the foundation for a definite work ethic that would arise, based on the principle of labour mobility. This monastic culture contrasted with that of ancient Greece and Rome, where labour was not a component of the good life, which consisted rather in political action, as ancient politics had no place for working people. In fact, work was for slaves (or servants); the free man did not work. Thus, monastic life, with its careful organization of even tiny details of daily life, provided the perfect location for developing the form of rational thinking that would later come to be known as instrumental rationality (means/ends rationality), to which Max Weber would devote such a substantial part of his work.

The Benedictine and Cistercian monasteries, in turn, were the outcome of the reflection on economic life that the Church fathers had begun as far back as the fourth century, with the rigorous subjection to Christian ethics of the faithful's relationship with worldly goods. Worldly goods and wealth were not condemned as such but were wrongly used, if they were considered as an end and not a means to our ultimate end, life with God. Basil the Great, of Caesarea, a monk who founded the charitable town known as Basiliad, made pointed observations on the morally right use of wealth: "The wells from which water is most drawn cause it to gush forth most readily and copiously; left unused, they putrefy. So too is wealth that remains immobile useless, while if it circulates and passes from one to another it is of common, fruitful use."[9] We see here an anticipation of the concept of common good that would emerge full fledged centuries later.

In the typical late-medieval city, citizens moved about freely and exercised what we might call a primitive form of participatory democracy in such places as the cathedral, the town hall, the merchants tribunal, the guildhall and confraternity, the market as the locus of trade and conflict, and finally the main square with its "parliament," that is, the political assembly of all citizens where public decisions were taken. This was when the modern idea of freedom originated, conceived both as "republican liberty" (i.e., the independence of the people organized as a commune separate from the power of the emperor) and as personal liberty (i.e., the freedom to decide one's own life plan). The economy of the Italian cities consisted of manufacturers and merchants and, in the coastal cities, seafarers. The merchants had the task of opening up new markets, even in distant cities, as export outlets for manufactures and sources of imported raw materials. The merchants were not only the most active agents of opening to other cultures but also the most active business innovators. Just think of such institutions as the "commendam," forerunner of the limited liability company; insurance; double-entry bookkeeping and business accounting (which the Franciscan monk Luca Pacioli established on a systematic basis in 1494); bills of exchange; pledge banks; and stock exchanges—all institutions without which self-sustaining, widely diffused economic development would have been impossible.[10]

The basis of this civic rebirth was a protracted process of economic and social evolution. In the economic sphere, this involved the rise of manufacturing, chiefly textiles, with significant technological advances (e.g., the broad loom) that allowed the institution of large workshops employing hundreds of workers. Meanwhile, the invention of the mechanical clock made it possible to measure work time and thus to monitor the productivity of wage labour. Finance and international banking developed so much that bankers were often decisive for the outcome of diplomacy or war between rival powers.

The most important development of all, however, was the cultural revolution, with the rebirth of the arts, philosophy, theology, and law. In spite of their countless differences, the civil humanists all shared the firm belief in the intrinsically social nature of human beings. This idea would be essential for the development of the market economy. Matteo Palmieri wrote in his *On Civic Life* (mid-1430s): "Of all beings, the most useful to man is man. He cannot hope to get from others those goods that he can obtain only from his fellow men."

As Remo Guidi's monumental work demonstrates, Christianity had to issue forth eventually in humanism because Christianity centers on the Incarnation[11]—which the Church fathers somewhat surprisingly called *Sacrum Commercium* to underscore the profound reciprocal relationship between the human and the divine and recall that the Christian God is a God of men living in history and that He takes an interest in their material condition. To love life, therefore, is an act of faith, not just of self-interest, since the Catholic ethic sees in one's love for others an instance of the love of God. This belief opens the way to optimism for the future, since man's works have not only an otherworldly purpose but also meaning and value here and now. So there is no break between medieval theology and humanism. This demonstrates the error of the thesis (still dominant in current historiography) that the rise of the market economy was a total novelty that broke with a Christianity built upon love. In other words, the dominant understanding of capitalist markets—that the culture of contract so central to capitalism today is opposed to the culture of reciprocity on which medieval community was based—is not credible. Contracts can exist outside the logic of capitalism, an insight behind the essays on contracts in this volume by Vincent Rougeau and Daniel Finn.

As Giacomo Todeschini has authoritatively observed, there is no solid foundation for the belief that a "charity economy" and a "profit economy" are utterly irreconcilable.[12] Sylvain Piron has shown that, even before the modern era, gift and market exchange were seen as complementary categories within a shared system of values. Building on Piron's work, Todeschini notes that the moral and legal justification of profit rested on the merchant's willingness to treat his customers properly, that is, not to make them pay the highest possible price given market conditions. The difference between the two—the theoretically possible price and that actually charged—was a gift, the product not of generic charity but of the need for an economic space occupied by persons who recognized one another as belonging to the same ideological universe. This is the sense in which charity and profit could be considered by medieval Franciscan scholars (Olivi, Duns Scotus, Bernardinio of Siena, Bonaventura of Bagnoregio, Ockham, and others) and by the most attentive medieval observers of urban civilization today as two sides of the same economic reality.

One of the crucial features of urban civilization is the market economy, properly conceived as a structure for governing economic transactions (not just the physical site of exchanges, which already existed in antiquity). Its governing principles discussed below all derive in one way or another from Franciscan thought, which was the first true school of economics, as Joseph Schumpeter himself acknowledged in his monumental *History of Economic Analysis*. Todeschini has shown that Franciscan thought introduced two major innovations to the intellectual horizon of the day. One was the idea that, although ownership is important for most people, for the friars, ownership is superfluous and only the use of goods and wealth is necessary, leading to the conclusion that "thanks to poverty, it could be easier to use and circulate wealth."[13] The second was the notion that if friars were to be able to exercise the virtue of poverty constantly, this poverty had to be sustainable over time. This is why they turned for help to lay persons, the spiritual friends of the Order, entrusting them with the management of money. The idea that some sort of functional division of labour was necessary took root and spread from here.

Starting with the first Exposition of the Rule in 1241, the Order's analysis of poverty was extended to all of society. Men of culture no longer saw the "deeply economic content of the choice of poverty made by St. Francis and his followers" solely as an option for individuals (Christian perfection) but also as "a socio-economic order for the community as a whole."[14] Around the same time, in the work of such men as Bonaventura da Bagnoregio, Hugh of Digne, and John Peckham, the principle began to form that the economic sphere, the governmental sphere (*civitas*), and the evangelical sphere (in the Franciscan sense) "are three degrees of the organization of reality, different but capable of being integrated."[15] If this integration occurs, it produces abundant fruits, so that the wealth that the voluntarily poor renounce can be used for the involuntary poor, until the latter eventually disappear entirely. And the integration of the three degrees can be attained only within an institutional arrangement—the market—that is founded upon three governing principles.

The first of the three principles is the division of labour, a way of organizing production, enabling everyone, even those less physically or mentally gifted, to perform useful work. Without the division of labour only the more gifted would be able to procure what they need by themselves. And the Franciscan maxim popularly known at the time—that alms help you survive but not live, because living means producing, which alms do not help you do—already contained an implicit condemnation of charitable assistance as unable to impart dignity. At the same time, the division of labour increases productivity through specialization and in practice obliges men to recognize in exchange their mutual bonds to others. For with the division of labour, exchange ceases to be marginal and episodic, but becomes a powerful agent of social organization. Recognizing their reciprocal dependence, wrote Erasmus of Rotterdam in *Enchiridion Militis Cristiani* (1503), men will be led to cooperate and to keep the peace because mutual dependence makes war too costly (an idea that would be taken up again by Kant and Montesquieu).

The second principle underlying the civil market is the notion of development, hence, accumulation. Wealth needs to be accumulated, in this view, not only as a reserve against future contingencies, setting aside a part of each year's output, but also out of responsibility to future generations. Thus, a portion of income must be allocated to productive investment, which expands the productive base and, ultimately, means making the economy into a positive-sum game. This spurred the organization of manufacturing labour, fostered the practice of training new workers through apprenticeship, and created an incentive to improve the quality of products by requiring craftsmen to produce a "masterpiece." A particularly eloquent definition of the concept of growth comes from Coluccio Salutati, who wrote, following his great predecessor Albertano da Brescia (ca. 1194–1250): "To dedicate oneself honestly to an honest activity may be a holy thing, holier than living in idleness and solitude. Because holiness attained through the rustic life serves only oneself . . . but the holiness of the industrious life raises up the life of many."[16] Clearly, here we are very far from the medieval canon condemning all economic production in excess of the strictly necessary ("Est cupiditas plus habendi quam oportet").

The third principle, finally, is freedom of enterprise. Those endowed with creativity (the ability to innovate), a good propensity for risk (the willingness to undertake an action whose outcome is initially not known), and the ability to coordinate the work of many others (*ars combinatoria*)—the three essential qualities of the entrepreneur—must be left free to undertake initiatives without the need for prior authorization from a sovereign or other authority because the active and industrious life (*vita activa et negociosa*) is a value in itself, not just a means to other ends. At the same time, freedom of enterprise implies economic rivalry, that is, the particular form of competition that takes place in the market. The *cum-petere* (seeking together) in the market is the direct consequence of freedom of enterprise and reproduces that freedom. In a competitive economy, the final outcome of the economic process does not follow from the will of some overarching entity but from the *free* interaction of a large number of actors, each rationally pursuing one's own objective in the framework of a definite set of rules. There are three elements necessary for any competitive market.

The first requirement is that interaction must be free. No agent may be constrained by force or induced to act by a state of necessity. This means that a person who is enslaved, or totally uninformed, or so poor that he is in no position to decide does not meet the condition of voluntary action that the play of competition demands.

The second element is the qualification of "pursuing interests rationally," which postulates economic agents' ability to calculate, including both the ability to assess the costs and benefits of the options available and the adoption of a criterion for choice. Note that this criterion, contrary to conventional wisdom in mainstream economics today, need not necessarily be maximum profit (or maximum utility). That is, competition does not have to be linked to the logic of profit. The objective of the participants in the market game may be either self-interested or mutual; they may aim at the special interests of a particular group or at the common interest. What matters is that everyone must be clear on the objective he or she intends to pursue; otherwise the rationality requirement fails.

Third, competition requires well-defined rules known to all participants and enforced by an authority that is not party to the game. The first instance of a law created directly by those to whom it will apply, and not by the sovereign, was the formulation of the celebrated *Lex mercatoria* and the *Law of the Sea* by merchants. These conventions had two fundamental provisions: a ban on the concentration of power in the hands of one or a few agents in the form of monopoly or oligopoly, and the ban on fraud and deceit in market transactions. It was not until the seventeenth century, after the Peace of Westphalia and the birth of the nation-state, that these laws came under state jurisdiction.

Through emulation, competition stimulates the spirit of enterprise and imposes rational calculation. Where there is competition, positions of rent[17] and privilege cannot obtain. To be sure, competition is costly, but it improves quality by leading to greater "individualization" of products, giving them an identity—as in politics, in which democracy certainly entails high costs but keeps the quality of civic life from deteriorating. As Bernardino of Siena said so forcefully in his "Vulgar Sermons" in 1427, if the end for which an enterprise is conducted is the common good, the social costs of competition will never be too high. In the thirty-eighth sermon, "On merchants and masters and how to conduct markets," we read, "For the common good trade must be exercised" (1101) and, further on,

> It is a necessary thing for a City or a Community that there are those
> who work products into another form. As there is wool and
> those who work it; it is legitimate that the wool-maker gain. Every
> one of those can and should gain, but with discretion. With this, it
> being always understood that in the trade you exercise you act only
> straightly. You must never use cunning; never falsify your goods, you
> must make it proper and if you know not how, first you should let
> it be, let it be done by another who can do it right, and then gain
> is licit (1138).[18]

So if the merchant uses his wealth for the common good, his activity is not only legitimate but also virtuous.

This passage from Bernardino nicely illustrates the difference between the civil market and the capitalist market. Then as now, the three principles (division of labour, development and accumulation, and freedom of enterprise) are the elements that identify a market economy of whatever kind. To specify the *kind* of market requires a fourth element, the one that identifies the specific end pursued by the participants. This may be the *common* good or the *total* good (defined as the sum of all individual goods). The common good is the object of the civil market economy; the total good, that of the capitalistic market economy. The Catholic ethic is basically the ethic of the common good and is thus perfectly compatible with the spirit of the civil market economy—indeed, it is at its origin. What makes market activity moral is the fact that exchange takes place in the framework of networks of solidarity, in other words, within a community. We can exchange to mutual advantage because before anything else we are bound by an obligation, a tie that ensures that the exchange will be civil. Essentially, for the Catholic ethic, what saves the market from degeneration is the logic of reciprocity. (For a thorough and deep examination of the notion of the common good, see Albino Barrera's contribution in this volume).

Starting in the late sixteenth century, the civil market economy began to be transformed into the capitalistic market economy, even though the definitive triumph of capitalism as a social order did not come until the Industrial Revolution. The role played by the intellectuals of the day was not irrelevant to the transformation. As Davide Canfora observes, the pro-republican literature of civil humanism was gradually supplanted by a courtly literature revolving around the rulers.[19] There was thus installed a general inclination on the part of the "intellectuals" to surrender to the blandishments of the rulers, abasing civil engagement. At most, the intellectual was allowed to serve as educator or coun-sellor to the prince. Capitalism gradually replaced the logic of the common good with that of the total good, that is, the "profit motive." Productive activity was directed to a single purpose, the maximization of profit for distribution among all the investors in proportion to their share of the capital. With the Industrial Revolution, the principle *fiat productio et pereat homo* (roughly, "Produce and let the worker perish") was finally established, sanctioning the radical separation between the suppliers of capital and the suppliers of labour and definitively abandoning the old principle that man is the measure of all things (*omnium rerum mensura homo*) that originally underlay the market economy.

The simplest way to see that the profit motive as such was not a constituent element of the market economy is to refer to the writings of the civil humanists (such as Leonardo Bruni, Matteo Palmieri, Antonino of Florence, and Bernardino da Feltre) and the civil economists of the eigh-teenth century (Antonio Genovesi, Giacinto Dragonetti, Cesare Beccaria, Pietro Verri, Giandomenico Romagnosi). A constant theme in their work is that market activities need to be oriented to the common good, from which alone they derive their prime moral justification. Among the earliest applica-tions of the concept of common good to the medieval commune is *De bono comuni* (1302), a treatise by the Florentine Dominican Remigio dei Girolami. The central idea is that you cannot have the good of a part without the good of the whole to which it belongs; without an orientation to the common good, society destroys itself, and ultimately, its individual members.[20]

The question arises: what exactly is the difference between "common good" and "total good"? A metaphor may serve. While the total good can be rendered by the concept of the algebraic sum, in which the addends represent the good of the individual parties, the common good is more like a product, in which the factors are the good of the individuals. The meaning of the metaphor is intuitive: in a sum, even if some of the addends are zero or negative, the total can remain positive. Indeed, it could happen that if the objective is maximizing the total good, it may be best to cancel the good (or the welfare) of some, if the welfare gains of others are large enough to offset the loss. In a multiplication, this is not the case, because the reduction to zero of even a single factor makes the entire product nil. In other words, the logic of the common good does not admit substitutability. You cannot sacrifice the basic welfare of one person—whatever his life situation or social position—to increase that of others, for the fundamental reason that this person has a God-given human dignity and always enjoys basic human rights. Within the logic of total good, however, this person is simply an individual, that is, a subject identified with a particular utility function, and utilities can be readily summed up (or compared) because they are faceless; they do not express an identity, a personal history. Being common, the common good does not concern the person as an isolated individual, but in relation with others. That is, it is the good of relationships between persons; it is the good of life in common. Common is that which does not belong only to oneself (as it is the case with private good) nor indistinctly to everyone (as it is the case with public good).

Basically, the key to the legitimacy or illegitimacy of market economic activity is reciprocity. Market exchange is ethically acceptable if it complies with—does not destroy—the principle of reciprocity. This means that the gift as reciprocity becomes, in the modern economy, the "exchange road."[21] The conclusion is that the modern notion of the entrepreneur and the category of profit are products of medieval Catholic culture, which managed—not without difficulty—to insert the market, the true novelty of the times, within the corpus of the scholastic theological elaboration thanks to the notion of the common good. The Franciscans were in the forefront in comprehending the positive aspects of markets and crafts. Both were considered as necessary activities for the "city," as long as they were directed to the common good, in that "no thing contributes so greatly to the common good as the utility of crafts and of the goods that are sold and bought."[22] The very same "Friars Minor" who had made the vow of poverty their rule of life became the great specialists in wealth—an irony indeed!

The civil economy tradition teaches us that there is no necessary conflict between the pursuit of profit and the Catholic ethic. You can be a good Christian by being a good merchant or craftsman. What ensures the absence of conflict between faith and economic agency is the orientation of economic action to the common good.

Weber's Thesis

In the late sixteenth century, the spearhead of the European economy started to move to the North, which began a slow but unstoppable process of cultural, social, and political transformation that continued into the second half of the eighteenth century—that is, until the Industrial Revolution, when all the preconditions for the transition from the civil market economy to the capitalistic market economy had been established. The causal factors in the transformation were multiple. The first was the influx of gold from the Americas, which immediately raised the level of prices, and eventually tripled them. The consequence was twofold: the gradual impoverishment of the social classes that lived on fixed incomes, notably the nobility and the clergy; and the swift and unexpected enrichment of the merchant bourgeoisie that lived on "profits upon alienation," that is, the proceeds from the difference between the purchase and sale price of goods. Economic historians underscore this transfer of wealth from the old ruling classes to the nascent bourgeoisie as one of the fundamental factors in the primitive accumulation of capital.[23]

A second factor in the move from civil to capitalist markets was the growth of long-distance trade thanks to the Age of Discovery. The consequent rise of commercial and industrial centers revived the class of merchant-manufacturers, leading to radical changes in the organization of production. The need for greater stability of supply prompted tighter control over the production cycle on the part of merchants. At the start of the seventeenth century, the putting-out system used two centuries earlier in Italy and Flanders began to become widespread in England and France. At first it was the merchant himself who supplied the craftsman with the raw material and commissioned the finished product, while the work was done independently in craft workshops. Later, the merchant took over the ownership of the means of production and hired wage labourers, thus controlling every phase of the production process. The worker no longer sold a finished product to the merchant but only his labour capacity, which became his sole source of livelihood. In the countryside the process was facilitated by the spread, along with the putting-out system, of enclosure[24] and by population growth. In the cities, the rise in prices impoverished those workers—the lowest strata of the old guilds—whose incomes were set by custom; and at the same time it drove out of the market craftsmen whose products were no longer competitive with those produced by the merchant-manufacturers. The latter alone could handle the new risks of enterprise.

A third factor in the transformation is worth mentioning here: the birth of national states after the Peace of Westphalia in 1648. This was a long historical process whose roots stretch back to the struggle among communes, papacy, and empire, but it gained decisive impetus in the second half of the seventeenth century with the need to unify markets and conduct economic policies in support of economic development. The centralized birth of the nation-states, in the end, took the administration of public affairs out of the hands of the citizens, relieving them of all responsibility for the common good and giving them an incentive for self-interested opportunism. The world of what had been common was transformed into a world of "common interests," hence, the opposition between public and private. What is public is the location of what is common, and this is set in opposition to what is private, which is the location of what is one's own. If the action of the State is always directed to care for that which is public, then the individual need only look out for himself. For the next three centuries, war in Europe becomes war between nation-states, in which *raison d'état*, the national interest, prevailed over all else, even when, as in the Wars of Religion, there appeared to be a powerful ideological component.

So we can see why the category of the common good was no longer adequate to interpret events, and why it receded as a useful guide to economic action. It was gradually supplanted by the notion of the total good. Here, the influence of the Reformation was crucial; its effects on economic life can never be overstated. The mutations in ecclesiastical organization, in the legal treatment of the goods of the Church and in relations with the secular authorities, all shook the pilasters of the preceding social order. For our purposes, within the Reformation, special importance attaches to Calvin's doctrine of predestination and more broadly to his stress on the individual's direct, exclusive relationship with God. Far from inducing loss of interest in this world in favour of the next, as one might expect, this doctrine served to mould patterns of conduct that ultimately proved to be of the greatest economic relevance. The Calvinist "secularization of holiness" led to the sanctification of labour and generally stimulated a powerful this-worldly activism.

This, then, is the context in which to place Max Weber's celebrated thesis that the Reformation encouraged—not, let us note, caused—the development of modern capitalism through the Protestant work ethic and the notion of "vocation" tied to the Calvinist idea of individual predestination. *The Protestant Ethic and the Spirit of Capitalism* (1904–5 and 1920) opens with a highly specific question: "What concatenation of circumstances resulted in the manifestation in the West, and here only, of cultural phenomena that, nevertheless, formed part of line of development of universal significance and validity?"[25] Seeking a meaningful answer, Weber begins by observing that "Protestantism has the effect of freeing the acquisition of wealth from the inhibitions of traditional ethics. It breaks the chains limiting the search for gain, not merely legalizing it but seeing it as the direct expression of the will of God." In particular, it is the Calvinist notion of asceticism—for Calvin, unlike the monastics, asceticism meant productive engagement in the world while controlling one's passions and impulses with reason—that, according to Weber, establishes the link between Protestantism and modern capitalism. The Benedictine rule *ora et labora* (pray and work) is replaced by Calvin's *laborare est orare* (work is prayer), converting Catholicism's other-worldly asceticism into the this-worldly asceticism of Calvinist spirituality. And this is the cradle from which grew the modern capitalist spirit.

According to Weber, what needed explaining was not so much capitalism as modern capitalism and especially its rapid diffusion throughout northern Europe. It is worth noting that unlike Luther, Calvin was fully conscious of the financial business carried on in his stronghold of Geneva and of its economic and social implications. So it is reasonable to argue that even though bourgeois values such as thrift, perseverance, and hard work all received recognition in Calvin's theology, modern capitalism as Max Weber defined it was more a side effect than the deliberate aim of that religious persuasion.

And there is more. Becker and Woessman's careful empirical study of Prussia, Weber's own region, has found that while there is indeed a significant positive correlation between Protestantism and economic success, this was due not specifically to Calvinist ethics but to the fact that the Reformation fostered literacy and schooling in general.[26] Luther and Calvin insisted that people needed to be able to read the Scriptures for themselves and in their own language. (Luther, in fact, produced the first German translation of the Bible.) The resulting mass literacy had the unexpected side effect of increasing the productivity of labour and hence economic prosperity. So it is true that Protestantism had a significant impact on economic growth where it became established, and in this sense the Weberian thesis is not disproved by research such as that of Iannaccone or Delacroix and Nielsen, according to whom no systematic influence on the development of capitalism in the countries of Europe can be ascribed to the Protestant ethic.[27] But Weber was mistaken about the channel through which this influence was exerted: the decisive factor was human capital, not Protestant ethics. This is also the conclusion reached, by another route, by Niall Ferguson, whose careful historical inquiry shows that the higher rates of growth in the Protestant countries starting in the seventeenth century depended much more on political and institutional factors (more efficient bureaucracy and administration, better representation of special interests, and a more equal distribution of wealth) than on theological ones.[28]

Max Weber opposed the arguments of historical materialist thinkers (such as Marx, Sombart, and R.H. Tawney) who held that Protestantism itself was generated by the rise of capitalism. Instead, with the support of the German philosopher and theologian Ernst Troeltsch, Weber inverted the causal relationship. And in this, I believe, he was right. Fanfani was among the first Italian scholars to contest the Weberian thesis in his celebrated 1934 essay.[29] The essay had a twofold aim: to back-date the rise of the "spirit of capitalism" to the late

Middle Ages, when the modern market economy took shape, and at the same time to show that this spirit was a deviation or at least a moving-away from Christian ethical principles. Both of these theses conflict with Weber. As Fanfani himself would write in 1976, in his mature years as an historian, "the weakening influence exerted by the social conception of medieval Catholicism is what explains the rise and growth of the capitalist spirit in the Catholic world."[30] In Fanfani's judgment, the Reformation strengthened but did not initiate the degeneration of the evangelical message, a development that had long been perceptible even within the Catholic world.

Underlying Fanfani's "strengthening" was the typically Protestant belief that salvation is an individual and not a community matter. Whereas in Catholic theology sin destroys the unity of mankind, in Protestant doctrine it is a rupture of the bond between the individual person and God. And thus salvation became an eminently individualistic question. The practical consequence of this alteration of perspective was the elimination, in the Reformation, of the social works of Catholicism: the resources spent on church buildings and rites within them, which is to say the abandonment of one of the highest expressions of the essential role of the common good. And this in turn resulted in the transfer of an enormous mass of resources from the social sphere to the economy, thus favouring the accumulation of capital. To put it another way, the Reformation affected not only the demand side, as is nearly universally believed, by shifting people's preferences toward a greater propensity to work and save, but also the supply side, with an appreciable reduction in the cost of religious services and practices. The elimination of the ecclesiastical hierarchy, of indulgences, of pilgrimages and other rites, of opulent churches, and so on, all freed scarce resources (labour and capital) and channeled them to other, economically more productive uses.

In the light of the analysis above, we are now in a position to locate the origins of Fanfani's incomprehension of the Weberian thesis.[31] The market economy did not arise as the antithesis to the Catholic ethic—as Fanfani believed—but was one of its most mature fruits. The key insight here is that at first the market was not a capitalist but a civil market. Its purpose was to serve the common good, not the total good. The decline of the Italian cities, beginning at the end of the fifteenth century, had a series of causes, one of which was the establishment of profit as the main driving force of economic activity. The era of civil humanism, and its civil economy, was a brief one. The age of freedom and the republics gave way to autocrats, principalities, and absolute monarchies, which paved the way to an epoch of authoritarianism far removed from the *libertas fiorentina* and the model of urban civilization. This explains why this brief period, with the institution of equality of citizens and freedom, including economic freedom, was followed in the seventeenth and eighteenth centuries by the forceful assertion of works of political and social theory in which Leviathan was given the task of uniting a civil society that had proven unable to govern the dynamics of community life and above all of making the process of economic development self-propagating.

The idea was gaining ground, sustained and justified by Protestant theology, that although man does indeed live in society, he does so only driven by necessity and interest and not because, as Aristotle taught, he is by nature a social animal. Life in community was seen as a phenomenon of the human condition and was experienced as a constraint from which it was impossible to escape. Man is a fundamentally egoistic and rational being, interested in maximizing his utility subject to constraints that a theologically guided ethics points out. This vision precludes reciprocity—and hence the free gift—as an essential dimension of being human, rejecting the anthropology of Augustine, Aquinas, and the early Scholastic school. It was against this illiberal and "noncivil" view of society that the Enlightenment, not only in France but also in Scotland and Italy, would react against with such vehemence, and not against humanist reciprocity, which actually was later adopted as "fraternity" by the French Revolution.[32]

In other words, in Latouche's terms, the advent of the Reformation broke the link that until then had held the two dimensions of reason together: the "elder daughter" of Minerva, *Phrònesis* (wisdom, reason), and the "younger son," *Logòs epistemonikòs* (geometrical reason). In the Reformation, these two spiritual children of Minerva were separated. "Protestant rationality" was identified with *Logòs* and "Mediterranean reason" with *Phrònesis*. The paradigm of instrumental rationality (the rational choice model), which is the true core of modern capitalism, thus found a hospitable terrain in Protestant spirituality.[33]

Our interpretation explains why, as early as the first half of the nineteenth century, there was a substantial shift in Protestant opinion both in Europe and in America, a move to a severe critique of the theory and practice of capitalism considered as the spirit of evil, the corrupter of all things. As Giovanni Rizza notes with great precision, Ritschl and his school sought to reinforce the social side of Christian morals.[34] In England, F. D. Maurice (1805–72) and then W. Temple (1881–1944) offered theological support for the protests of the working class, with unsparing and audacious criticism of the capitalist system. The same happened in Germany, with the work of F. Naumann (1860–90), and in Switzerland with the Christian Socialist movement of L. Ragaz and W. Monod.

In polemical intensity, these lines of thought and action rivaled those of the Catholic world, as represented by W. von Ketteler (1811–77), the Bishop of Mainz and the founder of what would come to be known as "social Catholicism";

Cardinal H. Manning of Westminster (1808–92), whose essay "Dignity and the Rights of Labour" prepared the way for *Rerum Novarum*; and L. J. de Bonald, Bishop of Lyon, who fought against the materialization of economic life under capitalism. But the most incisive critique of the theory and practice of capitalism as a system claiming to govern all the spheres of human life came from the neo-Calvinist movement led in the Netherlands by A. Kuyper and the neo-Orthodox movement inspired by Karl Barth and Emil Brunner. These Protestant thinkers were contemporaries of Max Weber, but he could not (or would not) take account of them. Had he done so, the whole debate would have taken a different course.

It is worth contrasting the most recent positions of neo-Calvinist theology with those of Michael Novak, one of the most influential students of the relationship between Catholicism and capitalism today. After a frontal assault on Fanfani, accused of "anticapitalist sentiments" stemming from the uncritical acceptance of Catholic corporativism, Novak seeks to show that a "democratic and liberal" capitalism that accepted democracy and recognized the primacy of politics over the economy not only would not conflict with the Catholic ethic but also would be supported and given legitimation by it.[35] Here we are facing a sort of reversal of roles among supporters of Catholic and Protestant positions vis-à-vis the spirit of capitalism. Once more, we see how the intellectual confusion engendered by the mistaken identification of market economy solely with capitalism spawns inconclusive diatribe.

Why Resist the Dissolution of an Intellectual Category?

Finally, let me turn to the third of questions that opened this essay, which proves to be particularly helpful in testing the fundamental hypothesis of the True Wealth project. Why has the perspective of the common good as formulated by CST begun to reemerge in the last quarter century, like an underground river, after vanishing from sight for centuries? How has the transition from national markets to the global market during that same time span made that perspective relevant and topical once again? Let me note in passing that these developments are part of a vast current of economic ideas whose subject is the connection between religious belief and economic performance. A new field of research has come into being of late, mainly in Britain and America: the economics of religion. Starting from the postulate that religious beliefs are decisive in shaping the cognitive maps of people and moulding the society's behavioural norms, this research program seeks to measure how much a given religion has influenced, in a given country or territory, the formation of categories of economic thought, welfare programmes, education policy, and so on. After a protracted period in which the presumed secularization of society seemed to have put an end to the religious question, at least in economics, this new turn of events is certainly paradoxical. (For more on this, see Mary Hirschfeld's essay in this volume).

So we return to the original question, with the observation that beginning in the first half of the nineteenth century, the civil vision of both the market and the economy in general began to disappear from scientific research and from political and cultural discourse. The reasons were many and varied. Consider just the two most important.

The first was the slow but steady spread throughout high European cultural life of Jeremy Bentham's utilitarian philosophy. His main work, in fact, dated to 1789 but would take decades to become hegemonic within the field of economics. It was with the utilitarian moral view that mainstream economics came to enshrine the hyperminimalist anthropology of *homo oeconomicus* and simultaneously its socially atomistic method.[36] The clarity and deep significance of this passage are notable: "The community is a fictitious body, composed of the individual person who is considered as constituting as it were its members. The interest of the community then is, what is it?—the sum of the interests of the several members who compose it."[37]

The second reason was the Industrial Revolution and the definitive establishment of industrial society. An industrial society is one that produces commodities. Machines dominate everywhere; the rhythm of life has a mechanical cadence. Human and animal muscles were very largely replaced by more powerful forms of energy, explaining the enormous increases in productivity that accompanied mass production. Energy and machinery transformed the very nature of work. Personal skills were broken down into their elementary components, hence the need for coordination and organization. A world was thus ushered in where men were seen as "things" because it is easier to coordinate "things" than people, and where people are separated from the roles they perform. Organizations—first and foremost, productive enterprises—deal with roles, not people. And this happens not just in the factory but all throughout society. Fordism and Taylorism represented the highest-level successful effort to produce a theory of this model of the social order. The rise of the assembly line has its correlate in the spread of consumerism, hence the schizophrenia typical of "modern times." On the one hand, the loss of the meaning of work (alienation due to the depersonalization of the worker) is pushed to extremes; and on the other, as if to compensate, the consumer becomes affluent. Marxist thought and its practical applications by the socialist movements sought in various ways, as we know, to try to find a way out of this social model.

The complicated interrelation of and conflict between these two forces (atomistic individualism and the industrialization of work) had important consequences for the theme treated here, namely the coexistence—even in today's society—of two opposed concepts of the market, each deeply flawed. One sees the market as a "necessary evil," an institution that we cannot do without because it ensures economic progress, but nevertheless an evil to guard against and to keep under control. The other sees the market as the best place for solving the problem of politics, just as the liberal-individualistic position maintains. In this second view, the "logic" of the market must be allowed to extend, albeit with the necessary adaptations and refinements, to all the spheres of social life, from family to school to politics to religious practices.

It is easy to pick out the weaknesses of these two mirror-image conceptions of the market. The first, perfectly summed up in the aphorism that "government must not row but take the helm," is based on the fight against inequality. It holds that only State intervention for income redistribution can diminish the differences between individuals and social groups. But that is not how matters actually stand. Inequality in the advanced Western countries, which had been reduced starting in 1945, has widened scandalously again in the last twenty years, notwithstanding massive State intervention in the economy. We know perfectly well the reasons for this tendency, involving the transition to post-industrial society: developments such as the application of information and communications technology to the production process and the creation of global labour and capital markets. But the point is to understand why redistribution cannot be an *exclusive* task of the State. The fact is that political stability is an objective that cannot be attained by measures to reduce inequality within the current model of democracy—the elitist competitive model in the sense of Weber and Schumpter—but only by economic growth. The endurance and reputation of democratic governments are determined much more by their ability to increase total wealth than to redistribute it fairly among citizens. And this is the simple, if unhappy, reason that the poor do not take part in the democratic game and thus do not form a constituency capable of influencing those who think exclusively in terms of political interest. So if we want to combat the endemic increase in inequality as a threat to peace and democracy, we must act primarily on the production of wealth and income, not only its redistribution.

The second view of markets—the monolithic free market mind-set of the "one best way"—is likewise mistaken. The financial crisis of 2008 reminded everyone of a basic principle of Catholic social thought. It is not true that the greatest possible extension of the logic of the (noncivil) market increases everyone's welfare. That is, the metaphor that "a rising tide raises all the boats" is false. The reasoning underpinning that metaphor is basically that since citizens' welfare depends on economic prosperity and since this is causally associated with market relations, the true priority of political action must be to guarantee the conditions for the greatest possible flowering of the market culture. The more generous the welfare state, therefore, the more it sets constraints on economic growth and thus runs counter to the diffusion of welfare and prosperity. Hence, this approach wants a selective welfare system designed only for those who have lost out in the market race. Others, those who manage to stay in the virtuous cycle of growth, should protect their own interests by themselves. Yet the simple observation of reality unveils the logical inconsistency of this line of thought: economic growth (i.e., the sustained increase in wealth) and civil progress (i.e., the expansion of the spheres of personal liberty) no longer march together. In other words, the increase in material welfare is no longer accompanied by an increase in well-being. Reducing the capacity to include those excluded from the market does not help those who participate in the market, and it reduces liberty, which is always deleterious to public happiness. (See the important contribution by Daniel Finn, in this volume, which addresses the same problem from a different, albeit complementary, perspective).

These two conceptions of the market, with their diametrically opposed philosophical premises and political consequences, have ultimately produced an unintended result at the cultural level (at least up until the recent financial crisis), namely, the dominance of an idea of the market that is antithetical to the idea of the market in the civil economic tradition. The new capitalist idea sees the market as a mechanism based on a twofold norm: the impersonality of relations of exchange (the less I know my counterparty the greater will be my advantage because you do better business with strangers!) and the exclusively self-interested motivation of all those taking part in the market (so that "moral sentiments" such as sympathy, reciprocity, fraternity and the like are allotted no space whatever in the market arena). And so it came about that the progressive, majestic expansion of market relations over the past century and a half ended up strengthening that pessimistic interpretation of human nature posited by Hobbes and Mandeville: only the iron laws of the market, supposedly, can tame perverse impulses and anarchic drives. The caricature of human nature that in this way imposed itself has helped accredit a twofold error: that the sphere of the market coincides with egoism, the place within which every man pursues his own individual self-interest as best he can; and, symmetrically, that the sphere of the State coincides with solidarity, the pursuit of collective interests. This is the foundation for the well-known dichotomous model State versus market, a model in which the State is identified with the public sphere and the market with the private one.

At this point it is not hard to explain the revival in contemporary culture of the debate over the concept of the common good, which is the cornerstone of the social Catholic code. As John Paul II made clear on any number of occasions, CST must not be seen as one more ethical theory on top of the many already set out in the literature but as a "common grammar" for them because it rests on a specific point of view, namely, that of care for the human good. In fact, where other ethics are founded either in the search for rules (as in positive natural law doctrines, according to which ethics is derived from legal norms) or in action (the neocontractualism of John Rawls or the neo-utilitarianism of John Harsanyi), the fulcrum of Catholic social doctrine is "being with." The meaning of the ethics of the common good is that in order to understand human action you must take the standpoint of the person who acts (see *Veritatis Splendor*, 78) and not that of a third party (as in natural law doctrine) or the impartial spectator (as Adam Smith suggested). For the moral good, as a practical reality, is known first of all not by those who theorize but by those who practice it. It is the latter who are able identify it and hence choose it with certainty whenever it is in doubt.

In John Paul II's Bull of Indiction of the Jubilee Year of 2000, *Incarnationis Mysterium*, we read: "There is also a need to create a new culture of international solidarity and cooperation, where all—particularly the wealthy nations and the private sector—accept responsibility for *an economic model* which serves everyone."[38] This passage is worth underscoring. Never in the long history of holy years had a Pontiff set out such a purpose—not just a more or less accidental consequence—for a Jubilee. Even more specific is the message for January 1, 2000, entitled "Peace on Earth to those whom God loves," which reads:

> In this context we also need to examine the growing concern felt by many economists and financial professionals when ... they reflect on the role of the market, on the pervasive influence of monetary and financial interests, on the widening gap between the economy and society.... Perhaps the time has come for a new and deeper reflection on the nature of the economy and its purposes.... Here I would like to invite economists and financial professionals, as well as political leaders, to recognize the urgency of the need to ensure that economic practices and related political policies have as their aim the good of every person and of the whole person.[39]

What is new, and somewhat surprising, is the call to tackle the issue we are dealing with at the level of theoretical foundations, or rather its cultural premises. In the face of the capitalistic squalor of the tendency to reduce all human relationships to the exchange of equivalent products, the spirit of contemporary mankind rises up and demands a different story.

The key word, the one that best expresses this need today, is "fraternity." It was, as we know, one of the watchwords of the French Revolution, but it was dropped by the postrevolutionary order and eventually erased from the political and economic lexicon. It was Franciscan thought, as we have recalled, that gave the word the meaning it retained over the centuries, which was at one and the same time to complement and to transcend the principle of solidarity. For while solidarity is the principle of social organization that enables unequals to become equals, fraternity is the principle that enables equals to be diverse. Fraternity allows people who are equals in dignity and in fundamental rights to devise different life plans and express their charisms distinctively. The nineteenth and the twentieth centuries were marked by major cultural and political battles—such as the labour and civil rights movements—in the name of solidarity, which was definitely a good thing. The point, however, is that a good society cannot be satisfied with solidarity only. A society with solidarity but not fraternity would be a society from which everyone would try to escape. For while a fraternal society is also characterized by solidarity, the reverse does not necessarily hold.

Consider, for example, the extensive ongoing debate on what Arthur Okun (1975) famously called "the big trade-off" between efficiency and equity (or distributive justice). Is it better to favour the exchange of equivalents, the principle of efficiency, or to give more power to government to improve the distribution of income? Questions like this have filled the research agendas of a host of economists and social scientists, with results that, to be honest, have been quite modest. The reason is certainly not a lack of empirical data or the inadequacy of analytical tools. Rather, it is that this literature has forgotten the principle of reciprocity, whose specific end is to translate the culture of fraternity into practice. The failure to produce a credible solution to the trade-off, despite the quality of the intellectual forces deployed, is due to the failure to remember that a human society in which the sense of fraternity is extinguished—in which the only aim is to improve transactions consisting in the exchange of equivalents or to increase public welfare transfers—is an unsustainable society. A society without the principle of fraternity has no future. That is, a society in which there is only "give in order to receive" or "give out of duty" is incapable of progressing, which is why neither the liberal-individualist worldview, in which nearly everything is for sale, nor the state-centred view of society, in which nearly all is duty, is a safe guide to lead us out of the quagmire in which modern society is now bogged down.[40]

What can be done so that the market can once again be an instrument of civilization, as in the humanist age, a means for strengthening social bonds?

This is the major challenge CST is posing today. That this is indeed an epochal challenge is confirmed above all by one question: in today's environment of capitalistic markets, is it possible that institutions whose *modus operandi* is based on reciprocity can not only emerge but also expand? To put it differently, what room is open for concepts such as fraternity, reciprocity, and gift in a sphere like the economic, in which the drive to impersonal relations and the irrelevance of interpersonal ties is not only strong but actually the condition for good business conduct? As I have suggested elsewhere, the answer of the followers of such scholars as Polanyi, Hirschman, Hirsch, and Hollis (to name but the most representative) is that economic agents, acting in a market governed solely by the principle of exchange of equivalents, are led into strictly self-interested decision-making. With time, they tend to transfer this way of thinking to other social spheres, including those in which the public interest demands virtuous acts (a "virtuous" act being one that not only *is* in the public interest but that is performed *because* it is for the common good). This is Karl Polanyi's thesis of contagion: "The market advances over the desertification of society."

A. O. Hirschman's position (1982) differs somewhat in line of argument but converges to the same conclusion. He holds that since virtue is a good action repeated many times and whose value increases with use, as Aristotle taught, virtue depends on a person's acquired habits. It follows that a society that favours economic and political institutions that tend to economize on citizens' exercise of virtue is a society that will run down its stock of virtue and will have great difficulty in reconstituting it. This is because, like muscles, virtues atrophy with lack of use. Brennan and Hamlin (1995), in fact, speak of the "moral muscle": economy in the use of the virtues crowds out the very possibility of producing virtue. So the greater the reliance placed on institutions bound to the exchange of equivalents, the more closely the society's cultural traits and social norms will conform to that principle. Martin Hollis reached a similar if more sophisticated conclusion, with his "paradox of trust": "The stronger the bond of trust, the more a society can progress. The more it progresses, the more its members become rational and thus more instrumental in their mutual representations. The more instrumental they are, the less capable they are of according or earning trust. So the development of society erodes the bonds that make it possible and of which it has a continuous need."[41]

Clearly, if these authors were right, there is little hope indeed of a positive answer to our question. Luckily, though, things are not so desperate as they may appear. First, to be acceptable the argument underpinning this reasoning needs to demonstrate that there actually is a causal nexus between virtuous dispositions and "institutions that economize on virtue," a nexus whereby agents, operating in the capitalist market, eventually acquire, by contagion, an individ-ualist uniform (self-interest plus instrumental rationality). Now quite apart from the fact that no such demonstration has ever been produced, the fact is that people with virtuous dispositions, acting in an institutional environment whose rules are forged on the assumption of self-interested rational behaviour, tend to get better results than egocentric individuals. The fact is that the vir-tuous person in a market based on the sole principle of the exchange of equiv-alents "flourishes" because he does what the market rewards, even though his motive is not to get the reward. As Brennan and Hamlin (1995) write, the reward reinforces his inner disposition because it makes the exercise of virtue less "costly."

Second, the thesis of Polanyi and the others requires that virtuous disposi-tions be the consequence of behaviour, but the exact opposite is true. Not even the most extreme behaviourism has gone so far as to maintain that behaviour causes one's natural disposition. And if the thesis were valid, there would be no explaining the fact that in today's societies dominated by institutions that "economize on virtue," we are witnessing an unprecedented flowering of orga-nizations of civil society (voluntary causes, social cooperatives, social enter-prises, nongovernmental organizations, and so on). This is because the motivation inducing agents to behave virtuously is critical. It makes a great deal of difference whether a person behaves virtuously for fear of legal or social sanction or because of an inner motivation.

How can we think that the idea of restoring the concept of the common good to the economic sphere is anything more than a consoling utopia? There are two verifiable considerations. One is the recognition that at the basis of the capitalist economy, there lies a pragmatic—not a logical—contradiction. The capitalist economy is certainly a market economy, that is, an institutional arrangement in which the two basic principles of the modern age are opera-tive: freedom of action and enterprise and the equality of all before the law. At the same time, however, the primary institution of capitalism—the capitalist enterprise—has been constructed over three centuries on the prin-ciple of hierarchy. A productive system has arisen consisting in a central structure to which a certain number of individuals voluntarily, for a price (a wage), transfer some goods or services of theirs, which once acquired by the enterprise entirely escape the control of those who supplied them.

Economic history has shown clearly how this came about, and we are also perfectly familiar with the great economic progress that this arrangement gen-erated. However, in this period of epochal transition from the modern to the postmodern era, more and more voices are noting how difficult it is to get the democratic and the capitalistic principles to advance together. The key problem is the so-called privatization of the public. Capitalist enterprises are increasingly taking control of the conduct of individuals—who spend well over half their living time at the workplace—and taking that control away from the State and other institutions, first and foremost the family. Ideas such as freedom of choice, tolerance, equality before the law, participation, and the like, coined and popularized in the age of civil humanism and reinforced during the Enlightenment as an antidote to the quasi-absolute power of the sovereign, are being appropriated and recalibrated by capitalist firms to transform individuals, no longer subjects, into the purchasers of the enterprise's own goods and services.

The dysfunction referred to above lies in the fact that if there are sound reasons for considering the greatest possible extension of democracy to be a good thing, then we shall have to start looking at what goes on *within* enterprises and not just at what happens between them when they meet in the marketplace. Robert Dahl has written, "If democracy is justified in the government of the State, then it is also justified in the government of the firm."[42] A society in which democracy applies only to politics will never be fully democratic. A good society to live in will not force its members into uncomfortable dissociations: democratic as citizens and voters, undemocratic as workers and consumers.

The second consideration turns on the increasingly common dissatisfaction with the way in which the principle of liberty is interpreted. As we know, there are three constituent dimensions to freedom: autonomy, immunity, and opportunity. Autonomy means freedom of choice. We are not free if we are not in a position to choose. Immunity means lack of coercion by outside agents. Essentially, this is the negative liberty ("freedom from") of Isaiah Berlin. Opportunity, or capability, as Amartya Sen uses the term, means the capacity to choose, to attain the objectives that the individual sets himself, at least in part. We are not free if we never at least partly realize our life plan. Yet while the free-trade approach ensures the first and second of these dimensions of freedom at the expense of the third, the state-centred approach, whether in the mixed-economy or social-market economy versions, tends to give the second and third dimension precedence over the first. The free-market approach can indeed serve as the motor of change, but it is not equally capable of managing the negative consequences, due to the substantial time lag between the sharing of the costs of change and that of its benefits. The costs are immediate and tend to be levied on the weakest members of the population. The benefits arrive with time and tend to go to the most talented people. As Schumpeter was among the first to see, "creative destruction" is at the heart of capitalism—which destroys the old in order to create the new and creates the new in order to destroy the old—but is also its Achilles heel. The social-market approach, in turn, in any of its many versions, assigns the State to deal with this asynchrony but does not modify the logic of the capitalistic market. It only restricts its sphere of operation and its incidence. By contrast, the distinctive characteristic of the civil market and its underlying common good paradigm is the attempt to keep all three dimensions of liberty together.

Conclusion

This essay advocates a point of view on the relationship between CST's criteria and an effective path to universal sustainable prosperity that is an alternative to the two inadequate views that are prevalent today. The first of these views holds that the Catholic conscience must be radically anticapitalist, seeing in capitalism an adversary to vanquish no less dangerous than Communism. This school appeals—too often naively and sometimes instrumentally—to the line of thought running from *Rerum Novarum* (1891) through *Quadragesimo Anno* (1931) and *Gaudium et Spes* (1968) to the *New Catholic Catechism* of 1992, which affirms: "The Church rejected the totalitarian and atheistic ideologies associated, in modern times, with 'communism' and 'socialism.' However, it also rejected, in the political practice of 'capitalism', individualism and the primacy of the law of the market over human labour." The second view—which is today in the minority—contends that at least since John Paul II's encyclical *Centesimus Annus* (1991) there has been the long-awaited turnabout. This is the thesis of Novak and other intellectuals known in America as "neoconservatives," who argue that the failure to connect what they call "democratic capitalism" with the Catholic ethic arises from the mistaken identification of the "bourgeois spirit" with a lack of faith.

My own view is that both these interpretations, legitimate and interesting as they may be, are reductive: one takes justice, the other liberty as the sole governing principle for gauging assonance or dissonance between Catholicism and capitalism. As we have seen, Catholic thought has always refused this kind of dichotomy. Rather, its intent is to hold together the three basic principles of any social order—exchange of equivalents, redistribution, and reciprocity—acting not only on the cultural but also on the strictly institutional plane. Truth to tell, this project has not always—or should we say, almost never—been fully realized. Historically, deviations from the mainstream—corporativist, capitalist, communist—have been the rule rather than the exception. Interestingly, where in 1891 Leo XIII identified the main problem as "the abuses of capitalism and the illusions of socialism," a hundred years later John Paul II decried "the abuses of socialism and the illusions of capitalism." But none of this warrants the conclusion that the Catholic ethic can be dragged to one side or the other and reduced to a partisan vision.

The guiding idea of CST is interdependence among basic principles. As the Compendium of the Social Doctrine reminds us (para. 162): "The principles of the Church's social doctrine must be appreciated in their unity, interrelatedness and articulation." Of course, the forms that CST may take change with time and place, but the Catholic ethic can never be called on for cultural support for modes of production or economic organizations that in practice deny the perspective of the common good that constitutes an overarching framework.

That a kind of revival of the concept of the common good is underway today is confirmed by numerous signs, which speak, in essence, of a renewed interest in seriously considering the civil economic viewpoint, at least as a working hypothesis. There is nothing to marvel at here. When one acknowledges the looming crisis of our civilization, one is practically obliged to abandon any dystopic attitudes and dared to seek out new paths of thought. This is the spirit of the True Wealth of Nations project.

NOTES

I would like to express my sincere gratitude to the Institute for Advanced Catholic Studies for having organized a most interesting and stimulating conference and to all the participants for their sympathetic reaction to this paper and their constructive criticism. The usual disclaimer applies. A somewhat different version of this chapter was published in Italian in the book edited by Giovanni Filoramo, *Le religioni e il mondo moderno* (Torino: Einaudi, 2009).

1. For a lucid analysis of how historical changes modify our interpretation of the principles of CST and how the Church has been able to provide an ever more accurate foundation and shape to these principles, see the contribution by Mary Hirschfeld in this volume.

2. For a survey of the recent literature, see R. Barro and R. McCleary, "Religion and Economy," 1–25; also L. Guiso, P. Sapienza, and L. Zingales, "Does Culture Affect Economic Outcomes?"

3. W. Sombart, *The Quintessence of Modern Capitalism*. Actually the word "capital" appeared in the various neo-Latin languages as early as the twelfth century but was not taken into early modern English until some centuries later.

4. Jacky Good, *Capitalism and Modernity*. In his celebrated *Origines du Capitalisme en France*, Bernard Groethuysen dates the origin of the "spirit of capitalism" in Catholic France even earlier, in the seventeenth century.

5. Fernand Braudel, *Civilization and Capitalism*. In Braudel's view, market economy and capitalism cannot be said to coincide, because in order to work, capitalism needs the State to ensure the execution of contracts. But the nation-state did not begin to form until the Peace of Westphalia, long after the advent of the market

economy. Marx himself, in *Capital*, never uses the term "capitalism" but prefers the expression "capitalist mode of production."

6. Oreste Bazzichi, "Valenza antropologica del discorso economico francescano."

7. E. Garin, *L'umanismo italiano*. It may be of interest to know that for centuries, the Catholic Church used the expression *doctrina civilis* to refer to teachings about political order and that it was only after the pontificate of Leo XIII that *doctrina civilis* became *doctrina socialis*.

8. It was humanism above all that passed this "desire" down to the future of all of Western civilization. The texts and archeological finds of Greek and Roman civilization were recovered, philologically reconstructed, and interpreted in the light of newly acquired knowledge, so as to produce new "fashions."

9. Basilio di Cesarea, *Il buon uso della ricchezza*.

10. The first pledge bank (*Montes pietatis*) was founded by a friar, Michele Carcano, in Perugia in 1462. It was intended to serve the poor but not the destitute, people who did need help but not charity. That is, the needy person had to learn to redeem himself: that was the purpose of this kind of "charitable credit." The idea behind the pledge banks was that goods—above all, money—must be used for the common good; in fact, merchants were recognized as guarantors of public well-being because they could bring together producers, consumers, and professionals together synergistically.

11. R. Guidi, *Il dibattito sull'uomo nel Quattrocento*.

12. G. Todeschini, "Credibilità, fiducia, ricchezza."

13. G. Todeschini, *Ricchezza Francescana*, 74.

14. Ibid., 81.

15. Ibid., 82.

16. Cited in O. Nuccio, *Il pensiero economico italiano*. See also M. Vitale, "L'impresa nell'Europa."

17. Economic "rent" is a payment to some productive element (whether a person or a thing) that exceeds the amount necessary to keep that factor of production employed in its current use.

18. Bernardino da Siena, *Prediche volgari sul Campo di Siena*.

19. D. Canfora, *Prima di Machiavelli*.

20. See F. Bruni, *La città divisa*, for a fine historical reconstruction of the notion of the common good as opposed to private good, from Dante's *Convivio* to Guicciardini.

21. "From Raterio to Olivi, and with the significant mediation of canon and civil law, gifts were more and more clearly seen as a form of economic behaviour that could bring back into the civil concourse those who had left it" (G. Todeschini, *I mercanti e il tempio*, 208).

22. Bernardino da Siena, *Prediche volgari sul Campo di Siena*, 118.

23. For a more detailed treatment, see E. Screpanti and S. Zamagni, *A Profile of History of Economic Thought*.

24. Enclosure is the process by which common land is taken into private ownership (fenced in or enclosed).

25. M. Weber, *Sociologia della religione*, 3. See M. Scattola, *Teologia politica* for a competent, thorough discussion.

26. S. Becker and L. Woessmann, "Was Weber Wrong?" This is one of a tiny group of works that have "tested" Weber's thesis using regional data (for nineteenth-century Prussia) and not cross-country data. International data notoriously suffer from severe problems of endogeneity, yet the bulk of the empirical literature has taken this approach. After isolating the positive effect of literacy on economic growth, Becker and Woessmann find that there is no significant difference, in economic success, between the Protestant and the Catholic counties of Prussia.

27. L. R. Iannaccone, "Introduction to the Economics of Religion," 1465–95; J. Delacroix and F. Nielsen, "The Beloved Myth," 509–53.

28. N. Ferguson, *Economics, Religion and the Decline of Europe*. In what has become a classic, the eminent Protestant thinker A. Bieler also maintains that Weber and his followers greatly exaggerated Calvin's influence in the rise of modern capitalism. A. Bieler, *La pensée èconomique et sociale de Calvin*.

29. A. Fanfani, *Cattolicesimo e protestantesimo nella formazione storica del capitalismo*. This truly major work, translated into any number of foreign languages, brought formerly unknown documents from archives in Tuscany to light. Ironically, it is much better known abroad than in Italy.

30. A. Fanfani, *Capitalismo, Socialità, Partecipazione*, 122. From a different analytical standpoint, Stark has recently come to the same conclusion, albeit with different arguments. See R. Stark, *The Victory of Reason*.

31. "So Weber's explanation is inadequate, and we have to ask whether there weren't other ways in which Protestantism encouraged or constrained the capitalist spirit...which, opposed and kept under control by Catholicism, became a social force when, *in the fifteenth century*, Catholicism began to decline, and was encouraged by Humanism, insofar as *Humanism weakened* Catholic ties" (Fanfani, *Cattolicesimo*, 166; emphasis added).

32. See L. Bruni and S. Zamagni, *Civil Economy*, for a more extensive treatment.

33. S. Latouche, *La sfida di Minerva. Razionalità occidentale e ragione mediterranea*.

34. G. Rizza, "On Economics, Ethics and Theology." Includes bibliographical references for the authors cited in the text.

35. M. Novak, *The Catholic Ethic and the Spirit of Capitalism*. More than a critique of Weber, Novak's essay is an effort to demonstrate the complete compatibility between "democratic capitalism" and the social doctrine of the Catholic Church as articulated in the prior forty years.

36. In the context of a clear discussion of the many definitions of social capital today available in the literature, John A. Coleman (in his essay in this volume) correctly stresses the point that the central thesis of social capital theory is antiatomistic, in the sense that "relationships matter."

37. Jeremy Bentham, *Introduction to the Principles of Morals and Legislation*.

38. John Paul II, *Incarnationis Mysterium*, para. 12.

39. John Paul II, http://www.vatican.va/holy_father/john_paul_ii/messages/peace/documents/hf_jp-ii_mes_08121999_xxxiii-world-day-for-peace_en.html.

40. For an extension of the argument. see D. Finn, *The Moral Ecology of Markets*.
See also A. Barrera, *Economic Compulsion and Christian Ethics*.

41. Martin Hollis, *Trust with Reason*, 73.

42. R. Dahl, *A Preface to Economic Democracy*, 57. See also M. Fleurbaey,
Capitalisme ou démocratie? L'alternative du XXI Siècle.

REFERENCES

Barrera, Albino. *Economic Compulsion and Christian Ethics*. Cambridge,
    UK: Cambridge University Press, 2005.
Barro, R., and R. McCleary. "Religion and Economy." *Journal of Economic Perspectives*
    20 (2006): 1–25.
Bazzichi, Oreste. "Valenza antropologica del discorso economico francescano."
    Miscellanea Francescana 105 (July 2005): 65–84.
Becker, S., and L. Woessmann. "Was Weber Wrong? A Human Capital Theory of
    Protestant Economic History." CES Working Paper 1987. May 2007.
Bentham, Jeremy. *Introduction to the Principles of Morals and Legislation*. London:
    Lincoln's Inn Fields, and E. Wilson, Royal Exchange, 1789 [1823], I, IV.
Bieler, A. *La pensée èconomique et sociale de Calvin*. Geneva: Librairie de l'Université,
    1959.
Braudel, Fernand. *Civilization and Capitalism, 15th–18th Century*. 3 vols. New York:
    Harper & Row, 1979.
Brennan, G., and A. P. Hamlin. "Economizing on Virtue." *Constitutional Political
    Economy* 6:1 (1995): 64–90.
Bruni, F. La città divisa. Le parti e il bene comune da Dante a Guicciardini. Bologna: Il
    Mulino, 2003.
Bruni L., and S. Zamagni. *Civil Economy*. Oxford: Oxford University Press, 2007.
Canfora, D. Prima di Machiavelli. Politica e cultura in età umanistica. Rome: Laterza,
    2005.
Dahl, R. *A Preface to Economic Democracy*. Berkeley: University of California Press, 1985.
da Siena, Bernardino. *Prediche volgari sul Campo di Siena* (1427). Edited by C. Delcorno.
    Milan: Rusconi, 1989.
Delacroix J., and F. Nielsen. "The Beloved Myth: Protestantism and the Rise of Industrial
    Capitalism in Nineteenth Century Europe." *Social Forces* 80 (2002): 509–53.
di Cesarea, Basilio. *Il buon uso della ricchezza*. Piacenza: Berti, 1931.
Fanfani, A. Capitalismo, Socialità, Partecipazione. Milan: Mursia, 1976.
———. Cattolicesimo e protestantesimo nella formazione storica del capitalismo.
    Milan: Vita e Pensiero, 1934.
Ferguson, N. *Economics, Religion and the Decline of Europe*. Washington, DC: Institute
    of Economic Affairs, 2004.
Finn, D. *The Moral Ecology of Markets*. Cambridge, UK: Cambridge University Press,
    2006.
Fleurbaey, M. Capitalisme ou démocratie? L'alternative du XXI Siècle. Paris:
    B. Grasset, 2006.

Garin, E. *Lumanesimo italiano* (1947). Rev. ed. Rome: Laterza, 1994.

Goody, Jack. *Capitalism and Modernity.* New York: John Wiley & Sons, 2003.

Groethuysen, Bernard. *Origines de l'esprit bourgeois en France.* Paris: Gallimard, 1927.

Guidi, R. Il debattito sull'uomo nel Quattrocento. Rome: Tielle Media, 1999.

Guiso L., P. Sapienza, and L. Zingales. "Does Culture Affect Economic Outcomes?" *Journal of Economic Perspectives* 20 (Spring 2006): 23–48.

Hamlin, A. P. and G. Brennan. "Economizing on Virtue." *Constitutional Political Economy* 6:1 (1995): 35–56.

Hirschman, A. O., "Rival Interpretations of Market Society: Civilizing, Destructive or Feeble?" *Journal of Economic Literature* 20 (1982): 1462–484.

Hollis, Martin. *Trust with Reason.* New York: Cambridge University Press, 1998.

Iannaccone, L. R. "Introduction to the Economics of Religion." *Journal of Economic Literature* 36 (1998): 1465–95.

John Paul II. Incarnationis Mysterium. *Origins* 28 (Dec 10, 1998): 445–53.

———. Veritatis Splendor. *Origins* 23 (Oct 14, 1993): 297–334.

Latouche, S. La sfida di Minerva. Razionalità occidentale e ragione mediterranea. Turin: Bollati Boringhieri, 2000.

Novak, M. The Catholic Ethic and the Spirit of Capitalism. New York: Free Press, 1993.

Nuccio, O. *Il pensiero economico italiano: le fonti* (1050–1450). Sassari: Gallizzi, 1987.

Rizza, G. "On Economics, Ethics and Theology." *International Symposium of the Society for Reformational Philosophy on Cultures and Christianity AD* 2000. Hoven, Netherlands, 2000.

Scattola, M. *Teologia politica.* Bologna: Il Mulino, 2007.

Screpanti E., and S. Zamagni. *A Profile of History of Economic Thought.* Oxford: Oxford University Press, 2004.

Sombart, W. The Quintessence of Modern Capitalism. London: Unwin, 1915.

Stark, R. The Victory of Reason: How Christianity Led to Freedom, Capitalism and Western Success. New York: Random House, 2005.

Todeschini, G. "Credibilità, fiducia, ricchezza: il credito caritativo come forma della modernizzazione economica europea." In *Prestare ai poveri,* edited by P. Avallone. Rome: CNR, 2007.

———. I mercanti e il tempio. La società Cristiana e il circolo virtuouso della ricchezza trad Medioevo. Edited by Età Moderna. Bologna: Il Mulino, 2002.

———. Ricchezza Francescana. Dalla povertà volontaria alla società di mercato. Bologna: Il Mulino, 2004.

Vitale, M. "L'impresa nell'Europa." *Appunti* 5 (2006).

Weber, M. *Sociologia della religione* (1920–21). Milan: Comunità, 1982.

4

The Political and Economic Impact of CST since 1891

Christian Democracy and Christian Labour
Unions in Europe

Vera Negri Zamagni

CST Comes from a Long-Standing Tradition

Christian faith requires a total conversion of life, penetrating
every corner of human action. Since only a few Christians opt
to live as hermits, all others must work out a pattern of life
inspired by Christian values in their normal activities: family,
education, work, business, leisure, community, and solidarity. As a
contribution to that process, the True Wealth of Nations project
seeks to investigate the practical implications of Christian faith
for economic life.

From the beginning of Christianity, its followers have looked for
the right way to live out their faith in the world. Prior to the recognition by Emperor Constantine of the right of Christians to practice
their religion and organize their own patterns of life, there was
tension sometimes resulting in open conflict between Christians and
non-Christians. The first real opportunity for Christians to develop
fully their own approach to economics and politics came centuries
later, with the breakup of the Roman Empire and the coming of the
age of Barbarians. This was a major dislocation of the previous order
and obliged Christians to construct a new civilization from scratch.
Monasteries and religious orders, guilds, confraternities and chambers of merchants, hospitals and conservatories, pawn banks and

public debt, municipalities and universities—these were the most important institutions of so-called Western civilization. And these were the institutional embodiments of the Christian values of dignity of every person, primacy of spiritual values over material goods, freedom understood as self-government and self-monitoring, along with subsidiarity, cooperative action, solidarity, and the common good.

Two aspects of this civilization should be stressed here. First, temporal ends (earthly goals) were ordered to God, the final End, a theme dealt with in depth by Mary Hirschfeld in her essay in this volume, and therefore political and economic power was at the service of the spiritual power. This limitation of power provided an early theoretical foundation for democracy and human rights. Second, economic thinking was developed, mostly by the Franciscan School, to provide a basis for the modern market economy and modern economic development, a theme developed in the essay by Stefano Zamagni in this volume. Even in the medieval period, the market was considered the best instrument for economic development for several reasons: it avoided wars through negotiations and compromises; it rewarded hard work; it promoted innovative solutions to problems; it gave to everyone an opportunity to be productive through specialization; and it tended to spread widely and inclusively, through investment.[1]

It is an historic fact[2] that the fundamentals of Western society *are* Christian, and this puts all the later developments of economic theorizing into perspective. In this context, we can say that the question raised by the True Wealth of Nations project, whether "the economic and cultural criteria identified in the tradition of CST provide an effective path to sustainable prosperity for all," was answered positively by Christians in the Middle Ages. In fact, the concept of "prosperity for all" was well known to Christians in the Middle Ages. For instance, the Franciscans developed the idea of the "prosperity of the city," as distinct from the enrichment of the individual. However, the battle in favour of a civilization inspired by Christian values, which seemed largely won, had to be fought again and again by subsequent generations because of the endless exercise of free will and humanity's enduring inclination toward sin.

Christians in every era have disagreed among themselves concerning the proper interpretation of the Christian message. At first these were "heresies" that could be marginalized, but at the end of the Middle Ages, major movements of dissent within the mainstream split Christianity into the fragmented religion it remains today. This is not the place to discuss in detail the main differences between Catholicism and the Protestant churches in matters of politics and economics. However, it must be noted that for a host of reasons, the churches of the Reformation ended up putting much less emphasis on keeping a Christian inspiration in economic and political activity than the Catholic Church. The real challenge, however, to the civil framework established during the Middle Ages came from those who did not share any version of the Christian religion and increasingly reverted to principles such as materialism, inequality, self-interest, self-judgement,[3] and the moulding of a new economics and a new politics through the Enlightenment, the Industrial Revolution, and the spread of universal suffrage.

The Catholic Church reacted first to the Reformation with the Council of Trent, which reaffirmed the presence of the Church in all aspects of public life, even though this presence was mainly restricted in practice to nations with a majority of Catholics. The delay in the industrialization and democratization of these Catholic nations produced a similar delay in the understanding by the Catholic Church that the traditional institutions developed in the Middle Ages were outdated and insufficient to meet the challenges of a new era. Large areas of public life had progressively been de-Christianized—economics and politics first—while the religious orders, still present in the fields of education and assistance, were losing ground.

It is in this context that modern Catholic social thought (CST) was born, with the aim of disentangling the ambiguities existing in modern economic growth, that had its roots in Christian inspiration but had moved away into materialism and self-interest. There are, today, many ways of contributing to CST such as, discussing its philosophical and theological underpinnings, analyzing modern economic and political theory to see where they conflict with CST, or reviewing the practical efforts to introduce it in society. This chapter takes this last approach, and on the basis of an historical account will evaluate the type of organization put in place and the impact of the activities of the many Christians engaged in politics and in economics in Europe in the last century.[4] As their work was supported by bishops and popes who produced an updated body of CST, the chapter will also discuss encyclicals and other official documents of the Catholic Church. There is obviously a distinction between CST in theory (encyclicals, bishops' documents) and CST in practice, the former laying down general principles (see the essay by Albino Barrera in this volume) and the latter producing a set of policy decisions inserted into a particular national context at particular moments of time. The interrelations between theory and practice of CST are themselves of the utmost interest and will find some reference in this chapter.

This chapter will sketch the beginning stages of modern CST in Europe between the nineteenth century and World War II in section 2 and will then discuss the flourishing of Christian Democratic parties after the end of World

War II, their crucial contribution to the launching of the process of European integration and to the "economic miracles" of many European nations and their subsequent decline in section 3. The concluding section will look at some of the issues that Catholics must face if they want to uphold their testimony of the Christian message today.

CST and Its Applications in Europe from Leo XIII to Pius XI

Already in the first half of the nineteenth century, there arose a preoccupation to reconcile the Catholic Church with the major changes taking place in European societies. The main issue at the beginning was how much to accept of the liberal thinking that had been developed by the bourgeoisie of the Industrial Revolution, which reclaimed freedom of enterprise and democratic governments together with various liberties (conscience, cult, teaching, publishing, association). The first major figure of the so-called liberal Catholics who tried to build a bridge between Catholicism and liberalism was Félicité Robert de Lamennais,[5] whose positions were condemned in the papal documents *Mirari Vos* (1832) and *Singulari Nos* (1834) because they conceded too much to "secularism." However, others followed, among whom were Antonio Rosmini (recently rehabilitated), Charles de Montalembert, Auguste Cochin, Henry Dominique Lacordaire, and Vincenzo Gioberti. These in general struck a more balanced compromise with liberalism and were active in the cultural and political arena of their times, playing "important roles in the development of the parliamentary system and the awkward compromises that supported political moderation."[6]

These Catholic liberals never won the open support of the Catholic Church. Rather Pius IX went a long way in mobilizing the Church in cultural battles in several nations against liberalism, particularly against civil marriage and state control of education. The liberal Catholics did not win a wide popular backing either, but they were successful in using arguments derived from liberalism to advance Catholic interests, and they produced some of the earliest examples of Catholics active in parliamentary discussions. Pius IX is in any case to be credited for having left an important mark on the history of Catholicism. He "advanced the organisational and doctrinal centralization of the Church" and "helped Catholic believers to overcome their prevailing deference, mobilising and energising them into becoming politically and socially active, and to formulate collective demands,"[7] although his intransigentism[8] retarded an effective political organisation of European Catholics.

The next major breakthrough into modern times was the creation of hundreds of new Catholic associations and organizations springing from concern

by nineteenth-century Catholics over several current issues, from purely liturgical ones to educational, political, and social problems. To increase their
visibility and organizational capability, these associations started to rally
national "congresses" (conventions) in which they could focus on common
goals and communicate them to society. The first such congress[9] was held in
Mainz, Germany, in October 1848 and reached its climax when the then parish
priest Wilhelm Emanuel von Ketteler[10] proposed to discuss not only religious
and educational issues but social problems as well. It was followed by many
other meetings in Germany,[11] with similar experiments held in Belgium and
Switzerland.

But in Belgium more success was achieved by the type of meeting started
in 1871, when the first congress of Catholic workmen associations met in Mons.
In the same year at Nevers, France, the *Union des associations ouvrières catholiques*
gathered, but the subsequent organization created in 1873 by Albert De Mun,
Cercles d'ouvriers catholiques, was more successful. In Italy, the *Opera dei congressi* was put in place in 1874, forming a branch devoted to social and economic
issues in 1887. Through the work of the economist Giuseppe Toniolo the *Circoli
di studi sociali* were organized (1889). Similar social movements were present
in Austria, Hungary, Spain, and Denmark, while in Great Britain and Ireland,
Catholic organizations mostly supported other political causes such as Home
Rule, in spite of the great political sensibility of persons such as Cardinal Henry
Edward Manning.

An open recognition of this social dimension of Catholic engagement in
public life was produced by the publication on May 15, 1891, of Leo XIII's *Rerum
Novarum*, an encyclical that embodied some of the previous experience accumulated by Catholics engaged in social activities. In this document, Leo not
only openly recognized the need to improve the distribution of the fruits of
economic progress brought about by industrialization but also encouraged
Catholics to promote organizations aimed at supporting workers in their claims
and needs. He preached the superiority of the Christian vision of solidarity between capital and labour, both seen as indispensible factors of production,[12]
over the socialist vision of "class struggle." After that document, the Catholic
social movement strengthened considerably in several directions, becoming
known as Popular Catholic Action.

There were three principal fields of application of the message of the *Rerum
Novarum*. The first was the cultural diffusion of ideas. In 1892 the first "Social
Week" was held in Germany, followed by France (1904),[13] Italy and Spain (1907),
Belgium and Holland (1908), where Catholic social principles were discussed
and experiences were compared and evaluated, often with the help of Catholic
economic and social journals. The second field was the strengthening and

re-launching of the Catholic presence inside the workers' movements, as well as the foundation of cooperatives, banks and enterprises of Catholic inspiration.[14] The European Christian Trade Unions organized the International Secretariat of Christian Trade Unions and held their first Congress in Zurich in 1908.[15]

The third field was political.[16] In Italy the political aspect of Catholic engagement before World War I was connected with the creation of a movement labeled Christian Democracy that aimed at rallying Catholics with the socialists against conservative parties.[17] This spurred a reaction by the same Leo XIII, who, with the 1901 Encyclical *Graves de communi*, declared acceptable the expression "Christian Democracy" only if it would refer to "social" action,[18] that is, to the activity of Catholics in society outside of political parties.[19] In 1907, Pope Pius X, with the encyclical *Pascendi Dominici Gregis*, condemned "modernism,"[20] mostly attacking the philosophical-theological aspects of the movement but also its political application. As a result of this, Italy could not organize a Catholic political party (the Partito Popolare Italiano, PPI[21]) until January 1919, when *Non expedit* was abolished,[22] not without an ambivalent attitude by the Vatican.

But outside Italy, Catholic politics was of a more traditional type, having started long before the concept of "Christian Democracy" emerged. In Germany, Catholics had been politically organized earlier in the German Centre Party (in the 1874 elections they gained 83 percent of the Catholic vote and a quarter of the seats of the Reichstag). Belgium, the Netherlands, and Austria had strong Catholic parties (the Belgian Catholics governed with absolute majorities between 1884 and 1917), while France was the notable exception, having parties and political groups supported by Catholics, but no Catholic political party.[23] An interesting map of the formation of the most important Catholic parties has been developed by Kalyvas,[24] in which the author shows that such creation in Belgium, the Netherlands, Austria, Germany, and Italy was preceded by years of efforts by Catholics to participate in public life. Kalyvas supports the view that such parties were not the first choice for the Church and that they came into existence only after the Church had realized that Catholic mass movements were insufficient to counter anticlerical attacks, just as were the pacts with liberal and conservative parties. The lower clergy was instrumental in the organization of such parties, but lay Catholics became more and more assertive, while the Church reduced its aversion. We should recall that the first open acceptance of democracy by the Vatican came only in the Christmas address of Pope Pius XII in December 1944.

After World War I, other Catholic parties were created in Spain,[25] in some of the successor states of the Austro-Hungarian Empire (particularly Poland), and even in the Nordic countries (in Norway, the KrF, Christian Democratic Party, was founded in 1933).[26] The different context in which the Catholic

Church found itself, with the increasing threat of a socialist "revolution," paved the way to a lessening of the traditional antiliberal Church campaign in favour of an antisocialist campaign, which was coupled with a weakening of Church support for Catholic democratic parties. The acceptance of democracy by the Church had been half-hearted and fragile before World War II. In the face of the increasing problems of parliamentary government in meeting the economic and political challenges of the post-WWI era, the majority of the European Catholics turned to support more or less authoritarian forms of government, coupled with the idea of replacing parliamentary democracy with professional chambers, a political option often labeled corporatism.[27]

With the devastating impact of the 1929 crisis, Catholics "were increasingly tempted to desert 'their' parties for nationalist and fascist political formations....In doing so, they effectively played on the latent anti-modernist and anti-pluralist dispositions of many Catholics which had originally developed in ultra-montane opposition to economic modernity and liberal parliamentary politics in the nineteenth century."[28] Pius XI did issue strong and uncompromising Encyclicals against Fascism (*Non abbiamo bisogno*, June 29, 1931) and Nazism (*Mit brennender Sorge*, March 14, 1937), but the appeal for liberties included in such documents were inevitably limited to freedom for Catholic associations and religious practices, although some general principles against dictatorships were laid down.

Three other facts enfolding the interwar period proved important for later developments. First, the "left-Catholics," namely, those who remained faithful to democracy, established in December 1925 Sécretariat International des Partis Démocratique d'Inspiration Chrétienne (SIPDIC), which allowed those who had been exiled by the dictators of the time (such as don Sturzo) to remain active and to develop connections and discussions. The SIPDIC met in 1932 in Köln (where Konrad Adenauer was mayor) and proposed the creation of a European "common market," with the aim of reaching a free exchange of goods, capital, and people in Europe, and state support of the income of farmers.[29] These ideas were set aside at the time but became useful twenty years later. In the late '30s, SIPDIC compromised with the politically deteriorating context in continental Europe and was finally disbanded.

In the second place, all those Catholic politicians who were in exile outside their countries (or inside it, as was Adenauer) and looked forward to a return to politics could avail themselves of Pius XI's inspired Encyclical *Quadragesimo Anno*, issued on the May 15, 1931. With clarity of argument and attention to detail, Pius interpreted and deepened *Rerum Novarum*, openly sketching the middle way of CST equidistant from individualism and collectivism. On this latter theory, the pope came back with a public condemnation of collectivism in his *Divini Redemptoris*, on March 19, 1937. The final event that must be noted came in June 1920 when the International Federation of Christian Trade Unions (IFCTU) was created in the Netherlands, followed in 1928 by the Catholic Workers International (CWI, Köln). Again, this organization was not very active in the 1930s, but formed the basis for postwar developments.

There are four main conclusions that can be drawn from the preceding survey:

1. In the pre–World War II period, both the Catholic Church and European Catholic organizations elaborated enough new ideas and instruments to be able to enter decisively as Catholics into the field of economics and politics in the new era of industrialization and plural democracy;

2. The process by which Catholic parties—which were born confessional (with the exception of the late Italian PPI) but were built up from the inside an identity distinct from the Church and even from religion— was long and difficult, but it was already in place long before World War I, with the emergence of important lay political figures;

3. The flourishing of this renewed Catholic presence in society was hindered, but not dismantled, by the outbursts of authoritarianism registered in continental Europe in the interwar period;

4. Catholics successfully prevented a marginalization of Christianity from public life and were ready to become important players in the post—World War II era.

Christian Democratic Parties and Their Role after World War II

The legacy of the pre–World War I period is the most important factor explaining the geography of Christian Democracy in Europe in the postwar era. If we exclude those areas in which right-wing (Portugal and Spain) or left-wing (Eastern Europe) dictatorships prevailed,[30] we see Christian Democracy taking the lead in continental Europe, with the notable but short-lived inclusion of France. In the case of France, the Movement Republicain Populaire (MRP), of Christian Democratic inspiration,[31] was successful immediately after the war in rallying the Catholics who wanted to part company from the previous proclerical Vichy government, compromised during German occupation. Initially, the Church supported MRP because of the lack of a viable alternative, and MRP became the first party in France in 1946 (with 28.2 percent of the vote). But a few years later, Church support was withdrawn, and the success of MRP turned into failure.

> In decided contrast to the situation in Italy and Germany...the
> French Church and the Christian Democratic party were not able to
> forge a lasting alliance....The MRP sought, unsuccessfully, to
> transform France with the Socialists, while the Church wanted to
> restore its Vichy-granted prerogatives. And while the MRP was
> untenable as a long-term ally, French politics did not present the
> Church with a suitable alternative.[32]

The MRP, however, continued to play a role in the 1950s, with Bidault and
Schuman.

It is not the place here to analyze national politics and to follow the developments leading to the hegemony of Christian Democratic parties in Italy, Germany,
Austria, Belgium, and the Netherlands,[33] nor to sketch the role played by the many
other minority Christian Democratic parties existing in Europe. It must, however,
be noted that those Christian Democratic (CD) parties that led governments—to
be found, as mentioned above, precisely in the same nations with the most substantial legacy from earlier Catholic parties—were capable of organizing themselves in an entirely new fashion. Indeed, in the postwar years, Catholic parties
had largely to face the mass communist challenge,[34] and no longer the elitist
liberal one, and this suggested major changes in more than one of the nations in
which they were present. Also, a strong presence of Catholic trade unions can be
found in some places, but not in others: Belgium, the Netherlands, Italy, and
France had Catholic trade unions, while in Germany and Austria Catholics mostly
tried to organize pressure groups inside the unified trade union.[35]

Most important for our purposes is, however, a definition of the political
manifesto characterizing the Catholic parties that led European governments.
Can we assume that there was a *common* approach by these parties? The interesting, though not so surprising, answer is yes; there was much in common.
This is in itself a novelty in Europe; here we have a political movement capable
of crossing national borders. The liberal and the socialist movements were also
supranational, but for different reasons neither could play a unifying role across
the continent, though the latter one in its communist version tried hard to do
so. Before unfolding this argument fully, a summary of the main points of the
common approach of the leading Christian Democratic parties will be helpful.
A list of the values present in all Christian Democratic parties includes:

a) the centrality of the person, leading to the adoption of human rights
   and the special emphasis on of the family;
b) work as the founding value of society, leading to the diffusion of the
   welfare state and the commitment to relieve poverty by practicing a
   policy of full employment;[36] leading also to overcoming class struggles

through institutions of joint participation of employers and employees (social partnership, mediation, harmonisation);

c) an antimaterialistic vision that aims to be equidistant from capitalism and communism, both rejected because of their faith in material wealth;

d) a large role granted to self-organized civil society bodies that mediate between the individual and the state; of particular importance among these bodies, the educational agencies that must be allowed to deliver religious education as well as to develop the vision of the world stemming from religion;

e) subsidiarity as a basic principle of government;

f) support for international cooperation and peace;

g) a new application of "laicity," with lay Catholics being directly responsible for political action and the Vatican more and more refraining from direct intervention.

This list represents the mature fruit of previous efforts at elaborating a distinct political program stemming from Christian principles, going much beyond the defence of Church "interests." Indeed, what comes out very clearly from this synthesis is the sketch of a "third way," different from both the liberal and collectivist approaches. It is a third way that cannot be confused with the authoritarian versions of it prevailing in the interwar period (and still in existence in some of the European countries after the war) in as much as it fully embraces democracy. It is a third way capable of influencing Europe and the world so much that some of its basic tenets have become "common possession of all parties."[37] As Misner rightly concludes:

> The kind of third-way projects and realizations that prevailed after World War II in many western European nations drew from the social Catholic tradition. In the Christian democratic movements, with their political aspirations, the importance of subsidiarity, intermediate bodies, and social justice for a humane democratic regime was stressed. The system of "social partnership" represents a legacy of the third-way thinking that had such a notable career in European social and political Catholicism. Facing the challenges of globalization, the parties of Christian Democratic heritage retain a critique of capitalism that sets them apart from their American cousins in ways it will be increasingly important to note at the beginning of the third Millennium.[38]

These views were largely embodied in the new constitutions that were approved in Italy and Germany and in the political systems that were promoted in all the countries in which CD had a large impact.[39] The constraints of space prevent the many historical inquiries that would need to be developed to evaluate the success of the Christian Democratic parties in making their doctrine effective, but some details about one aspect will be helpful, namely, the role of CD parties in the process of European integration.

Indeed, the international context in the postwar era was more favourable for Catholic leaders to develop transnational cooperation: not only the encompassing presence of the United States pushed the Europeans to various forms of collaboration, but the very presence of a number of governments led by Christian Democratic parties proved powerful enough to give intergovernmental relations a sense of purpose and direction. However, it was from the inside of the Catholic tradition that the most powerful forces toward integration emanated: the old idea of unifying continental Europe, the mistrust of a centralized sovereign nation-state, the belief in both subsidiarity and universalism, and the appeal to mediation and peace.

It was already in 1946 that the first talks of convening a meeting of European Christian Democrats began.[40] Under the active role of the Swiss and the Austrians, the meeting took place in Lucerne in late winter 1947. The agreement to form a Christian Democratic party international was not reached, but a more informal organization was put in place under the insistence of the French and Belgian representatives—the *Nouvelles Équipes Internationales* (NEI)—which had its first meeting in Liège in May 1947. Only in June 1948 did the NEI decide to employ as a subtitle, *Union of European Christian Democrats*, but differences of opinions about membership continued for years. As the hot and pressing "German question" could not be publicly discussed, Bidault utilised private contacts with German political leaders as early as July 1947, while the MRP was moving toward dropping French territorial demands. The first meeting of officials from the MRP and CDU (the German Christian Democratic party) took place in November 1947 in Switzerland; it is unclear whether the next meeting, in March 1948, saw the presence of Bidault and Adenauer. Adenauer did certainly participate, however, in the June 1948 meeting, while Bidault was not there. The two leaders were certainly both present in the October 1948 meeting, which was also open to other politicians of NEI. These meetings, which came to be known as the "Geneva Circle," were subsequently regularly attended by Bidault and Adenauer up to June 1949.

In both the Geneva Circle and NIE, the old idea of building up a "common market" appeared to be the easiest objective to be proposed, although it was often pointed out that the economic targets had to be instrumental to the solution of political problems. The resolutions approved in the meetings included: (a) full reconstruction of the German economy (February 1948); (b) enhancement of European security through the diffusion of welfare (March 1949); and (c) a strong social dimension to be granted to the market-based continental European economies (June 1949). The first practical step proposed in the direction of a common market was that of putting the iron and coal sectors of France and Germany under joint control, an idea that Adenauer had advocated since 1923 and was strongly supported by him in the Geneva Circle meetings: "During his meeting with Schuman in Bassenheim in October 1948 and again in a subsequent letter to him, Adenauer once more suggested the 'organic inter-locking' of French and German basic industries as a solution to French secu-rity and an important step towards Franco-German reconciliation."[41]

Later, Adenauer even proposed including the chemical sector in the agreement, but this was not considered feasible. On the May 9, 1950, the creation of ECSC (CECA) was proposed by Robert Schuman, with the full awareness of the importance of the occasion. Here are some of the passages of the Schuman speech, in the translation done by Dean Acheson, U.S. Secretary of State at the time, in his book of memoirs:

> World peace cannot be safeguarded without the making of efforts proportionate to the dangers which threaten it. The contribution which an organized and living Europe can bring to civilization is indispensable to the maintenance of peaceful relations. In taking upon herself for more than 20 years the role of champion of a united Europe, France has always had as her essential aim the service of peace. A united Europe was not achieved; and we had war. Europe will not be made all at once, or according to a single, general plan. It will be built through concrete achievements, which first create a *de facto* solidarity. The gathering together of the nations of Europe requires the elimination of the age-old opposition of France and Germany. The first concern in any action undertaken must be these two countries. With this aim in view, the French government proposes to take action immediately on one limited but decisive point; the French government proposes to place Franco-German production of coal and steel as a whole under a common higher authority, within the framework of an organization open to the participation of the other countries of Europe. The pooling of coal and steel production should immediately provide for the setting-up of common foundations for economic development as a first step in the federation of Europe, and will change the destinies of those regions which have long been devoted to the manufacture of munitions of war, of which they have been the most constant victims.[42]

As Milward[43] rightly commented, this new French approach produced the self-exclusion of Britain from the process of European integration, on the one hand, while on the other hand it guaranteed the inclusion of Italy, which at the time did not have a true economic stake in the iron and coal sector.[44] The Christian Democrats also had several other "transnational" aims, among which were the European Defence Community (EDC) and the Green Pool. With the former, the CD parties of the six ECSC nations aimed at pushing their countries to collaborate in military matters, but the French Parliament did not approve the treaty; with the latter, they wanted to promote the restructuring of the European agricultural sectors, including other European countries beyond the six of the ECSC, but negotiations failed. Being defeated over both, the CD leaders considered the "common market" line as the only viable option, up to the signing of the Treaty of Rome in 1956. This treaty, embedded in the Christian Democratic vision, included the putting in place of a CAP (Common Agricultural Policy, effectively started in 1962) and the creation of a bank (the European Investment Bank, EIB), which would finance development projects in Europe. The very successful settlement of the consequences of World War II can be ascribed in no small measure to the transnational alliance of the European continental CD parties.

After having truly dominated European politics in the 1950s, the Christian Democratic parties of continental Europe showed a progressive weakening, though they have certainly not become irrelevant even today. The causes of this downward trend have been clearly identified in the literature:[45]

a) the socialist parties opened to middle classes and became less anticlerical;

b) communist parties in the West lost any hope of winning majorities in parliaments;

c) the UK and northern countries joined the EU and enlarged the platform of non-CD parties;

d) "secularization" of society decreased confessional voting, in part due to libertarian and leftist movements starting with the French demonstrations in May 1968;

e) more recently, the wave of liberalization of the economy and containment of welfare programs is running counter to the established "third way."

The legacy of Christian Democracy remains, however, in the very pillars of continental European economy and society. The alliance between the "corporatist" welfare state of Christian Democratic origin and the Nordic social-democratic welfare state has rooted the welfare state as an intrinsic dimension of European societies.[46] The "social partnership" in industrial relations is another feature that characterizes Europe as different from the Anglo-Saxon model, together with the more important state role and the efforts at regulating markets more extensively. The formation of a supranational "core Europe" is another Christian Democratic feature, which has resisted the attacks of the British and the subsequent enlargement rounds, showing a capability of institutions such as the Commission to work out agendas that could lead to substantial integrationist steps,[47] much beyond the vision and the original intentions of individual national governments. It must be mentioned, for instance, that at least two of the most important Commission chairmen—Jacques Delors and Romano Prodi—were both Catholics rooted in the Christian Democratic tradition (although Delors was a member of the Socialist Party and Prodi led a centre-left coalition): the first was instrumental in the building up of the common currency (the Euro), the second in the solution of the "Eastern question" through the latest massive enlargement of the EU by the inclusion of nations formerly under Soviet control.

What is more, European Christian Democrats have remained an important political actor in Europe. In 1965 the NEI was transformed into the EUCD (European Union of Christian Democrats), made up of parties, not individual politicians. In view of the direct elections of European MPs in 1979, the EUCD further transformed itself into the EPP (European Popular Party), choosing to become the home of centre-right parties from different ideological origins. In doing this, it played an important "socializing" role for politicians of the new member countries, but at the same time lost many of its "Catholic" dimensions. At the national level, all CD parties shrank, but perhaps the greatest blow was suffered in Italy, where the alliance of CD with PSI (the Socialist Party) in the 1980s dragged the Christian Democrats into becoming more and more corrupt, up to the breaking up of the party in the early 1990s.[48] In any case, Catholics today in continental Europe no longer vote for a single party, showing different voting preferences and dispersing their votes across a wide spectrum of parties.

CST in Europe after Christian Democracy

There is no doubt that "Christian" parties in Europe have played a crucial role in supporting Christian values in society and granting the best possible conditions for the Church to carry out its mission in an ever-changing historical context. Today, however, they appear more and more inadequate. The growing power of CD lobbies has multiplied corrupt practices, and the general shift of politics away from ideology has increased the readiness of other parties to accommodate values and aims dear to Christians. All this suggests that the Church should be more cautious and open to more than one political option. In addition, at least three of the original targets of Catholic "battles" in modern society—individualism, secularism, and materialism—now permeate society more than ever, raising the problem of what should be done to resume these battles more effectively.

The idea is spreading that involvement in the internal affairs of CD parties has perhaps for too long focused the attention of European Catholics on the survival of the party rather than on the promotion of Christian values, something that might be easier if Catholics are spread throughout different parties and bear no unique responsibility for their structure and financing. Also, excessive reliance on politics has diverted Catholics from their presence in the economy, while the state-run welfare systems have largely bureaucra-tized solidarity, reducing personal involvement in assisting the poor, thus encouraging a more individualistic view of human life.[49] The time has come, therefore, to rethink the application of CST in Europe from scratch. No more than some thoughts in this direction can be provided here, leaving to others a fuller treatment of this issue.

There should be three priorities, the first of which is politics. If Catholics are no longer rallied in one single party, they need to develop common ideas on how to deal with sensitive issues such as family, education, the defence of life, and the role of intermediate bodies. To form a "critical mass,"[50] forums for the discussion of the issues must be created outside and across parties. Not being able to count on parliamentary majorities generated by a single party, Catholics must press for influence of civil society in forming public opinion and in trans-forming democracy from an elitist-competitive type to a deliberative type, in which counting votes in parliaments comes after an exhaustive discussion of the issues has taken place with the involvement of civil society. Secularism today can best be contested on the basis of cultural battles like the one in support of families with children or the one in favour of the dignity of life from conception to natural death.

The second priority should be economics. Materialism and individualism are hegemonizing economic life to the point of causing many Catholics to revolt against the market. It is critical to clarify today that it is not the market that is wrong from a Christian point of view but the capitalist version of mar-kets in recent centuries. Catholics need to once more take an initiative in the field of economics, putting in place corporations such as cooperatives and social enterprises, in which production is carried out with attention to the truly humane dimensions of work and consumption, both with reference to employees and clients. Even in capitalist companies, things can be largely improved by the reintroduction of a corporate social responsibility that is not merely a profit-maximizing strategy.

The third priority should be society. The welfare state must be replaced by the welfare society, in which the state still plays its redistributive role, but the responsibility for delivering services is given back to civil society and the involvement of people in caring for others is widespread, thus opposing individualism. We must reject the dualistic theory, according to which only "efficiency" rules are to be applied in production and then the resulting negative externalities are to be rectified by the State through redistribution. Methods of production that keep negative externalities to a minimum must be devised, and it is a primary responsibility of Christians to be on the forefront of this battle. Redistribution will still require State financing through taxation, but welfare services must increasingly be shaped and provided by civil society organizations, especially by nonprofit organizations. Welfare services must be tailored to the needs of people (in-kind services) and not be made up simply of a transfer of money, since those who receive it are often in no position to spend money prudently.

As the gospel reminds us, the good and the bad will live together until the end of times. It is therefore no surprise that even the most startling success of Christian action in society will not last. History shows that it is indeed quite possible to have, as Christians, an impact on institutions, economic structures, and ways of life, even a large impact. But every generation of Christians must be engaged in finding the best ways to diffuse God's message in their own time. Here the words of Saint Augustine are apt: "You say: these are bad times, times of difficulty, times of oppression. Live virtuously and you will change the times by living virtuously; change the times and you will no longer have to complain."[51] The True Wealth of Nations project is right to assert that Catholic social thought can lead the way to sustainable prosperity for all. CST has been influential in public life before, and our challenge is to render it effective in our day as well.

NOTES

1. This capability of inclusion is hindered by the many imperfections markets have, but especially by monopolistic positions.

2. This has found recently an authoritative recognition in A. Greif, *Institutions and the Path to the Modern Economy.* Here is a crucial passage:

> There is much to suggest that the late medieval institutional development had direct impact on later institutions. The modern business corporation grew out of the traditional legal form of the corporation, as developed for

medieval guilds, municipalities, monasteries and universities. The operation of the late medieval corporations led to the development of particular knowledge, laws, and other institutional elements that manifested in current practices such as trading in shares, limited liability, auditing, apprenticeships, and double-entry bookkeeping. European commercial law, insurance markets, patent systems, public debt, business associations and central banks were developed in the context of medieval institutions" (p. 394).

3. Self-judgment here refers to the belief not only that the individual must make moral decisions, something the Christian view holds, but also that there is no moral standard outside the individual, something Christianity rejects. The document of Pius IX, *Quanta cura* (1864), collected all these "errors" in a long list, in which one can read: "The human reason is the sole arbiter of good and evil (III); ... the entire control of state schools ... must be in the hands of state authorities (XLV); ... no other forces can be recognized but those expressed in material goods and all efforts must be placed in accumulating and increasing individual wealth and in satisfying individual passions (LVIII)."

4. I have kept my discussion limited to Europe because there are remarkable differences in the application of CST in other areas of the world, and documentation is not easily found. However, a large number of the arguments developed in this paper apply quite generally.

5. A. R. Vidler, *Prophecy and Papacy.*

6. R. Grew, "Suspended Bridges to Democracy: The Uncertain Origins of Christian Democracy in France and Italy," *European Christian Democracy*, ed. T. Kselman and J. A. Buttigieg (Notre Dame: Notre Dame University Press, 2003), 21.

7. W. Kaiser, *Christian Democracy and the Origins of the European Union*, 22. The author supports the view that the mass movements of Catholics were started by Pius IX's encyclical *Quanta cura* and only later strengthened by Leo XIII's encyclical *Rerum Novarum.*

8. Intransigentism defines the position of the pope against the loss of temporal power.

9. "Catholic Congresses," in *Catholic Encyclopaedia*, drafted in 1905–14 and now available at www.newadvent.org, with substantial later additions.

10. He was later appointed bishop of Mainz and became known for his sensibility to the social questions.

11. In 1890, the German Catholics founded People's Union of Catholic Germany, in which workers' Catholic organizations had the lead.

12. Leo XIII used very effective expressions in explaining his vision opposite to the socialist vision of an inevitable "class struggle": "Harmony produces beauty and order of things, while a perpetual conflict cannot but give rise to confusion and barbarism. Now, to compose conflicts, eradicating their same roots, Christianity has a marvellous comparative advantage" (*Rerum Novarum*, no. 15).

13. France was a place where this movement was more consolidated. See J. D. Durand, *Les semaines sociales de France.*

14. For the Italian case, see V. Zamagni, "Movimento cattolico e trasformazioni dell'economia e della società in Italia." It would be of the utmost interest to gather a number of historians who could provide a comprehensive and comparative view of the activities of Catholics in the economic and social fields in Europe up to World War I (and also later).

15. P. Misner, *Social Catholicism in Europe.*

16. The literature on this aspect is immense and contrasts sharply with the dearth of literature on the economic and social activities carried on by Catholics.

17. S. N. Kalyvas, *The Rise of Christian Democracy in Europe.*

18. Quoting from the Encyclical: the label Christian Democracy "must be employed without any political significance, so as to mean nothing else than...benefi-cent Christian action in behalf of the people." The "Opera dei congressi" was disman-tled in 1904 because it endorsed the political meaning of "Christian Democracy." Most of the people active in it gathered in other Catholic associations.

19. In Italy, the "*Non expedit*," a decree issued by the Pontiff in 1874, which prevented the participation of Italian Catholics in politics, was still in place. The *Non expedit*, though not an encyclical, was a directive issued against the annexation of the pope's temporal possessions by the Italian State in 1870.

20. Among the most important representatives of this movement are the Italians Romolo Murri and Ernesto Buonaiuti; the Irish George Tyrrell; the French Alfred Loisy and Lucien Laberthonnière.

21. Its founder, the priest don Luigi Sturzo, did not want to use the adjective "Christian" or "Catholic," because he considered his party lay and a-confessional, though inspired to Catholic values, and wanted the church to be free from direct involvement in political matters.

22. Single exceptions were permitted since 1904 mostly for Catholics to take part in local elections and only in 1913 to the national elections in support of Catholic candidates within the liberal party.

23. The absence of a successful French Catholic party is considered a puzzle by the literature. No mass organization (the French Church believed for a long time in monarchical restoration) existed; fragmentation (factionalisation) and elitism were part of the French unsuccess. Indeed, when a Catholic party was finally organized (the *Action Libérale Populaire*, ALP), it was not electorally successful in the 1902 and 1906 elections and could not take root.

24. Kaylvas, *The Rise of Christian Democracy*, 25.

25. Christian Democracy in Spain was always a minority party, and it never played an important role even after the end of Franco's dictatorship.

26. In Finland, one such party was crated only in 1958, in Sweden in 1964 and in Denmark in 1970. They were all minority parties, but some of their leaders did occasionally contribute to legislation, mostly on issues of education and the family.

27. M. Conway, *Catholic Politics in Europe, 1918–1945.*

28. Kaiser, *Christian Democracy*, 59.

29. P. M. R. Stirk, *European Unity in Context.*

30. Different still was the Irish case, in which Catholicism was so widespread that both existing parties (Fine Gael and Fianna Fáil) offered enough guarantees to the Church so that the necessity for an explicitly Catholic party did not arise, although Fine Gael often defined itself as the Irish Christian Democratic Party.

31. Most of its leaders had been members of Action Catholique. See C. M. Warner, "Strategies of an Interest Group."

32. Ibid., 149.

33. In Switzerland, too, the Catholic SKVP was a quite successful party.

34. Communist parties were very strong in continental Western Europe in the immediate postwar period, while the socialists either were allied with communists or lacked an attractive political proposal for the rural and middle classes.

35. See P. Pasture, *Christian Trade Unionism in Europe since* 1968. The book contains scanty references to the period 1950–68.

36. K. van Kersbergen, *Social Capitalism.*

37. P. Misner, "Christian Democratic Social Policy," 88.

38. Ibid. See also E. Lamberts, *Christian Democracy in the European Union.*

39. E. Lamberts, "Christian Democracy and the Constitutional State in Western Europe 1945–1995." One should recall that in the fifty years from 1946–1995 Christian Democratic parties were in power for thirty-six years in Germany, forty-seven years in Italy and Belgium, and forty-nine in the Netherlands.

40. R. Papini, *The Christian Democratic International.*

41. Kaiser, *Christian Democracy,* 225.

42. D. Acheson, *Present at the Creation,* 383–84.

43. A. Milward, *The Reconstruction of Western Europe 1945–51.*

44. Surprisingly, Italy under ECSC became the second producer of steel in Europe. See V. Zamagni, *Economic History of Italy 1860–1990.*

45. E. L. Evans, *The Cross and the Ballot.* See also Lamberts, *Christian Democracy.*

46. Even Britain and Ireland have a welfare state incomparable with the American one.

47. M. A. Pollack, *The Engines of European Integration.*

48. After that major blow, smaller Christian Democratic parties were founded, but Italian Catholics dispersed into almost all parties.

49. If the State bears responsibility for welfare measures, it is enough to pay taxes to produce the result and there is no personal involvement into solidaristic activities by the part of citizens.

50. In democracy, to have a "critical mass" is a priority, if proposals must find ways of being approved. Not necessarily a majority is always needed, but a substantial support in politics and/or in civil society (a "critical mass") is instrumental to be able to argue publicly in favour of a position. I can say that in the Italian context, after a long time in which Catholics found themselves fragmented and divided on many issues, now they appear to have understood the need for a "critical mass," and in such recent issues as artificial insemination and the family they have shown a common front.

51. Augustine of Hippo, Sermon 311 in Natali Cypriani Martyris. Trans. "Et dicitis: 'molesta tempora, gravia tempora, misera tempora sunt. Vivite bene, et mutatis tempora vivendo bene; tempora mutatis, et non habetis unde murmuretis."

REFERENCES

Acheson, D. *Present at the Creation: My Years in the State Department.* New York: Norton and Co., 1969.

Augustine of Hippo. *Sermons.* Hyde Park, NY: New City Press, 2000.

Chadwick, K., ed. *Catholicism, Politics and Society in XX century France.* Liverpool: Liverpool University Press, 2000.

Conway, M. *Catholic Politics in Europe, 1918–1945.* London: Cambridge University Press, 1997.

Durand, J. D., ed. *Les semaines sociales de France. Cent ans d'engagement social des catholiques français 1904–2004.* Paris: Parole e Silence, 2006.

Evans, E. L. *The Cross and the Ballot: Catholic Political Parties in Germany, Switzerland, Austria, Belgium and the Netherlands 1785–1985.* Boston: Humanities Press, 1999.

Greif, A. *Institutions and the Path to the Modern Economy: Lessons from Medieval Trade.* Cambridge: Cambridge University Press, 2006.

Grew, R., "Suspended Bridges to Democracy: The Uncertain Origins of Christian Democracy in France and Italy." In *European Christian Democracy: Historical Legacies and Comparative Perspectives,* edited by T. Kselman and J. A. Buttigieg. Notre Dame: Notre Dame University Press, 2003.

Kaiser, W. *Christian Democracy and the Origins of the European Union.* Cambridge: Cambridge University Press, 2007.

Kalyvas, S. N. *The Rise of Christian Democracy in Europe.* Ithaca, NY: Cornell University Press, 1996.

Kselman, T., and J. A. Buttigieg, eds. *European Christian Democracy: Historical Legacies and Comparative Perspectives.* Notre Dame: Notre Dame University Press, 2003.

Lamberts, E. "Christian Democracy and the Constitutional State in Western Europe 1945–1995." In *European Christian Democracy: Historical Legacies and Comparative Perspectives,* edited by T. Kselman and J. A. Buttigieg. Notre Dame: Notre Dame University Press, 2003.

————, ed. *Christian Democracy in the European Union 1945–95.* Leuven: Leuven University Press, 1997.

Milward, A. *The Reconstruction of Western Europe 1945–51.* London: Methuen, 1984.

Misner, P. *Social Catholicism in Europe: From the Onset of Industrialization to the First World War.* New York: Crossroad, 1991.

————. "Christian Democratic Social Policy: Precedents for Third-way Thinking." In *European Christian Democracy: Historical Legacies and Comparative Perspectives,* edited by T. Kselman and J. A. Buttigieg. Notre Dame: Notre Dame University Press, 2003.

Papini, R. *The Christian Democrat International.* Lanham, MD: Rowman & Littlefield, 1997.

Pasture, P. *Christian Trade Unionism in Europe since 1968*. Aldershot: Avebury Ashgate, 1994.

Pollack, M. A. *The Engines of European Integration: Delegation, Agency and Agenda Setting in the EU*. Oxford: Oxford University Press, 2003.

Stirk, P. M. R., ed. *European Unity in Context: The Interwar Period*. London: Pinter, 1989.

Van Kersbergen, K. *Social Capitalism: A Study of Christian Democracy and the Welfare State*. London: Routledge, 1995.

Vidler, A. R. *Prophecy and Papacy: A Study of Lamennais, the Church and the Revolution*. New York: Charles Scribner's Sons, 1954.

Warner, C. M. "Strategies of an Interest Group: The Catholic Church and Christian. Democracy in Postwar Europe, 1944–1958." In *European Christian Democracy. Historical Legacies and Comparative Perspectives*, edited by T. Kselman and J. A. Buttigieg. Notre Dame: Notre Dame University Press, 2003.

Zamagni, V. *Economic History of Italy 1860–1990*. Oxford: Clarendon Press, 1993.

———. "Movimento cattolico e trasformazioni dell'economia e della società in Italia." In *Un secolo di vita italiana. Il contributo dei cattolici*. Bologna: EDB, 2007.

5

Just Contracts and Catholic Social Teaching

A Perspective from Anglo-American Law

Vincent D. Rougeau

The True Wealth of Nations project aims to specify what Catholic social thought recommends for economic life, both at a personal and institutional level. This inquiry is profoundly linked to law and public policy, for it is through the law that many economic ideas are sanctioned and vindicated as the best way to organize key aspects of our common life. In turn, one of the most fundamental parts of the law relevant for economic life is the law of contracts. But when Anglo-American contract law is evaluated in light of the understanding of justice in Catholic social thought, it does not appear particularly just, and, in some cases, it may even be a tool for perpetuating certain types of injustice.

The 2008 crisis in credit markets offers a particularly vivid recent example. It was brought on by a deregulation that allowed far greater freedom in the designing of financial contracts (e.g., credit default swaps without the government oversight that could have eliminated the riskiest of these deals). Thus, the financial crisis of 2008 and the accompanying worldwide economic downturn arose from an unwillingness to temper an enthusiasm for markets with regulatory mechanisms that might have restricted profits. Behind the stories of foreclosed homes and bank failures were people who lost their savings, their jobs, and their hope for the future. These problems had their genesis in earlier legal changes over the last quarter century designed to "free" the credit markets from "burdensome" regulation. These changes obviously went too far, and policy makers responded with proposals to reverse the trend. Of course, the regulations that had been cast off were designed in large degree to prevent, or at least to temper, the kind of economic crisis that the deregulation engendered.

Catholic social thought gives us a way of evaluating how the economy and the law impact people's lives when those lives are considered as a whole, in their material, social, cultural, and spiritual aspects. An important tool that Catholic social thought provides for this evaluation is a rich notion of justice, and it is through this inquiry about justice that we can see how the law of contract serves an extremely important role in any assessment of how economic policies and ways of thinking enhance human dignity, or degrade it by focusing excessively on one aspect of the human condition. With this in mind, then, what does it mean to say that a contract is just? What do we mean by justice when decisions are taken within the realm of contract law?

In modern Anglo-American law, answering these questions has been made more difficult by the influence of classical and neoclassical contract theory rooted in the work of late nineteenth- and early twentieth-century American scholars such as Oliver Wendell Holmes, Christopher Columbus Langdell, and Samuel Williston[1]. These scholars emphasized the "amoral" nature of contract law, stressed principles rooted in individual autonomy, such as "freedom of contract," and attempted to demonstrate the importance of clear and predictable rules that could be mechanically applied in individual cases to achieve the "right" result. Although neoclassical scholarship since the mid-twentieth century, notably influenced by the work of Arthur Corbin[2], has done much to modify the rigidity and formalism of highly rule-based classical contract law, at its core American contract jurisprudence in particular is rooted in a vision of highly autonomous individuals who are motivated primarily by self-interest and a desire to gain profit and advantage over others.[3] This has been demonstrated most effectively in modern contract law through the influence of the "law and economics movement," which has given explicit recognition to economic efficiency concerns as a primary goal of contract formation, interpretation, and enforcement.

The sections that follow will (1) describe the three major understandings of justice in the Catholic intellectual tradition; (2) relate those areas to a particular aspect of Anglo-American contract law and policy; (3) evaluate how the law addresses justice concerns and assess its strengths and limitations in light of Catholic conceptions of justice; and (4) offer some suggestions about the future direction of contract law and its potential for being a force for economic justice in society.

Justice in the Catholic Tradition

In their pastoral letter, "Economic Justice for All,"[4] the U.S. Catholic bishops offered a brief treatment of the vision of justice in Catholic social teaching by describing in detail the three dimensions of basic justice:

> *Commutative justice* calls for fundamental fairness in all agreements and exchanges between individuals or private social groups. It demands respect for the equal human dignity of all persons in economic transactions, contracts, or promises.... *Distributive justice* requires that the allocation of income, wealth, and power in a society be evaluated in light of its effects on persons whose basic material needs are unmet.... Minimum material resources are an absolute necessity for human life. If persons are to be recognized as members of the human community, then the community has an obligation to help fulfill these basic needs.... Justice also has implications for the way the larger social, economic, and political institutions of society are organized.

> *Social justice* implies that persons have an obligation to be active and productive participants in the life of society and that society has a duty to enable them to participate in this way. This form of justice can also be called "contributive," for it stresses the duty of all who are able to help create the goods, services, and other nonmaterial or spiritual values necessary for the welfare of the whole community.[5]

The relationship between human dignity and human community is integral to a Catholic understanding of justice. Human persons are not seen as isolated individuals working to promote their personal advantage, but as members of communities and societies influenced by history, religion, and culture. This socially rooted conception of personhood understands the good of the individual as inseparable from the common good, which nevertheless exists as something unique, something that includes but is larger than the sum of the goods of individuals. It is the common good that creates tension between the idea of justice in Catholic social thought and understandings of justice in an Anglo-American contract law, dominated as it is by notions of individual autonomy and economic efficiency. As Stefano Zamagni notes in an essay in this volume:

> at the basis of the capitalist economy there lies a pragmatic—not, clearly, a logical—contradiction. The capitalist economy is certainly a

market economy, i.e. an institutional arrangement in which the two basic principles of the modern age are operative, namely, freedom of action and of doing enterprise, and the equality of all before the law. At the same time, however, the primary institution of capitalism—the capitalist enterprise—has been constructed over three centuries on the principle of hierarchy.... Capitalist enterprises are increasingly taking control of the conduct of individuals...and taking that control away from the state and other institutions, first and foremost, the family. Ideas like freedom of choice, tolerance, equality before the law, participation and the like...are being appropriated and recalibrated by capitalist firms to transform individuals, no longer subjects, into the purchasers of the enterprises' own goods and services.[6]

These concepts—freedom of choice, tolerance, and equality—take on quite different meanings in a free-market economy in which radical individual autonomy is presumed. This in turn makes a coherent conversation about the common good extremely difficult. The Catholic understanding of the common good relies on the idea that "any good of a person that is a real good...is embedded in the good of the community. Conversely, any common good that is a real good is simultaneously the good of persons.... The good of an isolated self, therefore, cannot be a...genuine good. It is illusion or surrealist fantasy, for the individual cannot be self-sufficient in any literal sense."[7] Yet, it is this very illusion that is nurtured and disseminated in the language of autonomy and choice favored by mainstream economic theory and Anglo-American contract law.

At the most obvious level, Anglo-American contract law is directed primarily to commutative justice, raising the question of whether an emphasis on commutative justice alone is sufficient for a body of law to be seen as just or fair. If one is to take seriously the broader concerns of justice in Catholic social teaching, the short answer to this question would doubtless be no. Thus, a second question must be addressed: whether contract law promotes justice effectively when it is evaluated in the context of distributive, social, *and* commutative justice. A moral analysis of the unjust contract is undertaken by Daniel Finn in an essay in this volume, while this chapter provides a similar analysis of contract law from a legal point of view.

Contracts play a central role in the organization of the economic life of society, and they have profound implications for allocations of income, wealth, and power. Thus, a broader inquiry about the justice of contract law is essential, and the conclusion would have to be that justice here is anaemic. Indeed, one might fairly ask whether contract law is intended to promote justice at all, or whether it is more accurately seen, at least in the Anglo-American legal tradition, as a tool for ordering private relationships among individuals, with little reference to social and cultural context in which those individuals live. It is also worth considering whether much more than this can reasonably be expected of the law of contract in a pluralistic society.

Contract Law and Commutative Justice

Contract law orders private relationships based on terms and priorities set by the individuals who have chosen to bind themselves to an agreement. The law seeks to respect the autonomy of the individuals involved by enforcing the agreement they made, applying the terms of the contract based on the apparent assent of the parties. Of course, discerning what has been assented to is difficult. In many cases, it is not clear whether a legally enforceable agreement has been formed or, if the existence of the agreement is not in doubt, there is a disagreement about the exact meaning of the contract's terms. Finally, when one party has performed its obligations—or is ready, willing, and able to do so—and the other party has not, the courts are often called upon to specify the consequences of this breach of contract. In each of these instances—formation, interpretation, and enforcement—the preferred approach in Anglo-American contract law is to find the intent of the parties and to enforce the bargain they struck. When there is doubt, the courts employ tools that, as much as possible, judge the parties' actions and the language of the contract using standards of objectivity and reasonableness.

Whether an enforceable bargain has been struck is judged using what is known as the "objective theory." For example, in the heavily studied case of *Lucy v. Zehmer*,[8] the Virginia Supreme Court was called upon to determine whether a contract for the sale of a farm, which had been drafted in very simple terms on the back of a restaurant bill, was enforceable. The defendant, the seller of the farm, argued that the agreement was made in jest, after an evening of heavy drinking during the Christmas season. The plaintiff/buyer argued that he had negotiated with the defendant/seller in good faith and in all seriousness and that he had every intention of purchasing the farm. Indeed, the price he had offered was well above the typical market price for similar properties, and the plaintiff was ready, willing, and able to perform. Although both plaintiff and defendant had been drinking, the court found no evidence that either party was inebriated to the extent that he did not recognize the ramifications of his actions. In sum, apart from the defendant's insistence that he was joking, there was no objective evidence that would have communicated such an intention to the plaintiff, and in their opinion reversing a finding for the defendant in the trial court, the court stated:

> In the field of contracts, as generally elsewhere, we must look to the outward expression of a person as manifesting his intention, rather than to his secret and unexpressed intention. The law imputes to a person an intention corresponding to the reasonable meaning of his words and acts.... The mental assent of parties is not requisite for the formation of a contract. If the words and other acts of one of the parties have but one reasonable meaning, his undisclosed intentions are immaterial, except when an unreasonable meaning which he attaches to his manifestations is known to the other party.... The law, therefore, judges of an agreement between two persons exclusively from those expressions of their intentions which are communicated between them.[9]

If we consider this case in the context of commutative justice, the ruling and its underlying reasoning appear very just indeed. Why should one party lose the benefit of an apparent bargain based on the unexpressed intentions of the other? It hardly seems unreasonable to hold parties to account for their behavior and even for the intentions that they have made objectively obvious to those around them. If, objectively speaking, those with whom you deal cannot tell you are joking, it seems reasonable for the law to treat you as if you were not. So far, so good. Yet, one problem with this view is that certain behaviors mean different things to different people, and culture and social context matter in our attempts to discern meaning. *Lucy v. Zehmer* is a case from rural Virginia in the 1950s. The parties had lived together in a small community for many years, and both would have been familiar with—and involved in—a tradition of "trash talking" that has long been a part of the male culture of the rural South. The defendant made this social context rather explicit in his testimony, and that contextual information played a significant part in the lower court earlier finding in his favor: "[Defendant] Zehmer claimed that he was 'high as a Georgia pine,' and that the transaction was 'just a bunch of two doggone drunks bluffing to see who could talk the biggest and say the most.'"[10] If we take seriously the view that human beings are social, are we confident that we can promote justice when we rely heavily on an external, post hoc assessment of the objective meaning of an individual's behavior, divorced from social and cultural context? As John Coleman noted in his essay in this volume, sociologists have long pointed out that not everything in the contract is contractual. This is where we begin to see the signs of important distributive and social justice concerns that may not be adequately addressed in the current regime of contract law. Perhaps in *Lucy v. Zehmer*, the Supreme Court was very much aware of the context and did not find the defendant persuasive. However, the trial judge, who most likely would have been from the same county as the parties in the case, was convinced by the defendant's version of the events. In light of the contextual, cultural, and social considerations, which decision was more just?

Another important instance in which contract law must address commutative justice occurs when one of the parties to a contract has breached an otherwise legally binding agreement. The modern trend in contract law has been to keep parties within the framework of their agreement as much as possible: to compel the breaching party to fulfill the contract and to resort to a full damage recovery for the nonbreaching party only as a last resort. This preference can be seen in both American and English law, in the presumptive rule of damages when a contract is breached. The "normal" recovery is what is know as "expectation" or general damages: "The object of awarding damages for breach of contract is to put the injured party, so far as money can do it, in the same position as if the contract had been performed.... In upholding this principle the courts have stressed that the object is to compensate the injured party for his loss, not to transfer to him, if he has suffered no loss, the benefit which the wrongdoer has gained by his breach of contract."[11] One way of doing this in practice is through the distinction between material and minor (or immaterial) breaches. To determine whether a failure to perform obligations under a contract is material, the American *Restatement (2nd) of Contracts* looks to circumstances such as (1) the extent to which an injured party would be deprived of a benefit he reasonably expected under a contract; (2) the extent to which the injured party can be adequately compensated for that part of the benefit of which he has been deprived; (3) the extent to which a party failing to perform will suffer forfeiture; and (4) the likelihood of rectification by the breaching party.[12] Only after an assessment of these factors is the nonbreaching party able to determine with any certainty that a material breach giving rise to a total breach of the contract has occurred, thereby relieving the nonbreaching party of any further obligation to perform its duties. If the breaching party seeks to cure its breach, or if the loss to the non-breaching party as a result of the breach is relatively minor or economically insignificant, the contract between the parties remains in force, with obligations being adjusted to account for the deviation from the original terms.

A classic American case that demonstrates this principle is *Jacobs & Youngs, Inc v. Kent*.[13] Plaintiff had built an expensive country residence for the defendant and was suing to recover a substantial balance still owed under the contract. In the contract the defendant had specified that all of the plumbing be wrought iron pipe "of Reading manufacture." After plaintiff had moved into the home, he learned that a substantial portion of the pipe, although wrought iron, had come from companies other than Reading, and he argued that plaintiff's breach should relieve him from his remaining performance obligations under the contract. Plaintiff admitted that substitutions for the Reading brand of pipe had been made but argued that there was no difference in appearance or quality from the Reading pipe. Although the court found that plaintiff had breached the contract by not using Reading pipe, it determined that plaintiff had "substantially performed" its obligations and that its breach was trivial. One indication of the triviality of the breach was that the value of the house was unaffected by the failure to use the Reading pipe. To remove the pipe that had been installed, however, would require tearing down walls at substantial cost and inconvenience. Ordinarily, a breaching party would be required to provide the nonbreaching party with the benefit of his bargain, in this case, Reading pipe. But because the breach was immaterial and the plaintiff had substantially performed, the nonbreaching party was not relieved of his payment obligations and was only entitled to an adjustment to that obligation based on the decline in value of property caused by the breach. In *Jacob & Youngs v. Kent*, that meant the defendant homeowner received no adjustment at all. English law has long taken a similar view, with an early announcement by Lord Mansfield in *Boone v. Eyre* (1779) that a party who performs a contract substantially, but whose performance is defective in some way, may still sue on the contract for the price. Subsequent cases made it clear that defective performance would entitle the party proving defective performance to an adjustment of the contract price based on the cost required to put the defect right.[14]

How are issues of commutative justice addressed by this rule? The law recognizes that enforcing agreements to their letter is not always in the best interest of the contracting parties, or of society. If the matter in dispute is truly ancillary to the primary purpose of the agreement, why should one party be allowed to abandon the agreement entirely based on a minor deviation from the contract? The rule in *Jacobs & Youngs* maintains the integrity of the agreement that was negotiated by the parties by enforcing it holistically, in light of its primary purpose. If the primary purpose of an agreement is to construct a house and, for the most part, that purpose has been achieved, should a problem with the plumbing result in a total breach? Perhaps it should if the problem makes the house uninhabitable, but if the breach involves something that is indiscernible or of a purely psychic benefit to the nonbreaching party, an adjustment to the contract terms not only preserves economic resources but also allows for flexibility within a contractual relationship that can adapt to changes in circumstances while still acknowledging that specific obligations under the agreement have not been met.

Indeed, preventing economic waste and the distinguishing of trivial matters from those that go to the heart of an agreement both signal some attention in contract law to the common good, at least inasmuch as that good is enhanced by economic efficiency. Preservation of economic resources has important implications for both social and distributive justice, but economic efficiency is often the only area in which the law considers the broader impact of individual behavior on the community.

Unfortunately, the doctrine of "substantial performance" has also been used in ways that perpetuate injustice, often by allowing powerful political and economic interests to run roughshod over weaker individuals despite the existence of explicit obligations under a contract. In *Peevyhouse v. Garland Coal & Mining*,[15] the Peevyhouses, a farm family in rural Oklahoma, had been approached by Garland for permission to strip mine on a portion of the family's property. The Peevyhouses had long opposed mining in the area because in most cases once the mining was completed, the land was left scarred and unusable. After some negotiation, they relented to Garland's request to lease their land for coal mining on the condition that the land be returned to its original condition when the mining operations were complete. In order to secure this promise from Garland, the Peevyhouses agreed to forgo a $3000 payment at the signing of the contract. Nevertheless, when the mining operations were finished, Garland refused to restore the land, arguing that they had substantially completed their obligations under the lease contract and that the Peevyhouses had suffered little or no diminution in the value of their land as a result of the mining. Furthermore, restoration—something ancillary to the main purpose of the contract—would impose substantial costs on Garland. The Oklahoma Supreme Court agreed with Garland, finding that although Garland had breached its obligation to restore the land, the appropriate compensation for that breach was not the cost of the remedial work, or the benefit of the bargain, but diminution in the value of the land as a result of Garland's failure to perform its promise. For this loss, the Peevyhouses were awarded $300.[16]

Once again we see why context matters and how a lack of attention to the noneconomic aspects of the common good can be lead to injustice. The Peevyhouse case has generated controversy among legal academics for over forty years, but it is still prevailing law in Oklahoma, and its reasoning has been followed in a number of other states.[17] The mining industry was extremely influential in Oklahoma at the time of the case, and the Peevyhouses were not able to match legal talent available to a "deep pocket" such as Garland. The understanding of the common good was limited to the idea that strip mining was a quick and relatively inexpensive way to remove valuable mineral resources from the land, which provided jobs and other economic benefits to the state. Environmental destruction—and the question of which members of the community were most likely to bear its burdens—received little attention at the time. Although there is greater awareness of these issues today, prominent corporate interests still argue with some success that the economic benefits of low-cost operations and high profits for the companies should be at the forefront of how their activities are judged and regulated. Anglo-American contract law strives to promote the freedom and autonomy of individuals to create their own agreements and see them legally enforced. The courts typically do not seek to revise agreements based on some independent view of justice outside the contract, unless the agreement violates a fairly explicit notion of public policy or when a party seems to be acting in bad faith. Even when they do revise or interpret an agreement, courts tend to employ tools that stress an objective understanding of what the agreement means and often reason that the party negatively affected knew or should have known the revision or interpretation imposed upon him.

All of this might appear consistent with a Catholic notion of justice that empowers all individuals within a society to participate in economic, social, and political life on equal terms. In these cases, the law attempts to play a role of neutral arbiter, giving individuals the freedom to make their own choices and to fashion agreements suited to their individual needs and personal tolerance for risk. Nevertheless, at some point the law should recognize that not all people are similarly situated in society and that imbalances of power, income, education, and social status exist that might routinely place some individuals on the losing end of private agreements in a culture that prizes individual autonomy and free markets. As Daniel Finn notes in his essay in this volume, "a rejection of unjust contracts from a moral perspective within the Catholic social tradition focuses on the character of the freedom of the persons entering into that contract.... that somehow or other the more prosperous party to a contract made an offer which the less prosperous party to a contract 'had to' accept even though they would have wanted (and deserved) better."[18]

Distributive and Social Justice in Contract Law

Given the extraordinary respect American contract law has for individual autonomy and the free market, how successful can this legal regime be in addressing the more communally oriented concepts of distributive and social justice? For at least two important reasons, social and distributive justice present great difficulty for Anglo-American contract law. First, both take seriously the reality of human difference within societies and proceed from an assumption that those differences matter. Justice, when properly understood in the Catholic tradition, includes a kind of partiality to certain groups in certain cases (e.g., the poor), particularly when the rights of those groups are imperiled or ordinarily have not been respected.[19] Second, members of communities have responsibilities to one another that may from time to time involve sacrifice, solidarity, and sharing, values that are not typically nurtured when free markets and personal autonomy are prized.

It is important, however, not to paint the theoretical assumptions underlying contract law with too broad a brush. The law has long recognized, and continues to develop, important defenses to contract obligation that take seriously the notion that persons in a bargain are not always equally situated and that "unequal bargaining power" often creates contractual obligations that the law has no obligation to respect. At the most basic level, contract law proceeds from an assumption that all adults are equally capable of entering into bargains and negotiating the terms as they see fit. In most cases, the courts are not interested in policing the "fairness" of private agreements, for it is assumed that individuals value things differently and that it is not for the law to assess contracts to determine whether one party or the other got a fair deal. That said, both of these presumptions can be overcome in a number of ways.

The more unequal the bargaining power of two individuals in a contract, the more likely a court is to find something wrong with the bargain that will release the weaker party from her obligations. Fraud, duress, undue influence, mistake, and impossibility are all doctrines that excuse performance, and each operates in its own way to police the abuse of power in contractual relationships. These tend, however, to be reserved for extreme cases. For example, fraud tends to be difficult to prove, often requiring the plaintiff to demonstrate by clear and convincing evidence that (1) a statement or representation (2) was know by the maker to be false, (3) the statement was material to the formation of the contract, and (4) it was acted upon by the party claiming fraud in reasonable reliance of the truth of the statement resulting in injury or damage.[20] Duress and undue influence tend to arise from extreme factual situations, such as physical compulsion, threats, or criminal activity.[21] What links these defenses is that all proceed from a showing by the injured party that his ability to make a free and autonomous decision has been undermined in some significant way, making it unreasonable or unfair to bind him to a contractual obligation. The undermining of individual freedom, or the distortion of information central to making a fully informed choice, vitiates the binding nature of a contract because assent was improperly secured.

The proper functioning of free markets depends on respect for individual autonomy and, in a capitalist economy, the law must promote an atmosphere in which individuals have not only the ability to make independent choices but also broad access to the information necessary to weigh the costs and benefits of their decisions. In many ways, unfettered individual freedom provides the moral impetus for the enforcement of contracts. We are each freely capable of making our own choices, and we all have access to the same information about the costs and benefits of our actions. Once we have entered into a contract, it is not for the law to protect us from bad decisions, because our choices were made on a "level playing field." The consequences of contractual arrangements, if made under appropriate conditions, are not the law's concern unless there is an extreme violation of public policy (the selling of human beings, for instance) or when there has been an undermining, prevention, or distortion of an individual's freedom to choose. This makes it rather difficult for contract law to engage in the types of inquiries necessary for attention to distributive and social justice concerns.

Public policy has long served as a way for courts to prevent the enforcement of certain kinds of bargains, but "an otherwise valid contract is rarely invalidated because it is against public policy."[22] In a society with widely divergent values and beliefs, the concept of "public policy" has become increasingly vague and restrictions based upon it tend to be controversial. The primary public interest that courts seek to protect is the freedom of contract. Thus, in order for public policy to trump this interest, the policy must be clear—typically something fairly explicit from constitutional, statutory, judicial decisions.[23] As the *Restatement (2nd) of Contracts* explains:

> Historically, the public policies against the enforcement of terms
> were developed by judges themselves on the basis of their own
> perception of the need to protect some aspect of the public welfare.
> Some of these policies are now rooted in precedents accumulated
> over the centuries. Important examples are policies against the
> restraint of trade, impairment of domestic relations, and interference
> with duties owed to individuals.... Society has, however, many other
> interests that are worthy of protection, and as society changes so do
> these interests. Courts remain alert to other and sometimes novel
> situations in which enforcement of a term may contravene those
> interests.... At the same time, courts should not implement obsolete
> policies that have lost their vigor over the years.[24]

Somewhat more developed, but not much more likely to be successful as a defense to a contract obligation, is the concept of unconscionability. Although long recognized in the civilian legal tradition, which inherited the concept from Roman law, Anglo-American law has only recently came to embrace the idea that certain bargains were "grossly unfair" or shocking to the conscience of the court:

> During the first half of the twentieth century, economic and social changes made the problem of enforceability of unfair bargains more acute than at any previous time. Large commercial enterprises increasingly began using standard form contracts to conduct business transactions. The typical standard form contained numerous "boilerplate" provisions that are extremely favorable to the drafting party. Moreover, negotiation of such terms rarely occurs both because the terms are normally not read and also because the form is usually presented on a "take-it-or-leave-it" basis.... Thus, the emergence of the standard form brought into question the concept of mutual assent, a pillar of classical contract law. The same period also witnessed a growing public awareness of the problems of the poor and unsophisticated, potential victims for unscrupulous commercial parties.[25]

The unconscionability doctrine was given explicit form in American law through Section 2-302 of the Uniform Commercial Code (the "UCC"). Because this section does not define what "unconscionable" means in the context of the UCC, the specific language of 2-302 is not particularly helpful in providing guidance on when a court should refuse to enforce a contract. The official comment to the section, however, does provide some clarification:

> This section is intended to make it possible for the courts to police explicitly against the contracts or the clauses they find unconscionable. In the past such policing has been accomplished by adverse construction of language, by manipulation of the rules of offer and acceptance, or by determinations that the clause is contrary to public policy or to the dominant purpose of the contract.... The basic test is whether, in the light of the general commercial background and the commercial needs of the particular trade or case, the clauses involved are so one-sided as to be unconscionable under the circumstances existing at the time of the making of the contract.[26]

Both public policy and unconscionability demonstrate the difficulty of addressing issues of distributive and social justice in a legal system rooted in individual autonomy, freedom of contract, and free-market capitalism. By what standard is unfairness to be judged? Our concern for distributive justice should make us wary of bargains that further enrich the wealthy and the powerful at the expense of the poor and the weak, but free markets depend on these types of imbalances to deliver on their promise of wealth creation. Social justice concerns might lead us to question the justice of contractual arrangements that routinely place certain segments of the population into economic difficulty, that prevent them from effective participation in society due to excessive debt borne of their efforts to secure their basic needs or because of structures that advantage "free" labor relations over collective bargaining and union membership. Stefano Zamagni, after Schumpeter, describes this as the "creative destruction" of free-market capitalism, and although the free market is an effective motor of change, "the costs are immediate and tend to be levied on the weakest members of the population. The benefits arrive with time and tend to go to the most talented people.... 'Creative destruction' is at the heart of capitalism—which destroys the old in order to create the new and creates the new in order to destroy the old—but this is also its Achilles heel."[27]

The court case generally cited as moving unconscionability into the American common law of contracts is *Williams v. Walker-Thomas Furniture.*[28] The facts originated in the late 1950s and grew out of the sales practices of a Washington, D.C., furniture store that served a primarily low-income, African American clientele. When furniture was purchased at Walker-Thomas on credit:

> title would remain in Walker-Thomas until the total of all the
> monthly payments made equaled the stated value of the item.... In
> the event of a default in the payment of any monthly installment,
> Walker-Thomas could repossess the item. The contract further
> provided that "the amount of each periodical installment payment to
> made by [purchaser] under this present lease shall be inclusive of and
> not in addition to the amount of each installment payment to be
> made by [purchaser] under such prior leases, bills or accounts; and
> all payments now and hereafter made by [purchaser] shall be credited
> pro rata on all outstanding leases, bills, and accounts due the
> Company by [purchaser] at the time each such payment is made."[29]

In essence, a purchase made at Walker-Thomas on the installment plan that remained unpaid served as collateral for any future purchases. Walker-Thomas could, and did, repossess all previous items sold that were not yet been completely paid for no matter how little was still owed if a customer defaulted on a more recent purchase.

What makes this case so interesting after fifty years is the way in which the dynamics of the market collided with critical social, economic, and cultural issues of the time, providing a vivid example of both the efficient and destructive aspects of "economically efficient" capitalism. From an economic standpoint, Walker-Thomas Furniture was providing consumer goods to low-income people through a financing vehicle that may well have been justified based on the risks associated with their customer base. Many of the people with whom they dealt were on public relief or depended on irregular work at an hourly wage. These facts, however, were also significant in the court's finding that the financing contracts in question may have been unconscionable:

> Did each party to the contract, considering his obvious education or
> lack of it, have a reasonable opportunity to understand the terms of
> the contract, or were there important terms hidden in a maze of fine
> print and minimized by deceptive sales practices? Ordinarily, one
> who signs an agreement without full knowledge of its terms might
> be held to assume the risk that he has entered a one-sided bargain.
> But when a party of little bargaining power, and hence little real
> choice, signs a commercially unreasonable contract with little or no
> knowledge of its terms, it is hardly likely that his consent, or even the
> objective manifestation of his consent, was ever given to all the
> terms.... In determining reasonableness or fairness, the primary
> concern must be with the terms of the contract considered in the
> light of the circumstances existing when the contract was made.[30]

Here we begin to see a real attempt by an American court to grapple with distributive and social justice concerns raised by contract law, and we can also see the danger in too heavy an emphasis on economic efficiency, individualism, and market rationality without attention to context.

Shaping the court's response was the fact that Washington, D.C., was a legally segregated city in the late 1950s and early 1960s, although by this time segregation was certainly on the wane. It would be rare for black residents of the city, particularly those of lower income, to venture outside of their neighborhoods to shop. In the 1950s, certain major Washington department stores in the primary "F Street" downtown shopping area were open to African American shoppers only on specific days, and some shops did not serve blacks at any time. This social and economic reality offers a bit more insight into the circumstances of the customers of Walker-Thomas Furniture. Not only were many of these people poor and uneducated, but they would have had few, if any, shopping options outside of their immediate community. Does the existence of economic and racial segregation at the time mean that the contracts in *Williams v. Walker-Thomas Furniture* were unconscionable? Not necessarily, but it certainly helps us understand why the judge who wrote the opinion was particularly concerned about the store's credit practices. Like the county court judge in *Lucy v. Zehmer*, he was acutely aware of the economic and social conditions of the city in which he lived and worked, and he recognized that the theoretical construct of "freedom of contract" and certain philosophical ideas about individual autonomy were misplaced in this situation.

Should the courts play a role in adjusting agreements that may take advantage of entrenched social and economic inequalities within society? The doctrine of unconscionability allows judges to do this from time to time, but successful claims of unconscionability are infrequent for reasons similar to those claiming violations of public policy.

Although the social and cultural context of *Williams v. Walker-Thomas Furniture* may now seem dated—particularly as it concerns racial segregation—the issues of economic inequality and its tendency to limit effective bargaining in contracting situations remains a live one.

A more recent issue of unfair or unconscionable bargains that commanded a great deal of attention today in both the United States and the United Kingdom was the crisis of 2008 that developed in the financial services industry, notably the collapse of a number of major commercial and investment banks due to outrageous risks taken in the home mortgage lending market. Congress, the federal government, and the governments of most of the European Union nations were all called upon to relieve both lenders and borrowers from the consequences of ill-considered mortgage lending contracts and the securities backed by theses loans.[31] Although some of these contracts were products of outright fraud, most were the results of bargains that under classic approaches to freedom of contract and economic efficiency should be enforceable. Many of the homeowners who suffered in this crisis were first-time buyers, often members of minority communities, who were encouraged by lenders to borrow large sums of money to purchase homes during a run-up in prices.[32] These contracts had significant social and distributive justice implications when one considers the power of the lending industry in the marketplace and its ability to market expensive or risky loans to unsophisticated consumers desperate for a piece of the "American Dream" or to grab the first rung of the "property ladder."[33] As laws regulating the financial services industry were liberalized over the last twenty-five years, financial intermediaries have been enriched beyond the wildest dreams of their shareholders. Once the business cycle began its inevitable turn downward, both lenders and borrowers sought to avoid the downside risks of their contracts. With their powerful allies in government and the important connection their business has to the health of the overall economy, it is hardly surprising that the governments of the world's major economies ultimately chose to direct hundreds of billions of dollars, pounds, and euros into private companies to protect them from the downside risks of their business decisions.

Just Contracts and the Common Good

This brief overview of some key aspects of contract law jurisprudence in the United States can hardly do justice to the intricacies of this subject. Nevertheless, it is reasonable to conclude that contract law seeks primarily to promote justice between, or among, parties to an agreement with as little intervention as possible from external moral, cultural, or political considerations. The key values being promoted are individual autonomy, freedom of contract, economic efficiency, and the unfettered flow of information relevant to assessing contractual risk and reward. Thus, even inasmuch as contract law addresses commutative justice concerns, it does so based on an understanding of the individual that is rather feeble when compared to the Catholic view of the person. Commutative justice disconnected from the situation of an individual in community with others and from broader understandings of the common good is simply a shell without internal substance. Albino Barrera, in an essay in this volume, recommends a focus on the economic common good as a way of giving an overarching framework to the principles of Catholic social teaching in the context of a market economy. When the economic common good is achieved, there is space in society for the integral development of the self, integral human development for others, and care for the earth.[34]

> Unlike Marxism or laissez-faire capitalism, [Catholic social thought] pursues a more difficult path of balancing two-fold objectives in a mixed economy. It appreciates the beneficial services offered by market operations even as it calls for extra-market interventions to mitigate the market economy's unintended consequences and excesses.... For example, the principles of subsidiarity and socialization govern the delicate balance between private initiative and state action. Integral human development calls for the human person to flourish in body, mind, and spirit. The principles of stewardship, universal destination of goods of the earth, and primacy of labor affirm both private property rights and their attendant just-use obligations.[35]

In 1993, the city of Ypsilanti, Michigan, filed a lawsuit against General Motors Corporation in which it alleged that GM had breached a contract to keep a manufacturing plant open in Ypsilanti.[36] In 1984 and 1988, the city had granted GM tax abatements for a period of twelve years, and the city alleged that those abatements were made in consideration of promises from GM to remain in Ypsilanti at least during the abatement period. Although the court concluded that the statutory process through which the tax abatements were granted did not create contractual obligations under classical rules of contract formation, GM was found to have made a legally binding promise to the city to keep production of certain vehicles in Ypsilanti under the doctrine of promissory estoppel. Promissory estoppel binds the maker of a promise if the promisor should reasonably have expected the promise to induce action or forbearance by the promisee, if the promise does indeed induce such action or forbearance, and if injustice can be avoided only though enforcement of the promise.[37] In finding GM bound by promises made during the negotiation of the tax abatements, the trial court judge noted that:

> There would be gross inequity and patent unfairness if General Motors, having lulled the people of the Ypsilanti area into giving up millions of tax dollars which they so desperately need to educate their children and provide basic governmental services, is allowed to simply decide that it will desert 4,500 workers and their families because it thinks it can make these same cars a little cheaper somewhere else. Perhaps another judge in another court would not feel moved by that injustice and would labor to find a legal rationalization to allow such conduct. But in this Court it is my responsibility to make that decision. My conscience will not allow this injustice to happen.[38]

Promissory estoppel is a well-established basis for creating a binding legal obligation in American and English contract law, but the stirring words of the judge in the Ypsilanti case bring to mind issues of unconscionability and reveal the concerns of distributive and social justice that so often go unaddressed in contracts cases. Unfortunately, the appeals court cut this discussion off at the knees and reversed the lower court in a strongly worded opinion:

> The trial court's finding that defendant promised to keep Caprice and station wagon production at Willow Run is clearly erroneous. First, the mere fact that a corporation solicits a tax abatement and persuades a municipality with assurances of jobs cannot be evidence of a promise.... [T]he fact that a manufacturer uses hyperbole and puffery in seeking an advantage or concession does not necessarily create a promise.[39]

The appeals court noted further that, "even if the finding of a promise could be sustained, reliance on the promise would not have been reasonable."[40] Many courts are not so rigid in their need to see an explicit promise; the fact that there was an act in reliance on some promise or commitment, express or implied, is often enough. Most American courts use the "reasonableness" standard to evaluate the reliance in order to determine the existence of a promise, but whether or not reliance is "reasonable" and, therefore, whether some sort of actionable promise or commitment was made, is a judgment call that gives tremendous discretion to the judge deciding the case. In contrast, English courts do not look to the reasonableness of reliance on the promise per se but, once the party seeking enforcement has changed its position based on the promise, to whether it would be inequitable to deprive the party of the benefit of the promise.[41] That approach could have tipped the judgment in favor of Ypsilanti. Contrary to the appeals court ruling, it does not seem unreasonable for the city of Ypsilanti to rely on commitments from a corporation that had been part of its economic lifeblood for decades. At the very least, it is clear that reliance on the commitment did great harm to Ypsilanti and its residents, and one way to avoid inequity would have been to hold GM to the commitments it had made.

Anyone familiar with the economic devastation that the state of Michigan has suffered over the last two decades as the American auto industry has fallen into decline knows how many lives depend on the choices made by companies such as GM. Similar to what occurred in *Lucy v. Zehmer*, the judge at the trial court level, who was probably more intimately aware of the relationship between GM and Ypsilanti, was much more willing to interpret the facts of the case in a way that recognized unique aspects of the case rooted in the American automobile's relationship with the industrial workers of Michigan. How might that relationship have affected the parties' understanding of the commitments that were being made prior to the granting of the tax abatements? This case says a great deal about the power that corporate interests can exert over public entities when they control the economic life of a community. It also demonstrates what can happen when the legal system is unwilling to consider the consequences of such a power imbalance and treats the weaker party—in this case, the city of Ypsilanti—as an equal in a contract negotiation that not only demonstrated unequal bargaining power but also was rooted in a special relationship in which GM was viewed in an almost paternalistic way by the workers of Michigan.

There are no easy answers in cases such as *Ypsilanti v. General Motors*. GM must take seriously its obligations to shareholders to turn a profit, but that profit does not come about in a vacuum. GM succeeded in part due to the commitment of its employees and its relationship with the communities in which those people lived and worked. A Catholic understanding of justice demonstrates that parties to a contract dispute are not simply individuals in a private negotiation designed to secure personal advantage, but are also persons situated in community who have responsibilities to the common good. How we treat one another in light of the cultural, social, and economic relationships of strength and weakness that exist among us is an issue of tremendous importance, and the legal system provides a venue in which we might be able to consider our obligations to one another in community when we make promises that we expect the law to enforce.

In a pluralist society with an aggressive, free-market economy, is it possible for the law of contract to attend to notions of commutative, distributive, and social justice that require an understanding of personhood rooted in community and strengthened by solidarity, sacrifice, and sharing? Ian MacNeil's relational theory is an important school of thought in contract law that attempts to take seriously the role of relationships, fairness, and cooperation in contract:

> By now, we are so brainwashed as to be almost unable to conceive of exchange except in terms of markets and discrete transactions. But exchange is not simply the product of social relations so organized. Rather, exchange is the inevitable product of specialization of labor.... Understanding this is the first step towards freeing ourselves of the Hobbesian and utilitarian intellectual blinders which prevent us from understanding contract behavior and with it relational contract.... [W]e must recognize that discrete exchange—which itself is the product of particular kinds of social relations, such as markets permitting and encouraging it—can play only a very limited and specialized function in any economy, no matter how market oriented that economy may be.... That discrete exchange can never be the *only* economic function essential to production, distribution, and final consumption of goods and services should also go without saying. But it must be said because this so-called science of neoclassical economics presumes a model treating discrete exchange as the sole economic function essential to production, distribution, and final consumption. And this model or other less sophisticated Hobbesian alternatives dominates the conventional wisdom of Western economic thinking.[42]

MacNeil's observations support the idea that Anglo-American contract law is primarily concerned with a particular vision of commutative justice—the justice that applies to discrete exchanges—and his recognition of a broader range of social relations applicable to any appropriate understanding of the functioning of contract law is extremely sympathetic to justice concerns in the Catholic tradition. Yet, although MacNeil's relational contract theory is a well-known and important part of the scholarly discourse, it tends to be evaluated in light of its inconsistency with the approaches that I have discussed, and it has not had much influence in overcoming the tendency to rely on foundational principles rooted in neoclassical and utilitarian approaches in contracts jurisprudence.[43]

The best way for Catholic social thought to engage issues of justice within contract law may be through greater dialogue with such theories as those of MacNeil. Both offer more complex understandings of the needs of human persons beyond utilitarian self-interest, and both take seriously the fundamental importance of society and human sociability in any evaluation of whether a particular legal regime is just. Within such a dialogue, the justice implications of contractual relationships might be seen more appropriately in less libertarian terms, and more as a reflection of how we should conduct our affairs in a community in which we believe all are created in God's image and in which we understand our interdependence through the virtue of solidarity:

> Those who are more influential, because they have a greater share of goods and common services, should feel responsible for the weaker and be ready to share with them all they possess. Those who are weaker, for their part, in the same spirit of solidarity, should not adopt a purely passive attitude or one that is destructive of the social fabric, but, while claiming their legitimate rights, should do what they can for the good of all.[44]

What might this mean for contract law on a more practical level? To answer this question, let us return to the economic crisis of 2008. Before the massive deregulation of the financial markets, governments intervened heavily in mortgage lending to protect consumers and enhance the stability of financial markets. Mortgage loans were readily available in the United States, for example, due to massive support from the federal government in the form of insurance and other programs that took much of the risk out of mortgage lending for private financial institutions. The contracts between borrowers and lenders reflected the heavy government regulatory oversight that was a recognition of the importance Americans place on home ownership in their overall assessment of their quality of life. Thus, loans were widely available to consumers because the private sector bore little risk in making them. These loans, however, were not particularly profitable for the financial services industry.

Deregulation allowed new loans to be marketed with little oversight from the government, placing both consumers and lenders at increased risk, but offering new opportunities for both property ownership and profit-making. Once the market turns sour, should the risk-takers suffer the consequences of their choices, as the market model requires? A relational theory of contract or a view of justice rooted in Catholic social thought probably would have been much more reticent to eliminate government regulation in the first place, recognizing the devastating effects that market spikes and crashes could have on the social and financial stability of American households. Indeed, this is a recognition of the importance of social capital in the life of a society and the need to maintain it. John Coleman raises a related question, regarding Francis Fukuyama's discussion of how to increase social capital in the United States: "How [does] a consumption ethos fostered by the libertarian model...undermine the very social and cultural virtues...essential to wealth creation?"[45] The drive to liberalize mortgage markets in the United States and the United Kingdom is an object lesson in the consequences of disregard for the social, cultural, and relational aspects of contract and market behavior in a drive to increase wealth and profits through greater efficiency. It is inaccurate and irresponsible to think that the state, through the law, is "harming" individuals in their pursuit to maximize their wealth by regulating markets and individual freedom within the realm of contract. The state will be called upon either to structure markets by regulation or to resurrect them when they fail.

Catholics will understand this regulatory role for the law as an appropriate exercise of its responsibility to promote the common good. Perhaps the Catholic notion of justice, rooted as it is in solidarity and the recognition of a redistributive role for law and public policy, is a bit altruistic for the realm of contract. How, one might ask, can the economy of a pluralistic nation with a vibrant market economy function with such a vision? How can we possibly imagine a just society under the rule of law that does not see our relationships with others as a fundamentally important part of who we are as human beings? The provision of a level playing field for the quest of mutual advantage in the midst of great inequalities is simply an endorsement of the law of the jungle, in which the strong assert their dominance over the weak. As Vera Zamagni notes in her essay in this volume:

> Materialism and individualism are hegemonizing economic life to the point of causing many Catholics to revolt against the market. It is critical to clarify today that it is not the market which is wrong from a Christian point of view but the capitalist version of markets in recent centuries. Catholics need to resume initiative in the field of

economics, putting in place corporations like cooperatives and social enterprises, in which production is carried out with attention to the truly humane dimensions of work and consumption, both with reference to employees and clients. Even in capitalist companies, things can be largely improved by the re-introduction of a corporate social responsibility that is not merely a profit-maximizing strategy.

Law is a creature of society; it reflects the culture of the people it regulates. Anglo-American law reflects an increasingly individualistic and materialistic society in which citizens have too little interest in caring for others and certainly have little patience for bearing the economic cost of doing so. Catholics and others of good will must step up and challenge this worldview by living out values of solidarity, sharing, and sacrifice that are becoming countercultural. But living out this virtuous way of life provides not simply personal benefit. As the fundamental hypothesis of the True Wealth of Nations project indicates, implementing both the values and institutions recommended in Catholic social thought would place our economy on the road to sustainable prosperity for all.

NOTES

1. See, e.g., Christopher Columbus Langdell, *A Summary of the Law of Contracts*; Oliver Wendell Holmes, *The Common Law*; Mark DeWolfe Howe, *A Treatise on the Law of Contracts*.

2. See, e.g., Arthur Corbin, *Corbin on Contracts*.

3. Melvin A. Eisenberg, "Why There is No Law of Relational Contracts." Although legal formalism would eventually come under attack from mid-twentieth century Legal Realism, which itself would spawn movements such as Critical Legal Studies and relational theory, classical and neoclassical theory have remained an important part of American contract law. See, John E. Murray, Jr., "Contracts and the Rise of Neoformalism."

4. National Conference of Catholic Bishops, "Tenth Anniversary Edition of Economic Justice for All."

5. Ibid., paras. 69–71.

6. See Stefano Zamagni's essay in this volume.

7. David Hollenbach, *The Common Good and Christian Ethics*, 79.

8. 196 Va. 493 (1954).

9. Ibid., 502–3.

10. Ibid., 500.

11. Robert Upex and Geoffrey Bennett, *Davies on Contract*, 295–96.

12. American Law Institute, *Restatement of the Law Second: Contracts*, 241.

13. 230 N.Y. 239 (1921).

14. Upex and Bennett, *Davies on Contract*, 262–63.

15. 382 P. 2d 109 (162).

16. Ibid., p. 113.

17. For an extensive discussion of the case, its background, and the surrounding controversy, see Judith Maute, "Peevyhouse vs. Garland Coal & Mining: The Ballad of Willie and Lucille," 89 Nw. U.L. Rev. 1341 (1995).

18. See Daniel Finn's essay in this volume.

19. M. Cathleen Kaveny, "Discrimination and Affirmative Action."

20. See, e.g., *Pitre v. Twelve Oak Trust*, 818 F. Supp. 949 (1993).

21. See generally, American Law Institute, *Restatement of the Law: Second: Contracts*, 161–77.

22. Randy E. Barnett, *Contracts*, 18.

23. Charles L. Knapp, Nathan M. Crystal, and Harry J. Prince, *Problems in Contract Law*, 642–43.

24. American Law Institute, *Restatement of the Law Second: Contracts*, Sec. 179, Comment *a*.

25. Ibid., 585.

26. American Law Institute, *Uniform Commercial Code*, Section 3-302, Comment 1.

27. See Stefano Zamagni's essay in this volume.

28. 350 F.2nd 445 (D.C. Cir. 1965).

29. Ibid., 44.

30. Ibid.

31. See generally, N. Eric Weiss, *Government Interventions in Financial Markets*.

32. Greg Allen, "Facing Foreclosure."

33. See, e.g. Thomas Hüetlin, "British Families, Drowning in Debt."

34. See Albino Barrera's essay in this volume.

35. Ibid., p. 31.

36. *Ypsilanti v. General Motors*, 61 U.S.L.W. 2563 (1993) (unreported opinion, Michigan Circuit Court).

37. American Law Institute, *Restatement of the Law Second: Contracts*, Section 90.

38. *Ypsilanti v. General Motors supra*, n. 34.

39. *Ypsilanti v. General Motors*, 201 Mich. App. 128 (1993).

40. Ibid.

41. Upex and Bennett, *Davies on Contract*, 47–48.

42. Ian R. MacNeil, "Relational Contract," 485–86.

43. See, e.g., Jay M. Feinman, "Relational Contract Theory in Context."

44. John Paul II, *Sollicitudo rei socialis*, para. 39.

45. See John Coleman's essay in this volume.

REFERENCES

Allen, Greg. "Facing Foreclosure, One Home at a Time, National Public Radio." Online. Available:http://www.npr.org/templates/story/story.php?storyId=89856332.

American Law Institute. *Restatement of the Law Second: Contracts 2d*, 3 vols. St. Paul, MN: American Law Institute, 1981.

The American Law Institute and National Conference of Commissioners on Uniform State Laws. *Uniform Commercial Code.* Eagan, MN: West 2009.

Barnett, Randy E. *Contracts.* 3rd ed. New York: Aspen, 2003.

Corbin, Arthur. *Corbin on Contracts: A Comprehensive Treatise on the Rules of Contract Law.* St. Paul, MN: West, 2008.

DeWolfe Howe, Mark. *A Treatise on the Law of Contracts (3rd).* Edited by Samuel Williston. Mt. Kisco, NY: Baker, Voorhis, 1957.

Eisenberg, Melvin A. "Why There is No Law of Relational Contracts." *Northwestern Law Review* 94 (2000): 805.

Feinman, Jay M. "Relational Contract Theory in Context." *Northwestern Law Review* 94 (2000): 737.

Hollenbach, David. *The Common Good and Christian Ethics.* Cambridge, UK: Cambridge University Press, 2002.

Holmes, Oliver Wendell. *The Common Law.* Cambridge, MA: Belknap Press, 1963.

Hüetlin, Thomas. "British Families, Drowning in Debt." *Business Week* (August 20, 2008).

John Paul II. *Sollicitudo rei socialis.* 1987.

Kaveny, M. Cathleen. "Discrimination and Affirmative Action." *Theological Studies* 57 (1998): 286, 301.

Knapp, Charles L., Nathan M. Crystal, and Harry J. Prince. *Problems in Contract Law: Cases and Materials.* 6th ed. New York: Aspen, 2007.

Langdell, Christopher Columbus. *A Summary of the Law of Contracts.* Boston: Little, Brown, 1880.

MacNeil, Ian R. "Relational Contract: What We Do and Do Not Know." *Wisconsin Law Review* 483 (1985): 485–86.

Maute, Judith. "Peevyhouse vs. Garland Coal & Mining: The Ballad of Willie and Lucille," *Northwestern Law Review* 89 (1995): 1341.

Murray, John E., Jr. "Contracts and the Rise of Neoformalism." *Fordham Law Review* 71 (2002); 869.

National Conference of Catholic Bishops. "Tenth Anniversary Edition of Economic Justice for All: Pastoral Letter on Catholic Social Teaching and the U.S. Economy." Washington, DC: U.S. Catholic Conference, 1997.

Upex, Robert, and Geoffrey Bennett. Davies on Contract. 10th ed. London: Sweet & Maxwell, 2008.

Weiss, N. Eric. *Government Interventions in Financial Markets: Economic and Historic Analysis of Subprime Mortgage Options.* Congressional Research Service: Washington, DC, March 25, 2008.

6

The Unjust Contract

A Moral Evaluation

Daniel K. Finn

> Behold, this is the fast which I have chosen, says the Lord. Loose every bond of injustice...Release the downtrodden with forgiveness, and tear up every unjust contract.
>
> —The Epistle of Barnabas 3.3

A contract is a mutual agreement between two or more parties that something shall be done by one or both, typically accompanied by an agreed-upon transfer of money, goods, or services. The contract is a powerful tool that brings predictability to economic relationships, and the development of contract law has further improved the likelihood that the parties to a contract will follow through on what they promised. Thus, contracts are a morally important part of the creation of wealth and prosperity—and a critical subject of inquiry within the True Wealth of Nations research project.

At the same time, however, the moral rejection of unjust contracts is ancient. The biblical condemnation of the practice found its most basic argument in the protection of the poor. There was little need to worry about the well-to-do entering into agreements that abused them. It was, rather, the poor and unfortunate who, under the strictures of unhappy circumstance, might agree to a loan with unfair conditions or terms of employment that left a family without enough to survive.

The later history of Christian evaluations of contracts preserves this concern for the poor but expands it to articulate four distinct arguments in the condemnation of the unjust contract: the biblically based concern for the poor, the proper relation between human law and God's law, the character of justice, and the violation of freedom that unjust contracts entail. We will consider each of these and then consider an extension of one of them—the notion of justice—appropriate for Catholic social thought today.

Four Arguments

The first argument against unjust contracts is rooted in God's concern for the downtrodden, that the needs of all his people should be met by the fruits of the Earth. The variety of Israel's laws around the defense of the poor is well known.[1] These include rules against harvesting the corners of one's field of grain and against passing a second time through one's vineyard to pick the late-maturing grapes (Deut. 24:19-21, Lev. 19:9-10). This portion of the crop was to be left for the widow, the orphan, and the resident alien. Out of a similar concern, existing contracts were at times to be dissolved, as in the sabbatical (Exod. 3:11) and jubilee years (Lev. 25:1-7). The reason for such dissolutions of legally sanctioned contracts—whether debt bondage or the transfer of land due to financial distress—was God's concern for the weak and poor. Albino Barrera's essay in this volume articulates well the Israelite requirement of *sedeq* within economic life.

The rationale for these laws is frequently misunderstood by modern Christians and particularly by non-Christians. It is sometimes presumed that this is a sort of "divine command" ethic, whereby the Israelite was required to do these things simply because the Lord decided they should: "God said so." While this would have been sufficient motivation, it was not the primary reason that the Hebrew people understood behind their moral obligations to the poor. As the book of Deuteronomy expresses the Lord's view, "You shall remember that you were a slave in the land of Egypt; therefore I command you to do this" (Deut. 24:19-22). This is not a philosophical argument about the character of the universe as Christians would later develop, but it presents a religious foundation for Hebrew morality. Because their God was one who himself favored the downcast and poor—he had after all brought an enslaved people out of Egypt—Israelites were to do the same. This was to be reflected in all Israelite activity, including contracts.

Although many things have changed in the intervening centuries, life today continues to illustrate the temptation facing the well-to-do in taking advantage of the poverty of the poor. The 2008 subprime mortgage crisis included not only homebuyers who imprudently took on mortgages they couldn't afford but also fraudulent mortgage contracts that took advantage of the uninformed. (A number of other problems in U.S. contract law are investigated in Vincent Rougeau's essay in this volume.) Because of the pervasiveness of abuse, nearly all nations have laws, for example, restricting how much interest can be charged on a loan of money. In spite of this, we find throughout low-income neighborhoods in much of the industrialized world loan offices that provided check-cashing services and advance payments on wages and on income tax refunds that take advantage of low-income people. While the exigencies of poverty do at times require emergency financial transactions, and for this reason having such services available in low-income areas is important, without laws restricting the amount of interest that such lenders charge, the abuses would be even greater than today.

The second basic argument behind the Christian critique of unjust contracts is the broader relationship that the Judeo-Christian faith has always been between human law and God's law.[2] In the Hebrew Scriptures, this meant that God's laws should direct Israel's life. In those eras in which the Israelites were in control of their own political fate (for example, during the period of the united monarchy from Saul to Solomon), God's law was to be the foundation for the human laws that the authorities would establish.[3]

In New Testament times, of course, the local political elites in the Jewish community were securely under the thumb of imperial Rome. Thus, there was little scope for human law to be based fundamentally in God's law. In nearly all periods in which Jews or Christians have lived in a state controlled by others, teachings moved away from the claim that all human law should be based in God's law and instead developed a distance between the two, sometimes respectful, sometimes outwardly critical of existing human law. Thus, Jesus himself can teach his disciples to "render to Caesar what belongs to Caesar" without any explicit critique of the failures of Roman imperial law.

The relation of Christians to human law in the Roman Empire has been well documented.[4] For the first three centuries, Christians were often persecuted and, as Philip Wogaman has argued, "Christians could not but regard much political authority as evil."[5] The great theologian Origen taught that although the emperor had been raised to his responsibilities by God, Christians were of a "different country" and were "created by the logos of God."[6] With the conversion of Constantine and the ongoing Christianization of the empire, Christians began taking more responsibility for human law or, as Wogaman puts it, "the accountability of power to God could be asserted and examined more directly."[7] Peter Brown reports "a new, Empire-wide patriotism."[8] And then later, with the corruption and slow demise of the empire, attitudes shifted back toward a greater distance and lower expectations.

This kind of change in position based on the existing context is even demonstrated within the life of Augustine himself. In the year 392, a relatively stable period in the history of the Roman Empire, Augustine opposed the use of force against unbelievers ("I do not propose to compel men to embrace the communion of any party, but desire the truth to be made known to persons who, in their search for it, are free from disquieting apprehensions"). However, some twenty-five years later, after the sack of Rome in 410 (the first time Rome had been occupied by a foreign power in nearly 800 years), his attitude in the midst of social chaos was quite different ("There is a persecution of unrighteousness, which the impious inflict upon the Church of Christ; and there is a righteousness persecution, which the Church of Christ inflicts upon the impious"[9]).

Augustine's own treatise on civil law in the *City of God*, written in the decade after that first sack of Rome, represents this latter approach, understandably shaped by circumstance in which there was little hope of establishing a morally adequate civil state or, to put it another way, in which the standards for a morally adequate state were low.[10] As one commentary describes Augustine's later view, the civil magistrate "contributes 'terror,' ensuring a social stability within which 'the good can live more peaceably amidst the evil.'"[11]

Christian theology in the Middle Ages presents a far more positive attitude toward law and government, typical of eras in which Christians are in the majority and the civil authorities are themselves believers. Thomas Aquinas employed a theory of natural law to create what became the classic Catholic articulation of the relation of human law and morality. Eternal law is another name for God's plan for the universe, which, given God's omnipotence, has the character of law. Natural law is the eternal law imprinted on each creature by means of its "nature." Thus, trees are inclined to grow toward the sun and put out leaves in accord with their nature, defined by God's creative intention. Similarly, humans are social animals, and, for example, destructive behaviors such as lying are detrimental to human social well-being. Actions are morally wrong if they subvert human flourishing or, to say the same thing, if they violate the natural law for humans.

In his treatment of the roles and responsibilities of owners of property, Aquinas observed that not only do the wealthy have an obligation to share their surplus with those whose needs are unmet but also in an extreme and urgent need a person might morally take goods from someone else's surplus, and this would be neither theft nor robbery.[12] The argument here, of course, is that even private property laws, which Thomas in general endorsed, had to remain subservient to God's more ultimate purpose, in this case, God's intention to meet the needs of all persons by means of the material world. This represents yet another example of the deference that human law and its many arrangements must show to the more fundamental law of God.

Human law is the set of rules made by the appropriate lawgiver—kings and princes in Thomas's day and democratic legislators today. But according to Thomas, human law must be in accord with the natural law, and if it violates that more fundamental law, it would not be a law at all. Thus, there is no assurance that laws passed by civil authorities are automatically worthy of being followed. As Thomas puts it elsewhere, "things which are of human rights cannot derogate from natural right or divine right."[13] This, of course, is the foundation for the moral endorsement of civil disobedience in Catholic doctrine.

Again and again in Catholic social teaching, the subordination of human law to natural and eternal law is clear. And beyond specifically Christian discourse, there are many examples of a similar recognition in civil law. The Nuremberg trials of Nazi military officers at the end of World War II were founded on the potential conflict between following human law and following a higher law to which all are called. Similar restrictions on an otherwise "free" market rooted in a law higher than merely human law—such as standards for contracts to prevent abuses—fit well within this tradition. Vincent Rougeau's essay concludes with an indication of what more adequate legal standards for U.S. law might look like.

In sum, the Catholic perspective rejects any argument that the legality of a contract between two persons is sufficient to guarantee its justice. Contracts are a wise human institution, but like all human inventions they must be subordinate to a higher purpose.

The third defense of the Catholic position on unjust contracts resides in the conception of justice itself. The classic Catholic view of justice, deriving from the work of Aquinas, distinguishes three basic types: commutative, distributive, and general (or "legal") justice.[14]

Commutative justice orders the relation of individuals to one another as individuals, and in this sense it is the most intuitively obvious form of justice for most people today. If I borrow something from you, I have an obligation to return it; if you enter into a contract to do something for me, you have an obligation to do it. Distributive justice relates to the proper order between the community and its individual members. In distributive justice the person or persons charged with responsibility for the community must render to each citizen that which is due. General or legal justice concerns the relation of the individual member to the social whole. This dimension of justice identifies the obligation of each person to contribute to the community, often described as a contribution to the common good.[15]

We will later see how these three parts of justice need to be reconsidered in light of institutional and intellectual change over the past few centuries, but for now it is important to recognize that the obligations of contract—what is owed from one party to the other—is, at first consideration, a matter of commutative justice. The question about unjust contracts concerns whether a contract that is unjust needs to be fulfilled and whether a contract entered into apparently voluntarily can be unjust in the first place.

The most vivid condemnation of the unjust contract in modern Catholic social thought is provided by Pope Leo XIII in 1891. In *Rerum Novarum*, Leo outlines a very strong version of private property ownership, somewhat stronger than that taught in the tradition before and after his own work.[16] Nonetheless, this pope says quite clearly that some labor contracts are unjust. In now-famous words, Leo taught that

> as a rule, workman and employer should make free agreements, and in particular should freely agree as to wages; nevertheless, there is a dictate of nature more imperious and more ancient than any bargain between man and man, that the remuneration must be enough to support the wage-earner in reasonable and frugal comfort. If through necessity or fear of a worse evil, the workman accepts harder conditions because an employer or contractor will give no better, he is the victim of force and injustice.[17]

Leo is working here from the natural law argument about God's intention in creating the material world to meet the needs of all. Workers have the right to have their needs met. In the premodern world, most people eked out their subsistence on the land, whether slaves in ancient Roman times, serfs in the medieval world, or subsistence farmers in early modern society. In the industrial world, the ordinary way for persons to have access to the goods of the earth they need is by getting a job, earning a wage, and then spending that wage in the market to buy food, clothing, and the other necessities of life. Thus, the requirements of justice that the prosperous share their surplus with those unable to provide for their own needs now in part becomes the obligation of those who offer jobs to ordinary workers—that the remuneration for any job be sufficient to meet the needs of the worker, including dependent family members.

Perhaps the most widely recognized example of such unjust wage contracts in our day is the third-world "sweatshop." Christian ethics would not find all objections lodged against factories in the developing world as worthy of support. In a nation with very low wages, the prospect of a factory job with higher-than-average wages may in fact be a real benefit for workers there, even though the wage is far beneath that in the industrialized countries. However, the demands of commutative justice do indeed impose responsibilities on employers, responsibilities that go far beyond those that may be negotiated in a wage contract between the firm and an individual worker. Press reports regularly publicize inhumane working conditions stretching from near slavery to sexual harassment and the denial of bathroom breaks to workers. Fundamental respect for human dignity is required in justice in all labor contracts or they are simply unjust.[18]

Put in more abstract terms, the obligations of commutative justice to fulfill contracts must not violate more fundamental obligations rooted in God's plan for the world. As Pope John Paul II taught, "even prior to the logic of a fair exchange of goods and the forms of justice appropriate to it, there exists something which is due to man because he is man, by reason of his lofty dignity. Inseparable from the 'something' is the possibility to survive and, at the same time, to make an active contribution to the common good of humanity."[19]

The fourth general argument behind a rejection of unjust contracts within the Catholic tradition focuses on the character of freedom of the persons entering into that contract. In a way, of course, this issue of freedom is implicit in the presumptions of the first three arguments: that somehow or other the more prosperous party to a contract made an offer that the less prosperous party to the contract "had to" accept even though they would have wanted (and deserved) better. This concern with freedom has become a primary issue only in the modern period, its importance rising with the general cultural shift toward greater appreciation of the dignity and rights of individuals. A very helpful framework for understanding the role of decision and autonomy in economic life is provided by Albino Barrera in his book *Economic Compulsion and Christian Ethics*.[20]

Barrera helpfully distinguishes between actions that are voluntary and actions that are compelled by circumstance. The fundamental insight here is that it is possible for someone voluntarily to choose one of two very unfortunate options due to the compulsion created by difficult circumstance. Here, Barrera employs Aristotle's notion of a "mixed action."

Aristotle cites the decision of a sea captain in the midst of a storm who decides to throw overboard all of the goods he had been transporting in order to save the lives of himself and his crew. On the one hand, he has certainly chosen to do this, and thus the decision can be described as "voluntary." On the other hand, everyone knows that in another sense he has done it "against his will," since without the duress of circumstance neither he nor anyone else would choose this course of action. We might ask whether we ought to consider this action of the captain a "free" one or not. A similar question, of course, arises in the case of the unjust contract.

If the stronger party to a contract were to threaten the weaker with some penalty for not entering into the contract—say a threat of bodily harm or death—no one would find that contract either voluntary or just. Here, however, the issue is whether a contract is just when entered into "voluntarily" by an individual choosing the least bad of highly unfortunate options.

Some philosophical points of view make a strong claim in this regard that would conflict fundamentally with Catholic social thought. For example, Libertarian philosopher Robert Nozick argues that "whether a person's actions are voluntary depends on what it is that limits his alternatives.... whether [the action of others] makes one's resulting actions non-voluntary depends upon whether those others had the right to act as they did."[21] From this perspective, an accident or natural disaster may severely harm a person but in no way can either limit his freedom, even though it would be violated by someone with a gun demanding money. In this view, of course, if a contract is entered into voluntarily, there is no worry that the person's rightful autonomy has been violated. For Libertarians, as long as both parties to a contract rightfully own what they agree to transfer to the other, there are no unjust voluntary contracts.

However, this is a peculiar definition of voluntariness or freedom. Consider Joe, who has a broken leg. If Joe broke his leg because he accidentally tripped and fell down a flight of stairs, his freedom has not been influenced in any way even though he be laid up in bed for weeks. However, if Joe's leg has been broken in a scuffle with a mugger who pushed Joe down the stairs (a violation of Joe's rights), Joe's freedom has clearly been violated. Yet, if Joe himself was the mugger and had been pushed down the stairs by his intended victim (a rightful act of self defense), Joe's broken leg represents no loss of freedom. This clearly is an unsatisfying definition of human freedom or voluntariness, where we cannot tell from the restriction itself whether the restriction violates freedom.

A more adequate understanding of the character of freedom would require that we take into consideration the exigencies pressed upon persons by their environment.

Barrera himself, following Joseph Raz, argues that the autonomy of persons in decision-making depends in part on the options open to them and that the worse the options, the lower the autonomy. As Barrera puts it, "personal freedom is severely curtailed if one is completely preoccupied, indeed driven, by the ceaseless need to scrounge for the essential means for survival and basic health."[22] That is, although all human choice faces opportunity costs—striving for one thing entails giving up another—if those opportunity costs are great enough and the circumstance dire enough, the effect of those costs is a reduction in freedom and autonomy. Since the confidence in the morality and efficiency of contracts that we can ordinarily have is rooted in the autonomy of the parties entering into a contract, this is a severe limitation, even if it may arise in only a small proportion of all contracts.

In sum, Barrera defines economic compulsion as "a condition in which market participants unavoidably incur profound opportunity costs. People give up nontrivial interests in order to satisfy, safeguard, or procure their other vital claims that are at even greater risk."[23]

Barrera's focus is not on formal contracts but on the less formal relations created by market opportunities. However, his analysis of compulsion will also demonstrate the difficulty in unjust contracts; it offers a way to understand them in more detail.

Examples of the coercive economic conditions under which millions daily live are plentiful. Consider the 60 percent unemployment in the port city of Chimbote, Peru. Chimbote is a fishing port, but due to overfishing of the Pacific, its fishing boats lie moored in the harbor month after month. In such a situation in which the majority of adults are unable to find work, the desperation created can lead parents to accept an abusive contract situation out of concern for the very survival of their children. An appropriately Catholic understanding of freedom requires that employers not take advantage of these quite real restrictions on people's freedom in the name of a greater profit for the enterprise. This and related concerns would quite naturally be a part of any reworking of the legal theory of contracts such as that suggested by Vincent Rougeau earlier in this volume.

Much more is said in the philosophical literature about contracts rooted in agency, autonomy, and freedom than has ever been articulated in the official Catholic social teaching on the issue. For example, Alan Gewirth focuses on the difference in power between workers and managers of large firms[24]: "from the standpoint of economic justice, the extreme disparities of economic power— the power to control the availability, remuneration, and conditions of work— violate the freedom criterion with its requirement that every actual or prospective agent to be able to control his behavior by his own unforced choice."[25]

There are at least two reasons for this difference between Catholic social teaching and philosophers' treatments of contracts. The first is that, as Albino Barrera argues in this volume, official teaching is typically a response to problems at a particular time and rarely takes the form of an academic treatise. The second and perhaps more important reason is that regardless of how we specify questions of agency and freedom, the Catholic conviction about the obligations of the well-to-do toward the needy intervenes in this debate early enough that the finer points of analysis of agency need not be appealed to. Nonetheless, this concern about freedom and compulsion is important enough to be listed here as the fourth argument within Catholic social thought against unjust contracts.

Third-World Debt

As suggested in Paulinus Odozor's essay in this volume, no treatment of the morality of contracts today can be complete without a view of the debate over third-world debt. Nearly all poor nations are currently saddled with large annual payments for principal and interest on debts undertaken years ago. In many cases those payments have already amounted to many times the original principle borrowed and thus the claim is widely heard that such loans are a type of unjust contract.

The latest available data on external debt for all developing countries taken as a whole (for 2006) shows a total amount of debt owed of $2.8 trillion, with annual principal payments of $417 billion and annual interest payments of $123 billion.[26] The average interest rate for private loans (e.g., from private banks) was 6.0 percent; the rate from official creditors (e.g., the World Bank, regional development banks) was 3.0 percent. The average of both types was 4.9 percent. The comparable figures for sub-Saharan Africa are an external debt of $173 billion, with annual principal payments of $17 billion and annual interest payments of $7 billion.[27] Interest rates were 5.6 percent to 1.37 percent for an average of 3.3 percent for the group identified as low-income countries. For the fifty-one poorest nations in the world, total debt was $352 billion, principal payments of $25 billion, interest payments of $10 billion, with interest rates of 4.8 percent to 1.8 percent. For an overall average of 2.2 percent.[28]

It should remain clear in this context that the standard Catholic teaching on borrowing is that it is not immoral to charge interest on a loan of money, but that in fact loans can often be of great service to the borrower. For example, wealthy nations such as the United States and Japan became industrially developed due in large part to the investments made by lenders in other countries that had developed before them. The same is true in developing nations today. Individuals and firms are willing to lend money for a profitable return, and if that money is invested in infrastructure and productive activity in a developing nation, the overall result can be a slow but steady rise in the prosperity of ordinary people there. However there are complications brought on by the fact that this transaction happens across the boundary between two financial systems.

Anyone who has taken out a thirty-year mortgage on a home knows that by the end of the thirty years, the borrower will have paid two to four times the value of the original principle, depending on the interest rate. This is simply how long-term loans work. However, the additional complication of an international transaction means that the payments must be made in the currency of one or another of the two nations involved in the loan. Typically, lenders denominate loans in the more stable currency, often choosing the U.S. dollar. Thus, if over time the second currency weakens in comparison with the dollar (as the currencies in many developing nations have tended to do over time), then it takes more and more of the local currency to make the same payment in dollars. Thus, whereas a typical homeowner may spend three times the value of the principal in paying off a mortgage, a second nation may spend six or ten or more times the value of the principal denominated in the local currency. The question then becomes whether the loan is immoral: either because the interest rate is too high or because lenders continue to insist upon regular payment even after it has become onerous for the borrowing nation.

Another significant complication is that political systems in developing nations tend to benefit elites in the country, as well as urban populations who are far more active politically than the rural poor. In addition, corruption is often a problem, as when governments take out large international loans, ostensibly for infrastructure projects, but a few individuals end up pocketing most of the benefits. Harvard economist Michael Kremer has proposed that some international body, perhaps the U.N. Security Council, should be empowered to cancel "odious" debt, that is, debt initiated by a dictatorial government, so that democratic governments that follow would not have an obligation to repay.[29] This would send a strong signal to lenders, that they should not make loans to dictators in the first place.

In the end, the justice of the loan contract between a developing nation and a private bank or even an international aid agency must be understood to be influenced by the obligations of the well-to-do to assist the poor. That is, these should never be solely understood as commercial transactions. But since developing nations do indeed need even purely commercial transactions for their own economic well-being, the line drawn between just and unjust contract will have to be made on a case-by-case basis. Perhaps the most important point here is that if wealthy nations took seriously their obligation to assist poor nations financially, much of the problem caused by international debt for developing countries would be resolved.

A Look to the Left

Given the current character of discourse about Catholic social thought and economic life in the industrialized North, the bulk of this essay identifies differences between Catholic social thought and influential perspectives farther to the right politically. However, it is appropriate to address here some fundamental presumptions widely held by partisans farther to the left that are deeply critical of contracts in many situations in which Catholic social thought is not.

The classic position here would be Marxism, which analyzes the relationship between capitalist employers and employees as essentially oppressive and exploitative. Catholic social thought has shared neither the Marxist analysis of class conflict nor its understanding of corporate profits as surplus value produced by workers but captured by their employers.

More recently, the theological movement named "radical orthodoxy" has renewed a fundamental critique of capitalism and markets based on an older theological perspective that rejects any endorsement of a relative autonomy between theology and other disciplines, as well as between religious commitment and a secular organization of economic life. Steven Long recounts favorably John Milbank's position concerning economic exchange. Although necessary, "these exchanges are to be narrated as liturgical performances within the church rather than commodity transactions solely relegated to the market."[30]

Our response here might be the same as that of Joseph Pieper commenting long before the rise of radical orthodoxy.

There are persons and movements who, in an unrealistic overevaluation of "community" ideals, regard the balancing of interests by contract as an inferior form of regulating human relationships, since they are based only on the "cold" calculation of one's own advantage.[31]

Catholic social thought has always appreciated the strengths of subsidiarity, even prior to the first use of that term by Pius XI. Individuals have rightful interests and an obligation to support self and family, and thus active participation in markets to reach such goals is an appropriate form of relationship with others. Compared to friendship or familial love, such relationships appear shallow, but as Pieper adds, "if the contract represents the balancing of interests, it also represents a form of mutual understanding." The opposition to unjust contracts in Catholic thought is not rooted in any rejection of contracts themselves but in the extent to which an unjust contract falls short of the standards of morality to which all contracting parties are called.

Further Developments Needed

The previous analysis raises broader questions that need further attention within Catholic social thought today. At stake here is the development of an intellectual framework within a living tradition, in which changes in historical and cultural context call for changes in official Church teaching, all the while maintaining a fundamental continuity with what had gone before. It will be helpful to consider a well-established economic example first, in order to understand this process of change in Catholic thought on economic life.

One of the classic examples of such change is the moral teaching of usury, the charging of interest on a loan of money. In the biblical era and the early church, the prohibition against usury was rooted in the concern for those pressed to borrow money under duress of hardship. For a lender to insist on an extra payment (interest) when the money is repaid was seen as a form of abuse of the poor on the part of those wealthy enough to make the loan.

Thomas Aquinas's own view of usury presumed that care for the poor was handled in his treatment of property, in which privately owned property was endorsed but with the proviso that those with a surplus of goods should share with those whose needs are unmet. Concerning usury, Thomas followed Aristotelean analysis: money is sterile, and thus when I allow someone else to use some of my money for a while, I should not ask for any extra when it is returned to me.[32]

For Thomas, loaning money was like loaning a bottle of wine to my neighbor. I take the bottle out of my wine cellar and hand it to him. He later brings back a bottle of wine (perhaps the same bottle, if he didn't open it, or else an equivalent bottle) and I put it back in my wine cellar. Since I have no loss, I should charge no extra. In Thomas's day, of course, the same held true in a loan of gold coins from the strong box in the cellar. Thus when my neighbor borrows and later returns three gold coins, I should charge nothing in addition.

However, Thomas argues that if I were to lend someone a house I owned, it would be perfectly moral to charge extra (something we call "rent") when the house is returned because the house is not "sterile." It provides "usufruct," as he called it, or what we in modern times call "a stream of services." Not having access to those services is a loss and thus an extra payment can be required in addition to the return of the thing borrowed.

It took hundreds of years for law and Church teaching to come around to the modern approach to usury, but over that time money itself changed in character.[33] Money became something no longer kept in cellars or under mattresses until needed. Money is a claim on resources, and today this claim provides a stream of services in a variety of markets. Money now is like the house and not like the bottle of wine, and if Thomas were alive today to apply his own analysis, he too would agree that charging interest on a loan of money is moral. Thus, usury is a classic case of a change in moral teaching about economic life arising from a change in economic life itself that presents us with a paradigm for thinking through other changes yet to occur: a change, but a change in fundamental continuity with the past.

One of the most fundamental shifts in the transition from the medieval to the modern period has occurred in the status of individuals and their place within social institutions, a pair of intellectual insights that on the one hand raises the status of the individual and on the other heightens our awareness of how much we as individuals are shaped by social forces around us. This shift was part of what Charles Taylor has called a move from a hermeneutic to prescriptive view of the relation of the human moral order to transcendent vision—a move from the medieval perception of the transcendent within and behind earthly reality to a stress on our being called by God to alter the world in line with a higher vision.[34]

The first change was the rise in status of the individual human person. Scholars have long debated the causes, but it is clear that over a couple of centuries, political philosophers Hugo Grotius, Thomas Hobbes, Baron de Montesquieu, John Locke, and others developed a view of political power that sees the moral root of power in the individual citizen and not in the king. Eventually, out of this conviction came democratic revolutions in nearly every nation of the world, insisting that not only do individual citizens have the right to alter their political institutions but actually have a duty to do so as well.

In the realm of moral discourse, this rise in the stature of the individual person can also be described by a different analogy: a shift of moral focus toward the individual person, a shift that has led to the use of language about human rights that was not employed in the premodern world. Thus to take a single example, the Catholic Church now speaks about the right to food, clothing, and shelter. When Aquinas spoke of the possibility of a man simply taking what he needs in a situation of great and urgent necessity, he spoke not of a right of the man but rather of the nature of the goods taken—goods that by God's intention should be used to meet human needs.

That is, in the modern world, the spotlight of Catholic moral attention broadened to include not only the nature of the goods but also the claim that the poor man has on those goods. Understanding this claim as rooted both in the nature of the goods and in the dignity of each human person, and thus ultimately rooted in God's creative intention for the world, Catholic social thought has adopted the language of economic rights.

Secular accounts of human rights, of course, no longer depend on an underlying conviction about God's intention. And in fact a number of secular accounts of human rights have come to argue that the rights of "noninterference"—freedom of speech, assembly, the press, etc.—are the most fundamental of human rights. Libertarians go even farther to argue that economic rights (such as a right to food) are unfounded and unjust claims because they can only be implemented by unjustly taking from some citizens through taxation the resources necessary to provide for needy individuals.[35] Brian Tierney, however, points out that in the history of human rights, the very first claims to be understood as belonging to everyone are not in fact the rights of noninterference but the rights to subsistence, today called "economic rights." Thus the conflicts we have already reviewed between human rights and legal contracts entail basic and not peripheral rights.[36]

Catholic social thought today speaks of the right to employment. As we have seen, this right arises out of the more fundamental conviction that all persons are to meet their needs by access to the fruits of the earth and that in an industrial society, employment as a worker is the ordinary way for this to happen.[37] This development, however, altered somewhat the Church's view of the employer. In one sense, of course, there have always been employers, including the master shoemaker who brought apprentice shoemakers along in the shoemaker's guild. But the notion that the fundamental contours of economic life are based on a large number of workers agreeing to work for another person and whose jobs are defined by that employer is a new development of the industrial era. And in response to this, Catholic social thought has understood the requirements of commutative justice as involving the payment of a just wage, adequate to allow the worker to then purchase in the market the fruits of the earth that God intended.[38]

The second great intellectual shift of the modern period entailed understanding the power of human institutions. Interestingly, where the first shift increases our appreciation of the uniqueness and dignity of the individual, this second shift more firmly roots that individual in a context of social life. In the seventeenth century, there grew an important awareness of political, social, and economic institutions that shaped human behavior and understanding. This awareness grew over time as more and more of the structures of political and economic life came to be seen as malleable and thus open to change by public action. The most important example here is the debate over the structure of government and the slow move from monarchy to democracy. But somewhat later similar debates occurred over the structure of the economy. One classic example here is the controversy in Britain over the "corn laws" in the first half of the nineteenth century, debating whether to allow the import of wheat from France.

With the rise of sociology and anthropology in the nineteenth century, intellectuals came to understand the relationship between institutions and individuals in a far more subtle way than had been possible before. One classic sociological articulation of this perspective occurs in the work of Peter Berger and Thomas Luckmann, *The Social Construction of Reality*. Here Berger and Luckmann argue that society is a human product, that society is also an objective reality, and that the human person is a product of that society. Prior to the modern world, it was widely presumed that the social order was a given, either by God's intention or by a more or less unchangeable history, not unlike the rules of the natural world. With this awareness of the social construction of reality came a conviction that social, political, and economic institutions can be changed, even if this is not easy to do. And since institutions have such great effect through the socialization of individuals, Christian moral analysis has come to understand how important it is—even for personal morality—to see that social institutions are well crafted.

This understanding of the relation of social structures and individual life also has had an impact on the view of justice in Catholic social thought, since we can now speak more precisely about the justice of institutions, about the impact that good or bad institutions can have on the sense of justice of individuals and on our moral obligation to shape those institutions properly. And it is not only legal institutions referred to here. As John Coleman argues in his essay in this volume, even the most straightforward of legal contracts is understood, entered into, and lived out amidst a network of social understandings without which it could not function.

Recent popes have been quite at ease with speaking about the justice of political and economic institutions, as was demonstrated in the address of Pope Benedict XVI to the Latin American bishops during his visit to Brazil in 2007. Benedict taught that "just structures are a condition without which a just order in society is not possible." Christians need to be committed to "the creation of just structures."[39]

However, there has been considerable resistance by neoconservative Catholics to this broadening of the view of justice to include a description of institutions as either just or unjust. Samuel Gregg has argued that justice is a virtue for individuals and "structures in themselves cannot be good or bad."[40] Michael Novak has rejected the view of social justice articulated in Catholic social thought since Pius XI's *Divini Redemptoris*.[41] Novak instead cites libertarian economist Friedrich Hayek to argue that "social justice is a virtue, an attribute of individuals, or it is a fraud."[42] Pius XI, however, taught that social justice demands "for each individual all that is necessary for the common good."[43]

With a greater appreciation of democracy as fundamental to political life, Catholic scholarship has come to recognize a shift in the subject of the obligations of distributive justice. At one time, only the prince or king had such obligations. Now the obligations of distributive justice refer directly to democratically elected legislators and indirectly to all citizens in a democracy, who have an obligation to vote for representatives who will fulfill the requirements of distributive justice.[44] In premodern eras, the average person was involved in social and commutative justice but had little relation to decisions about distributive justice except as a recipient. Today, every citizen is involved in making decisions about all three forms of justice, another way a change in how the world works can bring about a shift in Catholic social thought.

More broadly, this concern about moral responsibility for economic institutions extends beyond the issues of the unjust contract and distributive justice.

Neoconservative Christians who have provided a moral defense of markets over the past forty years have built on an older secular tradition that argues that the cumulative, long-term effects of the prosperity generated by markets is the most fundamental reason why they should receive our moral endorsements. For example, Robert Benne, in *The Ethic of Democratic Capitalism*, identifies the economic productivity of markets as one of the primary virtues of democratic capitalism.[45] This line of thinking dates back at least to Bernard Mandeville more than three hundred years ago.[46] Where traditional Christian morality argued for the benevolent intention of each actor and the beneficent effect of each act, this newer approach argues that selfish action can and often does conduce to the well-being of society more generally. Put more concretely, a firm obviously harms those workers it lays off during a recession, but the moral argument in defense of capitalism is that an economic system with this flexibility to adjust the level of production can, in the long run, create more jobs at higher wage levels than any alternative and will in turn also be better for the poor than any other. Although dangerous when applied simplistically, this moral argument is an important one for Catholic social thought.

Put in the language of justice, this argument shrinks the obligations of commutative justice, requiring simply the voluntary agreement on both sides in every wage contract. This, of course, is why the just wage doctrine has such difficulty in a market economy; it conflicts so fundamentally with the logic of the market. There is not room here to develop further this line of thinking, but it would seem clear that any move to endorse markets morally by restricting commutative justice in this way would need to be paired with an expansion of the notions of distributive and general justice. Catholic social thought, particularly in its official expressions, has shown a determination to maintain the fundamental conviction that all people of the earth have a right to have their needs met. If, for example, the harm caused by a market system to workers laid off during a recession is to be justified by reference to a future prosperity of the descendents of those unemployed workers, distributive justice must in turn be expanded to provide a vibrant assistance to the unemployed so that their lives are not badly damaged in the meantime.

And not only distributive but general justice also changes in the modern period. Since ordinarily in an industrialized world individuals find a job and use their wages to provide access to what they need, the view of general justice must include not simply the obligation of each person to contribute to the community, including contributions to gainful employment, but also an obligation on the part of society to provide an adequate number of jobs so that individuals can indeed make that contribution and support themselves and their families.[47] This is at the heart of the modern Catholic endorsement of the right to employment.

Neoconservatives are correct in cautioning against the dependency that some welfare programs can create as a by-product. However, a more robust view of the obligations of distributive and general justice will require steps often avoided by those on the right. There will need to be more careful structuring of the conditions for contracts within markets, relating both to employment law and unions as well as in the home mortgage market and in lending more generally. The financial crisis of 2008 demonstrated how poorly structured financial markets can create risky new contracts that may serve well the parties to those contracts in good economic times but that impose great cost on the whole society in bad. In addition, society as a whole, often but not always acting through government, has an obligation to provide sufficient funding for education and training, at least to those who could not otherwise afford it. And in an economy based more and more on advanced skills, such education would need to extend beyond high school. A wide variety of efforts to assist those who suffer most from the economic compulsion of the market will be necessary if the obligations once associated with the person-to-person relation in commutative justice are loosened in favor of the broader consequentialist moral argument that endorses markets.

In sum, we can see that the discussion of the unjust contract opens up wider arguments about markets more generally, many of which are taken up by the various essays in this volume. The development of doctrine within Catholic social thought is a normal part of historical change, but as always, such developments must occur in basic continuity with what is gone before. The claim for a consequentialist defense of markets—that they improve the economic well-being of nearly everyone eventually—is well founded, but along with that must come changes in our view of both distributive and general justice in order to remain faithful to the tradition that we have inherited. Contracts, like so many of the legal and cultural relationships that make up markets, merit both moral approbation and limitation based on their service to a fully moral economic system, one that can generate sustainable prosperity for all.

NOTES

1. See, for example, Stephen Charles Mott, *Biblical Ethics and Social Change*, chap. 4, "God's Justice and Ours."

2. Ibid., chap. 10, "Creative Reform through Politics."

3. See John R. Donahue, S.J., "The Bible and Catholic Social Teaching," 19–24. For a broad perspective on the prophetic insistence on this subordination of human law to God's law, see Gerhard von Rad, *The Message of the Prophets*. For a view of the role of the bias toward the poor, see Norman H. Snaith, *The Distinctive Ideas of the Old Testament*, 70.

4. For a perceptive view of the relation of law and politics in the New Testament era, see Richard J. Cassidy, *Society and Politics and the Acts of the Apostles*, chap. 11. For a more comprehensive look at the political thought in the early church, see Oliver O'Donovan and Joan Lockwood O'Donovan, *From Irenaeus to Grotius*, 107.

5. Philip Wogaman, *Christian Perspectives on Politics*, 36.

6. Origen, "Against Celsus," Book 8, para. 75.

7. Ibid.

8. Peter Brown, *Power and Persuasion in Late Antiquity*, 17–19. Cited in Joerg Rieger, *Christ and Empire*, 73.

9. Timothy Renick, "Liberty as a Christian Value," 36. Taken by Renick from Robert Van Voorst, ed., *Readings in Christianity*, 109–10.

10. Augustine of Hippo, *The City of God*.

11. O'Donovan and O'Donovan, From Irenaeus to Grotius, 107.

12. Thomas Aquinas, *Summa Theologica*, II-II, Q66, a7.

13. Ibid.

14. German philosopher Josef Pieper has presented the predominant twentieth-century description of Thomas's views. See Joseph Pieper, *Justice*. See also Pontifical Council for Justice and Peace, *Compendium*, 201.

15. For a fuller treatment of the notion of the common good, see Albino Barrera's essay in this volume.

16. On the excessively individualistic view of property in Leo XIII, see, for example, Ernest Fortin, "Sacred and Inviolable," 203–33.

17. Pope Leo XIII, *Rerum Novarum*, 34.

18. For a discussion of the twentieth-century impact of Catholic social thought on labor relations in Europe under Christian democratic parties and movements, see the essay by Vera Zamagni in this volume.

19. John Paul II, *Centesimus Annus*, para. 67. The priority of meeting the needs of all over the opulence of the well-to-do is also articulated in the essays by Albino Barrera and Andrew Yuengert elsewhere in this volume.

20. Albino Barrera, *Economic Compulsion and Christian Ethics*, chap. 1.

21. Robert Nozick, *Anarchy, State and Utopia*, 262.

22. Barrera, *Economic Compulsion and Christian Ethics*, 17.

23. Ibid.

24. For a contrary view that sees agreements as almost always entailing obligations, see Margaret Gilbert, "Agreements, Coercion, and Obligation," 679–706.

25. Alan Gewirth, "Economic Rights," 16.

26. World Bank, *Global Development Finance*, 2.

27. Ibid., 20–22.

28. Ibid., 22–25.

29. Michael Kremer and Seema Jayachandran, "Odious Debt," 32–35.

30. D. Stephen Long, *Divine Economy*, 267–68.

31. Pieper, *Justice*, pp. 58.

32. Aquinas, *Summa Theologica*, II-II, Q78.

33. Similar change generated the development of new economic institutions detailed in Stefano Zamagni's essay in this volume.

34. Charles Taylor, *A Secular Age*, 162.

35. See, for example, Nozick, *Anarchy, State and Utopia*, 238.

36. For an extended argument about this shift, see Brian Tierney, *The Idea of Natural Rights*.

37. Pontifical Council for Justice and Peace, *Compendium*, p. 288.

38. Christine Firer Hinze, "Commentary on *Quadragesimo anno*," 159. Thomas Stork, "Just Wage." Stork observes that the German Jesuit economist Heinrich Pesch also considered an unjust wage as a violation of commutative justice.

39. Benedict XVI, "Inaugural Address," 445–60.

40. Samuel Gregg, *Challenging the Modern World*, 197.

41. Pius XI, *Divini Redemptoris*, para. 51.

42. Michael Novak, "Defining Social Justice," 11–13.

43. Pius XI, *Divini Redemptoris*, para. 51.

44. Pieper, *Justice*, 51. See also Bernard Haring, "Justice."

45. Robert Benne, *The Ethic of Democratic Capitalism*, chap. 7.

46. Bernard Mandeville, *The Fable of the Bees*.

47. See the definition of social justice provided by the National Conference of Catholic Bishops, "Economic Justice for All," para. 71.

REFERENCES

Aquinas, Thomas. *Summa Theologica*. Translated by Fathers of the English Dominican Province. New York: Benzinger Brothers, 1947.

Augustine of Hippo. *The City of God*. New York: Modern Library, 1950.

Barrera, Albino. *Economic Compulsion and Christian Ethics*. New York: Cambridge University Press, 2005.

Benedict XVI. "Inaugural Address to the Fifth General Conference of the Bishops of Latin America and the Caribbean." *Acta Apostolicae Sedis* 99, no. 6 (June 1, 2007): 445–60.

Benne, Robert. *The Ethic of Democratic Capitalism: A Moral Reassessment*. Philadelphia: Fortress Press, 1981.

Berger, Peter, and Thomas Luckmann. *The Social Construction of Reality: A Treatise in the Society of Knowledge*. New York: Anchor Books, 1966.

Brown, Peter. *Power and Persuasion in Late Antiquity: Towards a Christian Empire*. Madison: University of Wisconsin Press, 1992.

Cassidy, Richard J. *Society and Politics and the Acts of the Apostles.* Maryknoll: Orbis Books, 1987.

Donahue, John R., S.J. "The Bible and Catholic Social Teaching: Will this Engagement Lead to Marriage?" In Himes, et al., *Modern Catholic Social Thinking: Commentaries & Interpretations,* 9–40.

Fortin, Ernest. "Sacred and Inviolable: Rerum Novarum and Natural Rights." *Theological Studies* 53 (June 1992): 203–33.

Gewirth, Alan. "Economic Rights." *Logos* 6 (1985): 7–28.

Gilbert, Margaret. "Agreements, Coercion, and Obligation." *Ethics* 103 (July 1993): 679–706.

Gregg, Samuel. *Challenging the Modern World.* Lanham, MD: Lexington Books, 1999.

Haring, Bernard. "Justice." In *New Catholic Encyclopedia: Second Edition.* Washington, DC: Catholic University of America, 2003.

Himes, Kenneth R., O.F.M., Lisa Sowle Cahill, Charles E. Curran, David Hollenbach, S.J., Thomas Shannon. *Modern Catholic Social Teaching: Commentaries & Interpretations.* Washington, DC: Georgetown University Press, 2004.

Hinze, Christine Firer. "Commentary on *Quadragesimo anno.*" In Himes, et al., *Modern Catholic Social Thinking: Commentaries & Interpretations,* 151–74.

John Paul II. *Centesimus Annus.* Washington, DC: U.S. Catholic Conference, 1991.

Kremer, Michael, and Seena Jayachandran. "Odious Debt: When Dictators Borrow, Who Repays the Loan?" *The Brookings Review* 21 (Spring 2003): 32–35.

Leo XIII. *Rerum Novarum. Seven Great Encyclicals.* Glen Rock, NJ: Paulist Press, 1963.

Long, D. Stephen. *Divine Economy: Theology and the Market.* London: Routledge, 2000.

Mandeville, Bernard. *The Fable of the Bees: Or, Private Vices, Publick Benefits.* Oxford: Clarendon Press, 1957.

Mott, Stephen Charles. *Biblical Ethics and Social Change.* New York: Oxford University Press, 1982.

National Conference of Catholic Bishops. "Economic Justice for All: Catholic Social Teaching and the U.S. Economy." *Origins* 16 (November 1986): para. 71.

Novak, Michael. "Defining Social Justice." *First Things* 108 (December 2000): 11–13.

Nozick, Robert. *Anarchy, State and Utopia.* New York: Basic Books, 1974.

O'Donovan, Oliver, and Joan Lockwood O'Donovan, eds. *From Irenaeus to Grotius: A Source Book in Christian Political Thought.* Grand Rapids, MI: William B. Eerdmans Publishing Company, 1999.

Origen. "Against Celsus." Online. Available:http://www.ccel.org/ccel/schaff/anf04.toc.html.

Pieper, C. Joseph. *Justice.* New York: Pantheon Books, 1955.

Pius XI. *Divini Redemptoris. Seven Great Encyclicals.* Glen Rock, NJ: Paulist Press, 1963.

Pontifical Council for Justice and Peace. *Compendium of the Social Doctrine of the Church.* Washington, DC: United States Conference of Catholic Bishops, 2004.

Renick, Timothy. "Liberty as a Christian Value." *Christian Century* 125 (June 17, 2008): 36–37.

Rieger, Joerg. *Christ and Empire: From Paul to Post-colonial Times.* Minneapolis, MN: Fortress Press, 2007.

Snaith, Norman H. *The Distinctive Ideas of the Old Testament.* London: Epworth Press, 1944/1962.

Stork, Thomas. "Just Wage." *The Encyclopedia of Catholic Social Thought, Social Science and Social Policy.* Lanham, MD: Scarecrow Press, 2007.

Taylor, Charles. *A Secular Age.* Cambridge: Harvard University Press, 2007.

Tierney, Brian. *The Idea of Natural Rights: Studies on Natural Rights, Natural Law, and Church Law,* 1150–1625. Grand Rapids, MI: William B. Eerdmans, 2001.

Van Voorst, Robert, ed. *Readings in Christianity.* Belmont, CA: Wadsworth, 1997.

Von Rad, Gerhard. *The Message of the Prophets.* New York: Harper, 1967.

Wogaman, Philip. *Christian Perspectives on Politics.* Louisville, KY: Westminster John Knox Press, 2000.

World Bank. *Global Development Finance: The Globalization of Corporate Finance in Developing Countries, vol. 2, Summary and Country Tables.* Washington, DC, 2007.

7

From a Theological Frame to a Secular Frame

How Historical Context Shapes Our Understanding of the Principles of Catholic Social Thought

Mary L. Hirschfeld

The Catholic tradition stretches out over millennia and yet hopes to speak to each succeeding age. The Church witnesses to eternal truth but must express that truth in ways that are inflected by the contours of a given historical era. The difficulty of speaking across historical eras is particularly clear in the case of the tradition of Catholic social thought, which in its modern form addresses the dislocations caused by the advent of modern industrial capitalism while drawing on the thought of Thomas Aquinas, who lived in an era in which capitalism was at most nascent. Between Thomas's age and our own lie not only the rise of capitalism but also a profound transformation in the theological and philosophical environment. Signal changes include but are not limited to the rise of nominalism, the subjective turn in philosophy, the loss of a sense of natural teleology, and the development of the first truly secular culture in the history of the world. As a result of these transformations, our frame for understanding economic matters is likely to be quite different from the one used by Thomas. In order to apply the principles of the tradition of Catholic social thought in our modern setting, we need to be attentive to these differences.

However, our attention to historical setting should not be merely a matter of trying to get right the translation from one era to another. The changes that attended the transition to modernity were frequently not neutral with respect to Catholic truth. Insofar as our modern frame began with philosophical moves aimed at rejecting central principles of Catholic thinking, our acceptance of that frame jeopardizes the Church's mission of witnessing clearly to the gospel. The Church thus confronts the task of sorting through the various trends and influences in the modern world, in an effort to distinguish what is neutral or even salutary from that which ought to be rejected. We can see this difficulty in particular as the Church grapples with the phenomenon of capitalism, which has introduced a host of social and spiritual ills (e.g., exacerbated income inequality and materialism), but which has also brought real benefits (e.g., a reduction in poverty and an outlet for human creativity). So as we seek to apply the wisdom of ages past, we need also to evaluate the modern setting for its strengths and weaknesses.

Such a task cannot be done perfectly insofar as we ourselves are shaped by our era. We can therefore neither perfectly understand the eras that have preceded us nor objectively evaluate the contours of our own. Nonetheless, we ought not let the perfect be the enemy of the good. A part of Catholic teaching is that there is an eternal truth and we have at least some access to it. That gives us hope that we are able to enter into the spirit of systems of thought such as Thomas's, that come from a different setting. And one would hope that having learned from his wisdom, we would be able to see our own situation with a fresh perspective, which might prove fruitful as we seek to give witness to the gospel in our own times.

In this paper, I propose to offer up an example of how such historical analysis is necessary if we wish to implement the principles of Catholic social thought by examining the fundamental hypothesis of the True Wealth of Nations project—that *the economic and cultural criteria identified in the tradition of Catholic social thought provide an effective path to sustainable prosperity for all*—from a Thomistic perspective. Because a full analysis of the changes in our philosophical and theological frame is not possible in a single essay, I focus on just one key change: the rise of secularism. Focusing on secularism has the virtue of identifying most clearly how distant Thomas's thought is from our own intellectual world, with the additional benefit of being directly relevant to the question of how we understand the end of "prosperity."

After pointing out some key features of Thomas's theological framework and contrasting it with our own more secular perspective, I will focus on three issues. First, I will discuss how Thomas understood the end of this-worldly (earthly) human flourishing in relationship to our final end, which for Thomas lies in the beatific vision. Thomas by no means denies the real goodness of earthly human flourishing, which we would associate with prosperity, but adoption of his framework would require that we qualify the fundamental hypothesis we are investigating. Second, turning to the question of how we understand prosperity, I will discuss Thomas's understanding of the relationship between material well-being and virtue, which Thomas identifies with human flourishing. Again, Thomas does not deny the genuine goodness of material well-being, but he understands it as ordered to our end in a way that diverges from our own modern sensibilities. This discussion highlights some tensions in our own thought that are not present under Thomas's framework. Finally, I will examine Thomas's understanding of material well-being in itself, arguing that Thomas's understanding is quite different from our own. In particular, he understands our material well-being as resulting in desires that are both satiable and static. As it turns out, crucial aspects of Catholic social thought depend on Thomas's conception of material well-being. Insofar as our modern conception of well-being is open to the possibility that our material desires are not satiable or static, Catholic social thought cannot be applied to modern economies without some amendment. At the same time, Thomas's framework does provide resources that could help us address those difficulties, and it provides a useful point of contact with a branch of modern research on the question of the relationship between income and happiness. The paper concludes with an assessment of the degree to which we could or should incorporate Thomas's perspective into our own. The paper cannot analyze these issues fully but will mark out places where Thomas's thought is in tension with our own as a prelude to further inquiry.

Since both "Thomism" and "secularism" can have multiple interpretations, it is first necessary to say something about how I will use these terms before proceeding. Beginning with the term "secular," I follow Charles Taylor who argues that there are multiple, possibly interrelated ways of understanding secularism. For our purposes, Taylor's first and most salient characterization of secularism is that we live in an age in which

> as we function within various spheres of activity—economic,
> political, cultural, educational, professional, recreational—the norms
> and principles we follow, the deliberations we engage in, generally
> don't refer us to God or to any religious beliefs; the considerations we
> act on are internal to the "rationality" of each sphere—maximum
> gain within the economy, the greatest benefit to the greatest number
> in the political area, and so on.

The dominant mode of economic discourse is purely secular in this characterization and thus serves as a useful benchmark for drawing comparisons with Thomas. Second, Taylor himself focuses on the characterization of secularism as a world in which faith in God is no longer the default belief but rather is seen as one of many options. The two characterizations are closely linked, however, in that it is our default belief in the autonomy of the world that allows us to believe that we can study most things without reference to our belief in God. Thus, my own use of the term "secular" should be understood as pointing to the way these two characterizations interact.[1]

As it happens, Thomas can be read in a way that is at least compatible with secularism. Alasdair MacIntyre offers a good treatment of the many versions of Thomism that have emerged over the centuries.[2] The crucial dispute has been over how to understand the integration of Thomas's theology and his philosophy. A tradition emerged in the late renaissance and early modern periods of reading Thomas as though his philosophy were separable from his theology, which would require a pattern of thought compatible with Taylor's characterization of secular—that is, one wherein human modes of reason can function autonomously from modes of knowing informed by faith or grace. The result was a version of Thomism in which the natural and the supernatural are seen as parallel but noninteracting modes of existence, which some have dubbed "extrinsicism."[3] The principle critique of extrinsicism is that it allows us to imagine that our reasoning about our political or economic lives is unaffected by our faith in God. In other words, extrinsicism is entirely secular if we use Taylor's characterization. In reaction to neo-Thomism, a more historical approach to Thomas's thought emerged.[4] My reading of Thomas draws on the resulting literature that emphasizes the theological character of all of Thomas's thought,[5] and that above all insists on reading the *Summa Theologiae* as a whole.[6] On this reading, the philosophical foundations that Thomas largely finds in Aristotle are transformed (in ways large and small) by being placed firmly within a theological setting.[7] In other words, on this reading Thomas's teachings about everything, including economics, are shot through with theological reasoning and are thus susceptible to serious deformation if we approach them with secular assumptions.

Thomas's Theological Framework

Under secularism, the world is understood as autonomous, in that its processes can be understood in their own terms. Belief in God is not ruled out under such a view, but it does become purely optional. Along with a tendency to see the world and its functioning as autonomous, there is a tendency to privilege the temporal horizon. By that, I mean that human flourishing, understood in this-worldly terms, is held to be the primary good. We all share a default belief in our ability to reason about the world, and while there is not perfect agreement about what constitutes temporal human flourishing, there is little disagreement that it is an important end. Even those who believe that humans have some sort of transcendent end take our concern with temporal flourishing quite seriously. The Truth Wealth project, for example, presumes that humans have a transcendent end, yet its focus is on the achievement of the temporal human good. In part this is because whatever our beliefs, we all live in a predominantly secular age and cannot help being formed by the age's concern with temporal well-being. In part this is because concern for temporal human welfare serves as a sort of *lingua franca* in a pluralistic culture in which beliefs about the transcendent are quite divergent, but where (our differences notwithstanding) there is at least some basis for coming to agreement about the temporal. We will later take up the theme of how to understand our temporal end in light of our transcendental end, but the main point for now is that it is characteristic of our age that the center of gravity of both our thought and our concern is in the temporal world we experience and not in God.

Thomas, by contrast, structures his thought around God. Indeed, he argues that theology is the noblest science, the one to which all other forms of science are ordered (*ST*, I, 1, 5).[8] Moreover, theology itself has God as its subject. All other things theologians might consider like "things and signs; or the works of salvation; or the whole Christ, as the head and members" are part of theology "so far as they have reference to God" (*ST*, I, 1, 7). Thomas echoes this point in his description of the structure of the *Summa*, wherein the *prima pars* deals with God; the *secunda pars* with "the rational creature's advance *toward God*"; and the *tertia pars* with Christ, "Who, as man, is our way *to God*" (*ST*, I, 2, prologue). Thomas's teachings on economics are located in the *secunda pars*,[9] meaning that on Thomas's own account we must understand them as part of our "advance toward God."

To really understand how Thomas's framework, which places God at the center, alters his understanding of the created world as well, it is necessary to consider Thomas's understanding of the relationship between God and the created order. Thomas is part of the classical theological tradition that sees God as both radically transcendent and radically immanent with respect to the created world. According to Robert Sokolowski, the defining insight of this tradition is that the world is created, with the crucial implication that the world does not have to be.[10] God, by contrast, necessarily is. As Thomas puts it, God's essence is his existence (*ST*, I, 3, 4). Essence refers to what a being is, while existence refers to the fact that a being is. In created beings, our essence does not require that we exist. The essence of a kumquat does not require that there actually be kumquats in the world. God's uniqueness lies in the fact that *what* God is, is identical with the fact *that* God is. Since creation does not have being of itself (or by its own essence, to use Thomas's vocabulary), it depends on God in order to be sustained in being. Thomas refers to this as our "participation" in divine being (*ST*, I, 44, 1). Notice that, on this view, creation does not refer specifically to the moment the world began (in some Big Bang, perhaps), but rather its ongoing existence. We are being created at every single moment in time. The core truth about the temporal world, then, is that it is absolutely dependent on God. There is no aspect of creation that could subsist on its own, since that property belongs to God alone. Thomas's formulation thus moves the center of gravity away from the created world, which must now be understood as being radically dependent on God as the source of both its existence and its meaning. There is literally *nothing* that could exist apart from God, since God is the unique being whose essence is to exist.

But Thomas's framework decenters the temporal in a yet more radical way, by forcing us to recognize the limits of human reason and by reminding us that human understanding is measured by God and not the other way around. Thomas does this in his discussion of the way human language is inadequate to the strangeness that is God. Ordinary human language allows us to speak of created beings whose essences are distinct from the fact that they exist. To use Thomas's terminology, created beings are "composite." In the sentence, "Socrates is a man," we identify Socrates' essence (humanity) as something that is predicated of the being we call Socrates. God, by contrast, is "simple"— because his essence is his existence, there is no "attribute" we could ascribe to him that is really distinguishable from him (*ST*, 1, 3, 4). We have a twofold problem, then, when it comes to talking about God. First, we only know created beings in which essence and existence are distinct. We simply cannot comprehend an essence that is existence. Thomas thus strongly affirms the central apophatic claim that we cannot know God as he is (*ST*, 1, 3, prologue).[11] Second, the structure of our language cannot capture God's simplicity. If we say, "God is a being whose essence is to exist," we are not speaking truly. To predicate the term "being" of God is to grammatically ascribe composition to him. As Thomas works through the opening questions about the divine essence, he enlarges upon the theme of the strangeness of God and the inadequacy of our thought about God.

However, he then takes up the fact that we nonetheless "name" God. In particular, we say of God that "he is good" or "he is just" (*ST*, I, 13). Against a tradition that wanted to argue that technically we can only speak of God negatively, or apophatically, Thomas argues that there has to be a positive or kataphatic moment in our theology because when people say things such as "God lives," they mean more than just "God causes life in us" or that "God is different from inanimate bodies." Positive statements are always inadequate. We only know God from his effects, that is, the created world. God is perfect (*ST*, I, 4) and is therefore the source of all perfections that we find in creation. These perfections reflect God but are necessarily imperfect reflections of God. Nonetheless, insofar as perfection is found in a created being, that being is like God. Thus: "When we say, God is good, the meaning is not, God is the cause of goodness, or God is not evil; but the meaning is, whatever good we attribute to creatures, pre-exists in God, and in a more excellent and higher way" (*ST*, I, 13, 2).

This leads Thomas to his doctrine of analogy, which is that our talk of God is neither univocal, such that "good" as applied to created beings is the same as "good" as applied to God; but neither is it equivocal, such that "good" as applied to created beings has no relationship at all to "good" as applied to God. Such talk is, rather, analogous in the sense that the "goodness" of creation is related to the "goodness" that is God, in that we have some conception of what we mean when we say God is good, albeit a terribly inadequate conception of that meaning (*ST*, I, 13, 5). As we've seen, our need to use analogy in our talk about God is directly related to the way creation depends on and reflects God. In other words, analogy is not just a description of theological talk; rather, it is an essential aspect of the relationship between the created world and God.[12] This is the *analogia entis* (the "analogy of being"), which is central to Thomas's thought.[13]

Our difficulty is that analogical thought, and the belief that the relationship between God and creation is itself analogical, is not compatible with secularism. Were we to maintain a purely apophatic approach to theology, insisting that the term "good" as applied to God has no positive content, we would *de facto* separate our knowledge of the world from our knowledge of God. Analogy requires that we understand that there is a connection between the created world and God. Moreover, on Thomas's account, we need to inquire of analogical terms that application of the term is "primary." In order for the analogy to work at all there has to be a connection between the terms. In this case, the connection is that there is goodness in creatures because creatures are created by God who is good. That means that although we move from our knowledge of "goodness" in creatures to the claim that God is "good," the primary meaning of "good" is in God, not in the creatures who are his imperfect reflections (*ST*, I, 13, 6). To acknowledge that "goodness" as we understand it is an imperfect reflection of divine goodness decenters the human in favor of the divine. We have access to creaturely understandings of creaturely goodness, but in Thomas's framework, we have to recognize that this knowledge is provisional. In particular, insofar as we come to deeper knowledge of God, and the true good that he is, we should have a correspondingly better understanding of creaturely goodness. Theological knowledge in principle should perfect our knowledge of creation in itself.

As we will see when we turn to explicit consideration of the True Wealth project's fundamental hypothesis from a Thomistic point of view, the general principle of analogy affects the analysis at many points. But there are some particular theological consequences of analogical thinking that form part of the overarching framework of Thomas's thought that are worth observing here. First, we need to expand our understanding of how creation serves as an analogical representation of God. In particular, approaching creation as analogy allows us to see that it has a mysterious, surprising, and wondrous quality that requires that the exercise of human reason have moments of contemplation and surrender. In addition, it raises the question of how the overflowing of the fullness of infinite being can be reflected in created finite beings. The answer to that question teaches us that we need to learn to respect both the heterogeneity of created beings but also their necessary ordering to one another. Second, we need to take up the question of how human beings uniquely function as the image of God, which is the point of Thomas's theology that demands that we take analogical thinking seriously when we consider ordinary human affairs.

As discussed above, the essential analogical relationship between creation and God centers on the fact that created beings do not have existence by virtue of what they are, whereas God does. Created existence, then, must come from God. As Thomas puts it, created being is a "proper" effect of God, an effect that requires God's continuing presence to any created being. Insofar as existence is the innermost thing of any created being, God is present to, or is "found" within each and every created being (*ST*, I, 8, 1).[14] Divine being is an overabundant fullness. Insofar as created being participates in divine being in this way, there is an analogous fullness in the simple act of our being. While we should never confuse created being with divine being, the analogous relationship between the two explains why we sometimes experience the sense of wonder at our existence—or at the goodness, truthfulness, and beauty of being itself. Moreover, on the classical account, being expresses itself in the transcendental modes of the true, the good, and the beautiful. Existence and the three transcendental modes that are part and parcel of it defy understanding by human reason, which requires forms or essences in order to "understand." Our sense of existence and its refraction in the modes of the true and the good and the beautiful offer us a way of encountering the divine in its reflection in the created world. Once we recognize this, it is clear that a sense of contemplation (of that which cannot be fully grasped by human reason) and a sense of wonder are appropriate responses to creation. As I will discuss below, our secular world has little space for the contemplative, and we will have to ask whether that creates obstacles to our ability to respond faithfully to the created world in which God has placed us.

Creation's representation of God does not stop at the existence that we have from him—essence—or the variety of forms of created beings are also created by God and also serve the function of analogously representing God. God wills that creation represent his divine goodness. Therefore, according to Thomas, God produced "many and diverse creatures, that what was wanting to one in the representation of divine goodness might be supplied by another. For goodness, which in God is simple and uniform, in creatures is manifold and divided; and hence the whole universe together participates in the divine goodness more perfectly, and represents it better than any single creature whatever" (*ST*, I, 47, 1).

The notion that God's goodness requires a multiplicity of beings in order to be represented in finite terms reminds us of the superabundant fullness of divine being. One implication of Thomas's view is that in order for us to "see" the representation of divine goodness in creation, we need to be able to see goods as heterogeneous. It is in their particularity that we catch glimpses, like shards, of God's glorious goodness. Views of creation that obscure the distinctness of created goods blunt our ability to catch the reflection of divine goodness in creation and impair our ability both to understand and to interact with creation in an authentically meaningful way. We should be wary of such models of human reason, like utilitarianism, which encourage us to see created goods as fungible and fully interchangeable. While it might be a convenience to assign a price to apples and oranges so that we can trade them or add them up, we need to remember that this is a fictional contrivance and that the deeper truth is that apples and oranges are different kinds of things (and therefore cannot really be added up).

At the same time, Thomas's recognition of the heterogeneity of created beings does not imply that the world is hopelessly fragmented. God may need a multiplicity of created beings in order to represent the fullness of his being, but there must also be a unity to creation if creation is to give witness to the fact that God is one. God shows this unity by ordering created beings to one another and all things to him (*ST*, I, 47, 3).

This ordering turns out to be crucial to Thomas's thought in a variety of interconnected ways. First, God orders created beings to their proper ends (which in turn order them to other created beings and toward God) through the exercise of his providence, which is the act of governance of creation. God exercises his providence by working through "secondary" or created causes, whether they be natural, random, or voluntary. Nothing created escapes God's providence, and thus there is a deep ordering to everything, whether that order is accessible to human reason (as in our ability to discern the law-like behavior of natural processes) or not (as in our inability to understand randomness or contingency). The more deeply we can enter into and discern the order of things,[15] the more we grow in knowledge of the created world.

As intelligent beings, we exercise a special role in God's providence, both in being able to direct ourselves to our own end and in having God as our ultimate end (*SCG*, III-II, III). We are thus given a role in our own providence, which we exercise through the virtue of prudence.[16] Through the exercise of prudence we choose the means that move us toward our end (*ST*, II-II, 47, 6). Because prudence is the virtue that allows us to conform to God's providence, especially as it is expressed through his law (both revealed and natural), it is essential to prudence that we be able to discern the order of things. Thus, although prudence has to do with the choice of means to reach our end, it should not be confused with the description of practical reason offered by utilitarianism. It involves discernment about the order of things, as befits the sort of practical reason necessary to a world in which the heterogeneity of goods needs to be respected, rather than the calculation of utilitarianism, which collapses all created goods into a single metric.[17]

One could say at this juncture that this is all well and good, but it is not obvious how the theological frame really alters our way of coming to understand the created world. Would it make any difference to the way a botanist practiced her science? A skeptic could concede that a Thomistic botanist might well celebrate God as the ultimate cause of plants, and she might even be drawn into an ever-greater appreciation of God's ordering of creation through the exercise of her science. But the actual science itself would not be much altered.

There are three replies that can be offered here. First, a Thomistic botanist would recognize that her science as all her other activities must be ordered properly to her proper end. Thus, for example, she could not perform research with the aim of developing a pharmaceutical with which she could poison all of Manhattan. Indeed, if the purpose of seeking knowledge is to inflate our vanity, done to the neglect of other obligations, or is otherwise conducted without reference to God, it ceases to be a virtue and becomes the vice of curiosity (*ST*, II-II, 167, 1). Second, the accent on contemplation that Thomas's framework would urge might well lead to a different type of science. Although not working out of any kind of religious tradition, feminists have argued that a more "feminine" approach to science could well entail a more contemplative approach and that this could lead to a different practice of science.[18] But the strongest argument is the third. The study of human affairs differs quite a bit from the study of other parts of the created world because humans have their end not only in the created world but also and indeed primarily in God. We are created to the *imago Dei* (the image of God),[19] and that means that we cannot escape the issue of the analogy between the created world and God.

Thomas's doctrine of the *imago Dei* is treated in only one explicit question in the *Summa* but undergirds his approach to moral theology. For our purposes, the key points are as follows. The end for which humans were created is to know and love God as God knows and loves himself. We are endowed with a mind that gives us a natural appetite for knowing and loving God; with grace we can actually know and love God (albeit imperfectly); and we achieve the perfection of the image in glory (*ST*, I, 93, 4). There might be a temptation to read this doctrine as an argument that the *imago Dei* is to function in us like a mirror of God. In particular, it is a mirror of the trinitarian God, in that the reference to God knowing and loving himself is a reference to the processions of the Trinity.[20] But once we make that observation, we can see that Thomas is not talking about a simple mirroring. If that were the case, we would be called to know and love ourselves as God knows and loves Himself. Yet, Thomas explicitly rules out this interpretation (*ST*, I, 93, 8). We are like God not insofar as the structure of our mind reflects the trinitarian processions; rather, we are like God insofar as we *participate* in those processions. Those processions are centered on God; and we are most like God when our own knowing and loving is centered on God.

Thomas's first exposition on the *imago Dei* thus reminds us, again, that Thomas systematically decenters the temporal (in this case, us) in favor of the divine. In addition, the accent is on our receptivity, not our agency. We realize the image through grace. Indeed, as Jean-Pierre Torrell argues, the whole doctrine is about the indwelling of the Trinity in the soul.[21] That corresponds to the accent on the contemplative that characterizes Thomas's thought. And finally, it means that we cannot escape thinking analogically. We are finite, created beings who are called to participate in the divine in a special way. Our end is thus to enter into relationship with God in a way that calls us to transcend our created nature.

Having laid down this framework, Thomas then goes on to talk about the way in which human nature is analogous to God's nature. In the prologue of the *secunda pars*, Thomas argues that we are "made to God's image, in so far as the image implies an intelligent being endowed with free-will and self-movement" (*ST*, I-II, prologue). This definition places the accent on our nature as *agents*, who as "principles of their own actions" (*ST*, I-II, prologue) are like God in a way that lesser created beings are not. This is what allows God to entrust us with our own "providence," which we have already discussed. This is the notion of the *imago Dei* that serves to ground the notion of human dignity. God has gifted us with intellect and will, and that gives us a special freedom to direct ourselves.

The *imago Dei* thus reflects the essence of analogical thinking. The first description of human beings as created to the image and likeness of God places the accent on God's activity in creating, redeeming, and beatifying us. That is the measure of how we are *not* like God. That Thomas makes this point places the accent on our distance from God. Once the disanalogy has been established, Thomas is free to talk about the analogy. We are not at all like God; but having established that, we can observe that we are nonetheless meant to represent God in creation in a special way. Thus, human dignity is affirmed but in a way that retains the proper stance of humility toward God. The exercise of human agency is affirmed, but in a way that reminds us of our limitations. The pattern of saying and unsaying is one that we will see repeated below since any dealings with the human situation need to be seen through this analogical lens.

So Thomas's framework is focused on God, relies on analogical thought in order to understand creation in relation to God, and sees beings as ordered to one another and to God. Our task now is to use this framework to assess our fundamental hypothesis.

The Relationship between Our Temporal and Our Final End

The basic proposition of the True Wealth project is that: "The economic and cultural criteria identified in the tradition of Catholic social thought provide an effective path to sustainable prosperity for all."

It is best to begin with the most general question, which is how *any* temporal end should be viewed in relationship to our final end. It should not be surprising to learn that Thomas's monumental treatment of human life in the *secunda pars* begins by establishing that human actions are ordered toward an end.[22] Nor, since Thomas's framework centers on God, should it be surprising to learn that humans are not ordered to any created good as their final end but rather to God (*ST*, I-II, 2, 8). The question is how does our temporal end stand in relationship to our final end? As I mentioned in the introduction, there are a variety of Thomisms, and this question is a central point of contention among them. Do we have just the one final end in God, or do we in addition have a natural end? As Denis J. M. Bradley argues, what is at stake here is the issue of whether or not God creates us with an in-built (natural) desire for a supernatural end that nature cannot fulfill. The tradition of Thomism, which argues that we have two ends, is founded on the notion that God could not have implanted in us natural desires that can only be met with supernatural assistance.[23] From the point of view of unassisted human reason, such a position is paradoxical: how can we be endowed with a nature that desires an end that transcends our nature?

Yet, as Bradley argues, this is precisely Thomas's point. Thomas rejects the notion that any created good can be our natural end because in order to reach our natural end, our will must be "lulled" (fully met). Yet, our intellectual nature is oriented toward the universal, such that our wills desire the universal good and our intellects desire the universal true. Since all created goods are only good by participation in the universal good, they cannot "lull" our wills (*ST*, I-II, 2, 8). Notice that the argument explicitly appeals to the analogous relationship between creation and God. Created goods truly are goods because they participate in the universal good. But they are themselves not that good. In pursuing created goods as ends, we learn something of what we are destined for. But we do not thereby achieve what we are destined for. This is the formulation that allows us to say that any "natural" end is certainly good, but imperfectly so. Moreover, the "natural" end can only be properly pursued if it is understood as ordered to the final end. We pursue the natural end because that is how God is present to us now, analogously and imperfectly. Attainment of that end should leave us with a deeper appreciation of what we are truly destined for. In other words, human nature is meant to be open-ended. We are to discover that we are incomplete and cannot fulfill our own natures, and that should leave us open to God's invitation to be drawn into his divine life. Of its own, human nature is "endless," that is, insatiable, a conclusion that makes Thomas a potential conversation partner with postmodern philosophies that likewise stress the endlessness of human nature.[24]

If one of the characteristics of secularism is its tendency to treat temporal human flourishing as the end of human action, it risks falling into idolatry, that is, mistaking a lesser good for our ultimate good. The dangers of idolatry are subtle but worth attending to. The first concern (which is not so subtle) is that if our attention is absorbed in pursuing temporal human flourishing, we will find ourselves increasingly absorbed in the attempt, precisely because temporal human flourishing never "lulls" our will. The world can become such a distraction that the seeds of the gospel can get choked off by "thorns" and fail to grow (Matt. 13:7, 22), thereby making it more difficult to attain our proper end and our true happiness. To affirm the real but imperfect and analogous temporal good in a secular world risks encouraging pursuit of those distractions at the expense of being able to hear truly and be transformed by the gospel.

But more critically, the promotion of Catholic social teaching can be self-defeating if we do not attend to the way its strictures would play out to an audience that takes temporal flourishing as a final end, rather than as an end that is analogously related to our proper final end. There are a variety of ways this can play out, but let me offer some reflections on just a couple of them. First, we need to be careful about the claim that God intends for humans to flourish in this world. As with all theological truths, this is a statement that is both true and not true. It is true to the extent that God wills for us to flourish as a fore-taste of the abundance we will know in the life to come; it is a way of sharing his overabundant fullness with finite creatures. Albino Barrera, in an essay in this volume, is right to say that scripture offers up ample evidence that God intends abundance and flourishing for his people. But insofar as we are des-tined for a transcendent end, it is within God's providence to frustrate the temporal end if it serves the purpose of lifting us up to our proper higher end. Using the logic of analogy, God can use temporal flourishing to witness posi-tively to what is to come; and God can use temporal suffering to remind us that even in earthly abundance we are truly impoverished with respect to the end that awaits us.

The Compendium of the Social Doctrine of the Church explicitly makes this point, arguing that the prophetic tradition clearly rejects oppression and poverty as evils but also sees them as "a symbol of the human situation before God, from whom comes every good as a gift to be administered and shared."[25] Poverty that is "sought or accepted with a religious attitude" can lead to the "true" wealth as opposed to the rich man who "places his trust in his possessions rather than in God." Indeed, it can be a positive value if it "becomes an attitude of humble availability and openness to God, of trust in him."[26] Thus, the same scripture that gives us the passages cited by Barrera to the effect that God wills for us to enjoy abundance also gives us the book of Job, which reminds us that God can visit suffering upon the just, though his purpose is always to lift the just up to their final end of true eternal abundance.[27]

There is an understandable reluctance to make much of God's ability to lead us to him through suffering. In particular, there is a fear that it could breed an attitude of complacency toward poverty and suffering, when we are in fact called to respond to the needs of others with a sense of urgency. The analogical framework allows us to understand that in our agency we are called on to make God present in the world, and we experience God's presence in our flourishing. Yet, the analogical framework crucially reminds us to keep some distance bet-ween the genuine good of temporal flourishing and our notion of our highest end. Thus, the proper stance is to be fully committed to the promotion of temporal flourishing and yet be willing to bear unavoidable suffering in patience. Without that stance, there can be a temptation to utopian thinking, which becomes impatient with suffering and can be tempted to short-circuit it through means that directly deny our higher end (i.e., by violating God's law one way or another). Alternatively, the futility of achieving permanent human flourishing can lead to a sense of despair that undermines our enthusiasm for reaching out to those in need. The analogical framework best ensures committed engagement in a spirit of sustaining hope.

To give another example of how an emphasis on temporal flourishing outside of the analogical framework can undermine the goals of Catholic social teaching, consider the issue of sacrifice. There are times when the needs of others become a call to make sacrifices for others. For example, when the Magisterium calls on prosperous nations to be willing to give out of their "substance," that is, out of that which they "need," it is arguing that economic justice might well require sacrifice on the part of the wealthy.[28] In his discussions of the order of charity, Thomas does argue that ordinarily we are to attend to our needs first. But there are times when the needs of the community require that one subordinate one's own needs to the needs of others (ST, II-II, 26, 5; ST, II-II, 32, 6). The difficulty is that for Thomas, God created us to seek true beatitude or happiness. Voluntarily giving up our ultimate end for the sake of another would negate the very purpose for which we are created. In other words, true self-denial is unintelligible. Thomas can nonetheless affirm sacrifice as a part of moral life because he distinguishes between the true eternal good and the partial temporal good. In other words, we can sacrifice temporal flourishing for the sake of others, even to the point of death. But we can do this because such sacrifices do not cut us off from our true eternal happiness.[29] What we cannot do is sacrifice our highest good for another. In other words, we cannot sin in order to help others, not even to save them from sin (ST, II-II, 26, 4).

If Thomas is right about human nature and the unintelligibility of making a sacrifice of our true happiness, then there is a danger in urging sacrifice in a world in which people identify their highest end with temporal flourishing. In particular, since it really is against our nature to sacrifice our highest end for others, people who mistake temporal flourishing for their highest end might rightly conclude (given their false premise) that it does not make sense to sacrifice their temporal flourishing for others. There is a fairly widespread belief that such all-encompassing sacrifice is noble, but since a truly all-encompassing sacrifice would reject our ultimate beatitude in God, this belief erroneously cuts against human nature and lays a foundation for skepticism about the rationality of any self-sacrifice. One can find such skepticism in certain strands of libertarianism, for example. Alternatively, people might continue to believe that sacrifice of their temporal end is noble but find themselves unable to make that sacrifice precisely because they understand such sacrifices to be total, and human nature is not constituted to make such total sacrifices. In such a world, calls to social justice and concern for others, which include a notion we are called to that self-sacrificial giving, may go unanswered—even by people who are well meaning. As *The Compendium of the Social Doctrine of the Church* explains, our readiness to share with others is made possible by an understanding of the "relativity" of economic goods, that is, their analogous nature.[30]

Taken together, these reflections raise some questions about our fundamental hypothesis that would seem to require more attention. First, given that God's providential design is aimed at our ultimate beatitude and not our temporal beatitude, it is an open question to me whether the fundamental hypothesis is correctly framed. While I do believe that the principles of Catholic social teaching are fitting to human nature and therefore represent the best way for us to providentially provide for our own temporal flourishing, I am made uneasy by the apparent claim that we would actually achieve temporal flourishing as a result. God has his own design, which might or might not include blessing our economic and social activities with "prosperity." Thus, it might be safer to say that the principles of Catholic social thought would promote true prosperity, rather than provide an "effective" path toward it. This point should be understood as more of a hesitation than a strong critique.

Second, and I think more critically, we need to think much harder about how the principles of Catholic social teaching would work out if they were understood in a secular framework rather than in the Thomistic theological/analogical framework. The mutation of the meaning of "sacrifice" is but one example of places where Catholic teachings could be counterproductive if adopted with what is in essence a faulty understanding of exactly how those principles work. The issue of what love of neighbor means, for example, would also shift if it were understood not as a communion made possible in God but rather as something that transpired between two autonomous beings, as one might imagine in a secular frame. The notion of "common good" fundamentally shifts if we are talking about interconnected humans in communion before God rather than autonomous human beings. The world has essentially inverted since Thomas wrote, and this would suggest that a deeper reflection on the principles of the Catholic social tradition that are rooted in Thomas is needed if we are to successfully translate them to the modern world. Thus, it would be unsurprising if our empirical work found that the principles of Catholic social thought did *not* promote true prosperity. It would be more correct to say that if the principles of Catholic social thought were properly understood in their full theological context, then their implementation would promote true prosperity. But because of the radical shift in context, I am by no means convinced that the principles can be properly understood by a secular audience, especially if they are promoted in a form that tends to be detached from their theological setting.[31] My own experience of transitioning from a secular view to a Catholic/Thomistic worldview is that the changes involved reach very, very deep and that the task of translating from one worldview to the other is actually quite daunting. This awareness helps us understand just how difficult a task it would be, for example, to implement today the structures or attitudes of thirteenth- or fourteenth-century "civil economy," identified by Stefano Zamagni in his essay in this volume.

Thus far we have focused on the way the frame of thinking matters for our reflections on the Catholic social teaching, but many other transformations have taken place between our day and Thomas's. The next two sections take up two such examples. The first has to do with the role material goods play with respect to temporal flourishing properly understood. After discussing that, we will then take up the question of how our understanding of the nature of our material desires has also shifted.

The Contribution of Material Goods to Temporal Flourishing

In his essay in this volume, Andrew Yuengert argues persuasively that "true prosperity" should not be understood purely in terms of material goods or income.[32] That he has to argue against the possibility that income is an adequate measure of well-being is symptomatic of the distance that lies between Thomas and us. The question we need to put to Thomas is not whether there is more to well-being than material goods, but rather whether material goods play any independent role at all in contributing to human flourishing at all. Yuengert concludes that income plays a role *alongside of* the virtues, personal initiative, and social relations. For Thomas, material goods are of instrumental value only, necessary in order to pursue the virtues that constitute temporal human flourishing.[33]

Recall that for Thomas there is order in the created world. A part of that order is that there is a clear hierarchy. With respect to human flourishing, virtue is a higher good than any bodily goods. Indeed, the more our life of virtue mirrors the one we will enjoy in our true eternal happiness, the less we stand in need of the "goods of the body" (*ST*, I-II, 4, 7). The external goods are necessary only insofar as they provide the platform from which we can pursue virtue. Moreover, as Thomas argues in the *Summa Contra Gentiles*, beyond what is necessary for basic survival, further wealth is a matter of indifference with respect to pursuit of virtue. As he explains, wealth can be used for good or ill, and the same can be said of poverty (*SCG*, III-II, 133). In short, because

external goods are ordered to our higher temporal goods, their value is measured by the use we make of them. There are two implications that can be
drawn from this that are relevant to our project.

First, there is a quick practical observation that can be made. As Yuengert
observes, the tradition has long been well-aware of the evil uses to which wealth
might be put. Thomas's perspective simply strengthens the point. Income is
not an end in itself. Its contribution to our well-being is entirely dependent on
how we use that income to foster genuine well-being. In an economy widely
noted for its consumerism, and its attendant appeals to concupiscent desire,
the gap between income and genuine well-being can be quite large indeed. To
make a Thomistic point using economic jargon, there is a great deal of ineffi-
ciency in our consumption. One could argue that income is simply not a useful
measure of genuine prosperity, at least in a wealthy nation. Rather than using
income, it might be better to use measures that are correlated with actual
human flourishing, as Yuengert suggests.[34]

In addition to recent lines of inquiry among economists about the relationship between income and actual well-being, there is an old line of research
done by some women economists in the first half of the twentieth century that
sought to establish a subdiscipline in consumption economics that would
investigate the "science" of consumption with the same attention that economists have traditionally devoted to the "science" of production.[35] The leading
figure in that school was Hazel Kyrk, who published her dissertation, *A Theory
of Consumption*, in 1923.[36] Her argument was that while we can rely on the
profit mechanism to push firms to produce goods and services in an efficient
manner, there is no corresponding mechanism that would push households to
efficiently translate their income into genuine well-being. There is no single
metric, like income, by which households can measure their efficiency.
Moreover, there is no mechanism that would drive inefficient households out
of business. She then went on to argue that we should construct a theory of
consumption that would study consumption patterns, which she understood
as being organized around "standards of living," and seek to evaluate them.
Such a study could be used to improve the "efficiency" of our consumption patterns, that is, our ability to translate income into actual human flourishing.
Consumption economics died out as a branch of economics in the mid-
twentieth century, presumably because the kinds of studies involved did not
meet the standards of the mathematical rigor that were increasingly coming to
define the profession of economics.

There are a few aspects of Kyrk's line of thought that can usefully supplement our thinking about how to measure the "good" of material wealth properly. First, her willingness to evaluate consumption patterns serves as a forceful

reminder that income is of instrumental value only. It is efficiently used only to the extent that it is in service of standards of living that are genuinely in service of human flourishing and should therefore not be viewed as an independent variable in a general assessment of economic well-being. It makes no more sense to think that having more income is always better without consideration of how it is used than it does to think that using more resources in producing a commodity is always better without consideration of whether the resources were efficiently employed. Second, not only did Kyrk question the connection between income and well-being, but she also proposed that we actually start training consumers[37] in how to make wise consumption decisions. While we might balk at the idea of "training" consumers today, there is something to be said for a line of inquiry that seeks not merely to describe the relationship between income and consumption, but which would actually seek to improve our practical reasoning about consumption.[38] An inquiry that had practical application as its aim might be a nice complement to the Church's teachings on the hazards of materialism and consumerism, since it would provide real material that individuals could use to achieve a more virtuous pattern of consumption.

The second implication of the shift away from thinking of material goods as valuable only insofar as they are ordered toward virtue and toward thinking of income as an independent good is that on the latter view virtue and material well-being can come into conflict, whereas on the former view they cannot. Adam Smith provides a useful example of the problem I have in mind. If we put Thomas on one end of a spectrum saying that it is only virtue that matters, and neoclassical economists on the other end saying that it is only income that matters, Adam Smith lies directly in the middle. Although Smith famously argues for the social harmony that results from the pursuit of self-interest, he also argues that a society grounded *only* in pursuit of self-interest could at best hope to continue. By contrast, "where the necessary assistance is reciprocally afforded from love, from gratitude, from friendship, and esteem, the society flourishes and is happy"[39] Smith clearly values both material well-being and virtue.

Yet unlike Thomas, Smith does not order one to the other. As a result, the two ends can come into conflict. Indeed, the conflict is implicitly introduced at the beginning of his landmark work on economics, *The Wealth of Nations*.[40] Smith's central argument is that economic growth is fueled by expanding the scope of the division of labor. It is the division of labor that increases productivity, a point Smith famously makes by describing the workings of a pin factory. By assigning one worker to draw out the wire, another to straighten it, another to cut it, another to point it, and so on, twenty workers can produce tens of thousands of pins a day, where an individual might hope to make a few dozen if he were to carry on the whole project himself.[41] Yet much further on in the same work, Smith admits that one of the costs of the division of labor, which is *the* cornerstone of economic growth, is that it renders the working class to be incapable of virtue. It is worth quoting Smith at length on this point:

> The man whose whole life is spent in performing a few simple operations...has no occasion to exert his understanding or to exercise his invention in finding out expedients for removing difficulties which never occur. He naturally loses, therefore, the habit of such exertion, and generally becomes as stupid and ignorant as it is possible for a human creature to become. The torpor of his mind renders him not only incapable of relishing or bearing a part in any rational conversation, but of conceiving any generous, noble, or tender sentiment, and consequently of forming any just judgment concerning many even of the ordinary duties of private life. Of the great and extensive interests of his country he is altogether incapable of judging, and unless very particular pains have been taken to render him otherwise, he is equally incapable of defending his country in war. The uniformity of his stationary life naturally corrupts the courage of his mind, and makes him regard with abhorrence the irregular, uncertain, and adventurous life of a soldier. It corrupts even the activity of his body, and renders him incapable of exerting his strength with vigor and perseverance in any other employment than that to which he has been bred. His dexterity at his own particular trade seems, in this manner, to be acquired at the expense of his intellectual, social, and martial virtues. But in every improved and civilized society this is the state into which the laboring poor, that is, the great body of the people, must necessarily fall, unless government takes some pains to prevent it.[42]

Thus, for Smith, the main engine of economic growth carries with it the price of making it difficult for the workers to lead a life of virtue. Although Smith clearly laments the negative consequences of the division of labor on the worker, it is clear that he thinks that the resulting prosperity is worth the price. Moreover, Smith is not talking about generating prosperity for other segments of society on the backs of the unfortunate laboring class. On the contrary, his interest in studying "the wealth of nations" is that he thought increased income could enhance the quality of life for the many and that this was a good end.[43]

We could multiply examples of the tension. In addition to the soul-stealing nature of manufacturing processes, we can observe that economic productivity requires resource mobility. Whether this takes the form of capital abandoning a community, or of laborers having to leave their communities in order to find better employment, the dynamism of capitalism reduces our commitment to our local communities. Does this inhibit our ability to work together for the common good? If so, is the productivity associated from resource mobility worth the price we pay for it? In short, the tension between virtue and material well-being lies at the heart of debates over the question of whether capitalism is to be embraced or rejected. Proposals to reduce the sharp edges of capitalism very frequently come with the concern that such proposals would reduce the efficiency in economic production that capitalism delivers. And while my head sides with Thomas in saying that finding forms of economic life that are in service of virtue would be worth a substantial reduction in material wealth, my heart says that the economic growth of the last few centuries has reduced economic misery a great deal and that it would be hard-hearted to advocate a return to an earlier world. In any case, the point is that Thomas did not experience this tension. His teachings about the economy are therefore subject to the critique that they might impede efficiency. This is a trade-off—or at least a potential trade-off—that our project necessarily raises.

The tension is compounded by another feature of our world that differs from that of Thomas: our notion that not only is material wealth an independent good, but that living standards should grow over time. To that issue we now turn.

Are Material Wants Satiable?

We live in a world of rising expectations. It is not merely that we think material well-being is important. We also think that our standard of living should rise over time. Houses grow and wardrobes expand. We eat out more; we travel more; we have more cool gadgets. Our improved and improving standards of living have a good bit to do with our sense that we live in an age of progress. Economists sum up this sense in their axiomatic assumption that human desire is infinite. Economists go on to deliver the necessary corollary: the expression of infinite desire in a finite world means that scarcity is an inescapable fact of life. Thomas takes a position to the contrary. For Thomas, our natural wants are satiable. Now, Thomas is not insensible of the fact that in some there seems to be a desire for ever more wealth. But as he argues, such "artificial" desires are a result of disordered concupiscence. The problem arises when we seek temporal goods as if they were our supreme good. We covet them because we believe they will satisfy, but when we gain them we find that they are insufficient, since they are not, in fact, our supreme good. But if we retain the belief that our happiness is to be found in material goods, then we are committed to a life of endless desire. From a Thomistic perspective, an axiomatic assumption of economics is really the hypothesis that humans generally have disordered desires.

The notion that "natural" material wants are satiable plays a critical role in Thomas's thinking about economic matters. I have written about this extensively elsewhere,[44] but let me offer a brief summary here. Thomas teaches that those who are prosperous can distinguish between that income that is necessary to them (their "substance") and that which is due to be shared with those in greater need (their "abundance"). The income that is part of our "substance" is not simply that which attends to our basic needs but also whatever it takes to maintain a standard of living appropriate to our station in life. The world in which Thomas lived was very different from our own in this regard. In contrast to our own world wherein economic goods define status, in Thomas's world, status determined access to economic goods. Moreover, there were socially determined notions of what goods were necessary to maintain a given rank in society, and social pressure was brought to bear on those who sought to attain a higher standard of living than was appropriate for their station in life.[45] In such a world there were socially well-defined standards of living, Thomas was pointing to a clear marker of what we could properly keep for ourselves and what we would properly wish to share with others. Because our wants are satiable, there is no real sacrifice in giving to others out of our abundance, since that wealth truly is superfluous to us.

If we transport Thomas's thought on this subject to our modern world, however, a rather serious problem arises. We do not have socially defined standards of living that can serve as a demarcation between that which we need and that which is superfluous. On the contrary, the reason we pursue greater income is precisely so that we can raise our standard of living. But once we've adopted a higher standard of living, the goods that make up that standard of living become necessary to us, that is, a part of our "substance." In this world, to give to others really does entail a sacrifice. This is the mechanism that leads us to the predicament that we are the richest country in the world, but we feel that we cannot afford to be more generous with others who are in dire need. Insofar as maintenance of a standard of living really is necessary to us, we are in a bind. Our lack of generosity is not simply a matter of greed. For example, if it has become the custom for high school seniors to go to their proms in limousines wearing expensive clothes, parents might feel obligated to make such extravagant expenditures on behalf of their children, lest their children suffer socially because they cannot partake of the ritual in the socially expected manner.

Once infinite desire becomes accepted as simply being part of human nature, and a corresponding expectation for rising standards of living sets in, a mechanism is set in motion that generates a rising sense of what it takes merely to "get by." Thus, even if we do not have concupiscent desires, we live in a society that forces us all to act as if we do. Twenty years ago we didn't need personal computers or cell phones. Now we do. Twenty years from now we will possess things out of necessity that we haven't the faintest idea of desiring today. The rising tide of "need" keeps pace with our rising income, and there is never much distance between the two. As a result there is not much "abundance" available to be shared with those in real material need. Although in Thomas there is no serious tension between our natural duty to attend to our own needs and the needs of others, we must now choose between taking care of ourselves (and our families) and taking care of others.

Acceptance of the notion that infinite desires are normal and that rising standards of living are desirable puts us into the situation described by economists wherein infinite desires are launched into a finite world, and scarcity is the inevitable result. We can hope that ongoing technological improvements will help us put those finite resources to use satisfying more human wants. But if the wants themselves grow at much the same rate, there is no real progress in "satisfaction"—much as Thomas argued in his characterization of the desire for "artificial" wealth. Calls for social justice in such a world are less likely to be answered. Additionally, the relentless drive to extract more goods from our finite world put a strain on the environment and our ability to be good stewards of our planet. Many of the principles of the Catholic social tradition are more difficult to implement in a world in which rising standards of living are held to be a good.

The tradition is clear that materialism and consumerism are real dangers. In that vein, the *Compendium* argues that it is "necessary to create life-styles in which the quest for truth, beauty, goodness and communion with others for the sake of common growth are the factors which determine consumer choices, savings and investments" (360). This is not unlike Hazel Kyrk's call for an inquiry into the extent to which standards of living promote genuine well-being. My argument here is that proposals along this line need to be stressed along with the principles of subsidiarity, preferential option for the poor, the common good, and so on, that are typically associated with Catholic social thought. If we cannot achieve wisdom in our consumption, we will not be able to meaningfully achieve the social justice we all ardently wish for. It would seem that we need a theology of consumption that would help guide us in discerning virtuous patterns of consumption, both as a necessary supplement to Catholic social thought and because, as argued in the previous section, we should not call material goods "good" without attention to how they are actually used.

What might such a theology of consumption look like? While we cannot simply appeal to socially defined notions of a standard of living, as Thomas was able to do, we can bring three important insights from Thomas to bear on the question. First, Thomas's analogical framework and his conception of all goods as ordered to one another and to God provide a useful structure for thinking about how we might become virtuous consumers. As we have already seen, the primary focus in modern economic thought is on asking how we can maximize our income, that is, our means, while little attention is paid to the ends economic goods serve. A theology of consumption would refocus our attention on the question of the ends to which economic goods are ordered. From Thomas, we learn that we are created to the image and likeness of God, and so the question would be how our consumption choices serve that end. The issue would become not whether we should or should not acquire the latest new thing; but rather given our aims, what goods and services would be helpful to achieving them.

For example, some have observed that now that we have dishwashers it is inconceivable that we would want to do without. But that observation nowhere contains an argument about what end is served by having a dishwasher, except perhaps the implicit argument that dishwashers are labor-saving devices and labor-saving is intrinsically good. But that is actually still an argument about efficiency about means, namely, that having the dishwasher would free up time, which is also a resource, to be available for other uses. As Tibor Scitovsky has argued, a good deal of our modern day decision making is focused on maximizing means of one sort or another. In particular, we strive to maximize income, save time, or save effort. But nowhere in that set of decisions is there any thought about what we will do with all the extra income, time, or energy.[46]

By contrast, if our first question is to ask what the dishwasher would be ordered to, we might encounter the following sorts of considerations. In a family, the labor of preparing a meal and cleaning up after it is a service for loved ones. We could imagine a mother and one of her children working together to prepare dinner, and a father and another of his children working together afterward to clean up. Doing the dishes would then be labor, but not labor understood merely as a cost; the labor of dishwashing would be inflected by the fact that it is (or can be) a shared activity and that it is directed toward the well-being of the family. The introduction of a dishwasher into such a situation might serve to shift attitudes toward that time, such that the labor involved becomes viewed as something unpleasant that is to be done as quickly as possible so that individuals could quickly turn to unspecified activities. It is entirely possible that the dishwasher could be part of a set of choices that decrease both the sense of community in the family and the sense that labor done for the good of others is valuable of itself. By contrast, we could imagine another family that has chosen to entertain frequently, serving the needs of the larger community by providing gatherings where friends and more distant family can come together and share a meal. In such a family a dishwasher might well promote that end by making it easier to host larger gatherings, and might well then be a genuine addition to the good of the family (and the larger community). The question of whether the dishwasher promotes or hinders the flourishing of a household thus depends on what the dishwasher is really ordered to.

Notice that reflections like this invite us to look at goods and services in a larger context, asking what role they play in constructing the shape of our lives. What values are embedded in those goods and services? How are the goods and services ordered to one another in service of genuine human flourishing? Such a framework allows us to begin to move away from the fallacy that more is simply better, while also avoiding the static notion of standards of living that Thomas accepted as a given feature of his society. In addition, it would introduce into our lives a sense that our everyday choices are a type of art. Do the pieces of our lives fit together to form a harmonious whole? Or are they random choices that we make in a piecemeal fashion as we decide about goods and services without thinking carefully how they fit into the overall pattern of our lives? In ordering our lives in a harmonious way, we are exercising our particular providence in God's creation, which itself orders things to one another. In general, it would increase the sense of purposeful behavior in an arena of our lives that is too often overtaken by whim or by desires that are not thought through.

A second Thomistic notion relevant to a theology of consumption follows directly upon this. Our modern notion of practical reason is to understand it as instrumental reason, deliberating about means to reach a given end. Moreover, the means are considered as interchangeable or fungible. What matters is the effectiveness with which the means promote the end. The paradigmatic case of such logic is economic reasoning, which is centered on the thought that our principle aim is to maximize "utility," and which is indifferent to the means we use to do it. On this view, life is a series of trade-offs. Would I maximize my utility by buying a dishwasher or by taking a weekend trip to Chicago? In economic jargon, my opportunity cost of buying a dishwasher would be forgoing that weekend trip. Such language emphasizes scarcity, which in turn fuels the notion that more is better.

Thomas's virtue of prudence likewise centers on reasoning about the means used to achieve ends, but it differs from the instrumental reasoning of economists in crucial ways. First, it takes the end as given to us (namely, the realization of our creation to the image and likeness of God) rather than as being defined by our unreflective desires. Although the end is given to us, the function of prudence is to discern what that end looks like in the specific circumstances of a given human life. Part of living out our creation to the image of God is to become virtuous human beings, but that leaves open the question of what a virtuous response to various situations entails. This leads to the second point, which is that the means cannot be understood apart from the end. The path toward virtue is simply the practice of virtue. Because of the particularities involved in each individual life, virtuous practices cannot be set down as some sort of code to be followed. It involves discernment of the order of things, discernment of oneself, and a judgment of how to fit one to the other. Under the economic model of practical reason, the means are fungible because all that matters is whether or not they most efficiently move us toward the end. By contrast, under Thomas's understanding of prudence, the means themselves are part of the end.[47]

To go back to the example of the dishwasher, under the economists' model of practical reason, we get the dishwasher if we think it's an efficient way of maximizing our utility, but there's nothing intrinsic to the dishwasher as a dishwasher that determines what our utility is. Under Thomas's understanding of prudence, one family might prudentially judge that getting a dishwasher could not be part of the basic aim of living together virtuously as a family, because it would distract from values important to the family, while another family might prudentially judge that getting a dishwasher facilitates their way of practicing virtue (i.e., by entertaining) and that it is fitting to get it because there is nothing in the dishwasher that is incompatible with the aims of the family. The meaning (and value) of the dishwasher depends on the way it is fit into the overall pattern of the family's life.

Thus we have some key contrasts. Economic logic is a matter of calculation, whereas prudence is a matter of discernment. Economic logic lends itself to choices made in piecemeal fashion, whereas prudence judges how the particulars fit into the overall pattern of a virtuous life. Economic logic sees goods as fungible and measures them by the single metric of "utility," whereas prudence respects the qualitative differences of goods and functions by fitting those diverse goods into an orderly and harmonious pattern. Economic logic sees choice as a matter of trade-offs; whereas prudence sees choice as being more like the artist's discernment that painting a central figure with a blue robe rather than a red robe better fits the overall meaning and mood of the painting.

Not surprisingly, Thomas's understanding of the virtue of prudence harmonizes with his understanding of the nature of God's creation. Recall that God represents himself in a finite world by using the qualitative differences in individual goods as a way of representing his superabundant goodness and by ordering those heterogeneous goods together harmoniously as a way of representing his oneness. In exercising prudence, we enter into a pattern of thinking that respects the diversity of good and the unity expressed by their proper ordering. In seeing that order and acting on it, we move to conform ourselves to the image and likeness of God.

The third note that we can take from Thomas as a part of a theology of consumption would be to recognize that our decisions about which goods to deploy in service of our pursuit of human flourishing are not made solely as individuals. We are social creatures, and part of living together is sharing common notions of what constitutes human flourishing. Our culture sets the boundaries within which we can discern a pattern of living that is harmonious with the aim of living virtuously. Thus, for example, although we live in a culture that celebrates freedom of choice and individual expression, it remains the case that there are many choices we cannot make. There are many different styles of dress I can choose, but I cannot choose to wear a toga to work if it strikes my fancy. For our purposes, the significant feature of the fact that social norms constrain our choices is the problem of rising standards of living noted above. If we were to discern that a simpler standard of living would be a more virtuous form of life, it is not within our power as individuals to implement it without regard for the social norms. To the extent that we live in a culture that understands practical reason as a matter of economic logic rather than prudence, which values income apart from the question of the good to which that income is put, and which has ever-growing standards of living that are as a result not obviously in service of genuine human flourishing, it can be very difficult for us as individuals to consume in a virtuous manner. We can see one model for handling that difficulty in the Amish, who live apart from the wider society. Christians living within that wider society but who wish to think about consumption along the lines I have sketched would need to find some sort of community that could sustain social norms that are compatible with economically virtuous lives. It is not clear what that would look like in practice. But I raise this point as a reminder that we ought not expect individuals to be able to adopt on their own the sort of virtuous consumption I have suggested here.

Taken as a whole, a theology of consumption developed along the lines I have sketched here would allow us to distinguish between that which is necessary to us and that which constitutes our abundance, without necessarily committing ourselves to static standards of living. At the same time, the insistence that the addition of new goods and services to our standard of living be determined based on the way it harmoniously fit into our pattern of living would serve as a restraint against the compulsion to simply seek growth in income for its own sake. That in turn would allow us to answer the calls of Catholic social teaching more readily.

Conclusion

To return to the issues with which we began, the question of what constitutes a virtuous orientation to material goods is not unconnected with how we understand the relationship between our temporal good and our final end. If Thomas is right that we have a proper infinite desire for God and a proper finite desire for material goods, then it should not be surprising that a secular culture that identifies temporal flourishing as our final end would come to think of our desire for material things as endless.

The *Compendium* explicitly links these problems to our loss of a "metaphysical perspective" that manifests itself as "the loss of a longing for God."[48] As we consider how best to offer the fruits of Catholic reflection on social matters to our culture, we need to recognize that the task is profoundly complicated by the fact that the culture we address does not share our metaphysical perspective. In this paper I have merely indicated some of the difficulties involved. By identifying some of the features of the gulf that lies between us and Thomas, I hope to have indicated why it is important to think about historical context. The question of how to bridge that gulf is a difficult one. A better understanding of the road that led from Thomas's world to our own would be helpful. But in closing, it is worth observing that Pope John Paul II, whose writings form the backbone of the sections of the *Compendium* that deal with the necessity of setting our social reflections within an explicitly theological framework, himself frequently argued that the Catholic tradition is best witnessed to by the way we lead our lives. Thus, whatever insights may be gained by probing and testing the fundamental hypothesis of the True Wealth of Nations project that the economic and cultural criteria identified in the tradition of Catholic social thought provide an effective path to sustainable prosperity for all from a Thomistic perspective, both the means to be applied and the goal to be sought must be consciously located within the ordering of all temporal goods toward our ultimate good. Evangelization and our hope to build a better world go hand in hand.

NOTES

1. Charles Taylor, *A Secular Age*. Additionally, Taylor identifies a third common characterization of secularization as the process in which there is a decline in religious observance and belief within the population. The United States is a secular society with respect to the first two characterizations, but not with respect to the last. My own use of the term "secular" does *not* conform to this third characterization. (In other words, the United States is quite secular on my terms, although religious belief and practice continues to flourish here).

2. Alasdair MacIntyre, Three Rival Versions of Moral Enquiry, 58–81.

3. Henri de Lubac, *Augustinianism and Modern Theology*, provides an influential history of the development of this reading of Thomas, which he contested. Although de Lubac's own solution to the theological problems he saw in neo-Thomism provoked widespread debate, his rejection of "extrinsicism" has come to be widely shared as we

see in the works of both Karl Rahner and Hans Urs von Balthasar as is his association of extrinsicism with the secularism that prevails in the modern world.

4. Étienne Gilson is a major figure in this revival. See, for example, his *History of Christian Philosophy*.

5. My reading of Thomas is informed by Servais Pinckaers, *The Sources of Christian Ethics*; Jean-Pierre Torrell, O.P., *Saint Thomas Aquinas*; MacIntyre, *Three Rival Versions of Moral Enquiry*; Denys Turner, *Faith, Reason and the Existence of God*; Denis J. M. Bradley, *Aquinas on the Twofold Human Good*; and especially Robert Sokolowski, *The God of Faith and Reason*. For Sokolowski, Thomas is a good exemplar of a mode of theological thinking that characterizes the entire Christian tradition up until Thomas. See also Kathryn Tanner, *God and Creation in Christian Theology*, for a description of the theological framework I will invoke that sees Thomas as an exemplar of a larger tradition.

6. As Mark D. Jordan, in "The Summa's Reform of Moral Teaching," observes, the tendency to read the treatises of the *Summa Theologiae* without reference to the whole began almost immediately, with the parts of the *Summa* circulating separately. Indeed, Thomas's *Summa* was one of the last of the genre and was largely replaced in the following generation by the genre of the disputed questions, a genre that militates against the sort of holistic reading necessary in order to sustain Thomas's vision of the integration of philosophy and theology.

7. MacIntyre, *Three Rival Versions of Moral Enquiry*, chaps. 4–6, provides a detailed discussion of this.

8. All references to St. Thomas Aquinas, *The Summa Theologica*, will be noted in the text, hereafter abbreviated as *ST*.

9. Although the teachings on economics are in the *secunda pars*, the fact that we need to understand God in order to understand our advance to God means that the material in the *prima pars* is often quite relevant. Further, the *tertia pars* offers discussions of Christ's life, which also shed light on Thomas's understanding of our proper attitude toward temporal flourishing in general and material well-being in particular.

10. Sokolowski, The God of Faith and Reason, 12.

11. Questions 3 through 11 of the *prima pars* seem to be about positive statements about God—that is, that he is simple, that he is perfect, and so on. But as Thomas himself states in the prologue cited here, these are all questions that discuss how God is not, not how God is. Thus, what Thomas means by "simplicity" is that God is not "composite."

12. See Henk J. M. Schoot, *Christ the "Name" of God*, for a good discussion of the importance of grammar for understanding Thomas's theology.

13. Erich Przywara (1889–1973) is the theologian most responsible for reviving our understanding of the centrality of the *analogia entis* to traditional Catholic thought. See Thomas F. O'Meara, O.P., *Erich Przywara, S.J.*, 65–148, for a good discussion of the richness of Przywara's reflections on *analogia entis*.

14. It is useful as we think about God's intimate presence to each created being to remind ourselves of God's uniqueness. Because God has a mode of being

("simplicity") that is radically distinct from the mode of being of created beings ("compositeness"), we need to guard against thinking of God as a being that can be thought of as existing alongside other beings, only greater in some way. The uniqueness of God means there is no scale common to God and to creatures. Because of this, God can be more interior to us than we are to ourselves without thereby negating or overwhelming our existence. The absence of a shared scale means there is no competition between God and creation. This is the thought that makes it possible to believe that Jesus' divinity in no way threatens to displace or crowd out his humanity.

15. Thomas's treatment of providence in the *Summa Contra Gentiles* is his clearest exposition on the subject. The points above draw on chaps. 64–67; 70–79. Hereafter, references to the *Summa Contra Gentiles* will be noted in the text following the abbreviation: *SCG*.

16. See Daniel Westberg, *Right Practical Reason*, chap. 16, for a discussion of the connection between providence and the virtue of prudence.

17. Thus, Thomas associates the gift of counsel with the virtue of prudence (*ST*, II-II, 52).

18. See, for example, Susan Bordo, *The Flight to Objectivity*, and especially Evelyn Fox Keller, *A Feeling for the Organism*.

19. Thomas uses the locution "to the image of God" rather than "in the image of God" because Thomas focuses on the telos, the goal or end, of human beings. God created us that we would become his image, but we do not fully realize that image until we are perfected in the beatific vision.

20. See D. Juvenal Merriell, *To the Image of the Trinity*, for a good discussion of the Augustinian nature of Thomas's teaching on the *imago Dei*.

21. Torrell, *St. Thomas Aquinas*, 90–94.

22. This puts Thomas in tension with much of modern thought. Alasdair MacIntyre, *After Virtue*, offers an account of how the loss of a teleological framework for understanding moral theory has rendered our moral discourse chaotic, and he is very helpful in understanding how the teleological framework can work. Although he remains somewhat distant from Thomas in *After Virtue*, MacIntyre's pursuit of this line of thought led him back to Thomas, as is evident in his *Three Rival Versions of Moral Enquiry*.

23. Bradley, Aquinas on the Twofold Human Good, xii.

24. Ibid., 514–34.

25. Pontifical Council for Justice and Peace, *Compendium of the Social Doctrine of the Church*, para. 323.

26. Ibid., 324.

27. David B. Burrell, *Deconstructing Theodicy*, offers a lovely reflection on the way the book of Job deconstructs attempts to rationalize God's ways, especially when it comes to the question of suffering.

28. Vatican Council II, *Gaudium et Spes*, para. 69. As will be discussed below, this is a shift from Thomas's argument that we should be prepared to give out of our "abundance," that is, out of that which is left over after our needs have been met. For a

fuller discussion of the reason for this shift, see Mary L. Hirschfeld, "Standard of Living and Economic Virtue," 61–77.

29. We should not think of sacrifices like this as an exchange wherein we give up temporal flourishing in order to "earn" our highest beatitude. It is rather that, confident in our hope of receiving beatitude, we are able to be more generous with the lower good of temporal flourishing.

30. Pontifical Council for Justice and Peace, *Compendium of the Social Doctrine of the Church*, para. 324.

31. It is worth noting in this regard that the *Compendium* does situate itself in an explicitly theological setting. The difficulties I refer to are what happens when the principles laid out in that document get lifted out of their theological context and offered up to secular audiences without further clarification.

32. See Andrew Yuengert's essay in this volume.

33. For the sake of simplicity I'm collapsing all the spiritual and intellectual pursuits under the broad umbrella of "human virtue." It would not be difficult to incorporate some notion of personal initiative or good social relationships under that rubric. So the contrast here is really between material goods and everything else.

34. See Andrew Yuengert's essay in this volume.

35. Mary L. Hirschfeld, "The Old Home Economics."

36. Hazel Kyrk, A Theory of Consumption.

37. Like many women economists of her day, Kyrk found employment in the discipline of home economics in which one of the tasks was to train young women in how to run their households efficiently.

38. Mary L. Hirschfeld, "Methodological Stance and Consumption Theory," 191–211.

39. Adam Smith, The Theory of Moral Sentiments, 124.

40. Adam Smith, The Wealth of Nations.

41. Ibid., 3.

42. Ibid., 340–41.

43. Istvan Hont and Michael Ignatieff, "Needs and Justice in the *Wealth of Nations*," 1–5.

44. Mary L. Hirschfeld, "Standard of Living and Economic Virtue."

45. Stephen A. Marglin, *The Dismal Science*, 212–14.

46. Tibor Scitovsky, Human Desire and Economic Satisfaction, 70–82.

47. Jean Porter, *The Recovery of Virtue*, pp. 156–162.

48. Pontifical Council for Justice and Peace, *Compendium*, 554.

REFERENCES

Aquinas, Thomas. *Summa Contra Gentiles*. Translated by Vernon J. Bourke. Notre Dame, IN: University of Notre Dame Press, 1975.
———. *Summa Theologica*. Translated by Fathers of the English Dominican Province. New York: Benzinger Brothers, 1947.

————. *The Summa Theologica*. Translated by Fathers of the English Dominican Province. Allen, TX: Christian Classics, 1991.

————. "Watering the Earth from Things Above..." In *Selected Writings, The Classics of Western Spirituality*, edited by Albert and Thomas, translated by Simon Tugwell, 355–60. New York; Mahwah: Paulist Press, 1988.

Barrera, Albino. *Economic Compulsion and Christian Ethics*. New York: Cambridge University Press, 2005.

Bordo, Susan. *The Flight to Objectivity: Essays on Cartesianism and Culture*. Albany, NY: State University of New York Press, 1987.

Bradley, Denis J. M. *Aquinas on the Twofold Human Good: Reason and Human Happiness in Aquinas's Moral Science*. Washington, DC: The Catholic University of America Press, 1997.

Burrell, David B. *Deconstructing Theodicy*. Grand Rapids, MI: Brazos Press, 2008.

Fox Keller, Evelyn. *A Feeling for the Organism: The Life and Work of Barbara McClintock*. New York: Freeman, 1983.

Gilson, Étienne. *History of Christian philosophy in the Middle Ages*. New York: Random House, 1955.

Hirschfeld, Mary L. "Methodological Stance and Consumption Theory: A Lesson in Feminist Methodology." *History of Political Economy, Annual Supplement to 29* (1997): 191–211.

————. "The Old Home Economics: Hazel Kyrk's Institutionalist Theory of Consumption." Paper presented at the History of Economics Society Conference at Babson College, Massachusetts, 1994.

————. "Standard of Living and Economic Virtue: Forging a Link between St. Thomas Aquinas and the Twenty-First Century." *Journal of the Society of Christian Ethics* 26, no, 1 (Spring—Summer 2006): 61–77.

Hont, Istvan, and Michael Ignatieff. "Needs and Justice in the *Wealth of Nations*: An Introductory Essay." In *Wealth and Virtue: The Shaping of Political Economy in the Scottish Enlightenment*, edited by Istvan Hont and Michael Ignatieff, 1–44. Cambridge: Cambridge University Press, 1983.

Jordan, Mark D. "The Summa's Reform of Moral Teaching—and Its Failures." In *Contemplating Aquinas: On the Varieties of Interpretations*, edited by Fergus Kerr, O.P., 41–54. Notre Dame, IN: University of Notre Dame Press, 2003.

Kyrk, Hazel. *A Theory of Consumption*. Boston: Houghton Mifflin, 1923.

Lubac, Henri de, S.J. *Augustinianism and Modern Theology*. New York: Crossroad, 2000.

MacIntyre, Alasdair. *After Virtue*. 2nd ed. Notre Dame, IN: University of Notre Dame Press, 1984.

————. *Three Rival Versions of Moral Enquiry: Encyclopaedia, Genealogy, and Tradition*. Notre Dame, IN: University of Notre Dame Press, 1990.

Marglin, Stephen A. *The Dismal Science: How Thinking Like an Economist Undermines Community*. Cambridge, MA: University of Harvard Press, 2008.

Merriell, D. Juvenal. *To the Image of the Trinity: A Study in the Development of Aquinas Teaching*. Toronto, ON: Pontifical Institute of Mediaeval Studies, 1990.

O'Meara, Thomas F., O.P. *Erich Przywara, S.J.: His Theology and His World*. Notre
Dame, IN: University of Notre Dame Press, 2002.

Pinckaers, Servais, O.P. *The Sources of Christian Ethics*. Translated by Sr. Mary Thomas
Noble, O.P. Washington, DC: The Catholic University of America Press, 1995.

Placher, William C. *The Domestication of Transcendence: How Modern Thinking about
God Went Wrong*. Louisville, KY: Westminster John Knox Press, 1996.

Pontifical Council for Justice and Peace. *Compendium of the Social Doctrine of the
Church*. Washington, DC: United States Conference of Catholic Bishops, 2004.

Porter, Jean. *The Recovery of Virtue: The Relevance of Aquinas for Christian Ethics*.
Louisville, KY: Westminster John Knox Press, 1990.

Schoot, Henk J. M. *Christ the "Name" of God: Thomas Aquinas on Naming Christ*.
Leuven: Peeters, 1993.

Scitovsky, Tibor. *Human Desire and Economic Satisfaction: Essays on the Frontiers of
Economics*. Brighton, Sussex: Wheatsheaf Books, 1986.

Smith, Adam. *An Inquiry into the Nature and Causes of the Wealth of Nations*. New York:
Modern Library, 1937.

————. *The Theory of Moral Sentiments*. Amherst, NY: Prometheus Books, 2000.

Sokolowski, Robert. *The God of Faith and Reason*. Washington, DC: The Catholic
University of America Press, 1995.

Tanner, Kathryn. *God and Creation in Christian Theology: Tyranny or Empowerment?*
Oxford, UK: Basil Blackwell, 1988.

Taylor, Charles. *A Secular Age*. Cambridge, MA: The Belknap Press of Harvard
University Press, 2007.

Torrell, Jean-Pierre, O.P. *Saint Thomas Aquinas: Volume 2, Spiritual Master*. Translated
by Robert Royal. Washington, DC: The Catholic University of America Press,
1996.

Turner, Denys. *Faith, Reason and the Existence of God*. Cambridge, UK: University of
Cambridge Press, 2004.

Vatican Council II. "Gaudium et Spes." In *Catholic Social Thought: The Documentary
Heritage*, edited by David J. O'Brien and Thomas A. Shannon, 166–237.
Maryknoll, NY: Orbis, 1992.

Westberg, Daniel. *Right Practical Reason: Aristotle, Action, and Prudence in Aquinas*.
Oxford: Clarendon Press, 1994.

8

Wealth Creation, Social Virtues, and Sociality

Social Capital's Role in Creating and Sustaining Wealth

John A. Coleman, S.J.

From the beginning of the discipline, the founding fathers of sociology, Max Weber and Emile Durkheim, showed genuine interest in the creation and sustenance of wealth. At the same time, Catholic social thought on economic life has always refused to divorce economic actions of individuals from their social matrix. For example, moral concerns about the apparently "economic" issue of income inequality are made even more important by the ways in which such inequalities tend to undermine the right to equal participation and voice on the part of minorities marginalized by their economic standing. Thus it is quite appropriate that the True Wealth of Nations project should engage sociological thought in considering its fundamental hypothesis, that "the economic and cultural criteria identified in the tradition of Catholic social thought should provide an effective path to sustainable prosperity for all."

Sociology and the Creation and Sustenance of Wealth

In his Protestant ethic thesis, Max Weber stood Marx on his head by arguing that the cultural "superstructure" was absolutely essential to produce the economic "substructure" of capitalism. For Weber, the moral values inculcated by Puritanism, in particular, virtues such as honesty and reciprocity that transcended sib and family, made the modern capitalist world possible.

As Weber argues it, culture is a kind of uncaused cause of a great historical transformation in wealth production, the outcome of "charisma."[1] Weber reminds us that there are "economically relevant" causes and effects that are not "economically determined." Too often, these remain thought of as externalities. Recent scholars, picking up from Weber, contend that contemporary parallels to the Puritan ethic can be found among Pentecostal converts in Latin America who improve their economic status by embracing thrift, sobriety, and a work ethic.[2]

Like Weber, both Emile Durkheim and Alexis de Tocqueville lifted up what might seem "externalities" to economic contracts to raise issues of the primarily social matrix and consequences of wealth creation. Thus, in his classic, *The Division of Labor in Society*, Durkheim critiques Herbert Spencer and other theorists who overemphasized "the contract" as the radical source of society. For Durkheim, contractual solidarities in economics very much depend on a prior organic social solidarity. Because "there is nothing less constant than interest, such a cause can only give rise to transient relations and passing associations," society predates any contract and contracts presuppose a pre-existing solidarity:[3]

> For everything in the contract is not contractual. The only arrangements which deserve this name are those which have been desired by the individuals and which have no other origin except in this manifestation of free will. Inversely, every obligation which has not been mutually consented to has nothing contractual about it. But wherever a contract exists, it is submitted to regulation which is the work of society and not that of individuals and which becomes ever more voluminous and more complicated.[4]

Alexis de Tocqueville was primarily interested in democracy, associational life, and liberty, but in places he connected these with economic prosperity. He seemed to think that extensive social and local institutions not only safeguard liberty but also spur prosperity and progress. A recent study employed Tocqueville's theory to argue that the contemporary French economy suffers from overcentralization and a lack of spontaneously generated, smaller, innovative entrepreneurial business precisely because France lacks the kind of complex associational life Tocqueville observed in America.[5] As we will see, Catholic social thought, like Tocqueville, links economic prosperity to justice as participation and a vigorous associational life.[6]

Of course, even at the very source of modern economic thinking, Adam Smith linked his *The Wealth of Nations* to a social matrix of virtue, justice, and solidarity outlined in his *The Theory of Moral Sentiments*.[7] Like Durkheim,

Smith thought interest was legitimate and real in the process of wealth creation and the division of labor in a market economy, but he also understood that interest rests upon both preexisting organic solidarities in society and personal virtues, such as justice and benevolence. Economists, all too often, fail to recognize the relation between *The Wealth of Nations* and *The Theory of Moral Sentiments*. And as Stefano Zamagni argues in his essay in this volume, the economic creativity of fourteenth-century Franciscans reminds us that the capitalist markets that have developed over the last few centuries are not the only way markets can be organized.

Three sections remain in this chapter. The first evokes and expands the notion of social capital and argues that it plays an essential role in wealth creation. This provides a more substantive treatment of themes identified in other essays in this volume. Andrew Yuengert deals briefly with the social capital literature, and Simona Beretta recommends "a relational approach to the family, seen as a form of social capital in itself but also as an institution that contributes to social capital." Gunneman also has a brief evocation of social capital. Thus, the concept seems to need a more extended treatment.

The argument that social capital brings to discussions of wealth creation and sustenance is the homely truth that relationships matter. In a certain sense, social capital recapitulates the early concerns of Weber, Durkheim, and Tocqueville. Like Weber, social capital emphasizes the role of virtue (trust, honesty, a work ethic) in wealth creation. Following Durkheim, social capital plays up spontaneous, noncontractual sociabilities. Social capital theorists link it to Tocqueville's stress on "civil society" and an associational life located midway between state and family.

The second section examines arguments made for social capital and virtue by economist Francis Fukuyama's *Trust: The Social Virtues and the Creation of Prosperity*, the literature on social capital within firms and the use of social capital in World Bank strategies for wealth creation in developing countries.[8] A third section, a concluding coda, locates the literature on social capital in relation to Catholic social thought and, once again, addresses this volume's guiding proposition: "The economic and cultural criteria identified in the tradition of Catholic social thought provide an effective path to sustainable prosperity for all."

The Role of Social Capital in Wealth Production and Sustenance

The core argument for those who evoke social capital is that it is vitally important for the functioning of modern economies and is the indispensable root of stable liberal democracies. Social capital has been given a number of different definitions. For our purposes, a key element is the noun "capital." Physical or monetary capital is potential wealth that, when invested, creates new wealth. By analogy, human capital is a stock of skills and abilities, created by investment in various forms of education, that serve to increase productivity and wealth. Social capital refers to both the networks (who we know and are connected with) and the concomitant virtues of solidarity and trust, which, when plumbed and invested, generate new wealth. As we will see, some definitions of social capital tend to decouple civil society or networks from capital. Others insist on their close bonding.

The central thesis of social capital theory is that "relationships matter." Social networks constitute a valuable asset. Interaction enables people to build up communities, engage in commitment to one another, and knit or mend the social fabric. A sense of belonging and the real experience of being embedded in social networks (and the relationships of trust and tolerance these usually involve) can bring great benefits to people. Evidence exists that communities with a plentiful stock of social capital are more likely to have lower crime rates, improved health, higher educational achievement, greater volunteering, and stronger economic growth. Christopher Beem captures this nexus between social capital and political and economic flourishing:

> Trust between individuals thus becomes trust between strangers and trust of a broad fabric of social institutions; ultimately, it becomes a shared set of values, virtues, and expectations within society as a whole. Without this interaction, on the other hand, trust decays; at a certain point, this decay begins to manifest itself in enormous social problems. The concept of social capital contends that building or re-building community and trust requires face-to-face encounters.[9]

For preliminary purposes we can adopt this following definition of social capital from Francis Fukuyama:

> Social capital is an instantiated informal norm that promotes cooperation between two or more individuals. The norms that constitute social capital can range from a norm of reciprocity between two or more friends, all the way up to complex and elaborately articulated doctrines like Christianity or Confucianism. They must be instantiated in an actual human relationship: the norm of reciprocity exists *in potentia* in my dealings with all people, but is actualized only in my dealings with *my* friends [or networks of connections]. By this definition, trust, networks, civil society and the like which have been associated with social capital are all epiphenomenal, arising as a

result of social capital but not constituting social capital itself. Not just any set of instantiated norms constitutes social capital: they must lead to cooperation in groups and therefore are related to traditional virtues like honesty, the keeping of commitments, reliable performance of duties, reciprocity and the like.[10]

It should be noted that, in Fukuyama's definition, social capital always consists in a relationship. It is not really something an individual can possesses. Social capital seems to involve a focus both on networks and on virtues and norms of solidarity flowing from social integration.

Four Accounts of Social Capital: Lowry, Bourdieu, Coleman, and Putnam

No one knows who first coined the term "social capital." While the phrase is now also used by economists, sociologists popularized its meaning and use. The first use of the expression, it seems, was by L. J. Hanifin, a state supervisor of rural schools in West Virginia. In an essay written in 1916, Hanifin urged the concept to highlight the importance of community involvement for successful schools.[11] The social historian and critic Jane Jacobs referenced the term in the 1960s.[12] French sociologist Pierre Bourdieu evoked the concept in 1972 in his *Outline of a Theory of Practice* and in later writings has returned to the term to clarify it further, by contrasting it to cultural, economic, and symbolic capital.[13] Economist Glenn Loury proposed a use of the term in a 1977 book to help explain racial income differences.[14] James Coleman adopted Loury's definition in work that developed and popularized the concept of social capital.[15] In the late 1990s the concept gained ground and has served as a focus of World Bank research programs and the well-known writings of Robert Putnam.[16] It is helpful to attend briefly to the similarities and differences in the use of the concept by Loury, Bourdieu, Coleman, and Putnam.

Economist Glenn Loury critiqued the narrowly individualistic and atomistic understanding of human capital in neoclassical economic theory. He writes:

> The social context within which individual maturation occurs
> strongly conditions what otherwise equally competent individuals
> can achieve. This implies that absolute equality of opportunity, where
> an individual's chance to succeed depends on his or her innate
> capabilities, is an ideal that cannot be achieved....
>
> An individual's social origin has an obvious and important effect
> on the amount of resources that is ultimately invested in his or her

development. It may thus be useful to employ a concept of
"social capital" to represent the consequences of social position in
facilitating acquisition of the standard human capital
characteristics.[17]

In a sense Loury is here merely restating the obvious. Someone growing up in the South Side of Chicago or in the Bronx does not start from the same position as someone growing up in Glencoe, Illinois, or Manhasset, New York. Loury felt he needed to make the argument because this apparently self-evident statement of reality was not at all evident to human capital theorists. Many of them, following Chicago economist Gary Becker, had misconstrued human capital by severing it from its social nexus.[18] Instead of being understood as the inherently social process that it is—no one goes to school in isolation from the context in which that school is located, administered, and funded—human capital had come to be viewed almost completely as being about individual achievement and motivation, or lack thereof.

The French sociologist Pierre Bourdieu defines social capital in a vaguely Marxist way as closely linked to power. He provides one of the most theoretically sophisticated attempts to use the concept. Bourdieu defines it this way: "social capital is the aggregate of the actual or potential resources which are linked to possession of a durable network of more or less institutionalized relationships of mutual acquaintance and recognition."[19]

Bourdieu relates social to economic and cultural (or symbolic) capital as analytically distinct but interwoven concepts. He draws on the notion of social capital to understand better the production and reproduction of classes and class divisions in society. For Bourdieu, although social capital is constituted by social networks and relationships, it is never completely disconnected from economic capital. Capital, for Bourdieu, simultaneously involves both economic and power relations. The social interactions that constitute or precipitate social capital are not always, however, thought of as economic. Nor are any of the forms of capital, including social capital, ever inherently divided from power. While the possession of social capital does not necessarily follow from the possession of economic capital, in Bourdieu's view, it remains an attribute of elites, a means by which particular networks both hold onto power and advantage and also serve as gatekeepers for access to the network. Not all varieties of social capital—even in networks equivalently thick and dense—are equal. Nor do even equivalently dense networks yield equal access to economic capital.

Bourdieu distinguishes between the social networks an individual is embedded in (and out of which social capital emerges as a distinct relational property) and the outcomes of those social relationships. Social networks, for

Bourdieu, should not simply be equated to the outcomes of those social relationships. This is similar to the point made by Fukuyama in his definition of
social capital cited earlier: "By this definition, trust, networks and civil society
and the like which have been associated with social capital are all epiphenom-
enal, arising as a result of social capital but not constituting social capital itself."
The danger is that some very dense social networks might be rendered invisible
because they are unable to generate resources due to lack of access to economic
capital.

Unlike other theorists, Bourdieu never links social capital to virtue or
notions of civil society. Indeed, he assumes that social capital often functions
to mask naked profit-seeking for its holders and, therefore, is generally inimical to an open democratic society. The advantage of Bourdieu's treatment is
his insistence on connecting social capital to power and class structure in
society. He does not think social capital is always morally beneficial for society.
The weakness of his approach is that, unlike others, such as Putnam's or
Fukuyama's treatment, it neglects the notions of virtue, trust, and the wider
societal—and not just class-based—outcomes of social capital. In the end, like
so many appeals to Marx's thought, Bourdieu's account is stronger as a hermeneutic of suspicion than as a resource for better relations between groups in
society across social divides: what Putnam has called "bridging" and not just
"bonding" social capital.

Sociologist James Coleman was the first real advocate of the concept of
social capital in mainstream sociology, and, like Glen Loury, he stressed its
connection to human capital. Coleman appealed to the concept in several key
comparable studies of private, religious, and public school systems.[20] He
defines social capital in functionalist terms:

> Social capital is defined by its function. It is not a single entity but a
> variety of different entities, with two elements in common: they all
> consist of some aspect of social structures, and they facilitate certain
> actions of actors ... within the structure. Like other forms of capital,
> social capital is productive, making possible the achievement of
> certain ends that in its absence would not be possible. Like physical
> and human capital, social capital is not completely fungible but may
> be specific to certain activities. A given form of social capital that is
> valuable in facilitating certain actions may be useless or even harmful
> for others. Unlike other forms of capital, social capital inheres in the
> structure of relations between actors and among actors.[21]

Coleman's main contribution to the notion of social capital was to show
how it could also function in nonelite groups. He argued, counter to the claims

of Bourdieu, that social capital could also benefit members of the working class. As a theorist who generally relied heavily on "rational choice theory" (i.e., a kind of "economic man" model imported into sociology, assuming rational actors maximize self-interest in a large market of plural choices), Coleman supplemented this narrow model with a notion of social capital as part of his wider exploration of the nature of social structures. Coleman's work highlighted the possibility that some institutions and social structures were better suited to the cultivation of reciprocity, trust, and individual action than others. He lifted up especially the role of the family, kinship networks, and religious institutions in the creation of social capital.

One problem in Coleman's defining social capital by its function is that the same outcome could flow from very different processes. Unlike Bourdieu, who links social capital both to human capital and to physical capital, Coleman uniquely emphasizes its role in the generation of human capital. Nor does Coleman pick up on Bourdieu's link of capital to power. Coleman's definition has also been labeled "fuzzy." As one critic has put it: "Coleman himself started a proliferation by including under the term some of the mechanisms that generated social capital; the consequences of its possession; and the appropriate social organization that provided the context for both sources and effects to materialize."[22] John Field compares Coleman and Bourdieu's thinking about social capital:

> Bourdieu's treatment of social capital is somewhat circular; in summary, it boils down to the thesis that privileged individuals maintain their position by using their connections with other privileged people. Coleman's view is more nuanced in that he discerns the value of connections for all actors, individual and collective, privileged and disadvantaged. But Coleman's view is also naively optimistic; as a public good, social capital is almost entirely benign in its functions, providing for a set of norms and sanctions that allow individuals to cooperate for mutual advantage and with little or no "dark side." Bourdieu's usage of the concept, by contrast, virtually allows only for a dark side for the oppressed and a bright side for the privileged.[23]

More than anyone else, Harvard University political scientist Robert Putnam has popularized the notion of social capital and has been instrumental in its spread into areas of economics.[24] As Putnam explains it:

> Whereas physical capital refers to physical objects and human capital refers to the properties of individuals, social capital refers to

connections among individuals—social networks and the norms of reciprocity and trustworthiness that arise from them. In that sense social capital is closely related to what some have called "civic virtue." The difference is that "social capital" calls attention to the fact that civic virtue is most powerful when embedded in a dense network of reciprocal social relations. A society of many virtuous but isolated individuals is not necessarily rich in social capital.[25]

Putnam outlines the reasons social capital is important. First, by encouraging cooperation (rather than isolated individualism or mere free riding), social capital allows citizens to resolve collective problems more easily. Second, social capital greases the wheels of everyday business and social transactions; they become less time consuming, cumbersome, or costly. Third, social capital expands our awareness of linkages and dependencies beyond the self. Fourth, capital often serves as a conduit for the flow of useful information that facilitates the achievement of our goals.[26]

Not all social capital is equally useful. Putnam distinguishes between "bonding" social capital, which strengthens relationships within a group, and "bridging" social capital, which encompasses more distant ties of like persons. Bonding social capital can become fairly exclusive; it can turn in on itself and lead to a homogeneous in-group that resists outside influences. Bridging social capital is more outward looking and links people across different social divides.[27] Of course, bridging social capital presupposes and builds on some prior variant of bonding social capital.

Critics have objected to Putnam's thesis that social capital is waning in the United States, his tendency to view social capital as almost always a win-win situation, and his insufficient attention to the power relations that play such an important role in intergroup relations. As one critic of Putnam put it, pitting Bourdieu against Putnam: "simply put, certain social networks are in greater positions of power than others, and they can therefore yield much more substantial returns to their numbers when those networks are engaged in social and political conflict."[28]

In his books on social capital in America, Putnam tends to hew closely to a Tocquevillean line about civic virtue and civil society and their connections to a flourishing democracy. But in his earlier book on Italy, Putnam claims a more direct economic impact of social capital on wealth creation. "Studies of the rapidly growing economies of East Asia almost always emphasize the importance of dense social networks so that these economies are sometimes said to represent a new brand of 'network capitalism.' "[29] In comparing the economic prosperity in Northern Italy (with a rich history of city-states and civic associations) and its failure in Southern Italy and Sicily (with its immoral familism and closed circles of trust), Putnam argues: "These communities [in Northern Italy] did not become civic simply because they were rich. The historical record suggests precisely the opposite: they have become rich because they were civic. Development economists take note: civics matters."[30] Stefano Zamagni's essay in this volume addresses this very history as rooted in medieval concerns for the common good. The economist, Francis Fukuyama employs precise comparative studies to argue for this sociological account of the relation between social capital and wealth creation. Before turning to Fukuyama's economic account, I want to summarize the discussion so far and advert to some caveats about our use of the social capital metaphor.

Social Capital: Summary Description and Some Caveats about Its Possible Uses

To summarize, social capital refers to dense networks of interaction anchored in social space between the family and the state, which facilitate access to human capital (skill formation) and wealth opportunities. The distinction between bonding and bridging social capital is critical for understanding the potential of social capital to create wealth for the wider society and not just, as in Bourdieu, to further intraclass solidarity. Social capital also references the concomitant social virtues of trust, honesty, reciprocity, and a cooperative work ethic in successful economies. It encapsulates both a structural and a cognitive/ attitudinal aspect. Social capital should always include some clear linkages to other forms of capital, otherwise it may mistake mere civic associationalism with capital accretion.

There are three caveats to raise about the concept of social capital. The first is a reminder that social capital is a complicated notion, only analogously similar to physical or human capital. It does not become depleted by use (on the contrary!). Being embedded in a dense network of interaction does not always, per se, generate equivalent opportunities for wealth (class and power remain important differentials). Nor should all forms of social capital (e.g., from a bowling club or a labor union or a church) be collapsed into a single category. Social capital generated within religious groups may have unique properties, different from those generated in family networks or wider secular civic associations.[31]

As Putnam observed in his original essay "Bowling Alone," "social capital is not a uni-dimensional concept."[32] Thus, there may be dangers employing the language of capital. Not everything of value should be called capital. As we saw, Weber and Tocqueville did not use the word "capital" when addressing these issues. The term may blind us to deeper sociological aspects of group formation. It runs the danger of skewing our consideration of social phenomena and goods toward a utilitarian and narrow economic model. The notion of capital, moreover, brings with it a whole set of concomitant discourses and may link it, in contemporary discussions, to capitalism currently institutionalized.

Because it is not a unidimensional concept, we need to distinguish three elements within the notion of social capital: (1) a structural element (i.e., a network of interconnectivity and sociality); (2) a cognitive element (i.e., the claim that economic prosperity depends on an underlying nexus of social relations), and (3) a moral and/or affective component (i.e., the existence of trust and the other social virtues). It remains an empirical question how closely these three in any given case are correlated. Robust claims about the role of social capital in creating and sustaining wealth presuppose a close relationship between the structural and the moral/affective components.

A second caveat reminds us that social capital is hard to measure. Putnam and Fukuyama have tried to address this issue of differing ways to measure the amounts or extent of social capital.[33] Because it is difficult to measure and because it entails externalities more often than do other forms of capital, social capital is often dismissed in economic thought. As Fukuyama notes:

> The case could probably be made that social capital is the most intangible of all intangible assets and tends to be consistently under-valued by markets because it is so difficult to measure. Many mergers and acquisitions have involved radical down-sizing of company work forces. This achieved cost savings in terms of current wages, but undermined trust and, therefore, social capital among the firm's remaining workers—a process regularly known as "dumb-sizing." Wall Street is obviously better able to measure the immediate labor cost savings than the longer term impacts of such actions on the firm's social capital.[34]

Finally, social capital is too often thought of as something universally beneficial. We need to remember the possible shadow side of social capital. Social capital may not always be invested toward positive ends; consider the social capital in the Mafia or Ku Klux Klan. There are potentially four negative effects from social capital: (1) without bridging social capital, bonding groups can become isolated and can develop a strong in-group, out-group ethos; (2) for some marginalized groups or isolated individuals, only some form of bridging social capital will allow significant increases in social capital; (3) the bonding of certain groups together can be based on insular ties, a common radical ideal that disrupts social integration; (4) strong social capital in intermediate groups can overpower weak political institutions and democracy.

To prevent the reader from getting lost in these diverging, sometimes overlapping, sometimes contradictory uses of social capital in the sociological literature, a very simple working definition may be helpful: the idea behind social capital is that polities "with high civic participation, good channels of communication, widely shared cooperative norms and high levels of trust are the polities that prosper" economically.[35]

Economic Applications of the Sociological Concept of Social Capital

Francis Fukuyama

It would be very difficult to find a better primer and exemplification of the contribution of sociological thought to economists' conversation about wealth creation and sustenance than Francis Fukuyama's *Trust: The Social Virtues and the Creation of Prosperity*. Fukuyama mines Weber, Tocqueville, Coleman, and Putnam to make an impressive case for the power of culture and societal structures in the making of economic society. The wide range of his comparative analysis is impressive: overseas Chinese economies in Taiwan, Hong Kong, and Singapore; Korea; Japan; Italy, France, and Germany; and the United States. Social capital (which Fukuyama simplifies a bit by equating it with trust, on the one hand, and associational forms of spontaneous sociability, on the other) not only plays a key role in wealth creation but also predicts, to a large extent, the scale and organizational forms an economy will take.

Fukuyama also mounts the most basic economic arguments for social capital: it reduces transaction costs; it allows greater scale in organization without involving direct state intervention in the economy; it bolsters morale in the workplace, allowing cooperative forms (teams) of enhanced productivity; it significantly reduces the classic free-rider problem by reducing individualism; and because of shared norms and trust, it allows a society to rely less on laws to control behavior. Distrust imposes a kind of tax on all forms of economic activity.

A few illuminating citations from Fukuyama's argument will provide a helpful beginning prior to moving on to his comparative data:

> Law, contract and economic rationality provide a necessary but not sufficient basis for both the stability and prosperity of post-industrial societies. They must as well be leavened with reciprocity, moral

obligation, duty toward community and trust which are based on habit rather than rational calculation.[36]

The greatest economic efficiency was not necessarily achieved by rational self-interested individuals but rather groups of individuals who, because of a pre-existing moral community, were able to work effectively.[37]

Social capital needs to be factored into a nation's resource endowment. A high trust society can organize its workplace on a more flexible and group oriented basis with more responsibility delegated to lower levels of organization.[38]

Rational utility maximization is not enough to give a full or satisfactory account of why successful economies prosper or unsuccessful ones stagnate and decline. The degree to which people value work over leisure, their respect for education, attitudes toward the family and the degree of trust they show toward their fellow—all have a direct impact on economic life and yet cannot be adequately explained in terms of the economist's basic model of man. Capitalism is facilitated when its individualism is balanced by a readiness to associate.[39]

Fukuyama turns to comparative case studies to bolster his point. He contrasts low-trust societies, which are inordinately family centered (Chinese overseas communities, France, and parts of Italy), to high-trust societies with a wide associational ethos and institutionalized intermediate groups (Japan, Germany, the United States)."

Societies that have very strong families but relatively weak bonds of trust among people unrelated to one another will tend to be dominated by small family-owned and managed businesses. On the other hand, countries that have vigorous private non-profit organizations like schools, hospitals, churches and charities are also likely to develop strong private economic institutions that go beyond the family.[40]

While nearly all economic endeavors started out as family businesses, in some societies, such family businesses predominate and manifest systematic difficulty in moving toward public ownership and management. Consider, for example, the small scale of private enterprises (prescinding from state-owned or -promoted businesses) in Hong Kong, Taiwan, and Singapore. Virtually all private sector businesses in these overseas Chinese economies are family owned and family managed. Chinese society has high trust within family but much lower trust toward outsiders. It is relatively difficult in these overseas Chinese societies to move to vigorous forms of widely held stock ownership of firms. One drawback in such family business organizations is generational—the so-called *Buddenbrooks* phenomenon, in which, by the third generation of a wealthy business family, it often becomes difficult to pass on the business or replicate the founder's entrepreneurial skills and innovation. Family businesses generally do not achieve the size and scale of large publicly owned corporations. Scale is not always, to be sure, a benefit but seems essential in some industries (e.g., pharmaceuticals, energy, and aircraft and auto manufacturing). Family firms are limited in scale.

Fukuyama notes that Italy tends to spawn smaller family-based firms, a kind of Italian parallel to the Chinese overseas societies. Italy has fewer larger firms than comparable European economies. However, in some cases, as in the famous terza Italia (Tuscany, Umbria, and Emilia-Romagna), small, craft-oriented, high-tech firms have prospered because of their flexible specialization. These firms show that intense competition (as in California's Silicon Valley) can sometimes occur along with the cooperative sharing of ideas. These Italian firms, in close proximity to one another and in special economic niches, share innovations widely and show cooperation similar to that embodied in social capital, something lacking in most Chinese overseas firms. In general, Fukuyama follows the argument about Italian capitalism in Putnam's *Making Democracy Work*. A correlation exists between associational life and economic prosperity in the Italian North and in *terza Italia*, while a lack of prosperity in the South is characterized by "a-moral familism."[41] Italian regional variations in industrial development and economic prosperity "correlate very strongly with the degree of civic community or of spontaneous sociability that prevails in the respective regions. There are family firms in all parts of Italy, but those in the high social capital center have been far more dynamic, innovative and prosperous than those in the South, characterized by pervasive social distrust."[42]

As Tocqueville argued, because France lacks strong intermediate associations between the family and the state, it has inherent constraints on "the French private sector's ability to produce large, strong and dynamic enterprises."[43] Some form of substitute organizations must then be provided by state intervention and subvention, with the usual inefficiencies of state owned enterprises. French familism and dislike of direct face-to-face relationships beyond the family lead to worker reluctance to form teams. Cooperation between workers and managers in France is notoriously dicey. In effect, France has produced two opposed forms of capitalism. One is traditional Catholic, family centered, and producer oriented. The other is Jewish or Protestant and specializes in finance and banking.

Korean economic growth relied heavily, at least at the outset, on government subsidy and control. Without a doubt, Korean network *chaebols* show strong economic performance, but there has been a resistance in family-centered Korea to professional management and public stock ownership; and myriad problems of succession to management have arisen. Yet a long tutelage under Japanese rule predisposed Korea to adapt some organizational forms (the *chaebol* is similar in many ways to Japanese *keiretsu* networks between a firm and its suppliers or across firms), which allow effective networking and economies of scale. The move to adapt these Japanese organizational forms came, however, less from an abundance of social capital than from governmental initiatives, especially those led by former president Park Chung Hee.

Japan, for its part, evolved via a nonfamilial form—the *samurai* society of loyalties that transcend sib and family. Japan has negotiated the move to widely held stock ownership of corporations and to professional management more quickly and successfully than have Chinese or Korean entrepreneurs. As Fukuyama argues, Confucianism transformed itself in moving to Japan, where "loyalty to the *daimyo* trumps loyalty to the family."[44] He also notes that, at the time of the Meiji restoration, Japanese culture experienced a national form of governance in which the actual power holders did not have to correspond to the nominal power holder (the emperor), which had a spill-over effect in the move from smaller-scale family firms to public corporate forms of ownership and management.

Vertical integration in a *keiretsu* social-economic network allows a company, such as Toyota, to upstream its supply chain with contractors and suppliers. Intermarket *keiretsu* networks (across types of companies commonly owned), while not always following market rules for allocation, reduce the free-rider problem and agency costs. Finally, Japan had its own version of Weber's Protestant ethic, in a this-worldly ascetical Buddhist movement ascendant at the time of the Meiji restoration.[45]

Germany, like Japan, is a high-trust society. Its codetermination schemes in industry management favor smooth industrial relations. (For a discussion of the contributions of Catholic thought and culture to this phenomenon, see the essay by Vera Zamagni in this volume.) Germans maintained longer than elsewhere a sense of professionalism, work as a vocation, even in the craft trades:

> There is a high degree of pride in labor on the part of the German
> working class and a sense of professionalism that allows German
> workers to identify not simply with their social class but with their
> industry and its managers. This sense of professionalism and calling
> has moderated the inclination toward class warfare in Germany and

has led to a very different set of workplace relationships than might otherwise have been the case.[46]

As was not the case in France and England, German high-trust workplaces have allowed for flexibility in skills among workers, team organization, and quality circles that have resulted in greater economic productivity.

The United States has a dual heritage of individualism and group orientation. Profoundly nonstatist, Americans have nonetheless been strong proponents of voluntarism and communitarianism. Like Putnam, Fukuyama sees new threats to the classic American associationalism described by Tocqueville. There has been a steady increase in litigation costs and a decline in social trust, and "the balance between individualism and community has shifted dramatically in the United States over the past fifty years."[47]

Fukuyama ends his section on the American economic forms by looking at ways to increase social capital in the United States. He notes how inadequate are the theoretical research and empirical evidence about alternative routes to the creation of social capital or its replenishment when depleted. He argues forcefully that "the most successful forms of modernity are not completely modern."[48] Again, he contends that "a successful market economy, rather than being a cause of stable democracy, is codetermined by the prior factor of social capital."[49] Economists neglect the social sources and matrix of the economy at their peril:

> [Political and economic liberalism] at least in its Hobbsean/Lockean form, is not self sustaining and needs the support of aspects of traditional culture that do not themselves arise out of liberalism. That is, a society built entirely out of rational individuals who come together on the basis of a social contract for the sake of the satisfaction of their wants cannot form a society that would be viable over any length of time. Such a society can provide no motive for any citizen to risk his or her life in defense of the large community, since the purpose of the community was to preserve the individual's life. More broadly, if individuals formed communities only on the basis of rational long-term self-interest, there would be little in the way of public spiritedness, self-sacrifice, pride, charity or any of the other virtues that make communities livable. Indeed, one could hardly imagine a meaningful family life if families were essentially contracts between rational, self-interested individuals.[50]

The one major fault in Fukuyama's excellent mining of sociological resources to rethink the nature of wealth creation and sustenance is his reticence to ask about the role of the economy in hastening the destruction of social capital—and, hence, in its own eventual decline. He fails to probe more deeply how a consumption ethos fostered by the libertarian model can undermine the very social and cultural virtues he posits as essential to wealth creation. Fukuyama knows that it is an act of considerable intellectual hubris to believe that only economic goals in the narrow sense can be considered "rational." Yet, such a belief is widespread in current American economic thinking.

If the goal of a livable society and ultimate long-term economic prosperity rests on spontaneous sociability and social cohesion, we need to ask how particular economic policies and market arrangements affect those qualities for good or ill. Thus, if corporate mergers and takeovers tend to undermine the cohesion of corporations and communities and the larger social good, policy should probably weigh against the supposed efficiencies that result from such mergers and takeovers. Perhaps the United States should follow Japan and discourage such disruptions in its large corporate infrastructure.[51]

Social Capital within Firms

Using the notion of social capital to understand firms and organizations is relatively new. In part, the dominance of more mechanistic and system-oriented conceptions of organizations and their activity has "masked their deeply social nature."[52] As Cohen and Prusak note, a number of students of organizational development have become increasingly suspicious of the "people, processes, technology mantra, ceaselessly intoned as the sources of organizational effectiveness."[53] To be sure, there has been a significant emphasis by business organizational theorists on human capital. Yet those writing about human capital too rarely address the social nature of organizations and frequently fall into the trap of drawing only on theories and metaphors that derive uniquely from financial and physical notions of capital. The argument for social capital in business firms is that, when harnessed, it generates significant economic returns.

The benefits claimed for social capital in businesses include the following:

○ Better sharing of knowledge due to the established trust relationships, and the emergence of common frames of reference;
○ Lower transaction costs due to a higher level of trust and cooperation (both within the organization and between the organization and its customers, suppliers, or partners);
○ Lower turnover rates, reducing severance costs and expenses of hiring and training, avoiding discontinuities associated with frequent personnel changes, and maintaining valuable organizational knowledge;

○ Greater coherence of action due to organizational stability and shared understanding.[54]

Social capital, even if of diverse forms and origins, is part of organizational life in every business firm. The increasing complexity of organizations, the scale of informational activity, globalization, and external and internal volatility of these factors all call for greater attention to social capital *within* firms and not just in societies that host national economies.

The World Bank, Social Capital, and Development

One economic institution that has taken social capital quite seriously is the World Bank, which has commissioned many working papers on social capital and development.[55] Although it would take us too far afield to review this literature in detail, it is worth noting, for example, that World Bank reports have found evidence that schools are more effective when parents and local citizens are actively involved. Teachers are more committed, students achieve higher test scores, and better use is made of school facilities in communities in which parents and citizens take an active interest in children's educational well-being. Yet the Bank also notes some negative effects, attributed to intense bonding social capital when, for example, disgruntled local elites joined together to close health clinics in Uttar Pradesh. As a result, child mortality rates rose dramatically.[56]

The World Bank breaks down its strategic use of social capital (for example, in its Social Capital Implementation Framework) into five key dimensions: (1) Groups and Networks: collections of individuals who promote and protect personal relationships that improve welfare; (2) Trust and Society: elements of interpersonal behavior that foster greater cohesion and more robust joint action; (3) Collective Action and Cooperation: ability of people to work together in resolving communal issues; (4) Social Cohesion and Inclusion: mitigates risks and promotes equitable access to benefits of development by enhancing participation of the marginalized; (5) Information and Communication: breaks down negative social capital and also enables positive social capital by improving access to information. Together, these five dimensions try to capture both the structural (what Fukuyama calls "spontaneous sociability") and the cognitive (what Fukuyama calls "trust and the social virtues") aspects of forms of social capital.[57]

As a result of field work and sponsored research on social capital and development, the World Bank lists the following claims about the relationship between social capital and economic development and provides corroborating research data to justify the generalizations:

- Crime/Violence: Shared values and norms can reduce and keep low the level of community violence. People who have informal relations with their neighbors can look out for one another and "police" their neighborhoods. Transaction costs for providing security are reduced.
- Economics and Trade: Trade at the macro level is influenced by social capital, a common property resource whose value depends on the level of interaction between people.
- Education: Family, community, and state involvement in education improves outcomes.
- Environment: Common property resource management entails cooperation with a view to ensure the sustainability of resources for the benefit of all community members, now and in the future.
- Finance: A stable, secure, and equitable financial system is a precursor to sustainable growth.
- Health, Nutrition, and Population: The lower the trust among citizens, the higher the mortality rate.
- Information Technology: Information technology has the potential to increase social capital—in particular, bridging social capital, which connects actors to resources, relationships, and information beyond their immediate environment.
- Poverty Reduction and Economic Development: Social cohesion in low-income nations encourages a move to sustainable development and economic prosperity.
- Rural Development: Social capital increases rural people's capacity to organize for cooperative development and helps groups perform key developmental tasks more effectively and efficiently.
- Urban Development: Urban areas, with their anonymity and fast pace, can be unconducive to societal development because social capital and trust are more difficult to develop and sustain in large groups.
- Water Supply and Sanitation: Social capital contributes to the sharing of information about sanitation as well as the building of community infrastructure.[58]

Concluding Coda: Catholic Social Thought and Social Capital

Very little systematic thought seems to have been given to the voluminous literature on social capital by those who write about, think through, or teach Catholic social thought. This is a serious lacuna. Nor do those who explore the concept of social capital refer to Catholic social thought. Does this mean, then, that we ought to scuttle the guiding proposition of the True Wealth of Nations project, that "the economic and cultural criteria identified in the tradition of Catholic social thought provide an effective path to sustainable prosperity for all"? By no means! The end of this section will suggest how the literature on social capital and Catholic social thought might enrich each other. But, first, it will be helpful to rehearse the evidence for a larger claim that almost all the main elements present in the social capital concept are found fully and more richly in Catholic social thought.

Consider some elements of Catholic social thought that might provide a useful lens for a rereading of social capital literature on wealth creation, economic development, and wealth sustenance. Clearly, Catholic social thought maintains a strongly social sense of the human as profoundly relational.[59] It distinguishes between state and society and insists, through its doctrine of subsidiarity, on the importance of associational life in civil society. The radical social-relational character of the human means that the right to association (not only for labor unions but also more generally) is not simply derivative from state benevolence. It is an ingredient in the essential sociality of the human. Catholic social thought links subsidiarity to solidarity. Catholic theories of a limited state and a vigorous civil society shy away from state-owned and overly regulated economies. Yet they also stress that there is a social mortgage on all private property and increasingly speak of corporate social responsibility. Catholic notions of corporations link them, as well as the state and other associations in civil society, to the defining and implementing of a societal common good.[60]

In its doctrine of the dignity of human labor, the Catholic tradition insists on active participation of workers in society and the economic order, referenced in its notion of "justice as participation." Papal social encyclicals consistently contend that in spite of the economy's rightful laws of development and semiautonomy from the state and civil society, it must not be thought of as isolated from its social context. As the Catholic slogan famously puts it, the economy must serve people and not the other way around. Catholic social thought on the economy frequently stresses worker codetermination (representation on corporate boards) and a cooperative harmony in the work place among employers and workers, each recognizing their mutual rights and responsibilities. Indeed, Catholic culture and thought have had an impact on the German worker teams and structures Fukuyama refers to, as Vera Zamagni's essay in this volume explores.

Catholic thought on the economy and society, like social capital theory, looks to community and social virtues such as trust, honesty, reciprocity, a productive work ethic, and mutual recognition of the dignity of labor and capital.[61] Like the social capital literature, Catholic thought is likely to turn to the social matrix (most often best limned by sociology) to understand economy and society. Both in the social capital literature and in Catholic social thought, the understanding of the economic agent includes much more than the rational interest-maximizing individual of classic economic fame.

The Mutual Contribution of Social Capital and Catholic Social Thought to Each Other

In summary, Catholic social thought contains two of the three elements of social capital, and it would benefit from the third. As we noted earlier, this multidimensional concept contains three distinct but interrelated elements: (1) a structural element (the existence of relationality and embeddedness in social groups outside the market and the state); (2) a cognitive element (the claim that social capital is essential for the creation and sustenance of wealth); and (3) a moral/affective element (the existence of the trust and other social virtues). It is precisely the second element that Catholic social thought can learn from the social capital literature and that the True Wealth project lifts up for our consideration. In a way, social Catholicism has a very rich doctrine of social capital but neglects to spell out its relationship to wealth creation.

Catholic notions of the common good are much more nuanced and subtle than the thinner social capital concept. Alas, however, as Albino Barrera contends in his essay in this volume, the Catholic tradition often has difficulty in articulating the formal characteristics of the common good. Echoing David Hollenbach, Barrera notes the incomprehensibility of the common good for most economists.[62] As Barrera states the point: "The tradition's social principles are presented at such a general level that they risk becoming irrelevant both in public policy debates and in the conduct of economic life at a practical level." Dialogue with the social capital literature might help make Catholic social principles more concrete, perhaps even measurable in principle.

The social capital literature also helps to make clear the close interrelationship between economic theory and the theory of democratic participation. While contemporary Catholic social thought clearly espouses both a market economy and a participatory democratic form of political life, it often fails to demonstrate the link between the two. A dialogue with the social capital literature might nudge Catholic social thought to make that nexus explicit. As Kenneth Anderson has put it, drawing on social capital theory, that link is essential for any critical understanding of the true workings of a market economy:

> The market and democracy are both sustained by wells of social
> capital that stable material prosperity helps to deepen, but which are

not the moral logic of the market itself. The market of the market-state is not self-sustaining. On the contrary, it requires a form of social life that goes outside it in order to function in the long term. However, loyalty, sacrifice, gratitude to those who came before—these are not the evident virtues of capitalism, but they are necessary virtues in a liberal-democratic-capitalist form of life. Without them, society eats its seed corn, the social capital bequeathed by the past to bless the future.[63]

For its part, Catholic social thought understands sociality, trust, and societal virtues as good in their own right and not just for their utilitarian contribution to wealth creation. As a result it avoids the dangers noted earlier in employing the language of capital. Not everything of value should be called capital. The term runs the danger of skewing our consideration of social phenomena and goods toward a utilitarian and narrowly economic model and of diminishing, in a reductionist way, the richness of social relationality. Catholic social thought, then, can retain all the virtues in the social capital concept without risking their reduction to an individualistic or utilitarian view of economic life. Especially if Catholic social thought engages in dialogue with the social capital literature, the truth of the guiding proposition of the True Wealth project is clear: the economic and cultural criteria identified in the tradition of Catholic social thought provide an effective path to sustainable prosperity for all.

NOTES

1. Max Weber, *The Protestant Ethic and the Spirit of Capitalism*.

2. David Martin, *Tongues of Fire*.

3. Emile Durkheim, *The Division of Labor in Society*, 204.

4. Ibid., 211.

5. Jonah Levy, *Tocqueville's Revenge*; J. L. Benoit and E. Keslassy's *Alexis de Tocqueville* argues that Tocqueville seems to have a notion akin to our current concepts of human capital (in his comparisons of Birmingham and Manchester and his noting the higher pay for skilled labor) and social capital. Cf. also a review of Levy's book, Eugen Weber, "Tocqueville's Revenge," 113–23.

6. Cf. David Hollenbach's chapter, "Justice as Participation," in *Justice, Peace and Human Rights*.

7. Adam Smith, *An Inquiry into the Nature and Causes of the Wealth of Nations*. Adam Smith, *The Theory of Moral Sentiments*.

8. Francis Fukuyama, *Trust*.

9. Christopher Beem, *The Necessity of Politics*, 20.

10. Francis Fukuyama, "Social Capital and Civil Society," 1.

11. For varying uses of the term "social capital," see Alejandro Portes, "Social Capital."

12. Jane Jacobs, *The Death and Life of Great American Cities*.

13. Pierre Bourdieu, *Outline of a Theory of Practice*. Also Pierre Bourdieu, "The Forms of Capital," 241–58.

14. Glenn Loury, "A Dynamic Theory of Racial Income Differences" in *Women, Minorities and Employment Discrimination*, 153–88.

15. James Coleman, "Social Capital in the Creation of Human Capital."

16. Robert Putnam, *Making Democracy Work*. Robert Putnam, *Bowling Alone*.

17. Loury, "A Dynamic Theory," 176.

18. Gary Becker, *Human Capital*.

19. Bourdieu, "The Forms of Capital," 249.

20. James Coleman, et al., *High School Achievement*. James Coleman and Thomas Hoffer, *Public and Private High Schools*. Coleman attributes the superior achievement of Catholic schools in lifting up inner-city students to its store of social capital (eg., the sense of community values and involvement by parents, students, and faculty in supporting the institutions, etc.).

21. James Coleman, "Social Capital in the Creation of Human Capital," S98.

22. Alejandro Portes, "Social Capital," 1–24.

23. John Field, *Social Capital*, 28.

24. See also Robert Putnam, *Democracies in Flux*.

25. Putnam, *Bowling Alone*, 19.

26. Ibid., 288–90.

27. Ibid., 22–23.

28. James De Filippis, "The Myth of Social Capital in Community Development," 791–806. Citation on p. 791. On the same page, De Filippis, unfairly it strikes me, claims that Putnam by "conflating social capital with civil society…divorces social capital from *capital* itself" and claims that Putnam separates social capital from economics. While this seems an arguable assessment of *Bowling Alone*, it misses the centrality of social capital to wealth creation in Italy in Putnam's *Making Democracy Work*.

29. Putnam, *Making Democracy Work*, 38.

30. Ibid., 37.

31. I develop this point in my chapter, "Religious Social Capital," 33–47.

32. Robert Putnam, "Bowling Alone," 71.

33. For Fukuyama on measuring social capital, cf. his "Social Capital and Civil Society," 5–7. Putnam heads the Seguaro Seminar at the John F. Kennedy School of Government, Harvard University, which engages in The Social Capital Benchmark Survey.

34. Fukuyama, "Social Capital and Civil Society," 10.

35. Mark Wickham Jones review of Stein Ringen, *The Liberal Vision*, 9.

36. Fukuyama, *Trust*, 11.

37. Ibid., 21.

38. Ibid., 31.

39. Ibid., 351.

40. Ibid., 49.

41. For immoral familism in Southern Italy, cf. Edward Banfield, *The Moral Basis of a Backward Society.*

42. Fukuyama, *Trust,* 104.

43. Ibid., 114.

44. Ibid., 178.

45. For a classic argument to a Japanese parallel to the Protestant ethic, cf. Robert N. Bellah, *Tokugawa Religion.*

46. Fukuyama, *Trust,* 233.

47. Ibid., 308.

48. Ibid., 352.

49. Ibid., 356.

50. Ibid., 351.

51. For this critique of Fukuyama, see the review of his book by Jonathan Rowe, "Review of Fukuyama's 'Trust,'" 68–69.

52. Don Cohen and Lawrence Prusak, *In Good Company,* 6.

53. Ibid., 8.

54. Ibid., 10.

55. See Paul Collier, *Social Capital and Poverty.* Paul Francis, et al., *Hard Lessons.* Paul Francis, "Social Capital at the World Bank." Christiaan Grootaert and Thierry van Bastelaer, *The Role of Social Capital in Development.*

56. World Bank, "What Is Social Capital?"

57. Ibid.

58. Ibid., http://web.worldbank.org/WBSITE/EXTERNAL/TOPICS/ EXTSOCIALDEVELOPMENT/EXTTSOCIALCAPITAL/0,contentMDK:20186552~me nuPK:418214~pagePK:148956~piPK:216618~theSitePK:401015,00.html. Click on each major heading for links to the research data or papers substantiating the claims.

59. For two sources on Catholic social thought, see my article, "The Future of Catholic Social Thought," (which argues for the need for a richer dialogue between Catholic social thought and the social sciences) in Kenneth Himes et al., eds., *Catholic Social Thought,* and Pontifical Commission on Justice and Peace, *Compendium of the Social Doctrine of the Church.*

60. I treat these topics at some greater length in my essay "A Limited State and a Vibrant Society," 22–53.

61. Among books' treating of Catholic social thought and the economy I have found especially insightful John Medaille, *Vocation of Business.*

62. David Hollenbach, *The Common Good and Christian Ethics,* xiii.

63. Kenneth Anderson's review of Philip Bobbit, *Terror and Consent,* 9.

REFERENCES

Anderson, Kenneth. Review of Philip Bobbit, *Terror and Consent: The Wars for the Twenty-first Century.* London: Allen Lane, 2008. In *The Times Literary Supplement,* July 25, 2008.

Banfield, Edward. *The Moral Basis of a Backward Society*. Glencoe, IL: The Free Press, 1958.

Becker, Gary. *Human Capital*. New York: National Bureau of Economic Research, 1964.

Beem, Christopher. *The Necessity of Politics: Reclaiming American Public Life*. Chicago: University of Chicago Press, 1999.

Bellah, Robert N. *Tokugawa Religion*. Boston: Beacon Press, 1957.

Benoit, J. L., and E. Keslassy. *Alexis de Tocqueville: Textes Economiques—Anthologie Critique*. Paris: Pocket Agora, 2005.

Bourdieu, Pierre. "The Forms of Capital." In *Handbook of Theory and Research for the Sociology of Education*, edited by John Richardson, 241–58. New York: Greenwood, 1985.

———. *Outline of a Theory of Practice*. Cambridge/New York: Cambridge University Press, 1977.

Cohen, Don, and Lawrence Prusak. *In Good Company: How Social Capital Makes Organizations Work*. Boston: Harvard Business School Press, 2001.

Coleman, James. "Social Capital in the Creation of Human Capital." *American Journal of Sociology* 94 (1988): S95–S120.

Coleman, James, and Thomas Hoffer. *Public and Private High Schools: The Impact of Communities*. New York: Basic Books, 1987.

Coleman, James, Thomas Hoffer, and Sally Kilgore. *High School Achievement: Public, Catholic and Private Schools Compared*. New York: Basic Books, 1982.

Coleman, John A. "A Limited State and a Vibrant Society: Christianity and Civil Society." In *Christian Political Ethics*, edited by John A. Coleman. Princeton, NJ: Princeton University Press, 2007.

———. "Religious Social Capital: Its Nature, Social Location and Limitations." In *Religion as Social Capital: Producing the Common Good*, edited by Corwin Schmidt. Waco, TX: Baylor University Press, 2003.

Collier, Paul. *Social Capital and Poverty*. Washington, DC: The World Bank, 1998.

De Filippis, James. "The Myth of Social Capital in Community Development." *Housing Policy Debate* 24, no. 4 (2001): 791–806.

Durkheim, Emile. *The Division of Labor in Society*. Translated by George Simpson. New York: The Free Press, 1964.

Field, John. *Social Capital*. London: Routledge, 2003.

Francis, Paul. "Social Capital at the World Bank: Strategic and Operational Implications of the Concept." World Bank, 2002. Online. Available:http://www.worldbank.org/essd/sdvext.

Francis, Paul, et al. *Hard Lessons: Primary Schools, Community and Social Capital in Nigeria*. World Bank Technical Paper no. 420. Washington, DC: The World Bank, 1998.

Fukuyama, Francis. "Social Capital and Civil Society." A paper presented for the 1999 IMF Conference on Second Generation Reforms. Online. Available:http://www.imf.org/external/nubs/ft/seminar/1999/reforms/fukuyama.htm.

———. *Trust: The Social Virtues and the Creation of Prosperity*. New York: Free Press, 1995.

Grootaert, Christiaan, and Thierry van Bastelaer. *The Role of Social Capital in Development: An Empirical Assessment*. Cambridge: Cambridge University Press, 2002.

Himes, Kenneth, et al., eds. *Catholic Social Thought: Commentaries and Interpretations*. Washington, DC: Georgetown University Press, 2005.

Hollenbach, David. *The Common Good and Christian Ethics*. Cambridge: Cambridge University Press, 2002.

———. "Justice as Participation." In *Justice, Peace and Human Rights*. New York: Crossroad, 1988.

Jacobs, Jane. *The Death and Life of Great American Cities*. New York: Random House Modern Library Edition, 1993.

Jones, Mark Wickham. *Cities and the Wealth of Nations*. New York: Vintage, 1985.

———. Review of Stein Ringen, *The Liberal Vision*. Oxford: Bardwell Press, 2007. The *Times Literary Supplement* (July 25, 2008).

Levy, Jonah. *Tocqueville's Revenge: State, Society and Economy in Contemporary France*. Cambridge, MA: Harvard University Press, 1999.

Loury, Glenn. "A Dynamic Theory of Racial Income Differences." In *Women, Minorities and Employment Discrimination*, edited by P. A. Wallace and A Le Mund, 153–86. Lexington, MA: Lexington Books, 1977.

Martin, David. *Tongues of Fire: The Explosion of Protestantism in Latin America*. Oxford: Basil Blackwell, 1990.

Medaille, John. *Vocation of Business: Social Justice in the Marketplace*. New York: Continuum, 2007.

Pontifical Council for Justice and Peace. *Compendium of the Social Doctrine of the Church*. Washington, DC: United States Catholic Conference of Bishops, 2005.

Portes, Alejandro. "Social Capital: Its Origins and Applications in Modern Sociology." *Annual Review of Sociology* 24 (1998): 1–24.

Putnam, Robert. "Bowling Alone: America's Declining Social Capital." *Current* Issue 373 (June 1995): 3–9.

———. *Bowling Alone: The Collapse and Revival of American Community*. New York: Simon and Schuster, 2000.

———. *Democracies in Flux: The Evolution of Social Capital in Contemporary Societies*. New York: Oxford University Press, 2002.

———. *Making Democracy Work: Civic Traditions in Modern Ital*. Princeton, NJ: Princeton University Press, 1993.

Rowe, Jonathan. "Review of Fukuyama's 'Trust.'" *The Washington Monthly* 27:10 (October 1995): 58–59.

Smith, Adam. *An Inquiry into the Nature and Causes of the Wealth of Nations*. Edited by Edwin Cannan. Chicago: University of Chicago Press, 1976.

———. *The Theory of Moral Sentiments*. New York: Augustus M. Kelley Publishers, 1966.

Wallace, Phyllis A. and Annette LeMond, eds. *Women, Minorities and Employment Discrimination*. Lexington, MA: Lexington Books, 1977.

Weber, Eugen. "Tocqueville's Revenge: A Review." *French Historical Studies* 24 (2001): 113–23.

Weber, Max. *The Protestant Ethic and the Spirit of Capitalism.* Translated by Talcott Parsons. Introduction by Randall Collins. Los Angeles: Roxbury Publishing Company, 1996.

World Bank. "What Is Social Capital?" *Poverty Net,* 1999. Online. Available:http:// www.worldbank.org/povertynet/socialcapital.

9

What Do We Know about the Economic Situation of Women, and What Does It Mean for a Just Economy?

Simona Beretta

The economic situation of women today provides a critical test of the efficiency and justice of our economic system. A true account of the role of women in the contemporary world includes acknowledging enormous disparities and close interdependence among continents, as in the case of the "global care chain," in which poor women from developing nations travel to wealthy nations to care for the children of well-to-do families in order to send money home to care for their own children. It also requires addressing questions about women's empowerment and dignity, whose answers pertain to the sphere of relationships, perceptions, expectations, and beliefs. It is curious to observe widespread consensus about the essential role of women and families in economic and social development and yet so little reflection (let alone dialogue) on what it truly means to be a woman, or a family. Christian anthropology provides the basis for a convincing, and convenient, way to explore what "true" flourishing of women and society means. Such concerns must be addressed if the True Wealth of Nations project is to investigate whether and how applying the principles of Catholic social thought will provide a path to "sustainable prosperity for all."

The first part of this chapter offers a broad review of consensus indicators and empirical findings concerning women's economic situation, in both medium-high-income and low-income countries.

They provide a helpful map of poverty and inequality faced by women, but they seem unable to answer essential questions about the true situation of women. Most data refer to women as individuals or as a group and cannot capture the particularity of the "feminine," which makes sense only within a relational setting in which the "masculine" is also understood. Hence, a relational paradigm is required to assess women's economic situations adequately. One may think that the economics of the family offers a relational analysis, but a review of the literature shows that most economic models share the same individualistic perspective we find in "gender studies." Since the feminine and the family are essentially relational notions, they can be described as a special kind of human and social "capital" that requires investment. The paper offers the idea of "generation" as a plausible, unifying concept in defining the feminine and the family; since the experience of generation is central to elementary human experience, it can provide a reasonable basis for intercultural dialogue about many critical issues.

The second part of this chapter explores the issues of efficiency and justice faced by women in a framework in which generative actions occupy a central role. It reviews current lines of economic research about measuring well-being and societal progress beyond Gross Domestic Product (GDP) and suggests going beyond the measurement of women's "missing" GDP and rethinking the nature of the "care" economy. In particular, it critically assesses the notion of women's empowerment, suggesting human dignity as more appropriate. The paper elaborates the idea that "generation" is at the heart of wealth creation, suggesting an intertemporal, relational paradigm, in which "true" development of persons and societies requires a generative dynamism driven by free personal actions that gratuitously circulate "received" gifts.

What Do We Know about the Economic Situation of Women?

Women in High-Income and Emerging Countries: Focus on the Labour Market

The disadvantaged position of women is not a new issue in economics: John Stuart Mill wrote *The Subjection of Women* in 1869. Women's position has changed much over the years and is still changing today at a rapid pace.

Most analyses of the economic situation of women in high- and middle-income countries focus on their participation in the labour market, theoretically analyzing and empirically measuring which factors influence "gender gaps" in participation rates,[1] employment, and wages. Today, the broad picture of the working situation of women in high-income countries still shows that

female participation and employment rates are lower than for men; furthermore, women's wages are on average lower than those of men with similar
education and working skills. These gender gaps, though, appear to be declining
over time.

Statistical data providing information for both men and women have
become abundant in recent years, and their access is easy and free; two
extremely rich sources are Wikigender and the UNECE database.[2] Detailed data
show that the broad trends summarized above exhibit much variation across
countries, sectors, and ethnic groups; differences are obviously relevant for
policy making, but their presentation in detail goes beyond the goal of this
paper, which is to provide a brief summary and to critically assess consensus
evidence on selected issues.

FEMALE EMPLOYMENT AND THE GENDER GAP IN WAGES. In recent decades,
female employment (defined as working for a wage) has increased in all
developed countries. Technological advances have reduced the demand for
manual labour and made it easier and more socially acceptable for women to
work in the market. Changes in the structure of the economy have altered the
type of jobs available; manufacturing work has declined while jobs in services
expanded.

The long run trend for the United States shows that the proportions of
men and women in employment were 80 percent and 20 percent respectively
in the 1920s, while they currently are slightly above and slightly below
50 percent.[3] The cross-country comparison of the difference between male and
female employment rates in ten high-income economies shows the smallest
gap in Sweden (around 5 percent) and very high gaps in Spain, Italy, and Japan
(well above 20 percent). Country differences are very significant, but they are
expected to converge over time; since the participation rate among women aged
25 to 29 is currently the same in the European Union as in the United States,
hence female employment in Europe will eventually grow.[4] Female participation in "formal" (i.e., paid) jobs is also very high in the emerging East Asian
economies: in 2006, for every 100 men in the labour force, there were 83
women, a higher proportion than the average for OECD countries.[5] Women
have been particularly important to the success of Asia's export industries, typically accounting for 60 to 80 percent of the jobs in many export sectors, such
as textiles and clothing.[6]

Over the past decades, the gender gap in wages (defined as the difference
in wage for men and women not attributable to differences in education,
experience, etc.) also narrowed significantly both in high-income and emerging countries, while women have increasingly entered traditionally male

occupations. The two trends obviously reinforce each other, since many studies suggest that predominantly female occupations pay less, even after controlling for personal characteristics. This is not to say that discrimination in the labour market disappeared: average median wages for men in full-time employment in OECD countries are 15 percent higher than for women; male median earnings are 20 percent higher than female median earnings in Korea, Japan, Germany, Switzerland, Canada, and the United States; the wage gap is less than 12 percent in New Zealand, Belgium, Poland, Greece, and France.[7] This gap is likely to narrow, but it seems unlikely to vanish despite the fact that many OECD countries have laws that ensure equal pay to men and women in the same position. As of today, the gender gap in wages is in fact more pronounced among high-wage earners; it is usually suggested that this is a consequence of the underrepresentation of women in managerial positions.[8] Some forms of discrimination are subtler, as in the case of women with children; over the past few decades, as the pay gap between women and men has been narrowing, in the United States, the wage gap between women with children and those without children has been widening.[9]

The disparity between men's and women's wages has two possible components: the fact that men and women tend to access different types of jobs and actual discrimination. By simply looking at the data, such disparity it is not easy to interpret. Given legal provisions, it is unlikely that women get paid less than men for the same jobs (wage discrimination). But then we need to address the reasons why women do not reach (or do not pursue) high levels in the career ladder, why they choose (or have to accept) lower-paid occupations, such as nursing and teaching. In other words: is working in the lower-paid "care" sector a woman's free choice or a necessity out of lack of alternatives? Do women choose not to climb the career ladder, or are they actually discriminated against?

THE RISE OF "WOMANOMICS". Recent years have witnessed an important change in high-income economies, in which women have taken on new roles and gained significant economic status. Acknowledging this newly acquired market power has led some commentators to use the expression "womanomics," a neologism with a slight flavour of feminine revenge or maybe masculine fear.

For example, in some "trendy" urban environments, the gender gap in pay has turned favourable to women. According to the U.S. Census in 2005, earnings of young women amounted to 89 percent of their male colleagues earnings. But in major metropolitan regions, young women from 21 to 30 years old were earning more than their male counterparts: 120 percent of the salaries of male colleagues in Dallas, 117 percent in New York.[10] Among the explanations are higher rates of tertiary education for women combined with higher wages for graduates. Since both trends appear quite robust, they point to a further convergence and, possibly, even a reversal in wage gap in OECD countries, as women's contribution to GDP (which includes only work in paid jobs) becomes ever larger.

Women are becoming more important in the marketplace, not just as workers, but also as consumers, entrepreneurs, managers, and investors. Women have traditionally done most of the household shopping, but as paid workers they have more money of their own to spend; surveys suggest that women make perhaps 80 percent of consumers' buying decisions from health care to furniture to food.[11] The trend in reinforcing women's market power seems to be confirmed by different sources. A study by Catalyst consultancy found that American companies with more women in senior management jobs earned a higher return on equity than those with fewer women at the top. As an explanation, they suggest that mixed teams of men and women are better than single-sex groups at solving problems and spotting external threats. A survey by Digital Look, a British financial website, found that women consistently earn higher returns than men. A survey of American investors by Merrill Lynch also found that women were better at investing, apparently because women were less likely to "churn" their investments.[12] Similarly, during the financial crisis of 2008, a higher degree of "feminization" of management seems to have provided better resistance to turmoil.[13]

The gender gap in higher education is probably the fastest changing indicator of the economic situation of women. While women were a distinct minority of undergraduates in 1960, they now make up a clear majority, changing gender ratios on college campuses.[14] The trend showing increased participation of women in higher education is widely acknowledged in most countries and very well documented in the Wikigender and UNECE databases.

From the womanomics perspective, there is still a lot of scope for women to become more productive as they make better use of their qualifications: girls tend to get better grades, and, in most developed countries, they are now being awarded over half of all university degrees. In the United States, 140 women enroll in higher education each year for every 100 men; in Sweden the number is as high as 150; but in Japan the ratio is still 90 women for 100 men. At present, for example, in Britain more women than men train as doctors and lawyers, but relatively few are leading surgeons or partners in law firms; from the womanomics perspective, this trend will change and better-educated women will eventually take more of the top jobs.[15]

Evidence of the changing role of women is overabundant and is not limited to the Western world. Think, for example, of women's political role in Africa, Asia, and Latin America. However, the changing economic role of women in affluent societies takes place in a cultural environment in which it is particularly difficult to answer—and even ask—questions about the "feminine." We seem to face cognitive and symbolic problems in gender roles, for various reasons, often implicit in women's ambivalent feelings about having reached market and social power: "Are we just better men than men? Is this what it means to be a woman?"

CHILDBEARING. Modern contraception has radically changed the economic role of women in high-income societies; as the 1999 Millennium Special Issue of *The Economist* remarked, the birth control pill is the invention that defined the twentieth century. Let us just note that, unlike other forms of contraception, the pill allowed contraception to be a private, individual decision of the woman and not a "couple" or a "family" issue; legalization of abortion provided a further method for reducing unwanted motherhood—a very costly, but undeniably effective, method.

The ongoing decline in disadvantage for women in education and the workplace exhibits ambivalent features because better professional opportunities for women do not come without costs, as most individual female narratives could confirm. In general, women still tend to retain primary responsibility for housework, child care, and elder care; hence, they work a large number of hours when we consider work both within the family and in the market.

Another cost of being a professional woman could be a negative trade-off between working in paid jobs and childbearing—the latter being a uniquely "feminine" endeavour. In high-income countries there is indeed a "gender gap" due to the fact that a lower proportion of women have jobs than men have; but, quite surprisingly, nations with *larger* gender gaps tend to have *less* childbearing, not more;[16] this evidence is confirmed by data about fertility rates and employment rates, which are *positively* correlated with each other.[17] In low-income countries, though, lower fertility rates tend to follow increased per-capita income.

Both the negative correlation between personal income and fertility rates in low-income countries and the positive correlation between labour market participation and fertility rates in high-income countries leave many open questions; they neither confirm nor deny causation here. No "materialistic" explanation of childbearing is probably adequate: is postponing or avoiding childbearing a free choice, or does it reflect economic constraints? Do women need to work because they need income for raising the children they desire? Are they forced to avoid motherhood for professional reasons?

Two further considerations are in order. One is practical: the international differences shown above may not be explained by women's relatively more egalitarian participation to the labour market, but rather by missing economic variables, such as national "family policies" that support childbearing (e.g., removing obstacles that make it hard for women to combine work with having children, providing for parental leave[18] and child-care support, allowing flexible working hours, reforming those tax and social-security systems that make it costly for women to work, and so on). The second consideration touches a deeper cultural level: childbearing requires a "positive" view of children and of forming a "generative" family. This view shapes and is shaped by the set of current and anticipated relationships in which each woman finds herself, including the expected relationship with a child to come. Using an evocative expression, childbearing both requires and signals hope, and no public policy can substitute for hope. In other terms, family-friendly public policies are probably necessary, but not sufficient, instruments in sustaining women's decisions to "invest in the future," to enter the truly definitive mother-child relationship that arises when giving birth to a child.

Women's Situation in Low-Income Countries: Work, Education, and Health

All international institutions promoting development explicitly declare their concern with women's well-being;[19] this is clearly reflected, for example, in targets and indicators of the United Nations Millennium Development Goals, MDGs. The most clearly gender-related MDG is the third (MDG 3): to "Promote gender equality and empower women"; the UN target is to "eliminate gender disparities in primary and secondary education, preferably by 2005, and in all levels of education no later than 2015"; MDG 3 official indicators, which are meant to measure gender disparities in the household, the economy, and society, serve as monitoring devices and policy instruments; their importance lies in the wide consensus (and resources) they command; they are available for virtually all countries and are suitable for cross-country comparisons.[20] It is worth noticing that, while yet difficult to assess, the consequences of the global financial crisis of 2008 are most powerfully felt by the poorest worldwide and especially by women, who form the vast majority of the poor. In particular, this kind of economic contraction affects women working in the manufacturing export sectors and in the informal sector of low-income countries; lower migrant remittances also reduce local consumption and investment. Official foreign aid, chronically insufficient, further stagnates due to budgetary problems in donors countries, where private donations also suffer. Investing in female education is particularly significant from a development perspective: educating girls boosts future prosperity, and it is widely acknowledged to be the best investment in the developing world. In fact, better-educated girls will be more productive women as workers, and they also will raise healthier, better-educated children.

Choosing Indicators of Gender Equality and Empowerment

Building on previous research about equity and development,[21] the World Bank identifies gender inequality as the archetypal "inequality trap" that perpetuates inequalities, with negative consequences not just for women but also for their families and communities.[22] The World Bank identifies the provision of equal opportunities across population groups as both an intrinsic aspect of development and as an instrument for achieving poverty reduction and economic growth. The *Global Monitoring Report* for 2007 (GMR) by the International Bank for Reconstruction and Development of the World Bank Group offers an updated review of gender equality in development.[23] It systematically reviews the trends in the official UN MDG 3 indicators of gender disparities; in addition, it offers some criticism of them and proposes a sort of World Bank consensus about measuring gender inequality.

GMR criticizes the official MDG 3 indicators on three grounds. First, they only partially capture what they are meant to. Education enrollment rates say nothing about equality of learning or educational outcomes; ratios of female to male are not easily interpreted, as they may improve simply because of a worsening in the situation of the male population. The share of women in nonagricultural wage employment is of limited relevance for low-income countries, where wage employment is not a major source of jobs and the most relevant barriers that inhibit women from participating in labour markets are rather the time burden of domestic tasks and the limited access to complementary inputs such as credit, capital, and technology. Political participation is captured only at the national level, not at lower levels where decision making is likely to exercise an important impact on women's well-being. Second, the official indicators ignore completely some key elements of gender equality: health outcomes, which are a particularly important determinant of well-being and productivity, and disparities in access to productive resources. The third GMR criticism concerns official indicators' inadequacy in assessing women's empowerment. While in principle MDG 3 refers to the promotion of both gender equality and women's empowerment, the official indicators measure gender disparity (the rights, resources, and voice enjoyed by women relative to those enjoyed by men) rather than women's empowerment—that is, "whether women have the ability to exercise options, choice, control, and power."[24] GMR especially criticizes the official UN indicator of women's position in the economy, which severely underestimates the economic role of women in low-income countries by considering nonagricultural wage employment only. In fact, women play a crucial role in food security, in all its dimensions: food production and distribution and nutritional security; and they play this role facing enormous social, cultural, and economic difficulties.[25] For example, in Africa, women represent around 33 percent of the workforce but 70 percent of agricultural workers; they provide for 60 to 80 percent of food processing for household consumption and sale, 90 percent of household water and fuelwood, 80 percent of food storage and transport, 90 percent of hoeing and weeding, and 60 percent of harvesting and marketing.[26] The role of women entrepreneurs—not officially classified among "paid workers"—is also very remarkable.[27]

Different studies reported in GMR point to women's reproductive role as negatively affecting female labour force participation in general and work for pay in particular.[28] Women also face the time burden of domestic tasks, especially collecting water and firewood.[29] The amount of time and effort needed to complete these tasks is highly dependent on environmental conditions: if water and fuel are difficult to get, these tasks can take hours every day, reducing the amount of time women and girls can devote to out-of-home employment or to attending school. GMR also notices that some environmental health hazards fall disproportionately on women, as in the case of exposure to indoor air pollution such as cooking with biomass fuels.[30]

Choosing indicators is never a neutral endeavour: they are inevitably based on implicit or explicit conceptions of what gender equality and women's empowerment mean. According to GMR, important elements of empowerment that are not captured by the official MDG 3 indicators include the ability of women to work for pay in all sectors (economic empowerment) and the ability to control their own fertility (household empowerment). Hence, GMR recommends the use of the five complementary indicators summarized in Table 1.[31] Notice that both the World Bank consensus on what it means to achieve gender equality and women's empowerment and the official MDG 3 vision are of great practical relevance: they express positions that command both international respectability and conspicuous financial resources.

Measuring Women's Empowerment: Data and Open Questions

MDG 3 indicators on *equality in the household* show that, in the fifteen years from 1990 to 2005, there has been uneven but general progress in both female school enrollment and literacy.[32] As an overall trend, female participation in the economy and in political activities, as monitored by the third and fourth official MGD 3 indicators, also generally improved over the same fifteen years,[33] with the exception of political participation in Europe and Central Asia.

TABLE 1 MDG 3: UN official Indicators and WB Recommendations

MDG 3, Gender disparity in the Household		MDG 3, in the Economy and market		MDG 3, in Society
Official UN indicators	WB recommended indicators	Official UN indicators	WB GMR recommended indicators	Official UN indicators
Ratio of girls' to boys' enrollment in primary, secondary, and tertiary education (official indicator n.1)	Primary completion rates of girls and boys (currently MDG 2)	Share of women in nonagricultural wage employment (official indicator n.3)	Labour force participation rates among women and men aged 20 to 24 and 25 to 49	Proportion of seats held by women in national parliaments (official indicator n.4)
Ratio of literate females to males among 15 to 24 years old (official indicator n.2)	Under-five mortality rate for girls and boys (currently MDG 4)			
	Percentage of reproductive-age women, and their sexual partners, using modern contraceptives (currently MDG 6)			
	Percentage of 15- to 19-year-old girls who are mothers or pregnant with their first child (additional indicator)			

Source: Information taken from ⟨http://www.un.org/millenniumgoals/⟩ and World Bank Recommended Additional Indicators World Bank, GMR 2007, 120.

The modified and additional indicators offered by GMR are also helpful in providing insights on the situation of girls and women in low-income countries. Primary school completion rates have generally improved in the last decades, but girls still lag behind boys in most regions, although not in all regions.[34] Health indicators provide strong evidence of gender inequality, as is documented by the GMR indices of female under-five mortality rates as compared to male rates. Because of biological differences between the sexes, rates of under-five mortality are normally higher for boys than for girls in countries where there is no significant discrimination against girls.[35] Where such discrimination exists, this shows up in higher-than-normal under-five mortality for girls than for boys, due to unequal access to nutrition and health care during early childhood.[36] Sex ratios at birth also have important information content; they have been "excessively" masculine in much of East Asia for decades, compared with the "normal" ratio of 104 to 106 males per 100 females in most populations. In China and the Republic of Korea, the sex ratio at birth was around 107 in 1982, rising sharply thereafter with the spread of sex-selective abortion in the mid-1980s. In China it increased to nearly 120 in 2005. In the Republic of Korea, it peaked at around 116 in the early 1990s and has since declined to about 108 in 2005.[37]

The percentage of women reporting use of modern contraceptives has increased over the last two decades, from 47 percent in 1990 to 56 percent in 2000;[38] between 1985 and 2005 in all countries for which data from at least two Demographic and Health Surveys are available, the percentage of women aged 15 to 49 reporting use of modern contraceptives has also been reported to increase. Notice that in the language of these international institutions, access to birth-control techniques is usually found under the heading "reproductive health"; speaking about health, there is a crucial missing element for assessing women's situation in both MDG 3 and GMR perspectives. This is HIV infection, which disproportionately affects women. In Africa and the Caribbean, more than 50 percent of HIV-infected persons are women; in sub-Saharan Africa, 57 percent of infected adults are women; and it is 62 percent in Kenya; adult women are 1.3 times more likely to be infected than men, while young women up to 24 years old are 3 to 6 times more likely to be infected than young men.[39] As it is, any failure to deal with AIDS/HIV is a failure to intervene on behalf of women. This may induce the suspicion that the insistence of international institutions on reproductive health is more an ideological stance than a truly pro-women policy.

Childbearing among teenagers is employed as an indicator in the GMR based on evidence that adolescent motherhood brings both disproportionate health risks to mother and baby and other negative effects, such as early departure from school, lower human capital accumulation, lower earnings, and a higher probability of living in poverty.[40] Interestingly, empirical evidence on adolescent motherhood is definitely mixed, with different countries reporting different trends;[41] it seems is that this indicator is culturally sensitive and, hence, very difficult to assess.

Monitoring labour force participation among women aged 20 to 24 is meant to indicate the extent to which education and skills acquired in school are used in the labour market. Three broad geographic areas can be identified as exhibiting similar patterns. First: female participation rates are the lowest in countries of Middle East and North Africa, South Asia, and Latin America and the Caribbean. In these regions, there has been little change in women's participation between 1990 and 2005, and we observe the greatest gender gap in participation; this is somewhat paradoxical in some places, as with 20- to 24-year-olds in Latin America and Caribbean, given the region's success in educating girls and eliminating the gender gap in schooling. Second, in sub-Saharan Africa, female employment rates are high, the gender gap in participation is low, but women are concentrated in low-paying agricultural employment or self-employment in the nonagricultural sector. Third, in Europe and Central Asia and in East Asia and Pacific, female participation rates are high, gender gaps in participation rates are low, women's share in nonagricultural paid work is high, but women tend to receive lower wages than men.

A Remarkable "New Thing": Migrant Women in the Global Care Chain

Over the last forty years, almost as many women have migrated between nations as men, most of them for family reunification; for example, female immigrants to America have outnumbered male immigrants since 1930. Nowadays, Europe and Oceania are also currently reporting increasing proportions of female immigrants, above 50 percent since 2000. This new trend, though, is driven by female labour migrants and not by family reunification. Some Asian countries exhibit a very clear pattern: in 2005, over 65 percent of the nearly 3,000 Filipinos that every day left the country for work or residence abroad were women; from Sri Lanka, in 2002, there were two women for every male migrant; between 2000 and 2003, on average, 79 percent of all migrants leaving Indonesia to work abroad were women. Most are employed as domestic workers. In Latin America, 1990 was the turning point, with migrant women above 50 percent; women from this region clearly dominated migration flows to Spain and to Italy, where above 70 percent of the arrivals were women. Poverty, disease, land degradation, and high male unemployment lead to a steady increase in African female migration; women still make up less than 50 percent of all African migrants, but the rate of increase of female migration is faster than the global average. Most African women circulate within the region, but they are also moving to North America and Europe. As an example, women constitute 85 percent of all those who migrate to Italy from Cape Verde; employment opportunities in France attract an increasing number of educated women from urban areas of Senegal; African nurses are migrating to Canada, the United Kingdom, and the United States.[42]

It is truly remarkable that the many international domestic workers and caregivers who leave their homes to care for others abroad also have their own children and elders to look after back home. Migrant women usually rely on female relatives or hire lower-income domestic workers to manage their households after they have emigrated. Migrant women leave their family in order to economically sustain it; they provide care for their employer's children or elderly, in exchange for a wage that can improve the material quality of life of their own families, which they can seldom visit. This pattern creates a sort of "global care chain,"[43] which seems to be an "all women's story," obviously stratified by income considerations. The chain interlinks women who, in both the North and the South, bear double responsibilities, as (formal or informal) employers as well as employees.

Other dimensions of the international movement of women are surely more problematic than the global care chain: in particular, the trafficking in women, of refugee women and asylum seekers.[44] But the ordinary fact that the global care chain is structurally built on the disruption of the basic meaningful relations of the women involved is what might be called a "normal" tragedy, pointing to the need of a "relational" view of the economic situation of women in order to assess their true well-being.

What We Do Not Know about the Economic Situation of Women

The UN and World Bank consensus indicators on gender inequality and women's empowerment in low-income countries share a common cultural background, also featured in gender studies in advanced and emerging countries: the individualistic approach to assessing women's economic situation. Individualistic approaches in monitoring the economic situation of women are not adequate in highlighting the specificity of the "feminine" in economics; the same idea of "feminine" makes sense only in a "relational" paradigm.

RELATIONS MATTER: ATTRIBUTIONAL DATA VERSUS RELATIONAL DATA. The empirical evidence on women's situation is characterized by the overwhelming prevalence of "attributional" data, which refer to women as individual agents or as a group—namely, an aggregation of individual agents that exhibit one or more common characteristics. "Relational" data, measuring women's roles and positions within networks, are virtually nonexistent.

The prevalence of attributional data is common in most fields of economic analysis, but there is a growing body of literature and empirical evidence based on the idea that relational data are indispensable for understanding a wide variety of economic issues, from firms' decisions about location and innovative behaviour[45] to the deep structure of economic integration.[46] While attributional data do offer valuable information on the economic and social situation of women, we cannot ignore their structural limitations: they are embedded in a cultural framework dominated by the individualistic paradigm, while many relevant questions concerning the true situation of women simply cannot be answered by attributional data alone. This is particularly true for the most sensitive "feminine" issues, childbearing and birth control probably being the most prominent among them.

Two related steps need to be taken. First, we need to collect and publish relational data, and not just positional data; second, we need to address two basic questions explicitly: what is the "feminine," and how does defining the "feminine" relate to defining the family and the relation between sexes in society at large. There is some economic research dealing with these issues, which is reviewed below; but further study is needed.

WOMEN AND THE FAMILY IN ECONOMIC THEORY. One could argue that the existing economic analysis of the family can effectively complement the dominant individualistic perspective; hence, a quick review of the main findings about "the family and the economy" follows.

The economics of the family finds its foundational text in Gary Becker's *Treatise on the Family*, published in 1981. Becker's theory is based on the existence of production complementarities, in which rationally optimizing husband and wife specialize in paid jobs and in housework respectively; decisions concerning having and raising children are also framed as a production complementarities issue. The decreasing importance of household production complementarities today (due to the increases in female labour-force participation, to labour-saving technologies for housework, and the increasing share of marriages that involve no intention of generating children) has promoted a rethinking of the economic theory of family, in order "to push beyond the production of own children and traditional notions of specialization, and seek to uncover the forces that yield the modern family form."[47] Contemporary research extends the economic models of the family beyond the notion of a "productive" household and toward emphasizing consumption complementarities and reciprocal insurance as central to marriage.

Redefining the fundamental purposes of the family is thus done within the largely unchanged economic paradigm of optimizing individual decisions; there is scant attention to the household as a meaningful network of relations deserving analytical attention.[48] This is quite contrary to elementary experience[49] and scientific evidence, which indicate that family networks are valuable—both in terms of their relational-symbolic dimension[50] and in economic terms.[51]

While early economic models of the family treated marriage and household formation almost identically, more recent theories[52] take the decoupling of domestic arrangements from the legal (and social) status of relationships as the starting point, where cohabitation emerges as an important (informal) institution, which is at times a precursor to marriage, at times a substitute for it.[53] The authors note that the birth control pill reduced the cost of waiting to marry, by allowing sex outside of marriage with little fear of an unwanted pregnancy; they also consider the improved control over fertility as a factor that changes the timing of marriage and births and facilitates women's accumulation of human capital by reducing the risk of disruption to women's education or labour-market plans.

Curiously, out-of-wedlock births also increased following technological innovations in birth control. Akerlof, Yellen, and Katz[54] tried to resolve this puzzle by arguing that women's newfound control over pregnancy increased pressure on them to engage in premarital sexual relations and reduced their ability to extract a commitment to marry in the event of a pregnancy. Further, those who did not adopt the pill or suffered contraceptive failure gained the option of choosing abortion instead of pregnancy; but if the choice was pregnancy, they typically lost the offer of a subsequent "shotgun marriage." The inadequacy of any of these suggested answers seems to entail an implicit declaration that the individualistic paradigm can take the analysis only so far. In any case, this analysis leaves unanswered the question of whether, at the end of the day, women are indeed better off after the dramatic improvement in birth-control technologies and the ensuing social changes in sex and family choices.

In a rather "extreme" paper,[55] Cox suggests that evolutionary biology can help explain the diversity in male and female decisions concerning the family. Experience shows that the sex of family members making economic decisions makes a lot of difference in outcomes,[56] but this evidence is still unexplained by typical economic models. Cox's paper speaks of sons and daughters, fathers and mothers, grandfathers and grandmothers taking distance from generic "person one/person two" households and the "parent-child" distinction. The theoretical pillar of Cox's "bio-founding" of the economics of the family is Hamilton's rule, which holds that the costs and benefits of altruistic acts are weighted by the closeness of the genetic relationship. Since those costs and benefits are asymmetrically distributed due to biological differences between male and female, biology influences mating behaviour, decisions to marry and divorce, and how much to invest in family relationships and children. In particular, the asymmetric investments men and women make in childbearing explain why it makes economic sense for women to be concerned with assessing qualitative goods, such as friend's support and male's loyalty, in family decisions. Provided the biological approach is taken for what it is—illuminating, but partial—it represents a very interesting theoretical attempt at highlighting the distinctiveness of the "feminine" in family relations and the basic sexual and intertemporal structure of the family.

Actually, such accounts of the biological dimension of human families (incomplete but based on the "given" biological structure of human beings) are superior to ever more frequent alternative accounts in which "gender" identity is the cultural and social product of the interaction between the community and the individual, independent of one's sexual identity. The focus here is on the well-being of actual women, unique human beings who are gifted with the biological possibility of bearing and feeding babies. The economic analysis of the family ought to consider the family as a "relational" investment, not merely as a form of production or consumption. This makes perfect sense in the discipline: take the analogy with the economic analysis of the firm as an example. As a firm is the observable outcome of risky human actions and interactions—namely, investments that imply personalized and durable relations—so is the family. The firm is explored by economists as a "unit" of some kind, with a "common good" of its own; so it should be with the family. Furthermore, it has long been established that the actual value of a firm includes its symbolic dimension; the same symbolic analysis should be applied to the family.

WOMEN AND THE FAMILY: A SPECIAL KIND OF HUMAN AND SOCIAL CAPITAL. The underinvestment by economists in any economic analysis of the relational nature of the feminine and the family is quite puzzling, given that targeting women in order to improve the lot of families and local communities is a widely accepted operational principle in development policy. The empirical literature on women's role in development and on the role of the family in sustaining its members' personal and social achievement is abundant, especially in low-income countries. Women repay loans more than men do; they care for children more than for themselves. But, why is it so? What's so special about women?

And what is so special about the family—that is, the concrete set of intergenerational relations in which the woman, with childbearing, holds a structurally central role? Family occupies the first position in the list of the determinants of social capital that the World Bank identifies in the link between social capital and development:

> As the main source of economic and social welfare for its members, the family is the first building block in the generation of social capital for the larger society.... In addition to influencing the human capital development of children, the family's internal and external relationships model behaviors that are transmitted via children to future relationships. Relations within the family foster the development of trust, essential for the formation of all outside relationships. The family's ability to meet children's physical and emotional needs strongly influences their perceptions of the trustworthiness of others outside the family. Family dynamics also encourage reciprocity and exchange, two other important factors in social capital generation. The material and emotional support shared freely between family members generates an implicit willingness to return such support.[57]

In a 2004 paper[58] a colleague and I tried to contribute to a "relational" approach to the family, seen as a form of social capital in itself[59] but also as an institution that contributes to social capital generation.[60] We offered a simple theoretical model and some empirical results illustrating that investing in the family as a stable network of relations generates social capital in the cognitive sense, as a generalized expectation of cooperation in society at large.[61] The empirical results of our explorations may well be naive, but we mostly worked on the premises: going back to basics in identifying the family as an institution. We wanted a definition of the family that could broadly hold, irrespective of social and cultural variables related to time and space.

In our definition, a family, as distinct from other forms of "households," is a network of relations in which "generation" occurs and in which generations (parents, children, grandchildren) meet. Such networks can be very small, even a single mother with a child. Generation is different from reproduction: while reproduction simply requires mating, generation implies a significant investment in human and social capital, entailing personalized and durable relationships, In short, generation means taking care of relationships. In particular, for generation to occur, two kinds of investment are required: in bridging two families and in stably bonding a man and a woman to each other. (There is an interesting parallel here with the bridging and bonding forms of social capital discussed by John Coleman in his essay in this volume). In other words, the generative nature of the family is mirrored in its intergenerational structure, a network to which different generations belong, an intertemporal bridge. The bridging is not just across time: while bonding is essential for a family to exist, a new family can be created (hence, the intergenerational structure can survive) only by connecting—or bridging—two distinct families.[62] Hence, the family is inherently generative, both in the personal and the social dimensions: it takes care of the newborn individuals, and it is structurally open to covenants with other families, "thickening" social cooperation. I have further elaborated on the idea of generation, with its strong symbolic dimension, as a powerful metaphor[63] for understanding wealth creation and development.[64]

Women, Efficiency, and Justice: Assessing "True Prosperity"

Beyond GDP: Assessing Well-being and Progress

There is a widespread agreement in the economic profession on the idea that income measures are, at best, first approximations of societal well-being and development; qualitative elements should also be taken into consideration, such as income distribution, inequalities, social cohesion,[65] propensity to innovation, environmental quality, health and education levels, cultural dimensions, and last, but not least, gender issues. The concern here is certainly related to that of the True Wealth project with "true prosperity."

The quest for meaningful indicators of well-being has gained momentum in the last few years, the "capability" approach by A. Sen possibly being the most remarkable new idea and the UNDP Human Development Index (HDI) the best known non-GDP measure of well-being.[66] Building upon UNDP experience, an international network of agencies[67] has recently been involved in a project named "Measuring Well-Being and Societal Progress"[68] (we could call it measuring "true prosperity").

PERCEPTIONS, EXPECTATIONS, AND BELIEFS MATTER. Producing indicators of well-being and progress is a deserving task, but one should be aware of two problems. One, the risks of ideological drifts in defining indicators of well-being and progress are all too real.[69] Data simply answer our questions; duly "tortured," empirical evidence would confess almost anything. Presumed "objectivity" is especially dangerous if well-being indicators are meant to drive and monitor policy actions. In defining and using "prosperity" indicators we always face the uncomfortable, unavoidable questions about what it is to be human (and a woman); ultimately, they are questions about "truth."[70]

Any notion of progress and well-being comes from outside the system;[71] any "objective" indicator actually needs answering questions such as: what is a good life? What is a meaningful world?

Second, societal change—for good or for ill—is driven by human actions and interactions. People act in time and space, facing unavoidable uncertainty with personalized and durable relations they choose to invest in, on the basis of perception, beliefs, and expectations, which are relational and pertain to the cognitive/symbolic domain. Undervaluing the role of expectations, beliefs, and perceptions in defining indicators of well-being and societal progress can seriously distort the resulting understanding of prosperity. Expectations matter in well-being, as is evident in how poor persons describe their experience of poverty: "Poverty is pain; it feels like a disease. It attacks a person not only materially but also morally. It eats away one's dignity and drives one into total despair"; "Poverty is lack of freedom, enslaved by crushing daily burden, by depression and fear of what the future will bring."[72] In the economics literature we find much evidence that perceptions and beliefs matter. For example, the trust citizens of country A have in citizens of county B has been shown to influence the extent of international trade, according to an interesting pattern: for high-tech and differentiated goods, in which quality matters, trusting the seller turns out to be essential; for commodities, in which solvency matters, trusting the buyer is crucial.[73]

Perceptions, expectations, and beliefs can hardly be directly observed, but they can be inferred by measuring observable risky actions that generate progress.[74] Risky action requires and, at the same time, signals hope (notice, that hope is an inherently relational concept: it produces social capital and trust). A plausible list of risky actions leading to progress includes economic actions (job creation; innovation; entrepreneurship; investment in physical, human, and social capital; and obviously investment in that very basic driver of change and societal renewal, childbearing), political innovation (institutional investment, fostering institutional diversity), and societal innovation (openness, "plurality").[75] To summarize: in assessing women's situation and progress, relations matter (hence, we need to collect relational data, not just attributional data), but perceptions, expectations, and beliefs also matter (hence, we need to capture them "in action").

WOMEN AND THE "MISSING GDP". Many argue that the income dimension of complex measures of well-being should include women's contribution to the quantities produced and consumed, even when their activity doesn't entail market transactions. Women work in the home, looking after children, cleaning, and cooking. This unpaid work is not counted in the standard GDP statistics, underestimating the actual amount of produced quantities. Reasonable estimates of an enlarged version of GDP including unpaid work can be provided: the money worth of unpaid housework can be roughly measured as the product of the estimated hours worked, times the average wage rates of a domestic worker. If this estimated amount were added to the contribution of women to official GDP, which in high-income economies is slightly below 40 percent of total official GDP,[76] women would end up producing more than 50 percent of this enlarged GDP. A second "missing" dimension of GDP reflects women's discrimination in the economy. A report by the United Nations Economic and Social Commission for Asia and the Pacific[77] estimates that sex discrimination costs the region between US$42 and US$47 billion a year by restricting women's job opportunities; the poor state of girls' education costs a further US$16 to US$30 billion.

This is what you can find (if you look hard) in economic literature about the missing contribution of women; but something very important is still missing. It is worth noting that childbearing is the single most evident and least considered case of feminine contribution (investment) to society and to the economic system. In a very basic sense, human beings are the most precious of economic resources. This was clear among the fathers of modern economics but was soon forgotten in the discipline. Since the beginning of the twentieth century, Catholic social thought on the importance of labour and the ontological priority of labour over capital remained as a lonely but clear affirmation of the economic (not just moral) value of human creativity; this occurred well before economic analysis of the so-called knowledge society became fashionable. Today, in the abundant rhetoric about the crucial role of human resources in firms, human capital in development, and so on, one seldom recalls that the analysis should be talking about actual pregnant mothers who are investing in the future, about actual babies and youngsters whose full human development requires much more than food, shelter, and training. Human generation requires care for meaningful relations, questing for beauty, for understanding, and for an overarching sense of life; such a quest is the most powerful driver of innovation and progress.

If we take the peculiar nature of human generation to be an investment in meaningful relations, it becomes reasonable to ask ourselves whether the notion of "enlarged" GDP, including women's nonmarket production of good and services and women's investment in the actual future of humanity, makes sense at all. A recent economics book by a noneconomist, Edward Hadas[78] gives a fresh look at what the economy is about. Building from elementary experience and backed by an impressive historical and philosophical background, the author redefines the economy with amazing ingenuity (the details may be unconvincing, but the overall architecture is interesting to say the least).

In his words, the economic aspects of society include everything that has to do with jobs, shopping, production, and so on ("Economies produce stuff… enormous amounts of stuff"[79]); here scarcity, prices, and wages make sense. But focusing on prices and paid labour can only provide a partial and inadequate picture of the "caring economy" in homes, schools, hospitals, and the like, which is critical for human well-being.

Bringing Hadas's discourse probably too far, his approach can lead to the proposal that the enlarged notion of GDP including women's work of care and women's investment in human resources makes little sense: summing "stuff" and "care" through the mediation of the inadequate metric of prices would be like summing carrots and apples.[80] One alternative would be to produce two distinct measures: on the one side, GDP of stuff; on the other side, a sort of GDP of care—whether the care is being given for love or for money, in which focus is on the actual good produced. In the second measure, we need to assess care output in terms of results and not assume, as in typical GDP calculations, that the value of care output is equal to the value of inputs deployed, measured either at their market price or their opportunity cost. The symbolic dimension of care is particularly precious: a true smile, when we need care, has really no price.

Women's Well-being and Gender Equality: Elementary Experience

Some examples, building on elementary experience, may illustrate the relevance of a cognitive/symbolic, relational perspective. The first example is largely autobiographic; it refers to the role of the cultural environment on women's situation, including self-perception, beliefs, and expectations. It depicts the economic situation of women in the 1950s, in Lombardy, as seen from the eyes of a girl. The economic system is made of small to medium size, artisan family enterprises, in which women are always informally involved, though now and then they are formal co-owners or formal employees. Women usually keep the accounting of the family enterprise. They collect credits and keep contact with banks, while men produce "stuff." Women participate in a quite real sense in economic management, despite scant evidence of formal empowerment. In a formally patriarchal society, there is a deep-seated, informal matriarchal structure. This situation makes sense only in a relational setting in which it is reasonable to expect the family to be a stable set of relations, in which all members share equal dignity. Family and business tend to reinforce each other in an ambivalent way: sometimes families are kept together by business interests, and sometimes business are viable because of a solid family relationship. Women's self-confidence is very high, and it is intrinsically relational; their self-confidence is built on collaboration with men, both in the family and in society. This self-confidence is contagiously transmitted, horizontally in society and from one generation to the next.

This experience probably explains much of my own instinctive benign neglect of issues of political correctness and my acute awareness of possible ideological drift in gender studies and gender policies. A more thoughtful explanation, though, would situate the Lombardy of the 1950s within a much longer history, tightly intertwined with the history of Christianity that is constitutive of the same Italian identity. Many women, such as the Longobardian Queen Teodolinda or Matilde di Canossa, shaped medieval civilization and politics—real women, like the ones I mentioned, and symbols, like Dante's Beatrice. In the amazing flourishing of the Renaissance, women were still highly considered. As an example that relates to the True Wealth of Nations project, consider the Allegory of Good Government[81] painted in the main City Hall of Siena. It features as major characters a number of women (Wisdom, Justice, Concord, Peace, and all the virtues) but just one man, the City of Siena. Women were eventually diminished in their high symbolic and practical public role, but that was when most intellectuals definitely abandoned the conviction that the person is *imago Dei*.[82]

The second example of the crucial importance of perceptions, expectations, and relationships can be found in the same assertive official reports quoted above, in which at times elementary experience pops up in the form of questions ("reality never cheats," Chesterton would say). Take the "choice versus forcing" issue in women's work profile in low-income countries:

> When women are employed, it is often claimed that, relative to men, they are more likely to: (1) be self-employed rather than work for wages; (2) work in the informal rather than the formal sector; and (3) work as own-account workers, domestic workers, and contributing family workers, while men are more likely to work as employers and wage and salaried workers....[83] A key question is whether women prefer to work at home or in family-owned businesses because of the location or the flexibility of work hours, which allows them to more easily combine work, domestic chores, and care. Or, do prevailing gender norms condition women to assume this triple workload or restrict their mobility? Or, is this pattern a result not of supply considerations, but rather of the gendered demand for labor, which presumably reflects existing societal gender norms?[84]

Good questions indeed, impossible to answer outside of a relational perspective; they are elementary questions that also arise in the supposedly advanced countries, where gender gaps tend to shrink and where "womanomics" is in the air. Why do women's work situations in the Western world deviate from men's? Is it discrimination, or is it choice?[85]

Perceptions, expectations, and beliefs, along with an inherently relational self-awareness, seem essential in assessing true gender equality. But how can gender equality be defined?[86] The UN Office of the Special Advisor on Gender Issues' definition[87] includes two parts. The first says: "gender...refers to both women and men, and to their status, relative to each other. Gender equality refers to that stage of human social development at which 'the rights, responsibilities and opportunities of individuals will not be determined by the fact of being born male or female.'" This definition falls short for two reasons connected to elementary experience. One is practical: justice requires widespread recognition that physically difficult jobs are not suited for women; I would not fight for gender equality in mining, nor for affirmative actions to balance the sex structure in construction work. The second reason is personal: don't professionally successful women (those who have rights, responsibilities, status, and power) feel strange when they happen to think: "Are we just better men than men?" Instead I would rather support "no programme of equal rights between woman and men unless it takes fully into account that the man owes a special debt to the woman in their shared parenthood."[88]

The second part of the quote from the UN Special Advisor on Gender Issues goes on: "In other words, a stage when both men and women realize their full potential." Gender equality cannot be just a matter of relative rights, status, or power. True gender equality must mean nothing less than realizing one's full potential, in which both men and women accomplish whát they long for, what they perceive was meant for them.

WOMEN'S WELL-BEING, EMPOWERMENT, AND HUMAN DIGNITY. With the slogan, "Human development, if not engendered, is endangered," the UNDP Human Development Report represented the first global analysis of gender disparities over a few decades, highlighting the undervaluation and nonrecognition of women's work and the wide and persistent gap between women's expanding capabilities and limited opportunities. The report introduced two measures for ranking countries on a global scale by their performance in gender equality: the Gender-related Development Index (GDI) and the Gender Empowerment Measure (GEM).[89] Meanwhile, "women's empowerment" became the typical consensus expression in gender policies. There is no single accepted definition of empowerment, but this is curiously part of the attractiveness of the term. It is rather common that evocative but imprecise expressions command a wider political consensus than precisely defined concepts. In broad terms, though, there is a significant overlap in the words used to define the term "empowerment": availability of options, possibility of choice, and exercise of control and of power.[90] The general definition of empowerment as the ability of women to make decisions and affect outcomes for themselves and their families is widely acceptable; but—as it often occurs— the devil is in the details. When inadequate indicators of true empowerment feed into inadequate policy instruments, they end up being self-validating despite their shortcomings.

An example based on elementary experience may help illustrate the complexity. Consider the goal of empowering young girls to avoid adolescent pregnancies and motherhood—surely a deserving goal. How do you measure the actual level of empowerment in this field, and how do you promote it? The typical list of indicators and policy instruments includes access to contraceptive information, to modern technologies for birth control, to abortion, and so on. If you use these indicators (as international development institutions do) to indirectly assess this dimension of girls' empowerment, you will likely promote access to those instruments as an empowering policy. Once wider access to birth control techniques and to abortion is realized, the number of adolescent motherhoods will very likely decrease: at the end of the day, this policy will prove effective in enhancing girl's empowerment—at least, according to the definition you started with, in an obviously circular way.

But it is worth asking: is that true empowerment? Notice that the above indicators and policies are targeted on individual girls, each of whom gains the individual (lonely) power to avoid unwanted childbearing by using the instruments that are made available to her. Would this form of individual empowerment be the same, to the girl, as an alternative form of relational empowerment that touches upon the sphere of meaning and promotes the possibility for the girl to live in a familiar and social environment in which her right to be fully respected in her feminine dignity is an undisputed principle and a social norm? My answer is, "No, they are not the same;" and I would expect a similar answer from any girl. The individual power of avoiding unwanted births is a very miserable power, if you cannot avoid unwanted sexual relationships. Actually, it is not difficult to imagine that true relational empowerment might in fact deteriorate as individual empowerment is realized, since the latter ends up putting all the costs of reducing unwanted pregnancies on the (lonely) shoulders of the girl.

You may think that the above is a rather extreme example of inadequate understanding of women's empowerment. It is not. Take micro-credit as an economic empowerment opportunity for women; it is often targeted on women, and women repay the loans on schedule much more reliably than men. But personal and community development crucially depends on whether the focus is on the woman as an individual or if attention is given to the relational circumstances within which she lives. Where unbalanced relationships among males and females prevail, a woman may be pretending to borrow for herself and be personally responsible for repayment, while in fact she has little control over the use of the money borrowed. In the empirical literature, self-help groups of women are reported to be helpful in supporting individuals, and this evidence only reinforces the message that individualistic empowerment policies are inadequate.

This is not to say that there are easy roads to true relational empowerment: it requires time for building personalized trust relationships. But as a minimum we have the responsibility to speak the truth. We must rethink the standard reduction of the complex enhancement of women's ability to make decisions and affect outcomes to a matter of "power," as the word "empowerment" seems to imply. Even purifying the language helps: speaking the language of women's human dignity seems less ambiguous than a generic empowerment discourse. An important example here is Albino Barrera's essay in this volume, which stresses human dignity as the cornerstone of true wealth, or the economic common good. Human rights are not exhausted by "freedom from," they must include "freedom for" realizing the purpose of a meaningful life. As Eleanor Roosevelt once said:

> Where, after all, do universal human rights begin? In small places, close to home—so close and so small that they cannot be seen on any map of the world. Yet they are the world of the individual person: the neighborhood he lives in; the school or college he attends; the factory, farm or office where he works. Such are the places where every man, woman, and child seeks equal justice, equal opportunity, equal dignity without discrimination. Unless these rights have meaning there, they have little meaning anywhere.[91]

Roosevelt here highlights the relational nature of human rights, clearly founding human rights on human dignity, as prepolitical and apolitical rights;[92] she suggests a common responsibility in actualizing human rights, whose realization cannot be delegated to any national or international agency. This approach underlines the practical realism of the principle of subsidiarity in human development policies; it encompasses and completes partial visions of social justice, such as access to material goods and as individualistic empowerment.

In too many cases, the present rhetoric of human rights, including women's rights, is clearly "a move away from the protection of human dignity towards the satisfaction of simple interests, often particular interests,"[93] during which power prevails over human dignity. Consider human reproduction, short of generation: at the frontiers of science, possessing the roots of life consists in a totally asymmetric structure of power—all the newborn babies will keep being "given" life, having no say. In everyday life, the power over reproduction (the power to give life, for one, or to withhold it, for others) comes to be perceived as a right. In both cases, human dignity is objectively at risk.

WOMEN'S DIGNITY IN THE CATHOLIC TRADITION. Woman's dignity is rooted in the account of the very "beginnings." Reference to the beginnings is particularly appropriate in this paper, which suggests generation as the main pillar for understanding the true wealth of nations and women's dignity. The word "generation" comes from *genos*, "origin"—as in the word "gender" (male-female) and "genealogy" (the individual "I," embedded in his or her own personal history).[94]

Since the beginning, the human being "cannot exist 'alone'...he can exist only as a 'unity of the two,' and therefore in relation to another human person...in the image and likeness of God...the Triune God."[95] This account of our beginnings matches elementary experience: we are "given" life by someone else, and we definitely are not happy alone. Being "one, in relation with" (communion: with the other, with the totally other, with nature itself[96]) is indeed the core aspiration of the human heart. Christian anthropology expresses this being "one, in relation with" as a permanent tension among three constitutive polarities of elementary human experience: the dual unity of body and soul, the dual unity rooted in sexual difference,[97] and the dual unity of individual and community.[98] It follows that "male and female differentiates two individuals of equal dignity, which does not, however, reflect a strict equality, because the specificity of the female is different from the specificity of the male, and this difference in equality is enriching and indispensable for the harmony of life in society."[99]

Particularly important is the primacy of the ontological nature of the Christian good news, which founds the ethical dimension. "For in Christ Jesus...there is neither Jew nor Greek, neither slave nor free, there is neither male nor female; for you are all one in Christ" (Gal. 3:26–28). The "new" creation opens unexpected horizons to understanding women's dignity, unexpected, but fascinatingly corresponding to being "one, in relation." The Christian tradition, with all its human shortcomings, does in fact preserve a deeply "spousal" dimension, an archetype of all relationships (Creation, Alliance, Incarnation;[100] Christ, the Bridegroom, and the Church, his Bride and His own body; the Eucharist, the Communion of Saints). Human marriage and the generative structure of the family acquire a new profound symbolic dimension,[101] which is a powerful drive for social affirmation of women's dignity (as in Dante and Lorenzetti).

Women do in fact play a peculiar role in the story of Christianity. Narrative, central in the Catholic tradition,[102] tells of generative women that have left a mark in history; with good reason, they are still called "mothers." Obviously, one can notice that structures of power within the Church were and remain largely male;[103] this can, and maybe should, be reformed. It is a matter of priorities, though; I have learned to appreciate more and more "the power of the powerless" (as Vaclav Havel would say), both within the Church and without. The actual history of the Church, past and present, is driven by saints—men and women, married and consecrated to God, much more than by clerical (male) institutions!

True Prosperity: Toward a Dynamic "Generative" Approach

Better ethics and better economics, as pursued by the The Wealth of Nations project, need be rooted in a true anthropology, up to the demanding test of elementary experience. Considering the many unanswered questions that remain in assessing women's situation, the paper suggested "generation" as a key concept for understanding well-being and progress, in an intertemporal, symbolic/relational paradigm.

Intertemporal prosperity needs to be understood as a process, as a path to be trod not as a final outcome to be pursued by technical and political interventions, whose success will be measured at the end. The path matters, well above the final result (the adolescent pregnancy story illustrates the essential difference between the path and the outcome). And symbolic/relational experience confirms the centrality of actions and interactions in economic life—as opposed to deterministic behaviour (actually, machines and animals seem to be better than we are at efficient behaviour). Action is free, open, and ultimately unpredictable; it is driven by beliefs, perceptions, and expectations and is embedded in personalized and potentially durable relation. From experience, we know that personalized relations are required for most economic transactions to occur, be they good or bad, just or unjust. Hence, for true wealth creation and true progress, we do not simply require space for personalized relations and social reciprocity of some sort. Because human relations are deeply ambivalent, we need to keep permanently open the question: what is really good, beautiful, and just, here and now?

What does the generative approach imply for a just economy and for true prosperity? Generation[104] implies taking care of relationships over time, for personal and societal progress. In assessing true human flourishing, we can immediately tell the difference between reproduction and generation; by analogy, we can easily tell the difference between mere economic growth and true prosperity. Do we detect generative actions? True prosperity signals and requires a generative societal dynamism, in which efficiency and justice can be detected in action.[105]

Notice that justice implies more than distributional justice, more than reciprocity in personal relations. Social justice as participation is dynamically realized when each person is granted the possibility of being generative, of participating as a protagonist in the generative story of wealth creation. Actions are truly generative when they respect and promote the basic element of justice, namely the nondisposable nature of human dignity and the prepolitical, apolitical source of human rights; this holds for every man, every woman, and every child (with air in the lungs, or not yet).

The dynamism of generation is driven by gratuity and gratitude: we can actually give because we receive our own being (even receiving is an act of freedom). Well beyond reciprocal personal relationships, initiating and nurturing economic and social relations also requires some form of gratuitous gift. Gift is a risky relation;[106] hence, risky generative actions need to be humanly reasonable. Freely entering gift relationships is reasonable because of hope[107]—even in the partial, mathematical sense of an expected "good" outcome. In other words, generation signals and requires positive expectations about the future, rooted in the experience of receiving. In family life, for example, the grateful memory of being generated opens one to being generative, and it takes generations to regenerate the family. Something similar can be said, by analogy, for society.

We accomplish self-realization "through a sincere gift of self"[108]—in the words used in this paper—through free and gratuitous generative actions. This is a claim that can be tested against elementary experience. Avoiding free, generative giving actually harms ourselves: shrunk personality, alienation from ourselves and from others and from true prosperity in society. There will be fewer gratuitous generative actions, less investment, less satisfaction of human needs (both marketable and nonmarketable), less innovation—just the opposite of the hundredfold we are promised, just the opposite of wealth creation and true prosperity. Generative actions change daily life, from what happens in the household to social and political institutions—their drivers, gratuity, and gratitude are in fact the opposite of the "all-consuming desire for profit" and the "thirst for power" that impregnate unjust social structures.[109] Generative actions are a form of intertemporal solidarity, the virtuous awareness of intertemporal interdependence, including institution building and the deconstruction of institutions when needed. Generative actions are wealth creating, as opposed to structures of injustice, which are wealth accumulating or wealth appropriating.

I need to gratefully acknowledge that I have placed "generation" at the center of my thinking because of a gift I received and hope to circulate: the Catholic social tradition (CST). It is a "living" tradition, which is credible because of its deeds: hence, it is open to the test of elementary experience. It is not most basically about promoting and practicing Christian values; it is about new life in Christ, which becomes unexpectedly generative. I would describe the Catholic social tradition as a generative dynamism in itself: the Church offers a "global vision" for promoting "integral human development."[110] That is, Catholic social thought circulates a "received" gift: the priceless gift of Christ Himself, fully revealing "the whole man" to each person.

NOTES

1. Participation rates measure the proportion of women who are in paid employment or looking for it; hence, they include unemployed women.

2. The Wikigender portal (www.wikigender.org) was promoted by OECD; it covers labour issues and a full range of social and political indicators about the position of women in societies. Data can be accessed by country and/or by issues; the portal also provides information about different "innovative" issues, such as women's access to credit and entrepreneurship and women's political and social participation. The United Nations Economic Commission for Europe (UNECE, www.unece.org) offers a Gender Statistics database that presents social data disaggregated by sex, covering gender-related aspects of population, family, work, education, public life, decision making, health, crime, and violence.

3. "A World Fit for Women," *The Economist Millennium Special Edition*, December 23, 1999. See Figure 1, *The Economist*, "A Guide to Womenomics," April 12, 2006. I choose to quote *The Economist*, a widely read and influential source of information, which is attentive to the changing profile of the role of women in society and in the economy.

4. "A Guide to Womenomics," *The Economist*, April 12, 2006.

5. The Organization for Economic Cooperation and Development is a group of 30 of the wealthiest nations in the world.

6. "A Guide to Womenenomics," *The Economist*, April 12, 2006.

7. http://www.wikigender.org/wiki/index.php?title=Wage_Gaps_Between_Men_and_Women.

8. Francine D. Blau and Lawrence M. Kahn, "Gender Differences in Pay."

9. Jane Waldfogel, "Understanding the 'Family Gap' in Pay for Women with Children."

10. Sam Roberts, "For Young Earners in Big City, a Gap I Women's Favor."

11. "A Guide to Womenomics," *The Economist*, April 12, 2006.

12. The above studies are summarized in *The Economist*, April 12, 2006. During the July 2008 True Wealth of Nations Conference, Los Angeles, Stefano Zamagni commented on the economic "rationality" of having more women sitting on firms' boards on the basis that men have a comparative advantage in managing standardized production, while women have an advantage within the post-industrial knowledge society.

13. As an example, Michel Ferrary of CERAM Business School (Nice) uses data from companies in the French CAC40 to show that the fewer women a company has in its management, the greater the drop in its share price since the beginning of 2008. Women seem to avoid risk and to focus more on a long term perspective, balancing the behaviour of their male colleagues; hence, it is unclear whether the incidence of female managers per se or gender diversity is the relevant explanation. See http://www.ceram.edu/index.php/Latest-News/Latest/Financail-Crisis-Are-Women-the-Antidote-CERAM-Research.html.

14. Claudia Goldin, Lawrence F. Katz, and Ilyana Kuziemko, "The Homecoming of American College Women: The Reversal of the College Gender Gap."

15. "A Guide to Womenomics," *The Economist*, April 12, 2006.

16. "Womenomics Revisited," *The Economist*, April 19, 2007.

17. Table 3, *The Economist*, April 12, 2006, reproducing data from Japan's Ministry of Internal Affairs and Communication.

18. Allowances are indeed higher for high-income, high-fertility countries. Economist.com, July 15 2008.

19. Promoting gender equality is explicitly part of most official development aid initiatives, especially in education and health programs and in the sphere of political participation. (See figure 4.4, IBRD GMR, World Bank, "Global Monitoring Report," 159). This is probably good, but it is reasonable to suspect some lip service to consensus priorities. As GMR notices, many "non targeted" policies (such as environmental policies, AIDS/HIV health initiatives, rural policies) would dramatically improve the situation of women, who suffer most from not tackling the existing situation.

20. www.un.org/millenniumgoals.

21. World Bank, *World Development Report*.

22. "The World Bank has recognized that there is no investment more effective for achieving development goals than educating girls," http://web.worldbank.org/WBSITE/EXTERNAL/TOPICS/EXTEDUCATION/0,contentMDK:20298916~menuPK:617572~pagePK:148956~piPK:216618~theSitePK:282386,00.html. UNESCO estimates that of the nearly 137 million illiterate youths in the world, 63 percent are female (quoted in World Bank, "Global Monitoring Report," 114); hence, both fairness and efficiency require improving female education.

23. The report's title is "Millennium Development Goals: Confronting the Challenges of Gender Equality and Fragile States."

24. World Bank, "Global Monitoring Report," 2007, 120.

25. See also the extensive documentation in The World Bank, FAO, IFAD, *Gender in Agriculture Sourcebook*, The International Bank for Reconstruction and Development

/ The World Bank 2009, http://siteresources.worldbank.org/INTGENAGRLIVSOUBOOK/Resources/CompleteBook.pdf.

26. FAO data, quoted by Mercy Karanja, "Women and Food Security."

27. Annina Lubbock. IFAD, "Donne imprenditrici e ruolo delle istituzioni di sostegno."

28. In the Kyrgyz Republic, for example, but not atypically, 24.8 percent of women reported that "housekeeping, taking care of children, sick persons, or the elderly" kept them from working outside the home, but only 1.5 percent of men reported these reasons. Andrew Morrison and Francesca Lamana, *Gender Issues in the Kyrgyz Labor Market*, quoted in World Bank, "Global Monitoring Report," 108.

29. "In rural areas of Burkina Faso, Uganda, and Zambia, the potential time savings from locating a potable water source within 400 meters of all households range from 125 hours per household per year to 664" (Ian Barwell, "Transport and the Village," quoted in World Bank, "Global Monitoring Report," 108).

30. This evidence points to the fact that even nontargeted environmental interventions that reduce indoor air pollution, promote reforestation, and improve water quality can produce great benefits on women (World Bank, "Global Monitoring Report," 58).

31. The report describe the new indicators as "measurable, actionable, and parsimonious: "three of the five build on existing measures of other millennium development goals, so the data requirements for monitoring them are not onerous; besides that, some of them are also being considered for future inclusion in the millennium development goals as part of new targets for decent and productive work and for reproductive health (World Bank, "Global Monitoring Report," 105).

32. World Bank, "Global Monitoring Report," 111–16.

33. Ibid., 118.

34. See table 3.4 in "Global Monitoring Report," 121. There has been a general improvement in completion rates from 1991 to 2004, which remain very low despite improvement only in sub-Saharan Africa (56.9 for girls to 67.3 for boys in 2004). The gap in completion rates is unfavourable to girls in South Asia (83.0 to 90.2 for boys). Completion rates for both goys and girls are highest in Latin American and the Caribbean (101.1 for girls to 99.4 for boys) and in East Asia and Pacific (96.3 for girls to 95.8 for boys)—that is, they are actually higher for girls than for boys.

35. For example, in four countries considered to be characterized by high levels of gender equality (Denmark, Finland, Norway, and Sweden) the girl-to-boy ratio is between 0.81 and 0.88.

36. See figure 3.9 in "Global Monitoring Report," 122. Evidence of higher than normal under-five mortality ratios, girls to boys, is clear in South Asia, sub-Saharan Africa (where absolute under-five mortality rates for girls are respectively three and five times higher that in Latin America and Caribbean), and East Asia and Pacific (even though the absolute mortality of under-five girls is much lower than in South Asia and sub-Saharan Africa).

37. These data reflect sex-selective abortion but may also include some amount of female infanticide; the net effect of sex selection before birth, at birth, and after birth is

reflected in the sex ratios of children aged 0 to 4; see World Bank, "Global Monitoring Report," 124–25.

38. United Nations, Department of Economic and Social Affairs, Population Division 2002.

39. UNAIDS/WHO, 2004.

40. World Bank, 2006.

41. World Bank, "Global Monitoring Report," 127.

42. See United Nations Population Fund, *A Passage to Hope*, 23.

43. Ibid., 25.

44. Chapters 3 and 4 of United Nations Population Fund are devoted to these issues.

45. Mario Agostino Maggioni, Mario Nosvelli, and Erika T. Uberti, "Space vs. Networks."

46. As an example, information about who trades with whom (relational data) provides much more information that just the levels of one country's trade (attributional data). See L.Guiso, P. Sapienza, and L. Zingales, *Cultural Biases in Economic Exchange.*

47. Betsey Stevenson and Justin Wolfers, "Marriage and Divorce."

48. The mainstream approach to family economics evidently clashes with other disciplinary perspectives. Contrast with Francis Fukuyama's perspective, quoted in John Coleman's essay in this volume: "one could hardly imagine a meaningful family life if families were essentially contracts between rational, self-interested individuals." I personally do not object to rationality and self-interest: reason is what makes us human; and our "true" interest is what makes us searching higher and deeper for meaning. I object to their reduction, all too common not only in economics.

49. The expression "elementary experience" will be recurrent in this paper. It is a crucial notion in L. Giussani, *The Religious Sense.* It is the basic structure of our "I": a complex of needs and "evidences" that accompanies us as we come face to face with all that exist (p.7).

50. V. Cigoli and E. Scabini, *Family Identità.*

51. See, for example, the papers by David G. Blanchflower and A. J. Oswald on "Happiness Economics," reviewed in NBER Reporter, 2008, n.2.

52. Betsey Stevenson and Justin Wolfers, "Marriage and Divorce."

53. Evidence shows that those who cohabit before marriage have been historically more likely to divorce than those who do not cohabitate (Stevenson and Wolfers, "Marriage and Divorce," 38). This evidence is at odds with what the typical economic approach to the family would imply: cohabitation should have a high information content and, hence, help avoid erroneous marriage decisions.

54. George Akerlof, Janet Yellen, and Michael Katz, "An Analysis of Out-of-Wedlock Childbearing in the United States."

55. Donald Cox, "Biological Basics and the Economics of the Family."

56. For example, having mothers allocate family income tends to increase the consumption of children. This unexplained evidence is widely used in development policy design.

57. www.worldbank.org/poverty/scapital/.

58. Simona Beretta and Luigi Curini, Il ruolo della famiglia nel generare capitale sociale.

59. Andrew Yuengert's essay in this volume also places the family "at the heart of any network of social relations."

60. Building upon traditional social capital theory, accurately summarized in John A. Coleman's essay in this volume, our paper took distance from a notion of social capital as the "associational life located midway between state and family." We maintained that the family constitutes a basic form of social capital in itself. Within an economic perspective, we focussed on explaining how decisions of investing in this particular form of "generative" social capital come about.

61. In the 2004 paper, we used "trust," as in Fukuyama, to measure the cognitive dimension of social capital. The structural and the cognitive aspects are not exhaustive of social capital though. The symbolic perspective would be more adequate in understanding the family as social capital and as a source of social capital. I thank Eugenia Scabini for conversation on this issue.

62. Incestuous relationships are perceived as pathological in virtually all cultures.

63. See Jon Gunnemann's essay in this volume: "Symbols point to a reality, which itself escapes all human attempts to fully understand it."

64. Simona Beretta, "Wealth Creation in the Global Economy."

65. Equality and cohesion are undoubtedly part of the answer to the question, "Does economic life enhance or threaten our life together as a community?" in the 1986 US Bishops document "Economic Justice for All", quoted in the True Wealth of Nations project. See Preface of this volume.

66. After Sen, some measures of sectoral "functioning" have also been common practices—as in the case of PIPA measuring education output in terms of problem-solving abilities of 15-year-old girls and boys, and similar tests for literacy functioning.

67. They include national statistical institutes, ministries, environmental agencies, private foundations, and international institutes providing statistics, such as OECD, World Bank, and Eurostat.

68. Mario Maggioni and I got involved in "measuring well-being and societal progress" when the initiative was launched in a joint OECD—EU/JRC expert seminar at the Catholic University "Sacro Cuore," in June 2006; the subsequent seminar in Istanbul produced a final document, "Istanbul Declaration," approved by the representatives of the European Commission, the Organization for Economic Cooperation and Development, the Organization of the Islamic Conference, the United Nations, the United Nations Development Program, and the World Bank.

69. As Albert O. Hirshman, in "A Dissenter's Confession," maintains, there are no such things as "right" (wrong) cultural attitudes and beliefs as "prerequisites" for economic growth and societal progress.

70. Despite the reluctance to use the word "truth," especially in Europe, it is curious to notice that in a follow-up of the "measuring well-being" project, the EU Commission held a conference, "Beyond GDP," in Brussels, November 2007, (http://www.beyond-gdp.eu/) whose programme "had" to use the adjective "true"!

71. This should not come as a surprise. It is well known that in any axiomatic system there are propositions that cannot be proved or disproved within the axioms of the system (Gödel). Still, especially in Europe, there is a mounting reluctance to simply admit that the notion of "truth" cannot be disposed of.

72. Both are quotes from Deepa Narayan, with Raj Patel, Kai Schafft, Anne Rademacher, and Sarah Koch-Schulte. *Voices of the Poor: Can Anyone Hear Us?* 2000.

73. Guiso, Sapienza, and Zingales, *Cultural Biases in Economic Exchange.*

74. This is the basic idea in Simona Beretta and Mario A. Maggioni, "Building a Panel of Indicators," contributed to the OECD—EU/JRC Seminar. This reflects elementary experience: "there is a vision and an understanding of the world that shows itself in our action. It is in our action where we take a position about daily life situations and affirm ourselves in relation to a world of values" (Ivone Gebara, quoted in Maylin Biggadike's essay in this volume).

75. Andrew Yuengert's essay, in his paragraph on *Personal Initiative*, uses a similar notion: "actual initiative for the good…and the fruits of initiative…are integral to prosperity." His list of examples is indeed very similar to the one in Beretta and Maggioni, "Building a Panel of Indicators."

76. *The Economist*, April 12, 2006. Could it be that an increase in the number of women being in paid jobs could actually reduce the enlarged GDP? Probably not; it is true that the increase in female participation has meant fewer hours of unpaid housework, but this element has very likely been counterbalanced by the increased productivity in housework granted by new technologies (dishwashers, washing machines, etc.). Most working women are still responsible for the bulk of housekeeping work, so it would not be unfair to maintain that, on average, women being in paid jobs simply work more, enlarging GDP in net terms.

77. Quoted in *The Economist*, April 19, 2007.

78. Edward Hadas, *Human Goods, Economic Evils.*

79. Ibid., 3.

80. Measuring GDP was a remarkable innovation required by the "new things" of the industrial revolution. Today we definitely need innovation: "services" account for a very large proportion of GDP in advanced economies (in which even the value of produced "stuff" often incorporates important "service" dimensions), and paradoxically in very low-income countries, in which bureaucracies "produce" a large share of output. It is all too evident that prices and factor remuneration are particularly inadequate for measuring both types of "production."

81. Fresco crated by Ambrogio Lorenzetti, 1338–39, Palazzo Pubblico, Siena, Italy.

82. See Andrew Yuengert's essay in this volume.

83. UNDAW, "The Role of National Mechanisms in Promoting Gender Equality."

84. World Bank, "Global Monitoring Report," 130.

85. Susan Pinker, *The Sexual Paradox* (reviewed by *The Economist*, April 18, 2008) collects evidence on the issue of "discrimination versus choice" by interviewing men and women about why they end up in different career trajectories. The author's hypothesis is that "male is the vanilla gender," from which women deviate; her

conclusion is that in fact it is so because evidence shows that it was personally costly for women to choose to deviate from men's choices. Interestingly, all interviewed women asked to be anonymously reported, while no man did.

86. I thank Andrew Yuenger for raising this "simple" question in discussing my paper.

87. As quoted in Maylin Biggadike's essay in this volume.

88. John Paul II, *Mulieris dignitatem*, 18.

89. http://hdr.undp.org/en/statistics/indices/gdi_gem/.

90. Most often, all these terms converge in defining empowerment in the context of the ability of women to make decisions and affect outcomes that are important to them and their families (World Bank, "Global Monitoring Report," 146). Self-efficacy is also an element of empowerment: women should be "capable" of defining self-interest and choice and be able and entitled to make those choices (A. Malhotra, S. Schuler, and C. Boender, "Measuring Women's Empowerment as a Variable in International Development"). Availability of options and choice may proxy a formal notion of empowerment but may be a poor proxy of actual "self-efficacy"; control and power may be more relevant to "self-efficacy," but they risk being trapped in an individualistic approach to empowerment.

91. Eleanor Roosevelt, "In Your Hands, Address at the United Nations."

92. Jane Haaland Matlary, "Women: Dignity and Human Rights." Paolo Carozza, "Subsidiarity as a Structural Principle of International Human Rights Law."

93. Benedict XVI, UN Address, April 18, 2008.

94. Eugenia Scabini, *Famiglia e procreazione oggi*.

95. John Paul II, *Mulieris dignitatem*, 7.

96. Also as Maylin Biggadike's essay in this volume puts it, relatedness implies also focusing on "how best to be in *communion with* nature instead of subjugating the environment."

97. "Man and woman complete each other mutually not only from a physical and psychological point of view, but also ontologically.... It is the 'unity of the two,' or in other words a relational 'uni-duality,' that allows each person to experience the interpersonal and reciprocal relationship as a gift which at the same time is a mission." Pontifical Council for Justice and Peace, *Compendium on the Social Doctrine of the Church*, para. 147.

98. Angelo Scola, *La dottrina sociale della Chiesa*. A. Finkielkraut, *L'umanità perduta*.

99. Pontifical Council for Justice and Peace, *Compendium*, 146.

100. Incarnation mysteriously abolishes all dualisms, giving a new perspective to the aspiration of being "one, in relation."

101. The spousal mystery "is a profound one, and I am saying that it refers to Christ and the Church" (Eph. 5:32). Christian mysteries are not the unknown, but the "inexhaustible": they are eternal truths offered to us in a way we can receive.

102. I personally find it moving that, in his first two encyclicals, the "intellectual" Benedict XVI needs to name real people—famous saints, or simple ones, previously known to only a few.

103. In my understanding, male priesthood is a service to the church, not a structure of power. Here, I am talking of church power as concerning decisions about resources, strategies, planning: that is, the necessary human aspects of a mysterious experience, which affirms not to be exhausted by its worldly dimension. Otherwise, the Church would hardly have survived some clearly nasty characters who happened to hold the church's power!

104. "Generation" is similar to "creativity" in the True Wealth of Nations project (see the Preface) and "creative energy" in Jon Gunnemann's essay in this volume. I find it very suggestive that, in his paper, the basic "generative" relation is honor: "True wealth comes from economic activity that honors God, Creation, and neighbor, and contributes to the well being of this whole."

105. Wealth creation and justice are indeed inextricably linked, as stated by the 1996 CTBI document quoted in the True Wealth of Nations project (Preface). In fact, they are integral to the same "generative" framework.

106. Jacques T. Godbout, *L'esprit du don*.

107. Hope is required for generating (see Jon Gunnemann's essay in this volume).

108. John Paul II, *Mulieris dignitatem*, 7, quoting *Gaudium et Spes*.

109. In the language of Catholic social teaching, they are structures of sin: John Paul II, *Sollicitudo rei socialis*, paras. 36–40. See also Jon Gunnemann's essay in this volume: "On the level of . . . social institutions, sin is exacerbated by the natural tendency of institutions and groups to seek their own well-being whatever the intentions of the individual members (R. Niebuhr), and by the power, formal and informal, that social groups and institution can wield over (others) . . . power is a central social reality."

110. Paul VI, *Populorum Progressio*, para. 13.

REFERENCES

"A Guide to Womenomics." *The Economist*, April 12, 2006.

Akerlof, George, Janet Yellen, and Michael, Katz. "An Analysis of Out-of-Wedlock Childbearing in the United States." *Quarterly Journal of Economics* III (1996): 277–317.

Barwell, Ian. "Transport and the Village: Findings from African Village-Level Travel and Transport Surveys and Related Studies." *World Bank Discussion Paper No. 344, Africa Regiona Series*. Washington, DC: World Bank, 1996.

Becker, Gary S. *A Treatise on the Family*. Cambridge, MA: Harvard University Press, 1981.

Benedict XVI. UN Address. *Origins* (April 18, 2008).

Beretta, Simona. "Wealth Creation in the Global Economy: Human Labor and Development." In *Rediscovering Abundance: Interdisciplinary Essays on Wealth, Income and their Distribution in the Catholic Social Tradition*, edited by H. Alford, C. Clark, A. Cortright, and M. Naughton. Notre Dame: University of Notre Dame Press, 2006.

Beretta, Simona, and Luigi Curini. Il ruolo della famiglia nel generare capitale sociale: un approccio di economia politica, in Pierpaolo DONATI (ed), *Famiglia e capitale sociale nella società italiana*. Ottavo Rapporto CISF sulla famiglia in Italia. Edizioni San Paolo (2003): 290–339.

Beretta, Simona, and Mario A. Maggioni. "Building a panel of indicators towards measuring the political dimensions of well-being, CRELL/JRC/OECD Workshop on Measuring Well-Being and Societal Progress," Università Cattolica del Sacro Cuore, Milano, 19–21 giugno, 2006. Online. Available: http://farmweb.jrc.cec.eu.int/Crell/Well-being/Powerpoints/ Beretta&Maggioni_well-being.ppt.

Blau, Francine D., and Lawrence M. Kahn. "Gender Differences in Pay." *Journal of Economic Perspectives* 14 (Fall 2000): 75–99.

Carozza, Paolo G. "Subsidiarity as a Structural Principle of International Human Rights Law." *American Journal of International Law* 97 (2003): 38–79.

Cigoli, V., and E. Scabini. *Family Identity: Ties, Symbols, and Transitions*. Mahwah, NJ: Lawrence Erlbaum Associates, 2006.

Cox, Donald. "Biological Basics and the Economics of the Family." *Journal of Economic Perspectives* 21 (Spring 2007): 91–108.

Finkielkraut, A. *L'umanità perduta, Saggio sul XX secolo*. Torino: Lindau, 2009.

"From here to Maternity." *The Economist*, July 15, 2008.

Giussani, L. *The Religious Sense*. Canada: McGill-Queen's University Press, 1997.

Giussani, Luigi. *The Religious Sense*. Canada: McGill-Queen's University Press, 2007.

Godbout, Jacques T. *L'esprit du don*. Paris: Editions La Découverte, 1992.

Goldin, Claudia, Lawrence F. Katz, and Ilyana Kuziemko. "The Homecoming of American College Women: The Reversal of the College Gender Gap." *Journal of Economic Perspectives* 20, no.4 (Fall 2006): 133–56.

Guiso, L., P. Sapienza, and L. Zingales. *Cultural Biases in Economic Exchange. Quarterly Journal of Economics* 2009 124:3, 1095–1131.

Haaland Matlary, Janne. "Women: Dignity and Human Rights." International Conference of Women, Development and Peace. Pontifical Council for Justice and Peace, Vatican City, October 28–29, 2005.

Hadas, Edward. *Human Goods, Economic Evils: A Moral Approach to the Dismal Science*. Wilmington, DE: ISI Books, Culture of Enterprise Series, 2007.

Hirschman, Albert O. "A Dissenter's Confession: 'The Strategy of Economic Development' Revisited." In *Pioneers in Development*, edited by G. Meier and D. Seers, 87–111. New York: Oxford University Press, 1984.

John Paul II. *Mulieris dignitatem*. August 15, 1988.

———. *Sollicitudo rei socialis*. December 30, 1987.

Karanja, Mercy. "Women and Food Security." International Conference of Women, Development and Peace. Pontifical Council for Justice and Peace, Vatican City, October 28–29, 2005.

Lubbock, Annina. IFAD. "Donne imprenditrici e ruolo delle istituzioni di sostegno." International Conference of Women, Development and Peace. Pontifical Council for Justice and Peace, Vatican City, October 28–29, 2005.

Maggioni, Mario Agostino, Mario Nosvelli, and Erika T. Uberti. "Space vs. Networks in the Geography of Innovation: A European Analysis." *Papers in Regional Science* 86, no. 3 (August 2007): 471–93.

Malhotra, A., S. Schuler, and C. Boender. "Measuring Women's Empowerment as a Variable in International Development." World Bank Gender and Development Group Background paper. Washington, DC: World Bank, 2002. Online. Available: http://www.icrw.org/docs/MeasuringEmpowerment_working-paper_802.doc.

Morrison, Andrew, and Francesca Lamana. "Gender Issues in the Kyrgyz Labor Market." Background paper for Kyrgyz Poverty Assessment. Washington, DC: World Bank, 2006.

Narayan, Deepa, with Raj Patel, Kai Schafft, Anne Rademacher, and Sarah Koch-Schulte. *Voices of the Poor: Can Anyone Hear Us?* New York: Published for the World Bank, Oxford University Press, 2000.

"Oral Contraceptives: The Liberator." *The Economist Millennium Special Edition*, December 23, 1999.

Paul VI, *Populorum Progressio*. March 26, 1967.

Pinker, Susan. *The Sexual Paradox: Men, Women, and the Real Gender Gap*. New York: Scribner Book Company, 2008.

Pontifical Council for Justice and Peace. *Compendium of the Social Doctrine of the Church*. Città del Vaticano: Libreria Editrice Vaticana, 2004.

Roberts, Sam. "For Young Earners in Big City, a Gap in Women's Favor." *Wikigender*, August 3, 2007. Online. Available: http://www.nytimes.com/2007/08/03/nyregion/03women.html?_r=2&pagewanted=1&oref=slogin.

Roosevelt, Eleanor. "In Your Hands, Address at the United Nations," March 27, 1958. Online. Available: www.udhr.org/history/inyour.htm.

Scabini, Eugenia. *Famiglia e procreazione oggi: contesto psicosociale odierno e sfide culturali*. Mimeo. Milano: Università Cattolica del Sacro Cuore, 2008.

Scola, Angelo. *La dottrina sociale della Chiesa: risorsa per una società plurale*, Centro di Ateneo per la Dottrina Sociale della Chiesa, contributi, 1, Vita e Pensiero. Milano: Università Cattolica del Sacro Cuore, 2007.

Stevenson, Betsey, and Justin Wolfers. "Marriage and Divorce: Changes and Their Driving Forces." *Journal of Economic Perspectives* 21 (Spring 2007): 27–52.

UNAIDS/WHO. *Women and AIDS*. AIDS Epidemic update, December 2004.

United Nations Division for the Advancement of Women (UNDAW). "The Role of National Mechanisms in Promoting Gender Equality and the Empowerment of Women." Report of the Expert Group Meeting. Rome, Italy, November 29–December 2, 2004.

United Nations Economic Commission for Europe (UNECE). Online. Available: www.unece.org.

United Nations Population Fund (UNPFA). *A Passage to Hope: Women and International Migration, State of World Population 2006*. UNPFA 2006. Online. Available:www.unpfa.org.

"Vanilla Is Not the Only Flavor." *The Economist*, April 18, 2008.

Waldfogel, Jane. "Understanding the 'Family Gap' in Pay for Women with Children." *Journal of Economic Perspectives* 12 (Winter 1998): 137–56.

"Womenomics Revisited." *The Economist*, April 19, 2007.

World Bank. *World Development Report: Equity and Development*. Washington, DC: World Bank, 2006.

———. "Global Monitoring Report, Millennium Development Goals: Confronting the Challenges of Gender Equality and Fragile States." Washington, DC: World Bank, 2007.

World Bank, FAO, IFAD. *Gender in Agriculture Sourcebook*. The International Bank for Reconstruction and Development / The World Bank, 2009. Online. Available: http://siteresources.worldbank.org/INTGENAGRLIVSOUBOOK/Resources/CompleteBook.pdf.

IO

Truly Africa, and Wealthy!

What Africa Can Learn from Catholic
Social Teaching about Sustainable
Economic Prosperity

Paulinus I. Odozor, C.S.Sp

For many people today, the word "Africa" is synonymous with poverty, hunger, disease, violence, and death. So, the title of this paper might seem a bit preposterous: Africa and wealth do not go hand in hand. Europe and America are synonymous with wealth; Asia and the Middle East are wealthy. Africa? How can anyone dare imagine an Africa that is self-sufficient, an Africa that can educate its young, feed its people, and look after its health and other needs without need for assistance from the international community?

This essay has two central premises. The first is that such an Africa is possible—provided several important challenges are addressed. The second is that Catholic social teaching contains important insights that can help Africa address many of these challenges. This work is therefore an attempt to show how, as the True Wealth of National project proposes, the economic and cultural criteria identified in the tradition of Catholic social thought can provide an effective path to sustainable prosperity for Africa. As the late Pope John Paul II said years ago in the post-synodal exhortation on Africa, "Africa is not destined for death but for life."[1]

This essay is in four parts. The first section will be devoted to the clarification of terms, while the second undertakes a delineation of those features of Africa, including economic conditions there today, which are relevant to our project. The third section identifies some of the salient economic and cultural criteria in Catholic social teaching (CST), which, if taken seriously, would point Africa to the path of sustainable economic progress. The fourth and final section will offer concluding observations.

Clarifications

It is important to begin by clarifying two key concepts that can have multiple meanings: "prosperity" and "sustainability." What accounts for a prosperous life can sometimes be subject to widely differing cultural interpretations in different places. In many traditional African societies, for example, one is prosperous who has a large family and therefore many available hands to help cultivate large tracts of land. Such people were often revered for their ability to feed their families and historically in some of those societies have been honored with titles and other marks of achievement by the community. Today, the criteria for measuring prosperity in these same societies have changed or at least expanded to include other values such as good education, a fine house, and other trappings of the successful life, each defined according to the standards of Western modernity. In much of Africa still today, a fat bank account does not automatically translate into economic or social prosperity in the eyes of many people. How, for example, can a person be considered wealthy and economically prosperous without family and offspring? How can a person, even a multimillionaire, who has no concern for neighbors or family who are in need, be considered successful? And yet in spite of the cultural aspects of the notion of economic prosperity, there is still in all societies some minimum threshold to use in determining wealth and poverty, although specifying in this threshold requires great care.

A similar clarification is necessary with regard to the notion of sustainability. The United Nations document on sustainable economic development speaks of sustainable development as "development that meets the needs of the present without compromising the ability of future generations to meet their own needs."[2] Part of our concern here is to determine ways Africans and African governments can adequately take care of themselves and their people today without compromising the ability of future generations to do so. A related question is how the tradition of Catholic social thought can help Africa achieve this aim. The two important considerations here, as the UN document points out, are the needs of the peoples of Africa and the limitations that African governments and individuals face in trying to meet these needs: both are daunting, so great as to be almost unimaginable.[3] To put it in general terms, "nearly 300 million Africans—a number approximately equal to the population of the United States—live in extreme poverty, surviving on less that one dollar a day."[4] What would prosperity mean to such people, and what could sustainability mean?

Given the note of restraint on economic growth that is contained in the idea of sustainability, especially in the face of declining resources and environmental degradation, some people in the Southern Hemisphere are convinced that concern for sustainability is one more attempt by the global North to get the world's poor countries to underwrite its economic progress. The burden of restraint should be principally on the industrialized nations, or at least it should be shared for all of the world to bear, given how closely interconnected we are as inhabitants of the same globe. As it is today, the high standard of living in the countries of the Northern Hemisphere and their wasteful consumption of fossil fuels are largely to blame for the atmospheric pollution we are now witnessing all around the world. Until the industrialized world is ready and able to do something about it, there will be no progress on environmental issues and thus no real possibility for sustainable economic development for Africa.

A Brief Overview of the Economies of Some African Countries

Although a country by country analysis of the economic performance in all of Africa is impossible here, it will be helpful to review the data from a few countries chosen to try to highlight some common economic features of most African countries. One thing the data discussed below show is that nearly all African countries fall far short of acceptable standards in nearly all of the modern indicators of economic prosperity, including food, housing, jobs, life expectancy, per capita income, affordable health care, and environmental health. In much of Africa, the basic needs of the citizenry in these areas are simply not being met. Nor are the aspirations of most people for a better life being fulfilled. A quick comparison of some randomly chosen African countries—Nigeria, Kenya, Sierra Leone, South Africa, and Mauritania—with some equally randomly selected non-African countries reveals an immense disparity in many of the economic indicators of prosperity and well-being, with African countries nearly always at the bottom rung of the ladder.[5]

Of the African countries in this sample, Nigeria is the most populous with 144 million people. South Africa has 47.4 million, Kenya has 35.1 million, Cameroon has 16.7 million, and Sierra Leone has 5.6 million. The four non-African countries in our selection have the following population figures: the United States has a population of 301 million, Brazil 190 million, Japan 127.4, and Mexico 108.7 million. Even though Nigeria might be comparable to the four Western countries based on population, the two groups are not comparable in terms of population growth. While Western nations and Japan have population growth rates of less than 1.5 percent, the African nations in our selection have population growths way above that mark, except for South Africa, which has a growth equal to the United States (0.9 percent). The reason South Africa has a lower population growth rate than the rest of Africa might be related to Jeffrey Sachs's argument in *The End of Poverty* that nations with higher levels of industrialization and economic growth have lower levels of population growth than nonindustrialized, more agricultural nations.

South Africa has a real GDP growth rate of 4.4 percent, which is lower than the African average of 5.2 percent. However, most of its growth comes from industry and nonagricultural products. This lack of dependence on agriculture is also reflected in the percentage of land that is allocated for nonagricultural production: 87.1 percent of the land in South Africa is used for other than agricultural production according to 2005 data, and only 2.2 percent of the national GDP comes from agricultural activities. The salaries in skilled industries and services are also higher, which contributes to the South African per capita of US$10,600, which is much higher than the other nations. Some of the industries in South Africa include automobile assembly, machinery, textiles, chemical production, and commercial ship repair. Industrialization in South Africa has also contributed to higher levels of literacy than in Kenya, Angola, Cameroon, Zambia, Mauritania, and Sierra Leone. With a literacy level of 82.4 percent, South Africans face fewer issues with skill transfer into industrial and service jobs than a Sierra Leonean, who lives is a country with a literacy rate of 34.8 percent.

The issue with the South African qualitative data is that it does not accurately reflect the situation for all people across the nation. Rather, it comprises both very high and very low values that together paint an average that conceals the great inequality left over as a legacy of colonialism. Thus, in South Africa, there are pockets of wealth, just as there are pockets of extreme poverty. The Gini coefficient of income inequality (in which a higher number from zero to 100 indicates greater inequality) is of 57.8 for 2004, 74.3 being the highest in the region.

Out of the eight African countries in this study, Mauritania has the lowest Gini coefficient: 39. It also has the second lowest Gini index of all twelve countries in this study; Japan has the lowest with 24.9. One of the factors that explains the data presented in the Gini index is the number of people who are unemployed in each country compared to the published gross domestic product (GDP). Angola for example, has a GDP of US$74.4 billion, but over 50 percent of its population is unemployed. This means that unless they are under some sort of welfare system, over half of the population has no access to wages or income. Furthermore, the US$6,500 in GDP per capita is not representative of the money each person can use to cover bare human necessities. In Cameroon, the situation is seemingly better because the unemployment rate is 30 percent, but GDP per capita is US$2,300, and growth is only 3.9 percent, which will not change the situation in the country in the near future. Kenya has a GDP growth greater than the regional average at 5.7 percent, but it suffers a 40 percent unemployment rate and US$ 1,600 GDP per capita. Sierra Leone has the lowest GDP per capita of the countries in the study with a mere US$800 of GDP per capita and a GDP growth rate of 1.7 percent. This can be explained by the nature of the jobs available in the country, which generally involve farming or mining, both of which were adversely affected by the recent war in that country.

To put these numbers into perspective we need to compare them to the data we have for the non-African nations. Of the four selected nations, Brazil has the highest Gini index of inequality at 57.0, falling right above South Africa (57.8). The GDP per capita is US$9,700, and the annual average economic growth is 4.5 percent. The greatest problems with Brazilian statistics are that they do not account either for the indigenous populations in the Amazon jungle, who do not receive wages, or for the racial discrimination against Afro-Brazilians, which limits the employment opportunities available to this segment of the Brazilian society. In spite of this acute discrimination, the unemployment rate here is still below double digits at 9.8 percent.

Mexico is the second most unequal society in the non-African selection, with a Gini index of 46.1 based on 2004 data. Its GDP per capita is almost four times that of Cameroon at US$12,500, and its unemployment rate is 3.7 percent. This low unemployment rate is misleading because there is a 25 percent underemployment rate that has to be accounted for. The difference between these two is that levels of unemployment measure the percentage of the population not able or willing to work in the formal market. Underemployment levels describe the employment of high-skill workers in low-skill industries, for example, a college graduate working as a cab driver. This can be due to one of two things: there is either discrimination against the person or a lack of higher-skilled jobs.

The United States has levels of inequality similar to those in Mauritania, at 40.8 in 2000. More recently, the Gini index for the United States has risen to 45.0 (2007). However, GDP per capita is an ocean away from Sierra Leone at US$46,000, with an unemployment of 4.6 percent. Keep in mind these numbers are from before the United States entered the economic crisis it is in now. Also, it is important to keep in mind that the U.S. economy is based on high-skill service jobs (such as accounting and consulting), which explains the differential in GDP with nations highly dependent on agriculture such as Cameroon (44.3 percent of GDP comes from agriculture) or Sierra Leone (49 percent of GDP comes from agriculture). Of the United State's GDP, 0.9 percent comes from agriculture, 20.6 percent comes from industry, and 78.5 percent comes from services. Of the nations in the study, only Japan (73.3 percent), South Africa (70.9 percent), and Brazil (64 percent) come close to that percentage. Japan has the lowest Gini index of the twelve nations at 24.9, with a GDP per capita of US$33,800, an unemployment rate of 4 percent, and a real growth rate of 1.9 percent. Most of the Japanese revenue comes from the service sector, 25.2 percent comes from industry, and 1.5 percent comes from agriculture. The Japanese economy is recovering from the various economic crises in the late 90s, boosting its economic performance from a -2.6 percent growth rate in 1998.

A few points have to be noted here. It is telling that no African country—from Egypt to South Africa—is listed in the section "High Human Development" in the 2007–08 human development rankings of the UNDP. Some African nations appear in the section "Medium Human Development." However, all the countries that appear in the section "Low Human Development" are African. Thus, the picture of economic prosperity in Africa is mixed. Some African countries enjoy higher economic prosperity than others. More interesting perhaps is the fact that all African countries will continue to lag behind the rest of the world with regard to economic prosperity for some time. A noted African economist, Chu Okongwu, expresses the African situation in these words:

> Taking into account the pitfalls of statistical aggregates and projections there from, let us suppose that there obtains somehow in our period a magical situation whereby Africa enjoys a phenomenal growth rate of some 8 percent per annum in per capita real GNP, while the rest of the world, especially the set of industrial centers, stands still. From a base of some US$470 (1988) that would just about place sub-Saharan Africa after 50 years at a point (US$22,044) in a neighborhood where North America was in 1988 (US$19,850). This supplies a crude measure of the African predicament and the indicated effort in the global context.[6]

There are two important questions to ask about the African situation at this point. The first is why Africa is in the situation we have been describing in this paper. The second is what continues to fuel this situation and why people like Okongwu seem so pessimistic about Africa's prospects for redemption. These two questions are important to the task of this essay, which is a search for insights from Catholic social teaching (CST) which can help in the search for a path to sustainable prosperity in Africa.

There are a number of reasons why African nations continue to be poor and unable to generate adequate economic prosperity for their citizenry. These reasons can be grouped into external and internal. In addition to some well-known historical shocks such as colonialism and the transatlantic slave trade, which left festering wounds in nearly every sector of life in Africa, there are newer external shocks which are creating havoc on the African continent. Some of these include international debt, the instability in the world economies, the increasing pace of technological change, "a new scramble for Africa" (which as in the first scramble for Africa is driven by insatiable quest for African resources needed for development and prosperity in the lands of the new economic powers such as China, Japan, and India), a "religious scramble for Africa" (which is pitting African communities and peoples against one another), and the so-called war on terror. A more sustained discussion of external factors affecting Africa's economic growth will follow. Here I will pay attention to some of the internal factors that are at the heart of Africa's lack of economic prosperity.

Africa's economic woes cannot be blamed entirely on external factors. There are internal factors that impede sustainable economic progress. It suffices to mention just two of these, one cultural, the other political. Africa's cultural patterns, which tend to guarantee full humanity only to one's kith and kin, have had deleterious consequences even in the economic development of the continent. "This non-appreciation of the humanity of the other" figures prominently "in Africa's many ethnic clashes today."[7] The point is that in spite of a glorious history of respect and hospitality for the known other within one's own group, African traditional societies were not able to elevate this regard for the known other into a universal norm of human rights that can assure every citizen, irrespective of his or her other affiliations, equal protection before the law. As I have argued elsewhere, "in order to metamorphose into modern democratic [and economically viable societies] African countries must expand their understanding of citizenship and develop a sense of participation as essential for the development and sustenance of democracy" and of economically viable states.[8] I have already alluded to Africa's internal strife. These have become legendary as features of modern African life. From Liberia to Sierra Leone, from Angola to Eritrea, from Sudan to Morocco, from the DRC to Kenya, from Rwanda to Burundi, from Ivory Coast to Nigeria, nearly all African countries have experienced, are experiencing, or will experience civil strife with destructive consequences for their people, the environment, and ultimately for economic development.

The second internal factor leading to Africa's economic crisis is the failure of leadership at various levels and a lack of transparency in public finance. One area in which this failure has been quite disastrous is that of policy formulation and implementation. As two noted African economists, Thandika Mkandawire and Charles C. Soludo, point out, policy failure in African countries is evident in the

> indiscriminate allocation of resources and rent-generating resources without any guarantees of reciprocal action by recipients; irrespon-sible monetary and fiscal policy; failure to maintain infrastructure; negligence of markets as an effective means of resource allocation; failure to promote agriculture; and failure to introduce policies to support diversification of exports.[9]

The result of all these factors put together is not just economic stagnation but an endemic depression in most African economies, with no end in sight.

There are many other aspects to Africa's economic crisis, such as rapid and unplanned urbanization, the AIDS/HIV pandemic that threatens Africa's hope for redemption, the youth, massive corruption and looting of state treasuries in many African countries, and so on. The net effect of all these forces put together, as Okongwu puts it, is that "in the current shift of initiative from the Atlantic to the Pacific—when Atlantic-side location and global wind system mastery have been displaced by control of the microchip in the advantage set—Africa is again being sidelined...We may say that, structurally in terms of the construction of socio-economic progress, Africa is, once again, headed in the wrong direction."[10]

Keeping in mind the main thrust of this essay, we will now ask whether there are resources within Catholic social teaching that can be of help to Africa's search for economic prosperity for its peoples.

What Catholic Social Thought Can Contribute to the Search for Sustainable Economic Progress in Africa

Catholic theology up until the first half of the twentieth century was Eurocentric. This was especially the case with moral theology, where Catholic social teaching is located. As John Langan points out, "The moral teaching of Catholicism was deeply rooted in the institutions and practices of Western life. Marriage, mon-archy, military life, economic associations all had a Christian, and even more specifically Catholic form to them."[11] Thus Catholic social teaching in its ori-gins and for sometime was very much identified with the world of Europe. Although the message of *Rerum Novarum* (1891), with its emphasis on the right of the individual to private property, is in some ways applicable to Africa, it can be safely said that it was not intended with the African world in mind. Its con-cerns were European as was its theology, and for good reasons. For one thing, the African churches, to the extent that they existed at all at this time, provided a far different set of problems and were not considered much of a theological challenge for the Church. However, the day would arrive when the needs of the African countries and of the African churches would begin to command some attention from the teaching office of the Church, indicating what Karl Rahner would refer to as the emergence of a "world Church."

Catholic social teaching began to address issues of specific relevance to Africa during the pontificate of Pope John XXIII. In *Mater et Magistra*, Pope John addressed not only such topics as the common good and just wage, which had been a staple of Catholic social teaching, but also agriculture (*MM*, 123–49) and aid to the developing nations that were beginning to emerge from colonialism. He argued that such aid must both respect the indigenous peoples of these nations and foster a type of development that is homegrown and not an imposition from the more developed nations (*MM*, 170). As Marvin Mich points out, Pope John XXIII also "opened a new chapter in economic teaching with his emphasis on equitable distribution and social solidarity between nations."[12] The new chapter has since been continued in the important understanding first expressed by Paul VI in *Populorum Progressio* concerning the worldwide dimension of the social question (*PP*, 3, 9). Pope John Paul II explains later on in *Solicitudo Rei Socialis* that to say that the social question has assumed a worldwide dimension is to acknowledge that various social problems of the day "depend more and more on the influence of factors beyond regional boundaries and national frontiers" and that the solutions to many of these problems depend on concerted efforts from peoples all around the globe.[13]

Great wisdom and insight are contained in Catholic social thought. Like the Bible itself, the more one reads this material, the more one discovers new insights and fresh perspectives. The constraints of space here will not allow a detailed study of all the materials contained in this corpus, but four important principles or benchmarks of Catholic social teaching will be of particular help in the quest for sustainable economic progress in Africa.

Economic Prosperity Is about Persons

Gaudium et Spes expresses quite succinctly some of these core principles: "Developing nations should strongly seek the complete human fulfillment of their citizens as the explicit goal of progress."[14] Another way to express this view is to say that economic prosperity is about the human person living a fully human life. This entails further the respect and nurture of the humanity of every individual. Catholic social thought has developed a strong emphasis on human rights, and as David Hollenbach argues convincingly, the stress on human rights constitutes the soul of the CST.[15] Pope John XXIII gave a comprehensive view of these rights in *Pacem in Terris*. The Second Vatican Council and several later Church documents elaborate these rights as well. For example, *Familiaris Consortio*, the synodal exhortation of Pope John Paul II, has a comprehensive list of the rights of the family.[16] In all, these rights are anchored in the belief that the human person, made in God's image and likeness, has priority in the social order, including in the economy. Pope John XXIII expressed this view quite clearly when he stated that "the human society, if it is to be well ordered and productive, must lay down as a foundation this principle, namely, that every human being is a person.... Indeed, precisely because he is a person he has rights and obligations flowing directly and simultaneously from his very nature."[17]

Many of Africa's problems with coexistence among different tribal and ethnic groups can be traced to lack of sincere appreciation of the equal humanity of those who do not belong to "our" group, who are not one of "us." Ancient African societies were slave-raiding and slave-holding societies. These slaves were typically from other towns and from other ethnicities. African societies that were otherwise very hospitable and humane allowed themselves to do this nefarious deed because they were unable to accord the same level of humanity to those who were not of their stock and kind. In other words, African societies have not over time developed a comprehensive theory of rights based either on religious or philosophical assumptions. That lack is evident today in many aspects of the modern life of Africans. The intractable conflicts, the arbitrary attitudes of rulers over the ruled, the persistence of feudal structures of chiefs and emirs who insist on superiority over others as a birthright, the meaninglessness of citizenship are all evidence of the lack of respect for human rights.

The constitution of every African state has a bill of rights. One of the important insights from Catholic social teaching is the placing of these rights at the every heart of political and economic life.[18] Respect for human rights is one sure way toward peace on earth, an important prerequisite for human flourishing and prosperity in every aspect of life including the economic. In Africa today there is constant agitation by individuals and especially minority groups who feel deprived of their human rights. The economic consequences of such unrest are incalculable. Take the oil-rich Niger Delta, for example. The minority groups in the Niger Delta, who feel that their human and civil rights are being violated by the rest of the Nigerian state, have engaged in constant agitation for better treatment. The result has been a steady decline in Nigeria's earning potential as an oil-producing state, a reality that translates to lack of progress or even to deterioration in people's earning power.

As David Hollenbach has pointed out, the stress on human rights in Catholic social teaching as the normative center of the organization of human societies does not amount to "the prescription of any single economic, political or ideological system." Instead, "basic human rights set limits and establish obligations for all systems and ideologies, leaving the precise form in which these systems will be organized undefined."[19] The stress on limits to state power and on the obligation of the state to its people is important for both political and economic progress in Africa. Many African countries that claim to be democracies are no more than dictatorships, where the rulers feel no need to account to their people for anything. It is the limitless use of state power that has today brought Zimbabwe, a once thriving country, to hyperinflation and the brink of widespread disaster.

The Common Good

Since the publication of *Pacem in Terris*, Catholic social teaching has made a point of stressing human rights and the common good.[20] John XXIII wrote in *Pacem in Terris* that "every civil authority must take pain to promote the common good of all, without preference for any single citizen or civic group."[21] However, he adds that considerations of justice can sometimes make it necessary for government to pay more attention to the less fortunate members of the community who are least able to defend or fend for themselves. In *Mater et Magistra*, John XXIII defines the common good as "the sum total of those conditions of social living, whereby men are enabled more and more to achieve their perfection."[22] It is thus understood in Catholic social teaching that the common good includes both the material and the spiritual dimensions of the human person, that is, that it includes "all aspects of human living that make for human flourishing."[23]

Discerning and fostering the common good is crucial for peace and for sustainable economic prosperity. There are many lessons for Africa in Catholic social teaching on the common good. The first is that in the quest for unity in African countries, a requirement that is critical for any economic progress, people must think on a much broader canvass than the one provided by ethnicity and tribal affiliation. A second is that it is impossible to develop an economically prosperous nation when leaders consider the national treasury as their private property. The embezzlement of funds by state functionaries is one of the greatest setbacks to economic progress in Africa. President Mobuto Sese Seko ran the Democratic Republic of the Congo as a private treasury, meanwhile leaving what is perhaps the most mineral-rich country on earth in the worst state of misery. Sanni Abacha carted away so much money from Nigeria to private bank accounts in Europe and elsewhere that nearly twelve years after his death the search for his loots is still yielding millions of dollars almost monthly. While he was head of state, roads and Nigerian infrastructure fell apart completely. His successors, Abdulsalm Abdulahi and Olusegun Obasanjo, did not do any better. The EFCC, the corruption watchdog that Obasanjo himself established, is now discovering serious cases of financial irregularities and cronyism that might yet mean he will face prison or other penalties.

Perhaps more than anything else, instilling the sense of the common good in African leaders and peoples could be the greatest contribution anyone can make to sustainable economic progress in Africa. For by so doing, one would also be teaching the current crop of African leaders to use whatever resources are available to them to work for the flourishing of everyone and not just the members of their own families and friends.

A Proper Understanding of Development

Since the pontificate of Pope Paul VI, the word "development" has become prevalent in Catholic social teaching. In *Populorum Progressio*, his encyclical on development, Paul VI asserts that the reality of poverty "makes a claim on the consciences of all humanity, especially the affluent."[24] He paints a picture of a world in which poverty, diseases, unemployment, food shortages, and lack of adequate health care continue to be serious problems despite all efforts to change the situation. For Paul VI the answer to the situation thus described lies in rethinking the concept of development that is operative in the world of economic and political theorists and planners.

Development, properly conceived, cannot be defined as economic growth alone. Andrew Yuengert, in his essay in this volume, makes a similar point about prosperity. To be authentic, development must be well-rounded and "must foster the development of each person and of the whole person."[25] A proper type of development is one that helps people "to seek to do more, know more and have more, in order to be more."[26] The sad reality, according to the pope, is that a vast number of people in the world cannot realize this aspiration. A concerted effort is required locally and globally to rid the world of ignorance, hunger, and disease and to meet the needs of peoples everywhere for education, shelter, food, adequate housing, and health care.

The pope proposes in this encyclical a notion of Christian humanism that pays attention to both the vertical and horizontal aspects of the human person. Such humanism is one that also looks for a way to integrate economic, technological, and social advancement in service of the human person. Although economic prosperity is important, it is not the only goal of human development. Nor is the quest for material things without problems when pursued at the expense of other aspects of the life of the human person because it can become a source of enslavement. Despite his caveat with regard to material goods, Paul VI insists that care must be taken on all fronts in all parts of the world to help people out of the situation of misery that entraps so many. In sum, he insists on an "integral" development, development that takes all aspects of the human person into consideration, not just the economic.

In an encyclical twenty years later, Pope John Paul II was forced to conclude that, although there had been many laudable efforts to improve on the situation that made *Populorum Progressio* necessary in the first place, "one cannot deny that present situation of the word, from the point of view of development, offers a rather negative impression."[27] The various indices for measuring economic development had worsened in all parts of the Southern Hemisphere, according to the Pope:

> Looking at all the various sectors—the production and distribution of foodstuffs, hygiene, health and housing, availability of drinking water, working conditions (especially for women), life expectancy and other economic and social indicators—the general picture is disappointing, both considered in itself and in relation to the corresponding data of the more developed countries. The developing countries, especially, the poorest of them, find themselves in a situation of very poor delay.[28]

Most of the poor countries referred to are in Africa. The data from the UNDP referred to earlier indicates that Africa scores the lowest in all the categories the pope mentions here. This is troubling, especially given the fact that many African countries at various times in the 1970s and 1980s had adopted various "development plans" that were to move the countries to a certain economic point and goal in a given time.

It must be noted that during the 1970s and the 1980s, several theories of economic development that had either failed in other parts of the world or were designed for vastly different economic situations were unleashed on Africa. Most African countries had embraced the neo-Keynesian economic theory that metamorphosed into the neoliberal theory whose first principle is monoeconomics, "which insists on the universality of rational economic behavior and the existence of marginal substitution possibilities in production and consumption"[29] An essential part of the neoliberal agenda is reliance on markets as efficient and "minimal government intervention in the provision, especially in the provision of infrastructure and education." The idea was to "roll back the state" and to "unleash the market."[30] The application of the neoliberal approach to economic development in Africa has been a disaster of the first order.

Whatever the virtues of neoliberal economic theory, it presupposed a well-developed economy and a literate populace who had imbibed every capitalist virtue—a situation that was not the case in Africa. This was the theory behind the structural adjustment programs that the World Bank and the IMF insisted on for every ailing African economy. During the 1970s and 1980s, Africans saw a significant withdrawal of their governments from provision of social services and educational programs at all levels. State institutions and businesses, which had all been erected with public funds, were sold at ridiculously low prices to a few wealthy individuals who themselves were either friends or relatives or agents of people in power. Sometimes privatization simply meant the selling of national assets to non-Africans, especially in the crucial areas of minerals and energy. Thus it was that both political and economic power were handed over to a few self-serving elites, while the people were saddled with ridiculously high debt incurred originally to build up these nonprivatized institutions.

Catholic social teaching, by insisting on integral development, invites policy makers to pay attention to the greatest and most essential form of capital—human capital. No economic progress can happen when people are poorly educated, are hungry, or have nowhere to lay down their heads. The way to sustainable economic progress passes through a citizenry who can trust that their government is looking out for their welfare. Since development is about people, the lesson from Catholic social teaching is that each government must do everything necessary to protect the legitimate interest and welfare of its citizens. This implies, among other things, that government should undertake the provision of those services, which in a given country cannot be provided by anyone else, because they are very capital intensive or because they impact the lives of too many people to be left in the hands of a few entrepreneurs whose only motivation is profit. It is also the duty of government to provide at all times an effective oversight for those sectors of the economy and society that have direct impact on people's welfare, such as banking and finance. Failure here, as the financial crisis of 2008 demonstrated, can have immensely destructive consequences for ordinary people, even more so for the poor.

The International Ramification of Poverty and Economic Progress in Africa

In a very remarkable passage in *Populorum Progressio,* Pope Paul VI proclaimed that the social question had now become a global question. One commentator points out that by this assertion, Pope Paul VI was taking account of the fast-changing pace of the social situation all over the world since World War II:

> The Struggle against colonialism had reached a peak in the 1950s. Dozens of new nations were affirming their entrance by joining the United Nations. The new prominence of agencies concerned with international trade and finance (e.g., GATT, UNCTAD, the IMF and the World Bank) showed clearly that justice was no longer something

to be worked out within any given country but was first of all an international matter—even an inter-continental one. Above all it concerned relations between the industrialized nations and the former colonies in what had come to be called the Third World (which is now more commonly called "the South").[31]

Pope John Paul II described the "global question" of Paul VI as offering a moral evaluation of the social question and an invitation to Christians and peoples in the Northern Hemisphere to recognize the interdependence "which exists between their conduct and the poverty and underdevelopment of so many millions of people."[32] He concludes that just as the social question has assumed a worldwide dimension, so also is it true to say that "the demands of justice can only be satisfied on that level."[33] The international dimension of Africa's economic crisis is perhaps most evident in three areas: the debt, the question of the control of Africa's mineral resources, and as a corollary, a recent phenomenon that can best be described as "a new scramble for Africa."

In 1996, Africa's external debt burden stood at about US$300 billion. Due to debt repayment and debt write-offs, the debt stock as of March 2008 is believed to be still over US$200 billion. The figures here might suggest there is progress. That is not really correct. Let us take the case of two countries, Nigeria and Zambia, as examples. In 2005, Nigeria was forced to "buy back" its debt from the Paris Club of creditors with about US$12 billion and from the London Club of creditors with US$6 billion. Nigeria's debt stood at about US$19 billion in 1985. Ten years later, without any more significant borrowing, Nigeria was said to owe about US$35 billion, "even though the country had between 1985 and 2005 paid over US$37 billion dollars on its loans."[34] The detrimental enormity of this so-called debt repayment for Nigeria and its citizenry does not simply lie in the injustice of the reality that this debt was first arranged on terms that were absurdly detrimental to Nigeria or in the fact that the debt had been repaid about two times over, but must also be considered against the fact that over half the population of Nigeria lives on less than a dollar a day. The former president of Nigeria, Olusegun Obasanjo, in a speech he gave at Notre Dame on September 23, 2003, complained that Nigeria was having to service its debt "by an amount that is eight times the provision for health care" in the federal budget.[35] In spite of the attention the debt issue has received in recent years, it still constitutes a blind spot for most otherwise well-meaning people in the Northern Hemisphere mostly due to ignorance about the effects of the predatory lending practices of their governments and lending institutions on the lives of so many people.

Zambia is one example where predatory institutions are getting away with policies that are extremely harmful to the people due to lack of attention by many people in the richer nations of the world. Zambia was one of those so-called highly indebted nations that had received forms of debt relief in recent years. It is now becoming clear that for some countries like Zambia debt relief may not bring much relief after all, since the country is relapsing into debt due to the activities of the so-called vulture funds that make exorbitant profits at the expense of poor countries in Africa by buying back debts from creditor nations at a huge discount before it is restructured and relieved.[36] After the "buy-back" the company "sues the debtor for the original amount of the debt, often with interest and penalty fees added on top, making a tremendous profit."[37] In 2005, Zambia was granted HIPC (Highly Indebted Poor Country) status, which then qualified it for 100 percent debt relief from the G8 countries. A previous loan from Romania used to buy tractors (which turned out to be unusable) was not within the G8 debt relief package. This loan, which was originally worth $30 million dollars, was sold to one of the "vulture funds" at $3 million. By a mixture of official corruption under the government of President Chiluba and through a whole host of missteps the loan rose to about $40 million a few years later. The point is that Zambia is again saddled with a loan that is forcing it to divert scarce resources that could have been used for the provision of much-needed infrastructure and services for the people.[38]

Another notable reason for Africa's economic crisis is the extreme dependence of the continent's economies on external conditions. African economies are mostly resource-based. The resources fall broadly into two categories: agricultural and mineral. The prices of these resources are dependent both on the vagaries of the world markets and on other conditions such as weather and civil strife, which are outside the control of African policy makers. Whenever adverse conditions affect production in any way, African economies feel the shock almost instantly since there are usually few shock absorbers, financial or otherwise, that can dampen the impact and prevent it from directly hitting the masses. In such cases, governments cannot meet their obligations to the people. Even in those cases in which, as in oil-exporting Nigeria, the price of the mineral resource is stable or appreciates significantly in the world market, there is no guarantee that the positive effects will be felt by the people, since supply can be subject to disruption by marginalized groups within the community who believe that they ought to get a greater share of the mineral revenue. Thus, the Niger Delta, the main repository of Nigeria's oil wealth, is now home both to many legitimately disgruntled groups and to criminals who want to control the fortunes from petroleum. The recent brutal war in Sierra Leone was orchestrated by criminal elements who wanted to control the nation's diamond resources. Chad and Sudan are also examples, among many others.[39] These resource wars and conflicts are part of a new scramble for Africa, which is a major reason for lack of economic progress and prosperity in Africa today.

Currently there are two "scrambles for Africa." One of them is a religious scramble for Africa, whereby all imaginable religious groups and sects in the world are traversing the continent, intent on making converts and seeking to create spheres of influence for themselves. The second new scramble for Africa is an economic one and the one with which we are concerned here. This scramble is led by countries such as China and Japan, which have in recent years taken a new interest in Africa, largely because of is potential as a source of cheap natural resources or as a place to flex the might of an emerging military power and a big-time arms supplier. In this way, China, growing wealthy and needing to fuel its economy, is becoming a major player in Africa in all sorts of ways that are detrimental to Africa's economic, social, and political stability and progress. China's involvement is exacerbating existing tensions in many Africa countries since China has little regard for other local ethical considerations such as the way the local minorities are treated.[40] Japan is also an interesting case. Japanese companies are involved in extensive logging in the equatorial rain forests and are creating environmental disasters as a result. Also, the interest of the Japanese in exotic animals from African game reserves has led to illegal poaching, which is driving some animals to the brink of extinction and is affecting local lives and economies in many other ways. A further result of foreign involvement in Africa, as the United States bishops wrote on their 2001 pastoral letter on Africa, is that these foreign entities have sometimes "provided arms to African governments and non-governmental entities resulting in further instability and deeper human suffering."[41]

A second aspect of Paul VI's statement that the social question has turned worldwide is that it calls for solidarity among nations. The growing interdependence among nations should give rise to the practice of the virtue of solidarity among nations: "Solidarity is not a feeling of vague compassion or shallow distress at the misfortunes of so many people, both near and far. On the contrary, it is a firm and persevering determination to commit oneself to the common good, which is to say to the good of all and of each individual, because we are all really responsible for all."[42]

Solidarity is the path to true peace, which is in turn imperative for the achievement of economic growth and the sustenance of economic progress.[43] In their 2001 letter, the Catholic Bishops of the United States point out a number of ways the rest of the world can show solidarity with Africa: providing urgent assistance for strengthening health care, helping promote educational development on the continent, fostering trade and relationships as partners, and supporting peace making.[44] The best way to be in solidarity with Africa is to be an advocate for the continent, especially in those places where Africa is not represented or where her voice cannot count for much, such as in the boardrooms of multinational corporations. Many corporations and the Western governments in fact consider African countries as no more than gas stations where they go to fill up their tanks with the resources necessary to power their own economic growth at home.

Conclusion

At the root of Africa's economic crisis is an anthropological crisis that has left the entire continent in search of its soul and its place under the sun for the past four hundred years. This anthropological impoverishment began around the time of the transatlantic slave trade and continues today through the brutalization of the African psyche as a result of internal and external factors. Any African renewal must first address this anthropological impoverishment of Africa. In other words, Africans must somehow be helped to believe in themselves again. The greatest contribution of CST is that it provides a framework for African renewal. Although the contribution of CST to Africa can have economic impact, this is not its primary value for Africa. For, let us face it, Africa is not lacking in economic theorists who have studied and worked in some of the most sophisticated economics institutions in the world. Every African ministry of economic planning or of finance and development is reeking with files and hundreds of pages of economic theories that were touted as solutions for everything that was ailing the economy. CST is different. Its focus has been on the human person, adequately considered, in all the dimensions of human life. African economic planners need to read these texts not just as religious opinion but as resource materials to aid them in their appreciation of the human person who is the subject of all economic planning.

Finally, there are three other ways Catholic social teaching is of value to Africa. The first is that it offers African planners a rare lens with which to evaluate Western approaches to economic planning. Catholic social teaching has been in dialogue with all these theories over time. Thus even the most nonreligious-minded economic planner in Africa who wants an economic point of view not driven by economic theory but by a strong view of the human person as both agent and subject of economic planning can appreciate CST as a ready source of insights about the essential goals of any economic system or approach. Second, therefore, Catholic social teaching is good for Africa as a value-raiser. The values it articulates and seeks to preserve are universal truths about the human person. When Catholic social teaching insists on the rights of people to own property or the rights of the worker to a decent living wage or the right of families to education that is proper and good for their child, it is not making a case just for Catholics or for Christians; it is advocating for every human being. This is a singular strength and appeal of Catholic social teaching. Third, the universal ability of Catholic social teaching to inspire has been good for Africa as motivator to action within the African churches. A lot of conscientization has been going on in the African churches on the basis of the inspiration that believers, lay and religious, have received from Catholic social teaching. The work of men and women—lay, religious, and clerical—in Africa who press for social justice issues in political, social, religious, educational, economic, and other aspects of life is simply stunning. Many of these efforts are motivated by Catholic social teaching.

There is indeed solid reason for the hope embodied in the True Wealth of Nations project—that Catholic social thought can assist the nations of Africa to find a path to sustainable prosperity for all.

NOTES

1. Pope John Paul II, *Ecclesia in Africa*, no. 57.

2. United Nations, *Our Common Future.*

3. Ibid.

4. United States Conference of Catholic Bishops, *A Call to Solidarity with Africa*, 13.

5. The data provided in this section comes from the 2007/2008 Human Development Index of the UNDP. See http://hdr.undp.org/en/report/global/hdr2007-2008. It was obtained and compiled by my student research assistant, Andrea Torres Hermoza.

6. Chu S. P Okongwu, "Africa and the Emerging World Order in the 21st Century," 6–7.

7. Paulinus I. Odozor, "Africa's Double-edged Inheritance," 14–15.

8. Ibid.

9. Thandika Mkandawire and Charles C. Soludo, *Our Continent Our Future*, 23. Charles Soludo is now Governor of the Central Bank of Nigeria.

10. Okongwu, "Africa and the Emerging World Order in the 21st Century."

11. John Langan, "Catholic Moral Rationalism and the Philosophical Basis of Moral Theology," 33.

12. Marvin L. Mich, "Commentary on *Mater et Magistra*," 199.

13. John Paul II, *Solicitudo Rei Socialis*, 399.

14. Vatican Council II, "Gaudium et Spes," 226.

15. David Hollenbach, *Justice, Peace, and Human Rights*," 87–100.

16. John Paul II, *Familiaris Consortio*, 291.

17. John XXIII, *Pacem in Terris.*

18. Drew Christiansen, "Commentary on *Pacem in Terris*," 225.

19. Hollenbach, *Justice, Peace, and Human Rights*," 90–91.

20. Drew Christansen, "Commentary on *Pacem in Terris*," 228.

21. John XXIII, *Pacem in Terris*, 56.

22. John XXIII, *Mater et Magistra*, 65.

23. Hollenbach, *Justice, Peace, and Human Rights*, 103.

24. Allan Figueroa Deck, "Commentary on *Populorum Progressio*," 292.

25. Paul IV, *Populorum Progressio*, 14.

26. Ibid., 6.

27. John Paul II, *Solicitudo Rei Socialis*, 13.

28. Ibid., 14.

29. Mkandawire and Soludo, *Our Continent Our Future*, 41.

30. Ibid.

31. Okongwu, "Africa and the Emerging World Order in the 21st Century," 12.

32. John Paul II, *Solicitudo Rei Socialis*, 9.

33. Ibid., 10.

34. Paulinus I. Odozor, "Catholic Moral Theology and the World Church," 285.

35. Olusegun Obasanjo, "The Wind of Change in Africa Today," 298.

36. Cf. "Vulture Funds" in http://www.Africaaction.org/campaign_new/docs/spotlightonZambia2.pdf.

37. Ibid.

38. Cf. Marie Clarke Brill, "Zambia's Vulture Fund Challenge." http://www.Africaaction.org/campaign_new/docs/spotlightonZambia2.pdf.

39. The U.S. bishops make the same point in their pastoral on solidity with Africa: "Africa's wealth in natural resources—which should be such a rich source of blessings—has sometimes become a source of tremendous suffering. The relationship between natural resources and conflict in Africa is becoming clearer. Two natural resources, diamonds and oil are of particular concern" (United States Conference of Catholic Bishops, *A Call to Solidarity with Africa*, 17).

40. A recent editorial in one of Nigeria's leading newspaper, the *Daily Independent* puts this matter in proper perspective. Cf. http://www.independentngonline.com/edit/article01.

41. United States Conference of Catholic Bishops, *A Call to Solidarity with Africa*, 17.

42. John Paul II, *Solicitudo Rei Socialis*, 38.

43. Ibid., 39.

44. US Conference of Catholic Bishops, "A Call to Solidarity with Africa," Sect. III, B, C, and D.

REFERENCES

Brill, Marie Clarke. "Zambia's Vulture Fund Challenge." Online. Available: http://www.Africaaction.org/campaign_new/docs/spotlightonZambia2.pdf.

Christiansen, Drew. "Commentary on *Pacem in Terris* (Peace on Earth)." In *Modern Catholic Social Teaching: Commentaries and Interpretations*, edited by Kenneth R. Himes et al., 217–41. Washington, DC: Georgetown University Press, 2005.

Dorr, Donald. *Option for the Poor: A Hundred Years of Catholic Social Teaching*. New York: Maryknoll, 1998.

Figueroa Deck, Allan. "Commentary on *Populorum Progressio* (On the Development of Peoples)." In Himes et al., *Modern Catholic Social Teaching*, 292–314.

Himes, Kenneth R., Lisa Sowle Cahill, Charles E. Curran, David Hollenbach, S.J., and Thomas Shannon, eds. *Modern Catholic Social Teaching: Commentaries and Interpretations*. Washington, DC: Georgetown University Press, 2005.

Hollenbach, David. *Justice, Peace, and Human Rights: American Catholic Social Ethics in a Pluralistic Context*. New York: Crossroad, 1988.

Human Developmesnt Index of the UNDP. Online. Available: http://hdr.undp.org/en/report/global/hdr2007–2008.

John Paul II. *Ecclesia in Africa*. Washington, DC: USCCB Publishing, 1995.

———. *Familiaris Consortio. Origins* 11 (Dec 24, 1981): 437–68.

———. "*Solicitudo Rei Socialis* (On Social Concern)." *Origins* 17 (Mar 3, 1988): 641–60.

John XXIII. *Pacem in Terris*. Washington, DC: US Conference of Catholic Bishops, 2003.

———. *Mater et Magistra*. NY: Paulist Press, 1961.

Langan, John. "Catholic Moral Rationalism and the Philosophical Basis of Moral Theology." *Theological Studies* 50 (Mar 1989): 25–43.

Mich, Marvin L. "Commentary on *Mater et Magistra* (Christianity and Social Progress)." In Himes et al., *Modern Catholic Social Teaching: Commentaries and Interpretations*, 191–216.

Mkandawire, Thandika, and Charles C. Soludo. *Our Continent Our Future: African Perspective on Structural Adjustment*. Trenton, NJ /Asmara, Eritrea: Africa World Press, Inc, 1999.

Obasanjo, Olusegun. "The Wind of Change in Africa Today." *Origins* 33 (2003): 298, no.18.

Odozor, Paulinus I. "Africa's Double-edged Inheritance." *The Tablet* (July 5, 2008).

———. "Catholic Moral Theology and the World Church: Some Suggestions on How to Move Forward." *Louvain Studies* 30 (2005): 285.

Okongwu, Chu, S.P. "Africa and the Emerging World Order in the 21st Century: Challenges and Prospects." SEDOS Bulletin (May 31, 1999): 147–53.

Rahner, Karl. "Towards a Fundamental Interpretation of Vatican II." *Theological Studies* 40 (Dec 1979): 716–27.

United Nations. *Our Common Future*. Online. Available: http://www.un-documnets.net/ocf-02.htm.

United States Conference of Catholic Bishops. *A Call to Solidarity with Africa*. Washington, DC: USCCB Publishing, 2001.

Vatican Council II. "Gaudium et Spes." In *Catholic Social Thought: The Documentary Heritage*, edited by David J. O'Brien and Thomas A. Shannon, 166–237. Maryknoll, NY: Orbis, 1992.

II

Capital, Spirit, and Common Wealth

Jon P. Gunnemann

The economist, like everyone else, must concern himself with the ultimate aims of man.

—Alfred Marshall

Economy and religion are not two separate realms of our lives but each fully part of one world. Since economic activity is intrinsic to all of human life, it is intrinsic to Christian life and faith. As the farmer, poet, and theologian, Wendell Berry has put it, "To be uninterested in economy is to be uninterested in the practice of religion; it is to be uninterested in culture and in character. Probably the most urgent question now faced by people who would adhere to the Bible is this: What sort of economy would be responsible to the holiness of life?"[1]

Berry's question makes explicit that the "sustainable prosperity for all" that the True Wealth of Nations project focuses on is produced in an economy that is responsible to the holiness of life. The question and the point of view stand in sharp contrast to the far more common view that economic activity and thought comprise an autonomous realm of human action to which theology and ethics may try to bring principles derived from foundations outside the economic realm. But theology must ask Berry's question; and economics always asks, and answers, it, at least tacitly. Economics cannot be done without some view of what a good economy is.

A preliminary, if yet formal, answer to Berry's question can be found in his definition of "good work": good work is work that honors God's work, which means honoring the neighbor and Creation.[2] An economy that honors God, the neighbor, and Creation is an economy responsible to the holiness of life; and, I will argue, it is an economy that generates true wealth, true prosperity. The aim of this essay is to contribute to an understanding of "true wealth" by offering a theological (Protestant) interpretation of capital and economic institutions. This task, then, is to work out the meaning of these theological terms for our economy.

In this essay, I offer an argument in three parts: part 1 argues that what economists call "capital" is an abstraction that refers to various complex forms of energy—natural, social, and cultural—organized for specific purposes or ends; and that these same forms of organized energy are referred to by theologians and Christian believers as spirit. Grasping the underlying spiritual reality of what we call capital helps us understand the nature of common (and "true") wealth, its purpose or end. Part 2 examines the modern business corporation, the primary institutional form of capital in the modern economy. In principle, the corporation embodies positive elements of spirit but for structural reasons, the energies of the business corporation are increasingly directed toward goals antithetical to the holiness of life. Part 3 integrates the various parts of the argument with an analysis of financial capital and its tenuous, if not destructive, relationship to spirit, stewardship, and the holiness of life.

The remainder of this introductory portion offers a concise statement of the major assumptions on which the larger argument is based.

Theological assumptions. Like Berry, my theological framework is Protestant, but my argument yields conclusions that are certainly consistent with Catholic social thought on economics; and insofar as they aim at deepening Christian understanding of central economic conceptions, they may also inform Catholic thought. I stand in the Reformed (Calvinist) tradition broadly construed, informed especially by the work of H. Richard Niebuhr and James Gustafson.[3] Three theological assumptions from this tradition are especially pertinent to my larger argument and in establishing links with Catholic social teaching:

The first is that the Reformed tradition has a strong doctrine of Creation. This means two things: one, no sharp line can be drawn between the spiritual and the material. The created world is material all the way up and spiritual all the way down. God as spirit is present throughout physical Creation—this is why the Creation is holy. Hence, I assume that theologians and economists are talking about the same world, even if with different language. The conviction that the whole of the physical world is God's creation, and that God as spirit is present in it, has a direct implication for one aspect of economic life: no part of the created world can belong to anyone as an absolute right. Any rights to parts of the created world (such as property rights) must be understood as rights of use and/or stewardship; and these rights must be justified by reference to their ability to serve the well-being of the whole of the created order. Two, a strong doctrine of Creation implies that the world we inhabit has a moral order accessible to human reason, at least to some extent. While the capacities of human reason are limited in important ways (more on this shortly), moral thought and judgment are not condemned to subjectivity, relativism, or the special insights of one religious tradition. While Roman Catholic teaching may use somewhat different terminology, there is strong general agreement on the holiness or sacredness of the created order, on the moral structure of Creation, and on necessary theological limits to any rights claims that humans may make in relation to the rest of Creation.

The second theological assumption is that the world and we who inhabit it are profoundly relational—this is the distinctive contribution of the work of H. Richard Niebuhr and James Gustafson and is stressed by Simona Beretta in her essay in this volume. "Relationality" means: (1) that all parts of the world are related to one another, through the complexity of physical matter and the dynamics of energy and the relation of every part of Creation to God; (2) that who we are as human beings, including our identity and self-understanding, is profoundly formed by our social and historical relationships as well as by the physical and biological dimensions of our being; and (3) that our knowledge of the world and of ourselves is itself socially formed. A relational understanding of the world, self, and human knowledge is consistent with scientific understandings of the world, including especially the perspectives of physics on the nature of matter and energy and of biology and the environmental sciences on the workings of evolution and the interdependencies of ecological systems.

The third assumption is that sin is a "constriction of the self" (Gustafson), the loss of a capacity to love (Christian agapé) in the sense of "attending to the other" (Martin Buber, Simone Weil, Iris Murdoch, Marjorie Suchocki), and especially the capacity to love wider circles of humanity, of Creation, and of the whole of being. The constricted self is an anxious self, preoccupied with its own well-being and incapable of serious and sustained attention to the well-being of others, to the well-being of larger circles of humanity, or to the well-being of the whole of Creation. Love is an opening of the self, enabling one to see the world from the perspective of other selves, involving an imaginative transcending of one's own point of view. On the level of society and social institutions, sin is exacerbated by the natural tendency of groups and institutions to seek their own well-being, whatever the intentions of the individual members (Reinhold Niebuhr has offered the classic account of social sin[4]); and by the power, formal and informal, that social groups and institutions can wield over individuals and over other social groups and institutions. Power, in the sense of the capacity to dominate others, is a central social reality and is often a fundamental manifestation of sin. By implication, economic analysis that does not attend to power—which is to say, does not attend to political economy—is abstract and seriously deficient. This understanding of sin has counterparts in Roman Catholic theology, although I think it fair to say that Protestant theology has, at least historically, given somewhat more emphasis to the enduring power of sin in human judgment and actions and to its social and institutional manifestations.

Economic Assumptions. First, although I make reference at necessary points to economic theory, my first concern is with economic institutions such as property, the market, and corporations.

Second, it is important to distinguish between economics as activities and institutions that create goods and services for the common good and economics as the making of money.[5] The distinction raises profound questions about the triumph of finance capitalism in our current economy that has caused a profound distortion of economic life.

Language and Knowledge. All of our knowledge is mediated by language; and all language, and hence our knowledge of the world, is profoundly metaphorical. This means, first, that the language of both theology and economics is deeply metaphorical. Theology works self-consciously with metaphors, symbols, and myth, but economics less so. Nevertheless, fundamental economic ideas such as capital, labor, market, money, and more are not only abstractions but also metaphors. The remarkable overlap between central theological and economic ideas (credit, *credere*, belief, redemption, salvation, *salvare*, saving, wealth, weal, well-being, and more) signals deep connections between theological and economic language.

Second, the interpretation of central metaphorical ideas requires a kind of phenomenological analysis, an internal analysis of both the ideas and the realities to which they refer. A key aspect of such an analysis is to understand the purpose for which a metaphor is chosen and used.

It follows, third, that all human thought is teleological: we think in a particular way and use the metaphors we do because we have some purpose in our thinking, whether explicit or implicit. Hence, the interpretation of economic institutions and metaphors requires attention to ends, stated or implicit.

This argument, then, is not a theory but an internal interpretation and explication (a phenomenology) of central ideas in theology and economics that may serve to instruct both theology and economic theory.

Capital, Spirit, and Common Wealth

The Meaning of Capital

One might imagine that economists who write about markets and capitalism would work with a clear definition of capital, but it is not so. What we find instead is ambiguity and complexity, if not disagreement. The most commonly used economic textbooks in college economics courses give at most cursory definitions of capital, often not until late in the book and subsumed under other topics. The term is virtually never given sustained or nuanced analysis. For example, N. Gregory Mankiw explains late in one of his textbooks: "The essence of capital is that it is a factor of production that is itself produced."[6] Note the emphasis on production, and the point that capital is humanly created: the image is of a tool, machine, factory, or other physical asset that enhances the productivity of labor. This is close to the classical definition of capital as one of the three factors of production, along with land and labor. But "capital" is also used by contemporary economists to characterize the other two factors of production. Land itself—actually a stand-in for all natural resources— is often understood as a capital asset even though not humanly produced. Ever since Gary Becker's *Human Capital*, educated or trained labor has been understood as "human capital."[7]

These extensions of the idea of capital are only the beginning of an expansive (dare one say imperialistic?) use of the metaphor "capital." It is now applied by social scientists and others to just about everything, using the terms social capital, moral capital, intellectual capital, and even religious capital. So the first set of ambiguities lies in the tension between the narrow, technical meaning of capital as a factor of production and the expansive uses of the term for just about everything. It is a potent metaphor, permitting the crossing (some might say "transgressing") of conceptual and disciplinary boundaries.

But consider then the definition of capital as "a stock of goods yielding a steady flow of income" in which "income" can include money (as from various forms of financial capital), energy (the flow of energy from the sun or wind or other source in environmental economics), or even personal satisfaction (the "psychic income" of holding a capital good such as a vacation home or an Impressionist work of art).[8] This use of the term "capital" does not cohere easily with Mankiw's "essence" of capital: that it is "man-made" (some stocks of goods are, some are not) and is for the purpose of production (it may have as its purpose the generation of various kinds of income or simply the creation of more capital).

In fact, perusal of economic literature yields many more definitions and characteristics of capital, and there is reason to conclude that no one definition could satisfy all economists or embrace all of the uses of the word.[9] But it is possible, I think, to offer a classification of kinds of capital to give some preliminary order to our thinking. Paul Hawkens and Amory Lovins (considered heterodox or even maverick economists by many mainline economists) suggest that there are four kinds of capital:

- manufactured capital: infrastructure, machines, tools, and factories
- human capital: labor and intelligence, culture, and organization
- natural capital: resources, living systems, and ecosystem services
- financial capital: cash, investments, and monetary instruments.[10]

While this sorting does not resolve all the ambiguities and complexities of the meaning of capital, it provides a frame for thinking more deeply about capital. Three observations about this frame are in order.

The first is that the way one defines and uses the term "capital" depends on one's purpose. If the purpose is to understand what makes labor more productive, capital as defined by Mankiw is adequate. If the purpose is to discern why labor markets fail to respond to changes in supply and demand the way economic theory says they should, then the idea that companies have invested capital in the education of labor, producing human capital (in Becker's sense[11]), serves the inquiry well. If you want to grasp how production either depends upon or depletes natural resources, you need a conception of natural capital. The metaphor of capital changes as the end of inquiry changes. Purpose determines metaphorical referent and content.[12]

Second, the fourth classification, financial capital, differs from the first three insofar as it is related to all of them and is either derived from them (as a system of ownership claims on them) or serves as a system of metrics in relation to them. Its purpose, minimally, is to offer some measurement of the others, but there are times when the "world" of financial capital seems to develop its own purpose(s) at some remove from a system of metrics.[13]

Third, we are nevertheless faced with the question whether there is any common notion that holds these metaphorical uses together, anything that gets to the "essence" of capital. I think there is. All of the definitions of capital entail the *organization and storage of energy* for a specific purpose or end. A spade or a plow stores the energy of the labor, which made the tool (and of the physical material from which it is made), and now increases the productivity of labor using it; it is a form of fixed capital that enhances labor. A computer is a more complex capital tool composed of many more capital inputs: physical capital (metals, plastics, silicon, more); the natural capital of various energy forms used at all stages of design and production; and human capital in the form of skilled labor in creating the parts and assembling the final product as well as in the form of the broader intellectual and cultural capital that makes possible the creation of silicone chips, circuitry design, various forms of hardware, the complexities of intelligent software design, and more.

All of these capital resources are forms of organized energy. A tree is a capital resource providing wood for human use, but it is itself an extraordinary reorganization of energy, drawing energy from the rays of the sun, using the chlorophyll of its leaves to create oxygen through photosynthesis and serving as one of the most important absorbers of carbon dioxide in the ecosystem. Understood as organizers of energy, trees and forests are the earth's lungs. A church organ represents yet another complex synthesis of immensely varied sources of organized energy: the natural capital in its physical structure (wood, metal, leather valves, ivory keys, all organized natural energy) and the human capital represented in the ancient craft of organ-making, as well as the entire Western musical tradition's store of knowledge of chromatics, harmony, rhythm, the scientific and mathematical knowledge connected to these, and the history of composition and performance skills, simply to name the most obvious. All of these are forms of organized energy. And when an organ is played in a worship service, yet another synthesis of forms of energy is manifest: everything just mentioned plus religious symbols, a history of liturgy in its various parts, and communal forces and energies. To what end or purpose? Production? Christians say that the purpose is the praise of God. Robert Putnam says that it creates social capital. (See John Coleman's essay in this volume for a treatment of social capital.)

These examples of capital as energy organized for specific purposes do not include the fourth type of capital: financial. At first look, it may seem that financial instruments (stocks, bonds, money) do not represent organizations of energy (beyond the physical material from which they may be made, such as paper or metal) and that they are in no way productive. Aristotle's argument that money is sterile, and hence that interest on loans is not legitimate because money cannot produce anything, depended on this assessment; and Thomas Aquinas's later prohibition of usury followed him. But almost all modern economists think this judgment wrong. There is not sufficient space here to give this issue the attention it deserves,[14] but two brief and tentative points are pertinent.

First, there is a consensus in contemporary economic discussions that money and other financial instruments are profoundly based on trust.[15] Absent trust, currencies collapse—witness the end of the Weimar Republic in the 1920s, the financial and bank crisis in the United States and Europe in 1929, and the dramatic devaluation of the Russian ruble after 1990. The current financial crisis, beginning in 2008, demonstrates vividly how markets can "freeze up" when trust fails. Trust, an indispensable virtue of relational selves living together, is a form of organized social energy with multiple and complex sources: personal formation and social habits, the actual experience of social solidarity, and confidence in a variety of social institutions (government in the case of money, other institutions in the case of bonds, stocks, and a host of other financial instruments). But financial instruments are not themselves stored energy; they are related symbolically to other organized energy in two ways: in use, as metrics of wealth, they offer a sum of the other forms of capital; and insofar as they are perceived as having value in themselves, they depend on and point to the social institutions and arrangements that generate trust. The symbolic nature of money points to its quasi-religious nature, a point I will take up later.

Second, money itself is an instrument with a purpose: it facilitates exchange and hence is indispensable for a market economy. In helping realize this end, it also helps coordinate the activities of billions of people and hence seems to have organizing power in itself. But it is important to see that the actual coordination is accomplished by markets and the price system,[16] which are forms of organized energy, relying on human inventiveness, legal systems that secure property rights and more, and complex social and political ecologies.[17] They are themselves manifestations of spirit. Because money facilitates the working of markets, it can easily appear to do what market and exchange in fact do. When people make this mistake, money may be called "counterfeit spirit."[18]

Three things are gained by the understanding of various forms of capital as energy organized for specific purposes. The first is to make clear the deep ambiguity and arbitrariness in the naming of the three classical factors of production. It is worth dwelling for a moment on the etymology of "capital," derived from the Latin for "head" and cognate to the capitals at the top of architectural columns, capital cities as the center of government, and captains of ships and armies. The very notion is hierarchical, connoting a governing capacity, as does its close economic relative, "principal," implying the prince.[19] The strong implication of hierarchical government in the word "capital" is critically important because it means that the other two inputs of the productive process—labor and natural resources—are "headed" by capital and serve it. This hierarchy is written into our law that specifies that, in parsing the responsibilities of corporate managers, the primary (principal) responsibility is to shareholders, that is, to the source of financial capital.

The primary fiduciary responsibility of corporate managers to shareholders or the owners of capital is a legal construction. There is nothing in nature here, nothing natural about granting capital in the narrower economic sense a dominant or governing role, a point long ago made by Marx. Metaphorically, this is, at root, the meaning of capitalism: capital is the captain steering the economic ship, not labor or natural resources. The fact that capital is now often used to refer to the other two factors of production further demonstrates its metaphorical nature but also opens the possibility of a "democratization" of the factors of production. Perhaps all three steer the economic ship.

To speak this way, of course, "reifies" capital, labor, and nature. These metaphorically construed realities in fact "do" nothing. Only people act. But economic metaphors are often reified in the language of economics and business: business leaders are often quoted as saying that "capital will flow to investments yielding the highest rate of return," as if capital had a mind of its own. The financial pages of newspapers will report, "The market has already discounted the drop in…," as if the market had a mind. These ways of speaking indicate how powerful the metaphors are. But we need to penetrate beneath the reifications, even while noting their power.

Second, and following directly: the perennial struggle between capital and labor not only is based on an abstract and metaphorical distinction (since "labor," too, is a metaphorical notion) supported by the legal system but also obscures the multiple sources of organized energy that go into the production of all forms of wealth, whether goods, services, or capital stock and savings. Anything that is humanly produced is in fact composed of an extraordinarily complex array of sources or "factors": the natural base of physical matter (organized energy), ideas developed over centuries, educated labor, communities that provide educated labor, social trust, and disciplines of hard work, government support and regulation at all levels, and the sources of energy required at every level and within each of the other sources. Any one of the three classical factors of production can be broken down into myriad other factors, all part of a complex and interdependent ecosystem. Any decision to grant priority to one source of a particular capital formation—for example, that it is more important than others and hence deserves greater "rights" in relation to them—has to be justified with attention to all the other sources or "factors" and with attention to our normative purposes and ends. Historically, most justifications of claims to priority, to the extent that they are based on anything more than tradition or existing patterns of social power, have rarely been asserted with any attention to the complexity of capital formation.

Hence, a third point: we need to develop adequate normative criteria for the ethical evaluation of various forms of capital, including accurate accounting of the complex factors that go into it: determining real costs in terms of resources—natural, human, social/cultural—that are used, degraded, or depleted; ascertaining and evaluating the purposes or ends each form serves;

and deciding to whom it is accountable. The development of such criteria is a major and complex project; the papers in this volume may be understood as a contribution to their development, drawing on Catholic social thought. Here I hope to contribute a theological framework for developing criteria and principles.

Spirit and Capital

If capital is energy organized in relation to specific ends, it is not merely a metaphor connected to those ends but also an abstraction from an underlying reality that is far more complex than the metaphor itself reveals. That underlying reality, I argue, is what theologians and the Christian tradition call spirit in its multiple manifestations. "Spirit" is also metaphoric, but when used carefully by religion and theology, it aims at characterizing "ultimate reality,"[20] the whole of existence. A nontheological word used to name the underlying reality is "energy": spirit is energy, *energia*, that realizes certain purposes, just as capital refers to various specific constellations of energy for various specific economic purposes. In Genesis, it is the Spirit of God (as "breath" and as "word") that creates, organizing energy into purposeful forms. To use modern terms, spirit may be said to refer to the antientropic processes of evolution that borrow from the steady flow of energy from the sun and, through complex processes beginning with photosynthesis, produce ever more complex and intricate life-forms, including the language and thought that enable reflection on this process.[21]

There are important theological nuances and distinctions with respect to spirit, of course. The "Holy Spirit," when it refers to the gift of God at Pentecost as promised by Jesus, has as its fundamental purpose the foundation of the church, the organizing of the people of God into a new community. But God is also called "spirit" more generally, and the interpretation of "spirit" that I am giving here is not confined to post-Pentecost Christian faith nor to the "Third Person of the Trinity" but encompasses the whole of divine purposive energy in organizing and ordering both nature and all human institutions. I cannot develop a full theology of spirit here. My fundamental point is that when theologians use the word "spirit" carefully in relation to all its manifestations, it symbolically characterizes the purposeful organization of all forms of energy in the whole of Creation;[22] and when economists—and increasingly, other social theorists—use the term "capital" for a specific end, they are abstracting from this underlying spiritual reality.

The implications of this insight are of the utmost importance. Think here of how the "spiritual" or "religious" is commonly understood in contemporary

thought. After Marx and Max Weber, the social sciences have typically relegated the religious and spiritual to the "ideational" world of human culture and
society. For Marx, religion was part of the ideational "superstructure" that was
dependent on, and typically obscured (as ideology) by, the material substructure—the physical world, the means of production, and what he called the
social relations of production. Weber sought to correct this one-sided understanding of the relationship of *Idealfaktoren* and *Realfaktoren* by showing that
"ideal factors" such as the "Protestant ethic" had causative power in the
development of social and economic institutions. Far too many theologians (at
least in the Protestant tradition) have seen Weber as an ally, protecting religious ideas, symbolizations, and practices from Marxist reductionism. But in
my mind this "protection" is illusory and remains reductionist. Go back to our
four forms of capital: the religious and the spiritual become part of the category
"human capital: labor and intelligence, culture, organization." In more common
variations, the spiritual is associated with human meaning, but not with the
natural world (the province of natural science), nor with the world of productive activity and financial capital (the province of economics). Indeed, spirit as
human meaning puts religion and God into the province of the social sciences
all together. The reliance on Weber's work actually reduces religious faith and
activity to human subjectivity and gives them a sociological framing.[23]

Now it is obvious that religious symbolization, thought, and practices are
part of human culture and institutions. But while this is true of human religious activity, institutions, and thought, it is not true of God, of divine spirit.
God is understood by Christians as intrinsically related to, and present in, the
whole of reality: to and in nature (the entire universe), to and in society (institutions), and to and in the domain of culture (symbols and social meaning).[24]
The sociological characterization of religion as human activity carried on in
human institutions must not be confused with the theological understanding
of God and spirit.

What does the theological understanding of capital as an abstraction from
creative spirit add to the previous discussion of capital and organized energy?
Here, three pertinent implications may be noted.

The first is that while both economic language and theological language can
in principle apply to the whole of life, both the "whole" and the language used to
talk about it differ decisively because the purposes differ fundamentally. The
"economic point of view" can be and has been applied to the whole of experienced human reality: there are economic interpretations of law, of government,
of the family, of religion, and more. But any such interpretation inevitably
requires reductionistic abstractions. All human action, motivation, and thought
must be translated into economic language that does not correspond with the

self-understanding of living human beings and cannot grasp the complexity, nuance, and depth of human motivation, interaction, experience, and meaning. Hence the "whole" is inevitably reduced to what the specialized language and its theoretical frames permit. We can learn a great deal from such frames of interpretation, but what is learned needs to be placed within broader and less reductionist interpretations of reality.

It may be argued that theological language is also reductionist, and it can be so used. To claim that a church (let alone government or the market or the corporation) is a manifestation of spirit does not comprehend all of its aspects. Any existing church has physical, social, and institutional aspects that can be fruitfully studied by sociologists, political theorists, economists, and psychologists. To claim that theological language adequately characterizes the whole of reality would be a form of theological triumphalism (something seen in Radical Orthodoxy, I think). We must especially avoid any kind of theological triumphalism.

Religious symbolism is about the whole, but good theology and authentic faith understand that symbols (and abstractions) are indeed symbols, involving all the limits of human understanding. Symbols point to a reality that itself escapes all human attempts to understand it fully.[25] Thomas Aquinas said that human reason "is confounded equally by the elusiveness of poetic expression and by the superabundance of the Word of God."[26] (Mary Hirshfeld's essay in this volume explores this insight and its implications for economic life in some detail.) Hence, theological language requires humility in all of our attempts to interpret, understand, and, above all, explain. And theological language requires the language of other disciplines, including the language of economics, in order to understand the world more fully.

Second: if God is holy and present in all of reality as spirit, it follows that "we human beings do not own the world or any part of it: 'The earth is the Lord's, and the fullness thereof: the world and they that dwell therein.'"[27] This theological point entails limitations on ownership and property. The earth is given to humanity and to other living creatures, as common wealth, and at most we are stewards of those portions of the earth over which we have some rights or claims, with concomitant responsibilities. The point is consistent with Christian teaching on property by Thomas Aquinas and many others, including, albeit more ambiguously, by John Locke who is considered by many to be the "father" of modern views of property rights.

Third, the theological interpretation of capital as organized energy helps clarify the end of economic activity. The normative criteria we develop for evaluating economic activity and well-being must be framed by an understanding of the whole of the world and of our relation to God's purposes. This means something similar to Wendell Berry's understanding of the holiness of life and of "good work" as economic activity that honors God's work, Creation, and the neighbor.[28] These criteria are at a fairly formal level, but they are consistent with Christian notions of stewardship, referring to the care of the household, nourishing the resources over which one has responsibility and attending to the well-being of all those who live in the household.

It is a major undertaking to spell out the implications of these broad principles for the modern economy; the essays in this volume together attempt to work in that direction. The remainder of this essay will examine some structural characteristics of the current U.S. economy that work systematically against even these broad principles. They can be understood as social manifestations of sin, the constriction of the self and imagination.

The Corporation

When I went to New Haven, Connecticut, as a graduate student in 1966, I sought out General Bank, located near several other banks across from the New Haven Green but dwarfed by the others in size. The man who assisted me in opening my modest student account asked, suggesting some surprise, why I had chosen this bank. I told him that before coming to New Haven I had read about New Haven and learned that when Jewish immigrants had come there, they could not get credit from the predominantly Protestant-owned banks in the city and had to form their own bank, now called General Bank. Many years later when African Americans began to move into New Haven, they too found it difficult to borrow money from the mainline banks. But General Bank offered the Black immigrants housing mortgages and loans for business.[29] I wanted to do business with this kind of bank.

As I told this story, I was interrupted by the President of the bank who had overheard my story. He was visibly pleased and invited me to his desk, behind an office screen just a few feet away, for a conversation. He confirmed my story but told me that banks like General, which took in locally generated wealth and then reinvested it in the community, would not last much longer. Banks were increasingly growing larger and merging and were seeking opportunities in investments and loans in parts of the country (at that time, the Sunbelt) where higher rates of return were possible. He estimated that General had only a few years left, and he was right: when I returned a decade later as a member of the Yale faculty, General Bank was gone, several other banks had been renamed, having been taken over by large national banks, and capital was flowing out of New Haven, not only in banking but also through the closing of manufacturing plants and through the departure of numerous corporate headquarters, all seeking higher returns on investment elsewhere. Less wealth was being produced locally, much of the wealth that was still produced was being invested elsewhere, and the bonds of trust with the local community had been broken.

General Bank, and at least some other corporations based in New Haven at that time, exemplified a form of capitalism close to what Stefano Zamagni, in his essay in this volume, calls "civil market society," in which capital enterprises create new wealth that circulates through the market, increasing the wealth of the whole community. But the new larger banks had a different purpose: increasing profits for shareholders who often had little or no connection to local communities and hence no sense of stewardship in relation to the many other stakeholders of a bank.

I do not mean to suggest that all capital should remain in the communities in which it is first generated. There are many complexities here: capital investment in other communities can be of great benefit to those communities, and there are regions of both the United States and the globe that desperately need capital investment. There can also be no single definition of a community: does it refer to a town or city or to a state or to nation or even to the so-called global community? Judgments about these questions are a matter of *phronesis* (practical wisdom based on knowledge and experience), and it requires articulation in laws that embody that judgment, even if imperfectly. The point is that the modern corporation, whether productive or financial, is guided chiefly by the pursuit of profits in the market, not by practical wisdom. This has been most vividly illustrated by the current financial crisis, beginning in 2008, during which the pursuit of profits and willingness to risk were so intense that venerable banks and investment houses went bankrupt.

The Corporation: Public Charter and Public Trust

The corporation is an institution created by law and chartered by government to enable a group of persons to act as a single body or person, having the powers of self-governance and the right to own property, enter into contracts, and "perform legal acts through representatives."[30] In the Middle Ages, towns and cities were incorporated under existing law, as were hospitals, guilds, monasteries, and the church.[31] The articulation of a theory of the modern corporate form emerged from debates by theologians in the eleventh, twelfth, and thirteenth centuries.[32] Stefano Zamagni recounts much of this history in his essay in this volume.

Governments create corporations because they serve important public functions (as with towns or schools) or contribute to the well-being of society. Following my interpretation of spirit outlined earlier, the corporation is a form of spirit, organizing the energies of human, cultural, and material capital for specified purposes. The corporate form helps fulfill the Catholic principle of subsidiarity, permitting important social and economic tasks to be done at the appropriate level. Corporate law, first worked out by canon lawyers, specifies the duties and responsibilities both for governing the corporation and for the interactions among corporations and other social institutions, in effect ensuring that the purposes of the corporation in serving the larger good are realized. The corporation, then, is publicly chartered and entrusted with certain tasks; and corporate law assures that the trust is not misplaced.

The modern business corporation has its origin in the formation of joint stock companies in the seventeenth and eighteenth centuries, which limited the liability of investors and enabled complex and often risky undertakings, particularly in international trade.[33] Since the end of the nineteenth century, the corporation has developed into the most important institution of modern economies, with large corporations dominating most production, trade, and finance. Economically the business corporation is a remarkable institution in its proven capacity for the efficient production of goods and services and hence for the generation of wealth. But the corporation is also an important social institution, depending on contract and the common agreement of those who form it. From this perspective, the business corporation is often counted among those institutions of "civil society" that occupy a space between government and individuals, extending freedom of action, relying on consent, trust, and mutual accountability, and to some extent limiting the power of government.[34] All of these values are manifestations of "spirit," dependent upon and nurturing what social theorists call "social capital," as John Coleman articulates in his essay in this volume. Indeed, the consensual basis of the modern corporation has led some theologians to see it, along with notions of the social contract and of contract generally, as an important institutionalization of Christian conceptions of the idea of covenant, with roots in both Jewish and Christian teaching.[35]

But the immense size and power of the modern business corporation coupled with its ambiguous standing in American law minimize its accountability and constrict its purpose, distorting whatever positive aspects of spirit it may embody and undermining the principle of subsidiarity.

The Accountability of Corporations. Corporate law structures the responsibilities of corporations, in both their internal and external relationships. As business corporations have grown in size and complexity, government has had to respond continuously, creating new law to assure that they serve the public good. But U.S. law, most legal theorists agree, has no coherent definition of the corporation and lacks a coherent body of corporate law, giving corporations extraordinary powers and limiting their accountability to the larger society. The reasons for this are unique to American history. We can identify four chapters in this history.

The first chapter begins in the federalism of the U.S. Constitution. The framers of the Constitution gave the power of incorporation to the individual states, following Jefferson's and Madison's concern that corporations created at the national level might grow so large as to threaten the power of democratic government.[36] The unanticipated consequence was "a race to the bottom": states competed for corporations, attracting them by writing less restrictive laws (most of the largest corporations are incorporated in Delaware), with the ironic consequence that corporations grew larger than Madison could have ever dreamed. The largest corporations today transcend state and national boundaries, with assets and sales exceeding the budgets of most states in the United States and even of many national governments.

The second chapter explains how the corporation became a "fictional, legal person" with all of the rights, including property rights, of individuals guaranteed under the Constitution. This standing is not specified in the Constitution itself, nor is it the result of sustained legal analysis and democratic discussion, but is rather a matter of historical happenstance. The decisive moment was in 1886 when the Supreme Court ruled, in its *Santa Clara* decision, that the corporation was a "person," "subject to protection under the US Constitution."[37] Since this decision, corporations have been considered persons under the law, with the full protection of its property rights, appealing especially to the Fourteenth Amendment of the Constitution (ratified in 1866), intended to protect the property of freed slaves after the Civil War, and which protects all persons from being deprived of their individual rights, including property rights, by the government. There is more than a little irony is this historical turn of events. "In 1938, Justice Hugo Black noted that, of all the cases in which the Supreme Court applied the Fourteenth Amendment in the half-century following *Santa Clara*, less than one-half of 1 percent invoked it in protection of the Negro race, and more than 50 percent asked that its benefits be extended to corporations."[38]

This decision and the idea it founded are deeply contested by legal scholars, with many arguing that it has no rational basis in law and that it stands in tension with the power granted to the states to charter and regulate the corporation.[39] If corporations have all the constitutional property rights of individuals, the power of states to regulate corporations is profoundly weakened.

The third chapter is the separation of ownership and control in publicly traded companies, documented by Adolf Berle and Gardiner Means in 1938.[40] Although shareholders have the legal right to elect (and remove) the members of governing boards, effective control of a corporation requires only a small, unified fraction of the total number of shareholders—by some estimates, as small as 5 percent or less. This means that, except for occasional attempts to organize shareholders in the name of "shareholder democracy," the boards and management of most corporations are controlled by a very small number of shareholders, usually highly represented on the boards and in effect creating a very powerful and very wealthy elite. The effect of this chapter in the story is the disenfranchisement of most shareholders from effective democratic control of corporate assets, rendering them in the minds of many thinkers nothing more than "functionless *rentiers*"—no longer real owners at all.[41]

The fourth chapter delineates the lack of corporate accountability, given the preceding three. The law says that the primary fiduciary responsibility of the managers of a corporation is to their shareholders. But the laws specifying the primary fiduciary responsibility of managers to shareholders were written simply to clarify the relationship of management to shareholders as increasing numbers of business enterprises became publicly traded companies. In this narrow context there was no place for considering managerial responsibilities to other stakeholders, or even for situating the fiduciary responsibility of managers in a broader context of corporate relationships and purpose. So the primary legal specification of corporate responsibility is not based on a coherent theory or definition of the corporation but is rather one part of a hodgepodge of laws, at the state and national levels, all responding to specific issues. Nevertheless, this specification of the fiduciary responsibility of managers has had the effect of defining "what the corporation is"—that is, in effect defining the corporation as the shareholders and their management, conspicuously leaving out labor and all other stakeholders.[42]

This *de facto* definition stands in sharp contrast to the laws of many European countries. For example, German law requires that labor be represented on corporate boards; and in the United Kingdom, the Companies Act of 2006 specifies that boards of directors are responsible not merely to shareholders but also to employees, communities, various business partners (especially customers and suppliers), and the well-being of the environment. But the lax charters of U.S. corporations, the extraordinary property rights of the corporation, and the legal narrowing of the fiduciary responsibility of corporate management to shareholders disenfranchise nearly all stakeholders with vital relationships to the corporation. This includes workers who are a vital part of the actual working of a corporation and the ones who do the real productive work; the vast majority of the shareholders, who are "owners" in name only; local, state, and even national communities in which the corporations do their work, or from which they choose to leave; and of course the natural environment. Effective control is in the hands of a small elite who may or may not have a commitment to the various corporate stakeholders and may or may not have a sense of purpose beyond maximization of profit.

Given this history, it is not surprising that many corporate managers have come to see their primary purpose as maximizing profits for shareholders. Economist Milton Friedman long ago declared that profit maximization was the sole social responsibility of business,[43] and the idea has become common currency in both business and economic thought, one of the structural girders of free-market ideology.

Not all business people think this way, of course, and many offer complex motivations and purposes for being in business: they want to produce high-quality goods and services, they want to create jobs and take care of their workers, and they want to contribute to the well-being of their communities. For such managers, profits are often low on the list of their purposes. A vice president of IBM once told me, in a conference on corporate responsibility, that profits are like breathing: you can't live without breathing, but breathing is not the purpose of life; and profits are essential for an enterprise to live—indeed, an indicator of whether the enterprise is alive—but they are not the purpose of business. But such corporate leaders typically face an uphill battle because the playing field is tilted sharply in favor of those whose sole purpose is profit maximization. If a company exercises stewardship virtues, caring for its wealth as part of a broader vision of business activity, it is often punished. Successful corporations that steward their resources, saving capital so that they can sit through downturns in the market without laying off employees, are targets for hostile takeovers and leveraged buyouts by corporate raiders who see an opportunity for huge short-term monetary gain, using the saved capital to pay off the leveraged loans and often selling off portions of the company to maximize their return.

Note the undermining of good capital market principles: capital in its narrower economic sense is a result of saving, sacrificing present benefits for future return, and thereby creating true wealth. Short-term profit maximization and capital speculation destroy savings and hence burden the future. But the playing field rewards the short-term financial point of view and the more aggressive tools of finance capitalism. The decisions made are governed or regulated only by market mechanisms, and increasingly by financial markets, often at great cost to the human and natural ecologies.[44]

The Financial Point of View and Finance Capitalism

Let's revisit capital and spirit in order to understand why finance capitalism is not, and cannot be, responsible to the holiness of life. It is possible to think of capital, spirit organized for a particular end, in an ascending order from its natural base (the organization of the ecosystem) through forms imposed on it by human beings (including all of human culture, social and political institutions, and productive forms and institutions) to the abstract forms of capital that measure both natural capital and the many human forms of capital, including money and various instruments of financial capital such as stocks and bonds.[45]

At the ground level of an economy, a person organizes resources toward some end such as the production of food or shelter. This ordering is itself the work of spirit, now manifest in the purposes, intelligence, and organizing capacities of the human being. In a capitalist market economy, such a person is an entrepreneur, and what gets ordered—cultivated land, a machine, the coordinated labor of many persons, a factory—are new forms of capital, new wealth generated by the purposeful energies of spirit. These new orderings are typically called "assets" in economics. All are the result of human agency or spirit—of the entrepreneur and of labor—but the assets depend also on the social "agency" of education, laws, and government, and they are fed by the social virtues of cooperation and trust.

All of these assets have a price, determined chiefly by markets: there is the price of original capital investment; and suppliers must be paid, workers at all levels compensated, and the goods and services sold. Money is the unit of measure of the prices; and the capital value is the sum of all the assets, minus any liabilities. If all costs are paid, including social costs sometimes "externalized" into the environment and into human communities, and if the company makes a profit, new wealth has been generated, not simply in the profit (which measures the company's efficiency and health) but in the jobs created, the goods and services provided, and the replenishing and nourishing of the natural and social ecologies.

All of this together may be said to represent the true wealth of an economy, true prosperity. The financial instruments that measure this wealth depend on trust at several levels: the trust among parties involved in direct cooperation, the trust between the company and its various stakeholders, the trust implicit in the various markets (the more trust in an economy, the more efficient a market functions because, without trust, transactions have to be policed, adding substantial costs[46]), and trust in the monetary system.

The company's assets as a whole can also be converted into money when shares in the company are sold and traded publicly or when bonds (debt) are issued to raise capital. In principle, the value of these financial instruments is quite directly related to the underlying assets they measure and represent: shares of stock and instruments of debt are all claims on the company's assets.

But once stocks and bonds are traded in financial markets, their value can vary because of other factors, and these other factors may be far removed from the complex relationships characterizing true wealth, including beliefs about the future of a particular sector of the economy, of the economy as a whole, or of financial markets themselves. As a consequence, the financial instruments representing a claim on the company's assets may have a value that greatly exceeds, or understates, the actual value of those assets.

Once a corporation's value is represented by financial instruments, a new kind of "ordering" occurs that is quite different from the ordering required within a business: it is the ordering of capital itself. Andrew Yuengert has helped me see that these two orderings, even if they overlap, are different both in their purposes and in the kinds of skills and judgment required. Entrepreneurs and managers of corporations order the variety of capital assets just discussed in a complex process requiring practical wisdom (*phronesis*) that is deeply reliant on the forms of trust present in each kind of asset. This wisdom includes a powerful interest in replenishing the assets and the trust on which they are based—this is stewardship of capital. But those who order financial capital (in its metric function, also a form of spirit) have as their purpose the preservation of the capital, increase in the income from it, and growth in total monetary value. The skills involved in realizing these purposes are the skills of finance, which have little to do with organizing a business, and they function at some distance from true wealth, both conceptually and psychologically.

We can identify levels or tiers of distance between financial markets and the organizing energies of true wealth. The first is simply the fact that the organizers of financial assets aim primarily at increasing financial wealth. The seeds for this are already present in any business corporation that aims simply at maximizing profits for shareholders: prosperity is measured not by the stewardship of capital broadly understood as composed of many assets, but by maximization of return on investment. It is only a short step for managers so disposed to see the business itself as if it were nothing but an investment portfolio, to be deployed in order to maximize total return (remember General Bank's fate).[47]

The next level of distance is represented by the dramatically increased influence of mutual funds and pension funds in recent decades. In principle, such funds are helpful instruments for making the wealth of the economy available to large numbers of people. But the market in mutual funds tempts—or drives—fund managers to seek the highest possible rate of return for their investors, and so the funds put immense pressure on corporations to increase their short-term profits, made public in quarterly reports. The shareholders in such funds are no longer really owners of the corporations whose shares the funds hold. They have no interest in the businesses themselves, only in the return they receive. In a recent book, John Bogle, the founder and former CEO of the Vanguard group of funds, excoriated the changes in the financial system that have removed shareholders from ownership, undermined productive and social ideas, and damaged the market.[48]

The next step increasing the distance from true wealth comes in the form of new financial instruments such as currency speculation, the bundling of instruments of debt (mortgages sold in bundles to investors who know little of the actual value or risk of the pieces in the bundle, which was a primary culprit in the 2008 financial crisis), and the recent extraordinary growth of derivatives (futures, hedge funds, etc.). Originally, trading in currencies was closely tied to the flow of physical goods between nations but now is a speculative "betting" on anticipated fluctuations in currency values.[49] Derivatives are typically not considered real assets at all, since their value "derives" from other assets (stocks, bonds, currencies), and, more especially, they depend on perceptions of how the market will move. These financial instruments are so far removed from the organized energies of true wealth that they cannot be said to measure true wealth in any way; they have floated above the system of metrics. The fact that the apparent wealth they create can collapse overnight—the "bubbles" eventually burst—is clear evidence that they do not represent wealth at all. The billionaire Warren Buffett, well known for his commitment to underlying value and long-term investment, has called derivatives "financial weapons of mass destruction" and "a ticking time-bomb."[50] They may not be real wealth, but they have the explosive power to do immense damage to real wealth. Moreover, the damage is not inflicted equally. There are winners and losers, and many of the losers are persons of modest means who lose a lifetime of savings, homes, health insurance, and more.

It is helpful to use the notion of social trust to interpret these levels of increasing psychic and institutional distance from the organized energy that generates true wealth. An interesting pattern emerges.[51] With a cursory look, the greater the distance from actual wealth-creating processes, the more the economic activity seems to depend on trust. If my retirement assets are all in mutual and pension funds, I must trust that they have real value. They are not tangible in the way that my house is or that my employment is (or was). If I hold cash in the bank or in my wallet, I must trust that the currency will continue to have value. If I ignore Buffett and invest in a derivatives fund, I must trust that the markets will behave one way rather than another—or at least hope they will do so.

But on closer examination the kind of trust involved and what is trusted are very different at each level. If I am a worker in a corporation led by managers with a stewardship commitment to all the firm's stakeholders, my trust is rooted in the repeated patterns of behavior of known persons, within a community itself characterized by a high level of trust. Similarly with local banks of yore: the lenders knew those who borrowed money, and there were assumed mutual duties, embedded in broader concerns for the well-being of the persons involved—quite a difference from current patterns of mortgage loans and consumer debt. But move up to the level of financial markets: here the trust is rarely dependent on relationships with persons in a shared universe of meaning. The trust must be placed in the value of monetary instruments, in governments that issue currency, in large banks backed by the FDIC, in the ratings of bonds by Moody's and Standard and Poor, and in the reputation of large institutions. At still higher levels of financial capital, it is not clear where the trust is placed, hence, the very high risk. The trust is closer to blind belief, perhaps approaches something akin to the gambler's instinct for deep and possible high return. Such "trust" has a most tenuous relationship to the trust of organized energy. It is closer to a probalistic extrapolation from experience, so often untrustworthy, and in some case is based on little more than fantasy.

Consider loans and debt. Debt is an IOU, a claim on assets, based on trust that the debt will be repaid. As is well known, U.S. household debt has grown exponentially in recent years, passing $14 trillion in early 2008. Combined with the federal debt (over $9 trillion), U.S. debt is 146 percent of GDP, surpassing any such ratio in U.S. history.[52] Many people have been alarmed by this immense debt and have been highly critical of predatory lending practices by banks, not only related to subprime mortgages but also to credit cards that are offered profligately to consumers who are not qualified to carry the debt. Moreover, banks and other financial institutions have tried to protect themselves against the high risks connected to such debt by selling the debt, typically creatively bundled in the various financial instruments discussed above, to other institutions and investors. But the focus here is on trust: what do people trust when they take on high levels of debt as consumers? The answer lies somewhere between blind belief in the inevitability of continuing economic growth and the fantasies generated by a consumer culture: having more is better, having more is the purpose of life, economic gain and the promise of future returns is the god we worship—and "in whom we trust."

The human imagination preoccupied with fantasies of personal abundance is constricted and misdirected, incapable of opening to the well-being of the neighbor and Creation, unformed in the virtues of trust. No wealth lies beneath the debt incurred in the pursuit of the cultural fantasies of more, no energy organized for purposes of human and natural well-being, no cooperation rooted in trust. This form of debt—a form of money—is truly counterfeit spirit. The

2008 collapse of the credit markets, reaching into all parts of the economy, represents the day of reckoning for misplaced trust and false credit (*creditus* from *credere*, to believe, to trust).

Concluding Remarks

Capital is an abstraction from the purposefully organized energy present in every aspect of Creation and every aspect of our being. Christians call this underlying and ever-present reality "spirit," and see all of life as holy. True wealth and true prosperity come from an economy that is responsible to the holiness of life, honoring God, the neighbor, and Creation. The idea that such an economy can be realized within human history would be hopelessly naïve—prevented by the constrictions of the self and the propensity of self-interest to impoverish our moral imaginations. But informed by the principles of Christian teaching, our social and economic institutions could encourage economic activity that is more responsible to the holiness of life and nurture persons committed to the virtues that contribute to the well-being of others. Unfortunately, the same institutions can reward behavior inimical to human ends and true wealth. Modern business corporations, because of their great power and, in the United States, the absence of a body of law to govern them, routinely violate the public trust to which they owe their being. They do this not because the leaders of the corporations are themselves evil—as a group, they are like most everyone else, more and less virtuous—but because the responsibility of institutions, by their nature, depends far more on good laws than on virtue. In this regard, the primary challenge, especially in the American economy, is structural change in the conception and governance of corporations, articulated in and sanctioned by law, and the enactment of economic policies more consistent with an economy oriented to "good work" and true wealth.

There are no quick fixes, but it is possible to identify in broad outline the most important dimensions of the needed structural changes. (1) Legislation is needed that clearly defines the purpose of the corporation, clarifies its responsibilities to its stakeholders, structures its governance so that the capital it controls is accountable to all who have contributed to it, and gives states—or the national government—genuine power to write charters for achieving these ends and the power to revoke them if the public trust is betrayed. (2) Regulation of capital flows both within the national economy and globally because the capital market cannot be responsive to the requirements of true wealth.[53] (3) A rethinking of taxation is needed so that it is conceived not as the raising of revenue for government to meet "public" needs such as education, public works, and defense, but as a means for assuring that all sources of wealth—workers, communities, culture, the natural environment—are compensated for their contributions and replenished. (4) Government oversight and regulation are needed (likely requiring international cooperation) of credit markets and practices and of financial speculation in its many forms, likely including very high rates of taxation on speculative capital gains. (5) A method for measuring the true wealth of a nation is needed, one superior to gross domestic product (GDP) with all of its well-known deficiencies.[54]

We are all called to a life that honors God, the neighbor and creation—as individuals and in community and society more broadly. Christian faith and common sense require that both our individual choices and our economic institutions be ordered to more substantial purpose than maximizing private gain and the dream of consumer abundance. Understanding capital as a form of spirit provides a framework for addressing these issues and can help bring us closer to that goal focused on in the True Wealth project—sustainable prosperity for all.

NOTES

1. Wendell Berry, "Christianity and the Survival of Creation," 99–100.
2. Ibid., 104.
3. The names I cite in the text refer to contemporary thinkers who have influenced the language I use for the basic conceptions. The conceptions themselves are rooted in classical and ancient formulations—for example, Gustafson's notion of sin as a "constriction of the self" has roots in Augustine, Calvin, and others. And although the theological perspective I sketch is Protestant, I believe it is consonant in most places with much of the Catholic tradition.
4. Reinhold Niebuhr, *Moral Man and Immoral Society*. Although Niebuhr later modified some of the views in this early work, it remains the classic statement of the social nature of sin.
5. Berry, "Christianity and the Survival of Creation," 99.
6. N. Gregory Mankiw, *Principles of Microeconomics*, 406. Mankiw's book is one of the most commonly used textbooks in college introductions to economics. Note how late this definition is given in a 506-page book; and it is part of the chapter "Markets for the Factors of Production," itself a part of the larger section "The Economics of Labor Markets." Markets, exchange, and the price system have center stage in the textbook; capital plays only a minor role on the stage, large capital institutions, virtually none.
7. Gary Becker, *Human Capital*. According to D. McCloskey (*The Rhetoric of Economics*, 77), Becker's argument comes from Theodore Schultz at Chicago; and I have read somewhere that Adam Smith first coined the phrase.

8. Irving Fisher, *The Nature of Capital and Income.*

9. The "Cambridge capital controversy" between economists at Cambridge University and MIT in the 1960s displayed deep, and ultimately unresolved, disagreements on some technical aspects of the meaning of capital. I am grateful to Dan Finn for reminding me of this.

10. Paul Hawkens and Amory Lovins, *Natural Capitalism,* 4. I have reordered their list, but the classifications and terminology are theirs.

11. Becker's understanding of human capital as educated labor (see n. 8 above) is narrower than the broader sense of human capital offered by Hawkens and Lovins. For my purposes here, the broader classification is adequate.

12. It is easy to do ideological analysis here: if you are a capitalist, you think that traditional capital in one or more of its forms creates the most value in the process of production. If you are a Marxist, you think that labor creates the most value (and it is too often forgotten that his view originated with John Locke, the father of common notions of private property, who argued that labor contributes 99 percent of the value to the productivity of land). If you are an ecologist, you think that natural resources and the ecosystem provide most of the value of everything, through the use of energy in all its forms, but especially that form produced by the sun's energy through photosynthesis. Ideological purpose dictates the relative importance of man-made, human, and natural capital.

13. I am indebted to Andrew Yuengert for this valuable insight, as well as for many other perceptive critical comments that have helped improve on the first version of this chapter.

14. The classical sociological and historical account of religious teaching on usury is Benjamin Nelson's *The Idea of Usury.*

15. See, for example, Robert Heilbroner and Lester Thurow, *Economics Explained.*

16. I am indebted to Mary Hirschfeld for helping me state this clearly.

17. See Daniel Finn, *The Moral Ecology of Markets.*

18. Jon P. Gunnemann, "Capital Ideas."

19. These terms are also patriarchal, a point perhaps also worth exploring.

20. "Ultimate reality" is Paul Tillich's phrase for the divine dimension of existence, but it is also used by other theologians.

21. I am fully aware of the controversies surrounding the idea of teleology in the evolutionary process. I cannot address these here but must be content to assert (noncontroversially, I hope, in relation to those contributing to this project) that as theologians in the Christian tradition, we are ineluctably committed to a notion of the purposefulness of the created order.

22. To say that all organizations of energy are manifestations of spirit is not to say that all forms are good. Spirit can be organized for evil ends, and when it is so organized, it is the demonic. The demonic cannot have an existence independent of divine creative power (the point is as old as Augustine).

23. Compare here Stefano Zamagni's point, in his essay in this volume, that Weber's understanding of capitalism and its *Geist* is incompatible with Catholic ethics and social teaching.

24. While this tripart categorization does not precisely correspond to the four forms of capital, it is a framing of God's relationship to the world that is common in at least Protestant theology since the seventeenth century, and it overlaps sufficiently with the four forms of capital to make the point.

25. I am influenced here by Paul Tillich's notion of the cross as a "broken symbol," as well as by Paul Ricoeur's understanding of the symbolic nature of all thought.

26. This quotation is from Alex Ross, *The Rest Is Noise*, 471–72. Ross is discussing Olivier Messiaen's religious understanding of music (the book is about twentieth-century composition) and does not give a citation.

27. Berry, "Christianity and the Survival of Creation," 96.

28. See nn. 1 and 2 above.

29. This history is not unusual: Jewish communities were typically the last to join "white flight" in the 1950s and 60s, working to integrate schools and stabilize neighborhoods and committed to the civil rights movement.

30. Harold Berman, *Law and Revolution*, 215–56. Among many other points, Berman discusses the tension between the Germanic conception of the corporation as a "fellowship" with a "personality" and the Roman conception of the corporation as an "institution."

31. In Christian thought, the church is "one body with many members."

32. Berman, *Law and Revolution*, 215–21.

33. One of the first, and certainly the most famous, joint stock companies was the British East India Company, chartered in 1600, to help develop trade with India, but which also in fact served as an arm of the British government in administering the British colony in India.

34. For good overviews of the meaning of civil society, see Adam Seligman, *The Idea of Civil Society*; and Simone Chambers and Will Kymlicka, eds., *Alternative Conceptions of Civil Society*.

35. But this is a highly contested claim, for reasons I give in the following paragraphs. For a Protestant view of the corporation as an instantiation of covenant and "voluntary association," see Max Stackhouse, *Public Theology and Political Economy*. For a Catholic view, with an even more positive evaluation of the business corporation, see Michael Novak, *The Fire of Invention*.

36. For brief discussions of this history, see Harvey C. Burke, *A Primer on American Economic History*, chap. 3; and Edwin M. Epstein, *The Corporation in American Politics*.

37. Marjorie Kelly, *The Divine Right of Capital*, 163. For a legal discussion of the history of the corporation as a fictional creation of the law before the *Santa Clara* decision, see Daniel J. H. Greenwood, "Fictional Shareholders."

38. Kelly, *The Divine Right of Capital*, 163.

39. For a legal discussion of the history of the corporation as a fictional creation of the law before the *Santa Clara* decision, see Greenwood, "Fictional Shareholders." Earlier decisions that gave corporations rights similar to persons were decried by the states, which, according to the Constitution, alone had the power to incorporate and establish the legal standing of the corporation.

40. Adolph Berle and Gardner Means, *The Modern Corporation and Private Property*.

41. This chapter of the story also explains the extraordinary ballooning salaries of CEOs in recent decades as well as the highly publicized severance packages—"golden parachutes"—for managers who have, by all accounts, failed.

42. I am grateful to Vincent Rougeau who, during discussion of the first version of this paper, both confirmed and clarified the fiduciary responsibility to shareholders as the primary and decisive responsibility of corporate mangers in U.S. law.

43. Milton Friedman, "The Social Responsibility of Business Is to Increase Its Profits."

44. In European companies such as in Germany, where workers are represented on corporate boards, leveraged buyouts are very difficult because the workers are considered part of the assets of the company that must be purchased, dramatically increasing the price.

45. I am deeply indebted to Andrew Yuengert for much of the following. Although the presentation of the ideas here is my own—and may not find his agreement—it is based on some of his language and his careful and creative parsing of different notions of capital in response to the first version of this paper.

46. See Charles E. Lindblom, *Politics and Markets*.

47. Imagine that as a corporate manager you look at the average annual profits of your business and compare this (better to do so during a bull market) to the average rate of return in the stock market over time (typically estimated at 10 percent annually). It could well make rational sense, given your fiduciary responsibility to your shareholders, to sell all of the enterprise's assets and invest the proceeds in the stock market, maximizing return. If all corporate managers did this, we would have no productive capacities. Of course, the market would correct this because, if the supply of needed goods decreases, prices would go up and the incentive to produce them would increase. But why not let others produce the vital goods and services? Something like this has in fact already happened as manufacturing work and jobs have disappeared in this country, going to countries where the goods we need are produced more cheaply. This outsourcing of jobs frees up capital for higher returns and contributes to the general move toward a service economy in which financial institutions with large profits play a central role. A part of this trend, reported to me by numerous corporate managers, entails a preference of business school graduates for careers in finance rather than in other sectors of the business world. Business students have told me that the "best and the brightest" go into finance because that is where the money is. Vera Zamagni reports a similar trend in Italy in her essay in this volume.

48. John C. Bogle, *The Battle for the Soul of Capitalism*. Vanguard's funds had minimal loads and low operating costs. Bogle was committed to long-term ownership and stewardship conceptions, and he was considered a hero of people's capitalism. It should be added, however, that his interest is chiefly in stewardship for shareholders and the recovery of the power of shareholders as owners. In my mind, his views need to be supplemented by the broader conception of stewardship I have advocated here and more consistent with Catholic social teaching as well.

49. I am indebted to Paul Caron for this insight.

50. Reported on innumerable websites. The source, reportedly, was Buffet's 2002 letter to Berkshire shareholders. It should be added that there are virtually no laws regulating this part of the financial market and, insofar as most of the market is international, no government to enact the needed laws.

51. I am indebted to Daniel Finn for comments aiding these reflections on finance and trust.

52. Charles McMillion, *Manufacturing and Technology News*.

53. Albino Berrera addresses the need for regulating capital flow in his essay in this volume.

54. There are numerous proposals for such measures, including the GPI (General Progress Indicator) based on the earlier ISEW (Index of Sustained Economic Welfare) proposed by Herman Daly, John Cobb, and Clifford Cobb in *For the Common Good*. Amartya Sen has developed indicators based on his "capabilities" approach to economic development.

REFERENCES

Becker, Gary. *Human Capital*. Chicago: University of Chicago Press, 1964.
Berle, Adolph, and Gardner Means. *The Modern Corporation and Private Property*. Rev. ed. New York: Harcourt, Brace & World, 1968.
Berman, Harold. *Law and Revolution: The Formation of the Western Legal Tradition*. Cambridge: Harvard University Press, 1983.
Berry, Wendell. "Christianity and the Survival of Creation." In *Sex, Economy, Freedom, & Community*. New York: Pantheon, 1992, 1993.
Bogle, John C. *The Battle for the Soul of Capitalism*. New Haven: Yale University Press, 2005.
Burke, Harvey C. *A Primer on American Economic History*. New York: Random House, 1969.
Chambers, Simone, and Will Kymlicka, eds. *Alternative Conceptions of Civil Society*. Princeton: Princeton University Press, 2002.
Daly, Herman, John Cobb, and Clifford Cobb. *For the Common Good*. 2nd ed. Boston: Beacon, 1994.
Epstein, Edwin M. *The Corporation in American Politics*. Englewood Cliffs, NJ: Prentice-Hall, 1969.
Finn, Daniel. *The Moral Ecology of Markets*. Cambridge: Cambridge University Press, 2006.
Fisher, Irving. *The Nature of Capital and Income*. New York: Macmillan, 1906.
Friedman, Milton. "The Social Responsibility of Business Is to Increase Its Profits." *New York Times Magazine* 13 (September 1970).
Greenwood, Daniel J. H. "Fictional Shareholders: For Whom Are Corporate Managers Trustees, Revisited." *Southern California Law Review* 69 (March 1996): 1021–104.
Gunnemann, Jon P. "Capital Ideas." In *Religion and Values in Public Life*. Cambridge: Harvard Divinity School, 2000: 97–109.

Hawkens, Paul, and Amory Lovins. *Natural Capitalism*. Boston: Little, Brown, 1999.

Heilbroner, Robert, and Lester Thurow. *Economics Explained*. Rev. ed. New York: Simon & Schuster, 1994.

Kelly, Marjorie. *The Divine Right of Capital*. San Francisco: Berrett-Koehler Publishers, 2001.

Lindblom, Charles E. *Politics and Markets*. New York: Basic Books, 1977.

Mankiw, Gregory, N. *Principles of Microeconomics*. 4th ed. Mason, OH: Thomson-Southwestern, 2006.

McCloskey, D. *The Rhetoric of Economics*. Madison: University of Wisconsin, 1985.

McMillion, Charles. *Manufacturing and Technology News* 15, no. 2 (January 24, 2008). Online. Available: http://www.manufacturingnews.com/news/08/0124/art1.html.

Nelson, Benjamin. *The Idea of Usury*. 2nd ed. Chicago: University of Chicago Press, 1969.

Niebuhr, Reinhold. *Moral Man and Immoral Society*. New York: Scribner's, 1932.

Novak, Michael. *The Fire of Invention: Civil Society and the Future of the Corporation*. Lanham, MD: Rowman & Littlefield, 1997.

Ross, Alex. *The Rest Is Noise: Listening to the Twentieth Century*. New York: Farrar, Straus and Giroux, 2007.

Seligman, Adam. *The Idea of Civil Society*. New York: Free Press, 1992.

Stackhouse, Max. *Public Theology and Political Economy*. Grand Rapids: Eerdmans, 1987.

12

An Ecofeminist Approach to the True Wealth Project

Maylin Biggadike

The True Wealth of Nations project has taken on much-needed work in applying Catholic social thought to economic analysis and in addressing the ethics and economics of prosperity. This essay will take up the perspective of poor women in the two-thirds of the world, out of the conviction that we will not understand prosperity without addressing the ethics and economics of poverty. Poverty is not an abstract notion. In the voices of poor people themselves:

> Poverty means hunger, lack of medical treatment, and poor access to basic services such as electricity and water supply. It means being unable to send children to school, and often needing them to work instead. Poverty means a lack of assets—such as land or savings—and thus extreme vulnerability to shocks due to economic downturns, family illness or natural disasters. It means social exclusion, and a constant feeling of insecurity and stress based on an uncertain future.[1]

Contrary to the charges of some critics, using gender as an interpretive tool does not stress women's goodness, nor does it diminish the important struggles of other parts of the population. It does recognize, however, that the most important measure of a healthy society, of the true wealth of nations, lies in the predicament of its most vulnerable group.

Poverty research identifies women and children as the most vulnerable populations and the ones who bear the greatest burden in poverty-stricken areas of the world. Women are often hardest hit by poverty, and they constitute a majority of the world's poor. Noeleen Heyzer, executive director of UNIFEM, summarizes this situation:

> The modern global economy is now a reality. Yet everywhere in the world there are people working in conditions that should no longer exist in this 21st century, for income that is barely enough for survival. Home-based workers put in long hours each day, yet are paid for only a fraction of their time. Rural women spend back-breaking hours on family plots, often for no payment at all. Those in urban areas work in unregulated factories, earning pennies for products that are shipped via sub-contractors to markets far away, or they find jobs as waste-pickers, scavenging garbage heaps for items to sell. The working poor are both men and women. However, the further down the chain of quality and security, the more women you find. Yet it is their work—including their unpaid work in insecure jobs or small enterprises—that holds families and communities together.[2]

This essay will explore the global gender gap and the effects of economic policies on women. It will describe the approach of ecofeminism in the work of Ivone Gerbara and will examine some existing programs of solidarity and empowerment. It will evaluate the situation of Latin American women working in *maquilas*[3] with help of ecofeminist analysis and the work of Amartya Sen.

The Global Gender Gap

One way to assess the situation of poor women in the global setting is to look at their status in relation to men. Research on the global gender gap has shown a direct link between poverty and gender disparities. Data on women are often not even available, due to lack of census collection and measurement difficulties. And, where they do exist, they are typically statistical in nature and do not reflect the more complex sociological and political environment in which poor women find themselves. In trying to capture this more complex environment, the World Economic Forum[4] (WEF) made a first attempt "to assess the current size of the gender gap by measuring the extent to which women in fifty-eight countries have achieved equality with men in five critical areas: economic participation, economic opportunity, political empowerment, educational attainment, and health and well-being."[5] The WEF study considers gender as the overarching sociocultural variable seen in relation to other factors such as race, class, age, and ethnicity. What is most interesting about this study, besides giving a general and global assessment of the gender gap, is the researchers' interpretation of the five critical areas that they use as criteria.

The researchers adopt Amartya Sen's notion that societies need to see women less as passive recipients of help and more as dynamic promoters of social transformation. This view, they claim, is supported by evidence, which suggests that factors such as education, employment, and ownership rights of women are a powerful influence on their ability to be social agents. Thus, their criteria for economic participation not only measure women's participation in quantitative terms but also compare unemployment levels, the levels of economic activity, and remuneration for equal work.

The study found that "worldwide, outside the agricultural sector, in both developed and developing countries, women are still averaging slightly less than 78% of the wages given to men for the same work, a gap which refuses to close in even the most developed countries."[6] Furthermore, they argue that poor women have been excluded from the gains of globalization, since these gains are often concentrated in the hands of those who own resources and have access to capital. They conclude that globalization has intensified existing inequalities and insecurities for many poor women, who already represent two-thirds of the world's poorest people. They stress the importance of "gender budgeting"[7] by national governments, especially in the developing world, as a way of taking into account the large percentage of women who participate in the informal sector and who, in some parts of the world, provide upwards of 70 percent of agricultural labor and 90 percent of the food, but who are nowhere represented in budget deliberations.

Economic Opportunity

The study's assessment of *economic opportunity* concerns the quality of women's economic involvement, beyond their mere presence as workers. This is measured using maternity leave benefits, the impact of maternity laws on the hiring of women, availability of government-provided childcare, female professional workers as a percentage of the total, and equality between men and women for private-sector employment. The researchers found economic opportunity to be a "particularly serious problem in developed countries, where women's employment is concentrated in poorly paid or unskilled job 'ghettos,' characterized by the absence of upward mobility and opportunity."[8] They attribute this state of affairs to negative and obstructive attitudes and to legal and social systems in which maternity laws penalize women economically.

Their study shows that this "ghettoization" of female labor crosses all cultural boundaries and professions, affecting women in virtually all countries.

Internationally, women are most often concentrated in "feminized" professions and remain in lower job categories, which is another major obstruction to economic opportunity and advancement. They conclude that the "feminization of poverty" names "the fact that the majority of the 1.5 billion people living on US$1 a day or less are women and that the gap between women and men caught in the cycle of poverty has not lessened, but may well have widened in the past decade."[9]

Political Empowerment

On political empowerment, the researchers have used data on the number of female ministers, seats in parliament held by women, women holding senior legislative and managerial positions, and the number of years a female has been head of state in each of the fifty-eight countries. They look at the representation of women in decision-making structures, both formal and informal, and their voice in the formulation of policies affecting their societies. They explain that a study of Bolivia, Cameroon, and Malaysia showed that

> were women to have a greater say in spending priorities, they
> [national governments] would be far more likely to spend family and
> community resources for improving health, education, community
> infrastructure and the eradication of poverty, as opposed to the
> military, alcohol or gambling. The demand for changed priorities is
> heard from virtually all women's organizations, from the most
> advanced and politically savvy in developed countries, to fledgling
> women's NGO's in the developing world.[10]

Educational Attainment

The researchers regard educational attainment as the fundamental prerequisite for empowering women in all spheres of society because without adequate education, women have limited access to jobs, are unable to gain political influence, and are more likely to raise children unprepared for the future. The educational gap is measured by comparing male and female enrollment in primary, secondary, and tertiary education, average years of schooling, and adult literacy.

Results show that, although "girls outnumber boys in tertiary level education in a very few countries...an obvious gender gap appears early in most countries and grows more severe with each year of education."[11] They note that a study by USAID has found that "countless women in the developing world are further removed from the information age because of their lower levels of education and deeply ingrained negative attitudes towards other forms of achievement."[12] Because information and communication technologies are a potent driving force of the development process, and since women still constitute two-thirds of the world's illiterate, the gender gap in educational attainment is particularly serious.

Health and Well-being

The criterion of health and well-being also exposes a gender gap between men's and women's access to sufficient nutrition and health care and related to issues of fundamental safety and integrity of the person. This is measured by infant and maternal mortality rates[13], adolescent fertility rates[14], births attended by skilled health professionals, and effectiveness of government efforts to reduce poverty and inequality. The researchers note that

> according to the World Health Organization, 585,000 women die
> every year, over 1,600 every day, from causes related to pregnancy
> and childbirth. The Planned Parenthood Federation of America
> quotes estimates that of the annual 46 million abortions worldwide,
> some 20 million are performed unsafely, resulting in the deaths of
> 80,000 women from complications, accounting for at least 13% of
> global maternal mortality, and causing a wide range of long-term
> health problems.[15]

They also emphasize that the most obvious aspect of reduced physical security and integrity of women is their vulnerability to violence. Reliable data on violence against women is difficult to obtain due to a social stigma and fear of disclosure, so that only a small proportion of the crimes of sexual assault, child abuse, wife battering, and gun-related violence are ever reported.[16] The complexity of social and cultural issues plays a great part in stigmatizing and isolating the victims of violence. In some countries, women are "forced into marriage with their violators with little or no control over their own persons"[17]: "Each year an estimated two million girls, usually aged 4 to 8, are forcibly subjected to female genital mutilation (FGM), which routinely leads to death, chronic infection and bleeding, nerve tumors, obstructed childbirth, painful scarring, etc. Although most prevalent in Africa and the Middle East, the practice of some form of FGM has been reported among immigrant communities in parts of Asia and the Pacific, North and South America and Europe."[18]

Assessing the gender gap is important for several reasons. It measures the unequal distribution of resources and opportunities based on whether a person is born male or female. Disparities at work exist because of sociocultural factors such as race, class, age, and ethnicity. The gender gap appears most acute in developing nations and in nations struggling with endemic poverty and points to a direct link between poverty and gender disparities. This link is of particular concern when we look at economic development through the eyes of poor women.

Effect of Economic Policies on Women

The informal economy has grown in many developing countries, comprising 50 to 80 percent of total nonagricultural employment.[19] This has been partly due to the collapse of commodity prices and the persistence of agricultural subsidies in rich countries, which have led to the disintegration of many rural communities.[20] This situation has forced men and women into the informal sector in which there is no job security and no medical and other benefits. In nearly all developing countries (except North Africa) over 60 percent of working women work in informal employment outside agriculture, a much greater proportion than for men:[21] "Over the past two decades, as employment in the informal economy has increased, women have entered the labor force in large numbers. The connection between these two trends is not clear. Are women taking over 'men's jobs' that, in the process, are being informalized? Are women entering informalized types of work that men now avoid? Or are women being actively recruited for new forms of employment that are, by design, informal?"[22]

Trade liberalization has created many job opportunities for women in export-oriented light manufacturing. This accounts for the many country statistics showing increased women's participation in the workforce. However, such statistics do not account for the conditions and insecurities related to such work. These jobs are not covered by labor or social protections, and as these industries need more skilled workers, over time men tend to take over the jobs that women secured when the country first opened its economy. Mexico, which signed the 1994 North American Free Trade Agreement (NAFTA), is a case in point: "The growth in women's employment did not necessarily lead to an improvement in their living standards. Women found more jobs in the vegetable and fruit export sector in agriculture but, with an increase in working hours and in employment on a piecework basis, their general labor conditions often worsened."[23]

In the situation of the *maquilas* in Mexico, even though female employment grew in absolute terms, it fell in relative terms. As *maquilas* looked for more skilled labor and switched to electronics, men took over the jobs previously held by women. Since 2000, *maquilas* have shed almost 200,000 jobs, most of which were lost by women.[24] "As *maquila* employment contracted and the Mexican economy faltered, women were forced to look for other types of employment, often accepting lower wages and poorer labor conditions."[25] Jobs in the informal economy increased, with women representing more than half of the workers.

Real wages are lower today than when NAFTA was implemented.[26] These declines in real wages have occurred in a labor market that is highly sex segregated, with women consistently earning far less than men with the same education and in the same jobs. "Furthermore, three out of every four rural women in 2002 worked without receiving any kind of payment....The gender difference in wages in 2000 [is calculated to be] more than two weeks wages for a woman with a basic education, meaning that a woman must work two weeks more than a man to make up the difference in wages."[27]

The papal encyclical, *Centesimus Annus*, argues that the creation of wealth in a market-driven economic system could, in the right conditions, promote the common good. The operative phrase here is "in the right conditions." One example of how the creation of wealth under *wrong* conditions can place undue burden on the women who work in them can be found in the *maquilas* of El Salvador and Nicaragua. Free-trade zones were created in these countries to alleviate the hunger and unemployment of widows in the civil wars.[28] The theory from the government's perspective was to entice foreign companies to build factories in their country by offering lower taxes and lower wages, in hopes of alleviating the domestic unemployment crisis facing their countries. From the companies' perspective, this was a sound investment, as they could take advantage of cheaper labor, thus achieving a lower and more competitive price for their products worldwide.

While the *maquilas* brought work to a destitute population, they also ignored the health, education, and welfare needs of the women employed in them. Women work under difficult conditions: they are required to sign waivers of pregnancy, have few or no breaks, and are on their feet for ten-hour days for a nonsurvival wage.[29] In addition, with mothers absent, their teenage daughters often have to forego their education in order to take care of the rest of their siblings. From a purely monetary standpoint, these women may be better off than before, but at an unquantifiably high personal and social cost. The economic policy designed to raise their living standards excluded the social and human development of these women and their daughters. Under this economic policy, the women are caught in a cycle of deprivation and do not benefit from shared prosperity.

Issues of economic and social justice, like the situation found in *maquilas*, are important topics for Christian social ethics, which acknowledges the preferential option for the poor and the centrality of economic justice in the lives of the oppressed. The preferential option for the poor is scripturally based in both the Hebrew Bible (the liberation of Israel from Egypt in the Book of Exodus) and the New Testament (Jesus' proclamation of the kingdom of God as something to be furthered here on earth, e.g. Matt. 25:31-46). Extending such teachings on solidarity and love of neighbor, it has woven its way into the broader Christian tradition. We find it in Catholic social teaching, expressing special concern in distributive justice for the poor and the vulnerable: "As individuals and as a nation...we are called to make a fundamental 'option for the poor.' The obligation to evaluate social and economic activity from the viewpoint of the poor and powerless arises from the radical command to love one's neighbor as one's self. Those who are marginalized and whose rights are denied have privileged claims if society is to provide justice for all."[30]

The Ecofeminist Approach

Ecofeminist thought was born in response to the need for understanding the plight of poor women in developing countries. As Jorge Arturo Chaves notes, "the developments of Latin American theology are not simply different because of their emphasis on specific subjects of research, but because of a different formal object and method of study."[31] Ecofeminism and mainstream economics represent two different philosophical traditions and methodologies for research. Economics, on the one hand, draws from the anthropological worldview of nineteenth-century liberalism, which regards the human being as a rational autonomous agent; whereas ecofeminism sees the human being as interdependent, taking seriously her "affective" nature as a source of knowing. Economics studies consumers, firms, industries, and countries using variables such as profits, growth rates, inflation, and gross national products. It does so through the scientific methods of hypothesis testing, model building, statistics, and econometrics. The ecofeminist model, on the other hand, studies the impact of power structures on both the individual and the community through personal and communal life experience. Economics' primary language is mathematics, and its mode of analysis is linear causality, whereas ecofeminism's primary language is personal story and its analysis is descriptive. The one works in aggregates and abstractions, the other in concrete personal reality.

Ecofeminist Epistemology

Ecofeminism not only provides a new content but also is based on a new epistemology, a new understanding of knowing and knowledge. Women and the ecosystem have always been there, but they were not considered constitutive elements of explicit knowing in traditional epistemologies. When a poor Latin

American woman's situation is placed at the center of analysis, our ways of knowing are modified. An ecofeminist theological expression always starts from what has been lived, from what is experienced in the present. Consequently, it rejects an abstract language about life and those matters deeply affecting human relationships. It stresses the need to understand specifics before we are able to give meaning to what we call universal.

The ecofeminist perspective proposes a retrieval of the most profound kind of knowing that human beings possess—that of their lived experience. It is founded on the precept that to know is, first of all, to experience. In the Latin American context, this lived experience points to struggles in the face of poverty, gender discrimination, powerlessness, class differences, racial discrimination, and destruction of the environment. In this setting, epistemological issues cannot be divorced from the practical that which countless people wrestle with on a daily basis.

Why, we may ask, is it necessary to talk about epistemology? Is it not sufficient to bring to the fore issues that affect women and ecology? Philosophical theories within the Western tradition have tended to be anthropocentric (that is, human centered) and androcentric (that is, male centered). Women and ecology are often left out of the equation. An epistemology that only refers to the experience of a part of humanity is limited because it treats that experience as if it were the experience of all. The ecofeminist perspective treats issues of gender and ecology as a constitutive part of our human way of knowing and sees the relationship between ethics and epistemology as rooted in the concreteness of our lives.

Ivone Gebara, a Roman Catholic theologian and ecofeminist ethicist, has helped illumine the problem of poverty in Latin America and is credited with the development of ecofeminist thought. My main critique of her work lies in her uncompromising call for the dismantling of all hierarchical and patriarchal structures within the Church. There is no room for reform in her thinking. Her work in revisioning Christian theology questions the patriarchal doctrines that keep these structures in place. She calls for a broadening of our horizons beyond monotheistic discourse about God, beyond catechetical learning, and beyond a dogma that can become authoritarian and punitive. She accuses Christian theology of being complicit in accentuating the inferiority of women and in exalting an instrument of torture, the cross, using it as an excuse for justifying the misery imposed on the poor, especially women. (We might note here a tendency to "throw the baby out with the bathwater.") Likewise, she blames capitalism for all the economic woes poor women face on a daily basis and does not distinguish between unjust economic practices and the economic system of capitalism. She makes the claim that the suffering of Jesus, "even if it has become the Christian paradigm of suffering, is certainly no greater than that of prostitutes stoned to death, of a mother whose child is wrenched from her, of the mass murder of indigenous peoples, Africans, Jews, Arabs...of women who see their children die of hunger because of the greed of those who hold economic power."[32]

What Gebara offers us that I find extremely enlightening are the several categories that describe the ecofeminist enterprise and that are intrinsic to eco-feminist thought. These categories of interdependence, process, context, and affectivity present a new way of knowing that regards women and the eco-system as constitutive parts of human knowing.

Interdependence: "The central assumption of ecofeminist epistemology is the interdependence among all the elements that are related to the human world."[33] It is a relationship between life and its multiple interconnections and is not restricted to human relationships alone but encompasses nature, the powers of the earth, and the cosmos itself. This sacred interdependence introduces us to a new way of relating to one another and to the earth from the perspective of *communion with* instead of the perspective of *conquering* earth and space, always inviting "us to step somewhat outside the closed subjectivity that sees the world and other humans as objects subservient to our will."[34]

Knowing as Process: Ecofeminist epistemology upholds the complexity of reality-in-process, which is ongoing, is in constant flux, and does not necessarily follow a predictable causal path. Ecofeminist epistemology, then, does not "hold up any single moment in the past or the future as a paradigm for all time. Rather, [it] affirm[s] the extraordinarily dynamic nature of the knowing process, adapting it to the vital needs of the great variety of human groups."[35]

Contextual: Ecofeminist epistemology takes the "lived context of every human group as its primary and most basic reference point."[36] It recognizes the history that has shaped the particular group and tries to capture the logic present in each context, its system and values. Contextual epistemology does not deny that there are universal elements present in every context, but it does stress the importance of beginning at the most concrete level and only afterwards appreciating its universal elements.

Holistic: "Holistic epistemology attempts to underline the fact that we are not just parts of a greater whole [but that] the greater whole is also a part of ourselves."[37] This means that our approach to reality and the particular way in which we know is conditioned by the greater whole, an evolutionary process that went on before us and continues within us. Holistic epistemology, while not rejecting a rationalistic mode of discourse, does object to its limitations when it is the *only* mode of discourse. (W)holistic, knowing as the word suggests, acknowledges that there are multiple ways of knowing and it appeals to the diversity of cognitive capacities within us.

Affective: Ecofeminist epistemology takes seriously the role that emotions play in human knowing. This approach rests on the belief that emotions bring inspiration, wonder, passion, and creativity to the myriad of issues that humans face: "An epistemology that is characterized by affectivity will recognize that the immense spectrum of emotions and feelings is manifested in all men and women according to their individual characters, their life situations, and their cultures."[38]

The common theme that underscores all the ecofeminist categories discussed above is the notion of relatedness. Relatedness means "the connection, the correlation, and the interdependence that exists between and among all things. It refers to the very stuff that creates and sustains life, that nourishes life and allows it to grow."[39] It includes the affirmation of interdependence and difference.[40] It is relatedness that enables us to see our connectedness to one another and to the earth; to appreciate the indissoluble unity between our mind and body, between spirit and matter; to embrace our entire self and not only parts of it; to accept our feelings and emotions as capable of invigorating our reason; to perceive our histories as crucial to informing our present context; and to better understand the dynamic nature of our reality-in-process. Relatedness impacts the way we approach our relations among humans. It privileges the common good while respecting the integrity of all beings, individually and collectively. We not only consider the impact of any action on ourselves but also take seriously the effect that action may have on different social groups and communities of human beings who live together on the same planet.[41]

To live in accordance with the common good is to encounter God in the events of daily life (theopraxis). It is a freedom that allows us to go on hoping despite the temptation to despair, to love life in spite of suffering and poverty, and to live lives of sharing and solidarity however scanty the resources.

Programs of Solidarity and Empowerment

The ways poor women have sought to taste this freedom in their daily lives testify to their courage in the face of tremendous obstacles. There is an intuitive understanding of ecofeminist principles, a commitment to working in community and to lending a helping hand when possible as well as reaching out for help when necessary.

A Small Garden in Ecuador

Maria Peralta is an indigenous Quechua woman, a sixty-year-old farmer, who joined a family garden project sponsored by the OXFAM America (Oxford Committee for Famine Relief) through grants to the Center for Pluricultural

Studies (CEPCU): "It is a small piece of an innovative development plan for the entire San Pablo Lake basin designed to reduce pollution in the lake, improve the soil and reduce erosion, and help the 30,000 indigenous people in the area to improve their diet, health, access to education, and standard of living."[42]

Before Maria took part in this project, she only had enough money to buy seeds for five crops and did not know how to farm other vegetables. With the small loans she gets from CEPCU, Maria now grows other vegetables and raises cows and guinea pigs. It is a very small garden behind her house in Otavalo; but those sixty square yards, about the size of a tennis court, have made a big difference in Maria's life. She proudly says: "Everything we have comes from this garden. My older children couldn't go to school when they were little, but I was able to pay for school for them when they were older."[43]

This small garden feeds Maria and her four children—Rosita, Angelo, Juanita, and Clarita. Maria's children have also benefited and for the first time can hope for a brighter future. With the money from the sale of the animals and vegetables, Maria can now afford to buy books and uniforms for her children. Rosita, the oldest, not only finished high school but also will be the first in the family to attend university.

It is amazing what a small garden can do: an indigenous woman has been empowered, there is no hunger, the family diet has improved, all four children have access to education, and all this has contributed to a reduction in soil erosion and lake pollution. We can only imagine what 30,000 small gardens could accomplish.

Quilombola Dolls

"The sale of one doll pays for a bag of rice. It doesn't sound like much, but it can mean the difference between eating a decent meal and being hungry,"[44] says Bernadina Firmiana, whose face serves as an icon for the craft's trademark. Quilombolas are descendants of African slaves. Their ancestors fled slavery to found Conceição das Crioulas, now a community of around 4,000 in northeast Brazil. In the early twentieth century, white farmers took the Quilombolas' most fertile land, leaving them with little space to grow food.

In partnership with a local association, the Associação Quilombola de Conceição das Crioulas (AQCC), OXFAM is helping "the community's women develop craft products and marketing them through trade fairs and nearby shops. The community produces high quality pots, dolls, bags, and mats from caroa, a fibrous local plant."[45] OXFAM provides support by offering business

and marketing courses, providing funds for packaging, a community magazine, a website, and a brochure. In addition, after the Brazilian government
recognized the Quilombola land claims, OXFAM has supported the AQCC's
fight to reclaim their stolen land.

The choice of the Quilombola crafts has a dual purpose. Three hundred
years ago, their ancestors were cotton growers and made clothes, bags, and
tablecloths to sell. And it was with the money from their crafts that they eventually bought the lands that were taken from them. The Quilombola dolls, in
particular, tell the Quilombolas' story. Each is modeled after a woman from the
community. The doll's packaging introduces the women to the buyer and
explains the community's struggle to reclaim their land.[46]

This project embodies many of the ecofeminist categories, especially that
of interdependence between humans and the earth and how, after three centuries, women are actively reclaiming their ties to the land of their ancestors,
which they regard as sacred and priceless. The crafts provide an essential supplement to the small income the community receives from farming, but just as
importantly they represent the Quilombola culture. They contribute to keeping
the culture alive, speaking to future generations through the women and their
stories. These women have great hopes of developing their craft into a successful business. One woman eagerly exclaimed: "I wonder what it would be like if
we got a huge order. Well, you've got to be ambitious."[47] The women attribute
their progress so far to determination, and it is obvious that their determination, hope, and ambitions are driven by their history, their present context,
their links to their ancestors, and their ties to the land.

The Capabilities Approach

In the field of development economics, Amartya Sen has developed an
approach to poverty, inequality, and development that addresses many of the
concerns of ecofeminism. The touchstone of this approach is the view that
people must have the socially grounded capacity to make choices in accordance with their values. Sen refers to this as the "capabilities approach." He
takes the failure to survive (i.e., death) as a basic indicator of deprivation of
capabilities. For Sen, a purely income-based analysis of poverty leaves the
story half-told. He argues instead that poverty is the failure of basic capabilities to reach certain minimally acceptable levels. While acknowledging that
income is one important aspect of development, the capabilities approach
emphasizes "functioning" as it relates to other spheres of life, such as access
to education, health care, politics, the right to life, and avoidance of premature

death.[48] In Sen's model, the conventional criterion of GDP growth rate is no longer the ultimate test of success. Economic growth is important only to the extent that it helps eradicate deprivation and improve capabilities and the quality of life of ordinary people.

Capability has to do with what a person can or cannot do, can or cannot be. Thus, a person's well-being (what she has achieved) and a person's advantage (her potential for achievement) are crucial in any assessment of standard of living and poverty. The notions of well-being and advantage refer to a person's social agency: that is, are the social conditions in place so she can avail herself of the opportunities for a fruitful life? To speak of social agency is to speak of freedom at a very basic level. If a person is hungry, has no shelter or means of addressing her situation, then she has been stripped of *substantive* freedoms. If, in addition, she has no opportunity to use economic resources to make political choices about laws, to receive support when needed, or to question the state of affairs, then society has stripped her of the *instrumental* freedoms necessary for her to make morally responsible choices.

Maquilas *of Nicaragua*

An ecofeminist analysis of the *maquilas* of Nicaragua entails attentive and holy listening to all the parties involved, especially those most affected, the women workers. This approach reveals that there is much more to free-trade zones than a government economic policy to entice foreign companies to build factories by offering lower taxation and lower wages, in the hope of alleviating the hunger and unemployment of widows in the civil war.

I had the opportunity, in May of 2005, to experience firshand accounts from several people of varied backgrounds on the topic of *maquilas*. As I heard the reports of their involvement with *maquilas*, I asked probing questions and listened attentively to their answers, always keeping in the back of my mind the question: how would privileging the voices of poor women inform the total situation? What follows are summaries of my conversations with owners, managers, and architects of *maquilas* as well as the women who work in them.

Voices of Investors: The economist I spoke to, who is credited with bringing *maquilas* into Nicaragua, is very proud of what he has accomplished. He claims to have opened up employment for over 80,000 people who otherwise would have had no source of income. The architect I spoke with who was hired to design the *maquilas* for Levi Jeans and Gap, Inc. also spoke proudly of his project that would cover 300,000 square feet. It was to be designed in a way that allowed three working shifts per day, a total of 9,000 employees working at their stations for 8 to 10 hours a day. Another company would put down the capital for building the *maquila* and yet another company would contract directly with Levi Jeans and Gap, Inc. to organize the labor.

Everyone I spoke to at this level was extremely proud of what they were doing for the economic situation of their country. To them, it was obvious that everyone was better off. Levi Jeans and Gap, Inc. could get cheap labor, allowing them to compete in the global market. The banks received a fair return on their loans. The capitalists who financed the building of the *maquilas* would receive a good return on their investment. The architect took pride in his highly paid designs, which minimized cost and at the same time allowed for efficient manufacturing. The government economist sat back proudly surveying the foundation he had laid for economic growth in a country still trying to survive the vestiges of civil war. And all are satisfied and convinced that they have improved the lot for poor women in their country.

Voices of Women Workers: The conversation with the women workers, who asked for anonymity, revolved around their situation since the war (between the Sandinista government and the Contras) and what they did for a living. They shared that the work in the *maquilas* was hard because of its repetitious nature, the long hours, standing by machines in unbearable heat, and because permission to use the bathroom was often denied. Uppermost in their minds were their children, whose care was in the hands of their young daughters, children themselves. Those who had partners were worried about losing their jobs should they get pregnant. In exasperation, one said: "How is it possible to please your husband, obey the Church, and still retain your job?" One woman said that she worried about her ten-year-old son who tried to help by selling gum in the town square. She knows that he uses part of the money for glue—"you see he got addicted to sniffing glue to stop the hunger before, and now he can't stop." These were women who were burdened and afraid, and they made me promise not to denounce them; they did not want to appear to be complaining, because they felt lucky to work in an American *maquila*. They claimed to be much better off than their friends who worked in Korean and Taiwanese *maquilas*, where the conditions were worse. It struck me what a different picture these women were painting for me about *maquilas* compared to what I had heard from the owners and investors. In my mind, I translated their voices as saying: "Yes, it's good but it's not good."

Voice of Plant Manager: The plant manager's attitude was cautious. He was in charge of the production of bras for Victoria's Secret at a *maquila* in Masaya. He claimed he had to work long and hard hours, like the women, but that his job was to make sure the women stayed on task and met the daily productivity target. Like the women, he was pleased to be working for an American *maquila* because the salaries were higher. He said the women at his *maquila* were well paid at US$50 a week, which comes to about US$1 per hour. I asked him how much he estimated would be the cost of producing a bra from start to finish, including materials and transportation. His answer was US$5.00 for a bra that sells in the United States for around US$50.00. I was given various excuses for not being able to take a tour of his *maquila*, but I was able to visit it from the outside. I noticed that they were long barracks-like structures made out of tin with no visible windows. Since it was the rainy season, with temperatures close to 100 degrees and almost 100 percent humidity, I asked the plant manager whether they had air conditioners or fans for the women. His answer was a hearty laugh. I asked if the women had health care benefits, and the laugh was even heartier. He claimed it was unnecessary as they could all go to government medical clinics. But if they got sick, they would not be paid; if they got sick too frequently, there would be a long line of women wanting their jobs; and if they got pregnant, well, they would definitely be fired.

Who Benefits?

The justification for the existence of *maquilas*, as we have seen, is manifold. The resounding voice, even from the women, is: "The women are better off!" The question for social ethics is: in what ways are the women really better off? I posed this question to a prospective *maquila* developer who answered: "Nothing drastic has changed in their lives, they have enough for rice and beans now, which is more than they would have had otherwise!" He had just bought seventeen acres of land in San Marcos, a beautiful plantation of fertile land with oranges, plantains, and a variety of livestock. When I asked him why he would turn this fertile land into concrete blocks of factories, his honest reply was that it was the best investment available, with easy and assured profit. He was going to take advantage of the government's vision of increasing foreign investment in the country through the establishment of *maquilas*, making it profitable for foreign investors by relaxing local labor laws and profitable for domestic investors by providing easy credit. When I pushed him on the terrible conditions under which women work, his reply was that this was the concern of the middle person who negotiates with the foreign companies and had nothing to do with him. His part was only to supply the land and building and his conscience was clear. It became obvious to me at that moment that the piecing out of the various parts of *maquila* financing, construction, and administration was in itself a structural device that provided plausible deniability to the few who owned capital and who would benefit the most while the majority who labored to produce the final product continued to live from hand to mouth.

Maquilas *from the Lens of Ecofeminism and Capabilities*

The conversations presented thus far portray a complex scenario with multiple players. They give us a picture of the interdependence among the groups involved as well as the differential benefits accruing to each. At this juncture, it would be beneficial to ask whether *maquilas* pass the tests of the capabilities and ecofeminist approaches and assess the effectiveness of *maquilas* in meeting the needs of each group. Are they really the panacea for poverty reduction lauded by proponents of unfettered globalization and free trade?

Another way of asking this question is: are the poor women really better off? The answer is a definite yes, *if* the only determinant of well-being is income. However, if we assess well-being from the perspective of the capabilities approach, it cannot be said that work in the *maquilas* is something the women value doing or being, but rather what has to be endured for survival. If well-being is assessed by the ability to work in more humane conditions, the assurance that their children are safe while they work, that their jobs will not disappear because of pregnancy, then the situation in *maquilas* fails the well-being test and women are not better off. It also fails the advantage test in that these women have no other alternative but to acquiesce to the conditions imposed upon them. That is, they have no real opportunity to improve their lives. These women cannot be said to have social agency as they cannot act or bring about change according to what they value. The instrumental freedoms are not in place for them to achieve the basic capabilities they seek. If the central issue in economic development is to expand the social opportunities open to people, then *maquilas* have not met that requirement. It is one example of how inadequate it is to liberalize economic controls without first creating the social conditions necessary for economic growth to truly benefit all concerned. This insight is well known to Catholic social thought—and in the wake of the global financial crisis of 2008, even to many who used to preach "free" markets.

From the perspective of ecofeminism, any analysis of the situation begins by taking the lived context of the women as the primary and most basic reference point. This means it is not sufficient justification that *maquilas* have contributed to an increased gross domestic product, have alleviated an unemployment problem, and have increased foreign and domestic investments. The unasked questions that don't show up in the country statistics are of paramount concern to ecofeminists. Who takes care of your children when you are at work? What happens when your child is sick and you can't show up for work? Do you go to work when you are sick yourself, for fear of losing your job? How do you wrestle with pregnancy, husband, and job loss when your priest says artificial contraception is a sin and abortion is murder? How do you deal with the intense heat and long hours standing in front of a machine? What happens to you and your family if you were to lose your job? Do you have any other options? The answers to these questions would reveal an untenable situation for poor women in the *maquilas* who have no other recourse but to submit to what is demanded of them. These are questions of justice and equity. Where are the labor laws and safety nets, which are supposed to protect poor women, and why are there such disparities in benefits among owners, investors, managers, and workers?

It is obvious that only a small share of the profits derived from *maquilas* trickle down to the women workers. The women themselves were grateful to be working in an American *maquila*, since salary and working conditions were better than in Asian maquilas and they were now assured of having enough money to buy rice and beans for the family.[49] If income were the only determinant of well-being, then the women could be said to be better off. But when *maquilas* are tested against the capabilities approach, they fail the core requirements of well-being and advantage. From an ecofeminist perspective, the situation represented in the *maquilas* validates the ecofeminist critique of a society in which women's voices are excluded from consideration. It points to the nonexistence of safety nets and basic benefits for workers, the nonparticipatory nature of the work environment for women, and the nonexistence of free and sustainable agency. While the ecofeminist approach does not identify the root causes of poverty, it does provide a more holistic and comprehensive analysis of economic policies and their effectiveness, without excluding the most vulnerable members of society.

Capabilities, Ecofeminism, and Catholic Social Thought

Sen's economic development theory, ecofeminist liberation theology, and Catholic social thought employ different methods for research and analysis, but all acknowledge that wealth creation and the pursuit of social justice are inextricably linked. They recognize how inadequate it is to liberalize economic controls without first creating the social conditions necessary for economic growth to truly benefit all concerned. The conclusions of *Prosperity with a Purpose* outline the right conditions necessary for economic growth to serve God's purposes and encompass the concerns of both the capabilities approach and ecofeminist thought.

Under the right conditions, economic growth can serve God's purposes. The conditions are: that humanity is seen as one human family, with a universal bond of solidarity; that wealth creation and the pursuit of social justice are inextricably linked; that market forces encourage economic growth but are regulated in the interests of the community; that the environment is safeguarded by substantial efforts to mitigate the harm caused by pollution; that advancing prosperity leaves no one behind, not children, retired people, those who care for families, disabled people, nor any other section that is vulnerable or liable to neglect; that globally, priority is given to those whose economies are burdened by unmanageable international debt or are victims of unfair international trading conditions; and that the structures of civil society are renewed so that local communities can shape their own future.[50]

To see humanity as one human family with a universal bond of solidarity and to respect and safeguard the environment is consistent with the ecofeminist understanding of interdependence. A growing prosperity that leaves no one behind honors the plight of women in the two-thirds of the world, women who carry the greatest burden and whose voices are often not heard. The preferential option for the poor and solidarity with the poor commit us to examine what constitutes well-being, the capability to function, the achievement of substantive freedoms, and the exercise of instrumental freedoms. The principle of subsidiarity points to the central role that agency plays in economic development. Agency is the ability a person has to bring about change and to judge achievements in terms of her own values and objectives; it results in individuals effectively shaping their own destiny, thereby enabling them to make responsible social and moral choices.

The four general criteria of Catholic social thought (promoting the common good, human solidarity, the principle of subsidiarity and protecting the most vulnerable) encompass the central concerns of the capability approach in economic development and the ecofeminist approach in liberation theology. From the perspective of Christian social ethics, these criteria emerge from the radical command to love God above all and to love our neighbor as ourself. The greatest challenge facing economists and Christian ethicists may very well be designing economic policies that meet these criteria and moving individuals, communities, and governments to implement them. Even though the task is daunting, if the Church, governments, communities, theologians, and economists work together challenging and strengthening one another, the basic insight behind the True Wealth of Nations project will hold true: the economic and cultural criteria identified in the tradition of Catholic social thought will place us on an effective path to sustainable prosperity for all.

NOTES

1. World Bank, "Fighting Poverty in Pakistan," 3.
2. Noeleen Heyzer, "Preface" in *Progress of the World's Women*, 6.

3. *Maquilas* are foreign-owned assembly plants, usually for light garment and textiles, operating in free-trade zones, free from quotas, export duties, and labor laws.

4. The World Economic Forum is an independent, international organization committed to improving the state of the world by engaging leaders in partnerships to shape global, regional, and industry agendas.

5. Augusto Lopez-Claros and Saadia Zahidi, "Women's Empowerment," 1–16.

6. Ibid., 3.

7. Gender budget initiatives not only identify targeted expenditures on women, but also aim to "breakdown and identify the differentiated impact and incidence of general public revenue and expenditure on women and men ... [and] significantly contribute to overall objectives like equity, equality, efficiency, transparency, the realization of social, economic and cultural rights, and good governance" (Ibid., 3).

8. Ibid., 3.

9. Ibid., 4.

10. Ibid.

11. Ibid., 5.

12. Ibid., 5.

13. Since these variables are particularly affected by the level of poverty in a given nation, the data has been adjusted by the number of physicians available per 1000 people as an indicator of the quality of the country's health system in general.

14. This is used as an indicator of health risks among women aged fifteen to nineteen years and as an indicator of the lack of other choices available to young women.

15. Lopez-Claros and Zahidi, "Women's Empowerment," 5.

16. Ibid., 5.

17. Ibid., 6.

18. Ibid., 6.

19. UNIFEM, *Progress of the World's Women 2005*, 6.

20. Ibid.

21. Ibid.

22. Ibid., 18.

23. Maria Elena Cardera, et al. "Nafta's Impact on the Female Work Force in Mexico."

24. Between 1998 and 2004 women's share of the jobs in the maquilas fell from 63% to 54% (INEGI, Statistics of Maquiladora Export Industry).

25. Ibid.

26. Ibid. In 1997, three monthly minimum wages were needed to purchase a basic food basket. By 2000, the average household needed four times the monthly minimum wage to purchase a basic food basket.

27. Ibid.

28. Regina Sevilla Góchez, "The Role of Women, During the War and in the Postwar Period in El Salvador," 3.

29. Ibid.

30. United States Catholic Bishops, "Economic Justice For All."

31. Jorge Arturo Chaves, "On the True Wealth of Nations Project."

32. Ivone Gebara, *Out of the Depths*, 116.
33. Ivone Gebara, *Longing for Running Water*, 51.
34. Ibid., 53.
35. Ibid., 55.
36. Ibid., 61.
37. Ibid., 62.
38. Ibid., 64.
39. Ivone Gebara, *Out of the Depths*, 133.
40. Ibid., 139.
41. Ute Siebert-Cuadra, "La Persona Desde Una Perspectiva Ecofeminista: una Conversación con Ivone Gebara," 21.
42. OXFAM International, "Innovative Program in Ecuador Gets Big Results from a Small Garden."
43. Ibid.
44. OXFAM International, "Designs for Life in Brazil."
45. Ibid.
46. Ibid.
47. Ibid.
48. Douglas Hicks, "Gender, Discrimination and Capability."
49. "Having enough for rice and beans" does not mean that is all they eat. It is a local saying, which refers to meager subsistence and survival.
50. Churches Together in Britain and Ireland, *Prosperity with a Purpose*, 1.

REFERENCES

Cardero, Maria Elena, et al., "NAFTA's Impact on the Female Work Force in Mexico." UNIFEM: Mexico City, 2000.
Chaves, Jorge Arturo. "On the True Wealth of Nations Project: A Common Effort of Economics, Ethics and Theology." Paper presented at the True Wealth of Nations Conference. Los Angeles: Institute for Advanced Catholic Studies, June 2008.
Churches Together in Britain and Ireland. *Prosperity with a Purpose*. London: CTBI, 2005.
Gebara, Ivone. *Longing for Running Water: Ecofeminism and Liberation*. Minneapolis: Fortress Press, 1999.
———. *Out of the Depths: Women's Experience of Evil and Salvation*. Minneapolis: Fortress Press, 2002.
Góchez, Regina Sevilla. "The Role of Women, During the War and in the Postwar Period in El Salvador" (unpublished paper). UN Commission on Human Rights for Women, *Beijing Plus Five Platform for Action* 2000, NGO delegate, Lutheran Church of El Salvador (oral presentation and personal conversation).
Heyzer, Noeleen. *Progress of the World's Women*. New York: United Nations Development Fund for Women, 2005.
Hicks, Douglas A. "Gender, Discrimination and Capability: Insights from Amartya Sen." *Journal of Religious Ethics* 30, no. 1 (2002): 137–54.

Lopez-Claros, Augusto, and Saadia Zahidi. "Women's Empowerment: Measuring the Global Gender Gap." World Economic Forum, 2005. Online. Available: http://www/weforum.org.

"Maquilas: Preview of NAFTA." Adapted from a Maquila Solidarity Network Pamphlet, June 1995. Online. Available: http://www/web.net/~msn/5maq2.htm.

OXFAM International. "Designs for Life in Brazil," April 2005. Online. Available: http://www.oxfam.org/.Eng/programs_deve_samerica_brazil2.htm.

————. "Innovative Program in Ecuador Gets Big Results from a Small Garden," October 2005. Online. Available: http://www.oxfam.org/eng/programs_deve_samerica_ecuador2.htm.

Sanyal, Parth. "Interview with Amartya Sen." *Frontline* 22, no. 4 (February12–25, 2005). Online. Available: http://www.frontlineonnet.com/fl2203/stories/20050225005401300.htm.

Sen, Amartya. *Beyond Liberalization: Social Opportunity and Human Capability.* London: London School of Economics, 1994.

————. *Development as Freedom.* New York: Anchor Books, 1999.

Sen, Amartya, and Jean Drèze. *Economic Development and Social Opportunity.* Oxford: Oxford University Press, 1999.

Siebert-Cuadra, Ute. "La Persona Desde Una Perspectiva Ecofeminista: una Conversación con Ivone Gebara." *Con-Spirando* 17 (September 1996): 20–25.

UNIFEM. *Progress of the World's Women 2005: Women, Work and Poverty.* Chen, Vanek, Kund, Heintz, Jhabuala, and Bonner. Online. Available: http://www.unifem.org/attachments/Products/POWW2005_eng.pdf.

United States Catholic Bishops. "Economic Justice for All." Pastoral Letter on Catholic Social Teaching and the U.S. Economy. Washington, DC: U.S. Conference of Catholic Bishops, 1986.

World Bank. "Fighting Poverty in Pakistan." Online. Available: http://worldbank.org.pk.

13

Moving from Research to Action

Some Lessons and Directions (from a Catholic Social Ministry Bureaucrat)

John Carr

I am honored to be a part of this impressive initiative on this important and timely topic, but I am a little anxious. On the one hand, I am neither an ethicist nor an economist, nor am I an academic. My relation to academe is that I am a product of Catholic higher education and I pay for it for my children. On the other hand, I have spent decades trying to apply and advocate the principles of Catholic social teaching on Capitol Hill, at the White House, and in a myriad of gatherings—Catholic and otherwise—across the United States.

My own approach to the issues addressed by the True Wealth of Nations project is shaped by my service as a staff member at the U.S. Conference of Catholic Bishops, helping the bishops share and apply Catholic social teaching on a range of economic and other issues. My perspective also reflects my experience as a long-term advocate and analyst on these issues, including work with leaders in both political parties. My comments also reflect my everyday experiences as a parent, consumer, worker, and investor.

I am grateful for the opportunity to engage other perspectives and the chance to reread *Centesimus Annus*. This powerful and groundbreaking encyclical reflects its particular time and yet offers an enduring framework for thought and action. Unfortunately references to it in public discourse often come with rather selective citations and ideological analysis.

I have been asked to address "moving from research to action." The foundation for this task is not just my experience, but more important how the Church understands of the role of Catholic social teaching. As Pope John Paul II taught in *Centesimus Annus*, "As far as the Church is concerned, the social message of the Gospel must not be considered a theory, but above all else a basis and a motivation for action. Today more than ever, the Church is aware that her social message will gain credibility more immediately from the witness of actions than as a result of its internal logic and consistency."[1]

In light of this teaching, the premise and tasks of the True Wealth project are particularly important, provocative, and interesting: "The economic and cultural criteria identified in the tradition of Catholic social thought provide an effective path to sustainable prosperity for all."

And as the project has mapped out, it is critical to define, specify, and measure what is meant by:

- economic and cultural criteria
- the tradition of Catholic social thought
- effective path
- sustainable prosperity for all

This is important work, with implications that could have a significant impact on how we use and understand Catholic social teaching and how we apply it on key challenges in economic life. Based on the essays in this volume, I see the potential of the True Wealth project more clearly than I see an overall framework. Not surprisingly, it seems to me that the project needs to be more than simply the sum of the parts, and these initial parts don't yet make a whole. They represent an interesting start on a much longer journey, but just a start.

Initial Reflections and Reactions

I have been asked for my perspectives and advice based on my experiences as someone who applies and advocates the principles of Catholic social teaching on behalf of the United States Conference of Catholic Bishops. Here are some of my initial, outsider reactions:

In many ways this is very much an "insider" conversation. It includes both ethics *and* economics, but in this preliminary phase it represents a small circle of discourse and participation. Those who could most benefit from the conversation may need a form of "simultaneous translation" to really understand or participate in the discussion.

So far the discussion is focused more at "looking back" than "looking around" at contemporary realities or "looking ahead" to the future.

There is a nuanced and helpful discussion of wealth, its importance, its treatment in Catholic social thought, and its roles, responsibilities, and impact. It would be helpful to more clearly address the rights and responsibilities, related to private property and the larger and more central questions around the advantages and limitations of the market.

A central moral challenge is that so many people have too little to live a dignified life, rather than some people have too much, although these two realities are clearly related. There is a useful discussion of ways concentrations of wealth contribute to this, for example, in the essay by Andrew Yuengert. In simplistic terms, I see excessive wealth more as a spiritual issue, than as a moral one, in light of the biblical warnings about passing through the "eye of the needle." Anyone who looks at the ads in (the appropriately named) *Vanity Fair* or the *New York Times Sunday Magazine* cannot avoid a sense of scandal and outrage in a world in which half of humankind lives on less than $2 a day. Pope John Paul II's warnings on hyperconsumption seem very much needed.

I am both interested and confused by the references (in the basic True Wealth statement in the Preface) to widespread hostility to and skepticism of market economics and to the demonizing of affluent persons. This may be the case in academic circles, but not in ecclesial or policy circles with which I am familiar. I am unfamiliar with bishops and pastors who are outspoken in their criticism of market economics or who rail against the rich in their parishes or dioceses.

One major concern I have is that several of the papers seem to reflect a too-narrow definition and treatment of Catholic social tradition. This is a tradition of thought *and* action. What the Church and its members *do* exemplifies and develops what the Church *says*. The papers seem to neglect the "witness of action" that Pope John Paul II spoke about and the ways the Catholic community puts these principles into practice through institutional and individual forms of service and public action (including Catholic Relief Services, the Catholic Campaign for Human Development, Catholic health care, and Catholic Charities, to cite only official forms of Catholic action and presence).

The Catholic social tradition is not just a set of ideas and principles. It is embodied and expressed by a wide range of individuals, institutions, and movements through history and across our nation. This history includes Cardinal James Gibbons, Archbishop John Ireland, Fr. John A. Ryan, and Msgr. George Higgins, among others. In our times there are a wide variety of movements and organizations that carry out this mission: the pro-life movement, JustFaith, Pax Christi, the National Catholic Rural Life Conference,

St. Egidio, Catholic Worker, faith-based organizing, Legatus, Catholic Business networks, Woodstock Center, National Interfaith Committee for Worker Justice, as well as other significant ecumenical and interfaith action. One concrete example is the remarkable efforts of the Coalition of Immokalee Workers. This group of immigrant workers in and around Immokalee, Florida, has been funded by the Catholic Campaign for Human Development and actively supported by the local bishops and the Florida Catholic Conference, as well as many Catholic, interfaith, and secular organizations. The coalition has secured agreements with McDonalds, Burger King, and Taco Bell to provide better wages and working conditions for Florida's tomato workers.

The True Wealth project might be strengthened by greater analysis and assessment of the effort to apply the principles of Catholic social teaching to concrete situations, as well as advocacy on policies by the Holy See, national bishops' conferences, and state Catholic conferences.

The project might also benefit from greater focus on key questions involving work and workers rights, authentic human development, the concrete demands of solidarity, and care for creation.

I would also raise two additional concerns. The first is that the project has an overwhelming global focus and so far attends too little to United States realities and challenges. A project based in the United States needs to address moral dimensions of economic challenges in the United States. Second, most papers tend to be abstract. The elements of "sustainable prosperity for all" are impressively outlined in the Andrew Yuengert's essay: virtues, personal initiative, social relations, and material goods. However, it is important to remind us all that these are not simply abstractions, but matters of life and death, who moves ahead and who gets left behind, who goes hungry and lacks health care, who lives in dignity and with hope and who does not. Abstractions can drain away passion, urgency, consequences. In the end, this project and these principles are about people, not just principles, policy, and politics.

Foundations

It is essential to anchor this project in the biblical mission of Jesus Christ: "The Spirit of the Lord is upon me. The Lord has anointed me to bring Good News to the poor, liberty to captives, new sight to the blind, to set the downtrodden free" (Luke 4:18). Also important is the task outlined by Pope Benedict XVI at the White House: "The Church, for her part, wishes to contribute to building a world ever more worthy of the human person, created in the image and likeness of God (cf. Gen. 1:26–27). She is convinced that faith sheds new light on all things.... Faith also gives us the...the hope that inspires us to work for an ever more just and fraternal society."[2]

The centrality of the poor in the Church's mission and life has been made emphatically clear in the first encyclical of Pope Benedict XVI, *Deus Caritas Est*:

> Love for widows and orphans, prisoners, and the sick and needy of every kind is as essential to her as the ministry of the sacraments and preaching of the Gospel.... The church cannot neglect the service of charity anymore than she can neglect the sacraments and the word.[3] Charity must animate the entire lives of the lay faithful and therefore also their political activity, lived as "social charity."[4] The Church cannot and must not...remain on the sidelines in the fight for justice. She has to play her part through rational argument and she has to reawaken the spiritual energy without which justice...cannot prevail.[5]

This mandate and mission is carried out in economic life through a set of principles developed over time and expressed by the United States Catholic Bishops as a "Catholic Framework for Economic Life:"[6]

1. The economy exists for the person, not the person for the economy.
2. All economic life should be shaped by moral principles. Economic choices and institutions must be judged by how they protect or undermine the life and dignity of the human person, support the family, and serve the common good.
3. A fundamental moral measure of any economy is how the poor and vulnerable are faring.
4. All people have a right to life and to secure the basic necessities of life (e.g., food, clothing, shelter, education, health care, safe environment, economic security).
5. All people have the right to economic initiative, to productive work, to just wages and working conditions, as well as to organize and join unions or other associations.
6. All people, to the extent they are able, have a corresponding duty to work, a responsibility to provide for the needs of their families, and an obligation to contribute to the broader society.
7. In economic life, free markets have both clear advantages and limits; government has essential responsibilities and limitations; voluntary groups have irreplaceable roles but cannot substitute for the proper working of the market and the just policies of the state.

8. Society has a moral obligation, including governmental action where necessary, to assure opportunity, meet basic human needs, and pursue justice in economic life.

9. Workers, owners, managers, stockholders, and consumers are moral agents in economic life. By our choices, initiative, creativity, and investment, we enhance or diminish economic opportunity, community life, and social justice.

10. The global economy has moral dimensions and human consequences. Decisions on investment, trade, aid, and development should protect human life and promote human rights, especially for those most in need wherever they might live on this globe.

According to Pope John Paul II, the Catholic tradition calls for a "society of work, enterprise and participation," which "is not directed against the market, but demands that the market be appropriately controlled by the forces of society and by the state to assure that the basic needs of the whole society are satisfied."[7]

The economic context for the United States reflects a paradox. As the U.S. bishops have suggested, we live in the most powerful, productive economy on earth. In some ways that economy is pushing us forward and in other ways it is pulling us apart. We may be one nation, but we live in four different economies in which some are moving ahead and others are left behind, in which many are being squeezed and still others are in the shadows.

Moral Framework

In addressing these challenges, the Church brings a unique set of assets, including its everyday experience and institutions, global reach and local presence, and leaders and a large community of people. However, the most important assets for this effort are a way of thinking and a set of ideas. Catholic social teaching offers a consistent set of ethical principles that shape approaches and responses to economic life.

In the often ideological and polarized economic debate, perhaps the most important dimension of our ecclesial tradition is what I call "the Catholic AND," which brings together complementary ideas and values into a more coherent and integrated framework:

- Human Life *and* Dignity
- Rights *and* Responsibilities
- Family *and* Community

- Priority for Poor *and* Vulnerable
- Dignity of Work *and* Rights of Workers
- Solidarity *and* Subsidiarity
- Care for the Planet *and* People
- Common Good (which is all about *and*)

The Catholic "and" is also reflected more specifically in particular elements of Catholic teaching on economics:

- The free market has both clear advantages *and* specific limitations.
- Government also has both responsibilities *and* limitations.
- Private property is both a right *and* a responsibility.
- There is both a duty to work *and* a right to decent work, wages etc.

Another way of thinking about Catholic teaching in this area is to examine the paradoxes reflected in what I call "the Catholic BUT":

- The free market is the most efficient instrument for utilizing resources and effectively responding to needs, *but* there are many human needs that find no place on the market. It is a strict duty of justice and truth not to allow fundamental human needs to remain unsatisfied and not to allow those burdened by such needs to perish.[8]
- *Centesimus Annus* warns against *"social assistance state" but* also against "idolatry of the market."
- Private property is a right *but* has to be exercised for the common good (e.g., there is a "social mortgage" on all private property).
- Workers have a right to choose to join a union, *but* unions have a responsibility to seek the common good.
- Contracts are valid instruments, *but* some contracts are so unjust they should not be enforced (see, for example, the essay by Daniel Finn in this volume).

A Challenging Agenda

This initiative focused on "true wealth" can help define, specify, and assess what *Centesimus Annus* calls a moral and juridical framework. Economic freedom is to be "circumscribed within a strong juridical framework,"[9] and the state "has the task of determining the juridical framework within which economic affairs are to be conducted."[10] What are the moral boundaries, the ethical fundamentals within which economic actors, institutions, and markets need to function?

The True Wealth project can help specify what Pope John Paul II in *Centesimus Annus* called the "advantages…and limitations of the market." It can help identify which "human needs find no place on the market."[11] It can explore the linkages among and distinctions between solidarity and subsidiarity, helping to clarify what we can do as individuals and what we need to do together.

Like other Catholic contributions in this area, the work of the True Wealth project needs to be *authentic:* reflecting our faith, anchored in Scriptures, expressing Catholic social and moral teaching, and not a political or ideological agenda. It also needs to be *distinctive,* reflecting the perspectives of a community of faith, not an economic interest group or political faction. These efforts need to be principled without being ideological, in that they must not compromise on fundamentals, but should be open to different ways to apply those principles. They also need to be *modest,* acknowledging different roles and expertise, respecting differences on specific applications of principles and priorities.

In my experience, Catholic social teaching is more likely to shape the debate than to determine outcomes. It often offers hard questions more than easy answers. Helpfully, the True Wealth project insists that the pursuit of "sustainable prosperity for all" is a moral obligation and also acknowledges that that people of good will can and will differ on how best to achieve it.

From my perspective, the role of the Church and those who take this tradition seriously may include the following elements:

- make the case for the priority and moral urgency of "sustainable prosperity for all,"
- encourage debate on how best to pursue it,
- offer ethical criteria to help define economic choices,
- assess the moral dimensions and human consequences of alternative policies,
- insist on the participation of the poor, sometimes being a voice for the voiceless,
- contribute to discussion and advocate our principles/policies in the broader discussion.

One major institutional challenge is for the Church to practice what it preaches in economic life, including wages, working conditions, participation, and so on.

A huge challenge for all of us, but a special responsibility for academics within this project, is how to share the "secret" of Catholic teaching on economic and social life in individual and institutional ways. How is it integrated and applied in curricula and educational culture. What difference does it make if someone attends a Catholic university or college? Are our students prepared to practice everyday Christianity in their work, families, communities, and public life? Do they practice "faithful citizenship"? In the words of Pope Benedict XVI, "The church wishes to help form consciences in political life and to stimulate greater insight into the authentic requirements of justice as well as greater readiness to act accordingly, even when this might involve conflict with situations of personal interest."[12]

Will this project and our own contributions help "form consciences" and offer "greater insight" and greater "readiness to act" even against personal interest?

One of the most important potential contributions of the True Wealth project is to help build bridges and make connections. We can divide up the work, but we should not divide the Church. This important project can help bring down the walls between ethics *and* economics, theory *and* policy, research *and* advocacy, faith *and* life. At its best, it should remind us that we are all in this together. At its core, the True Wealth project should remind us that what is morally right is also economically wise.

NOTES

    1. John Paul II, *Centesimus Annus*, para. 57.

    2. Benedict XVI at the White House, April 17, 2008.

    3. Benedict XVI, *Deus Caritas Est*, para. 21.

    4. Ibid., para 29.

    5. Ibid., para 28.

    6. United States Conference of Catholic Bishops, "Catholic Framework for Economic Life."

    7. John Paul II, *Centesimus Annus*, para. 35.

    8. Ibid., para. 34.

    9. Ibid.

    10. Ibid., para. 15.

    11. Ibid., para. 34.

    12. Benedict XVI, *Deuis Caritas Est*, para. 16.

REFERENCES

Benedict XVI. Address at the White House. *Origins* 37 (May 1, 2008): 738–39.

———. *Deus Caritas Est*. *Origins* 35 (Feb 2, 2006): 541–57.

John Paul II. *Centesimus Annus*. *Origins* 21 (May 16, 1991): 1–24.

United States Conference of Catholic Bishops, "Catholic Framework for Economic Life." Online. Available: www.usccb.org/jphd/economiclife/.

Index

estate tax, 24
ethics: Catholic, 64; Christian
    social, viii, 337; Christian,
    economics and, vii; developments
    in, 15; criteria, viii; democratic
    capitalism and, 79, 159;
    development, 56; economic policies
    and, 337; principles, Christian, 77;
    Protestant, 64; theological
    social, 15; traditional, 75; versus
    economics, vii
ethnicity: clashes, in Africa, 273; gender
    gap and, 320
EU, 107: economy, 28; government, 27
EUCD: EPP and, 108; NEI and, 108
eucharist, 252
Euro, the, 108
Europe: core, 108; female employment
    in, 238; female immigrants
    from, 238; female immigrants
    to, 239; northern countries, EU
    and, 107
European Christian Democrats, 105
European Christian Trade Unions, 100
European Defense Community
    (EDC), 107
European Investment Bank. See EIB.
European Popular Party. See EPP.
European Union gender and
    employment in, 229
European Union of Christian
    Democrats. See EUCD.
evangelization, hope and, 192
evil confronted by God, 17
exchange, 243: of equivalents, 85; labor
    and, 136
Exodus (scripture), on the poor, 325
Expectations: action and, 245;
    importance of, 245;
    measuring, 244; women's, 247
extrinsicism, 168

fairness 3: courts and, 127
faith, 348: Christian, 11; Christian,
    requirements of, 313; economic life
    and, 9; lack of, 88; religious,
    human subjectivity and, 299
Fall, The (Gen. 3), 43, 44, 49
Familiaris Consortio (John Paul II),
    276

families, 40, 52, 87, 240: a-moral, 212;
    and community, 346; as an
    institution, 243; as center of
    communities, 211; as social
    capital, 201, 242; between state
    and, 208; biological dimension
    of, 242; business, 247; CD
    and, 103; Christian virtues and, 95;
    definition of, 243; determinant of
    social capital, 243; economic
    interpretations of, 299; economic
    life and, 211, 345; economic theory
    of, 240; education and, 217;
    business organizations, 212;
    family-based firms, 212; family-
    centered business, in Korea, 213;
    form, modern, 241; French, 212;
    immoral, 208; institutions and, 211;
    life, generation and, 254; new
    ventures by, 51; policies,
    national, 233; relational approach
    to, 243; role of women in, 320;
    social capital and, 206; support
    of, 160; with children, 109; woman
    as center of, 243
Fanfani, 76, 77, 79: Weber and, 77
farmers, 148
fascism, encyclicals against, 101
fathers, church, 3
federalism, U.S., 304
feelings and emotions, reason and, 329
female genital mutilation. See FGM.
Ferguson, Niall, 76
fertility rates, adolescent, 323
feudal structures, in Africa, 276
FGM, 323
Field, John, 206
Filipinos, female immigrants from, 238
financial crisis (2008), 3, 27, 28, 60, 81,
    117, 137, 280, 309, 311, 335
financial instruments, value of. 308
financial system, global, collapse of, 28
Finn, Daniel, 9, 12, 43, 68, 82, 120, 126,
    143, 347: moral ecology of markets
    and, 21
firm: family-based, 212; symbolic
    dimension of, 242; value of, 242
Firmiana, Bernadina, 330
Flanders, production in, 74
Florida Catholic Conference, 344

People of God, 17
people processes, 215
Peralta, Maria, 329
perceptions: action and, 245; importance
    of, 245; measuring, 244
performance: of duties, 203;
    substantial, 125
person, 40: abundance in creation, 19;
    centrality of the, CD and, 103;
    community, women and, 251;
    human, nature of, 39, 40;
    individual, 3; social orientation
    of, 42; the economy and, right
    to, 345; the subject of society, 41;
    whole person, 38
personal initiative, 56, 344
personhood, socially rooted, 119
personnel changes, 215
philosophies: androcentric, 327;
    anthropocentric, 327; political, viii;
    rebirth of, 67; subjective turn
    in, 165
phrònesis (wisdom, reason), 78,
    302, 308
Pieper, Joseph, 154
pilgrimages, 77
Piron, Sylvain, 68
Pius IX, 98
Pius X, 100
Pius XI, 98, 101, 154, 158
Pius XII, 100
planet and people, care for, 347
Planned Parenthood Federation of
    America, on women's health, 323
Plato: injustice and, 7; prosperity in, 39
pleasure, vi
plurality, 245: in culture, 169;
    in nation, 138
Pocock, J. G. A., 66
Poland, 100: gender gap in wages
    in, 230
Polanyi, Karl, 85, 86
polarities, human, 252
policies: economic, market arrangements
    and, 215; obsolete, 128
politics, 331: action, market culture
    and, 82; church and, 300; CST
    and, 285; empowerment, gender
    gap and, 320; in Africa, 285;
    international, family and, 52;

market and, 81; participatory and
    democratic, 219; problems, 99
pollution, vii: community and, 337
poor (people): and vulnerable, priority
    of, 347; as measure of economy,
    right to, 345; assisting the, 109;
    biblically based concern for, 143;
    Catholic action and, 99; Catholic
    tradition and, 127; central to
    church mission, right to, 345;
    commitment, 329; courage, 329;
    dependent, 6; exploitation
    of, 145; participation of, 46, 54,
    81, 348; preferential option
    for, 23; unfair provisions
    and, 129; women, untenable
    situation for, 336; women,
    freedom and, 329
population: food and, 24; growth, 74;
    urban and rural, 153
Populorum Progressio (Paul VI), 275,
    278–280
Portugal, dictatorship in, 102
possessions, 25: slaves of, 47
poverty, vi; 103: assets and, 319;
    describing, 245; elimination of, 17;
    ethics and economics of, 319;
    feminization of, 322; in Latin
    America, 327; inequality and, 53;
    international ramification of, 280;
    rates of, 53; reduction of, capitalism
    and, 166; reduction, economic
    development and, 217;
    romanticising, 19; stress and, 319;
    relief of, ix; vow of, 73; women
    and, 228
power, 253, 292: abuse of, 127;
    government, corporations and, 303;
    in Latin America, 327; kinds of, 65;
    thirst for, 254
PP. See Popularum Progressio.
pray and work, 76
predestination, 75
pregnancy: adolescent, 250; waivers
    of, 325; work and, 335
prices, products and, 247
primacy of labor, 24
principalities, 77
principles, modern social, scripture
    and, 22

Schuman, Robert, 103, 106
Schumpeter, Joseph, 68, 81, 87
science, Thomistic, 147: feminist, 174
Scitovsky, Tibor, 188
Scotland, Enlightenment in, 78
Scripture, 348: concrete economic, 17; economic life and, 13, 16; Hebrew, 3; New Testament, 3; on income, 45; precepts in, 23; preferential option for the poor, 325; social principles in, 25; to be read by all, 76; vulnerable and, 24
Second Vatican Council. *See* Vatican II.
Sécretariat International des Partis Démocratique d'Inspiration Chrétienne. *See* SIPDIC.
sector, formal or informal, women in, 248
secularism, 98, 109: interpretation of, 166, 167; today, 10
security, European, welfare and, 106
sedeq (biblical justice), 8, 144: as a quality of God, 16; as empowering divine gift, 16; as God's saving act, 16; as order in God's plans, 16; Exodus liberation and, 16; natural and moral order and, 18; restoration, postexilic and, 16; translation of, 16
segregation, racial, 131
Seko, Mobuto Sese, 277
self, entire, 329
self, development, 21, 96: gift of, 22, 26; family and, 52
self-awareness, 249
self good, isolated, 120
self support, 160
self-confidence, contagiously transmitted, 248
self-denial, unintelligible, 179
self-employed women, 248
self-government, 96
self-interest, 86, 97: Christian view of, 7; economic life and, 6
self-judgement, 97
self-monitoring, 96
self-perception, women's, 247
self-realization, gift of self and, 254
self-sufficient, law and, 120
self-understanding, human, 300
Sen, Amartya, 5, 45, 87, 244, 320: on poverty, 331, 332; on slavery, 48;

economic development theory of, 336; on women and social transformation, 321
Senegal, female immigrants from, 239
sentiments, moral, market and, 82
serfs, medieval, 148
servants, 66
services: a stream of, 155; basic, access by the poor to, 319; in-kind, 110; public action, 343
severance costs, 215
sexes, data about the, 237, 240
sexual harassment, 149
Shank, Judy, 11
shareholders: as owners, 308; democracy, 305; profits of, 306
sharing, 136, 139: Catholic tradition and, 127; resources and, 329
shelter: needs of, 278; right to, 345
Sicily, circles of trust in, 208
Siena, city of, 248
Sierra Leone: CPD per capita in, 271; economic indicators in, 269; GDP from agriculture, 272; GDP per capita in, 271; literacy in, 270; war in, 282
Sierra, civil strife in, 273
Silicon Valley, California, 212
sin, 40: as rebellion, 44; as "constriction of self," 291; in Catholic theology, 77; power and, 292; social, 292; Thomas on, 179
Singapore: economy, 210; family businesses in, 211
Singulari Nos (1834), 98
SIPDIC, 101
skill formation. *See* human capital.
skills, 214
slavery, 24, 48, 66, 70, 128, 149, 273, 276; Christian teaching and, 6; former, 330; in ancient times, 148; property of, 304; reminders of, 144
Smith, Adam, 83: on prosperity, 39; on wealth, 7; on wealth of nations and virtue, 200; Thomas and, 183, 184
sobriety, Puritanism and, 200
sociability, spontaneous, 210, 212, 215, 216
social bonds, 84
social capital, 209: benefits of, 215; caveats about, 208; civil society

women (*continued*)
    self-help groups of, 251; social
        transformation and, 321; the GDP
        and, 245, 246; True Wealth Project
        and, 319; truth about being a, 244;
        vulnerable populations, 319; wages
        of, 229; well-being of, 242, 247;
        working, treatment of, 334
womanomics, 230, 249
Woodstock Theological Center, 12, 344
work, vii, 87: anthropology of work, ix; as
        prayer, 76; as vocation, 213; at
        home, 248; Christian virtues and, 95;
        coordination of, defined, 70; dignity
        of, 24; duty and right, 347; family
        and, 52; family-owned businesses,
        248; gender gap and, 321; good, 289,
        311; in Scripture, 21; industrialization
        of, 81; leisure and, 211; meaning
        of, 80; measuring, 67; religion
        and, 63; slaves and, 66; subsidiarity
        and, 22; sufficiency and, 19; unpaid,
        FDP and, 245, 246; volunteer, 53;
        wealthy and, 6; women in low-
        income countries and, 233
workers: agricultural, 235; as moral
        agents in economic life, 346; as
        source of wealth, 313;
        codetermination of, 218;
        movements, 100; pregnant and, 333,
        334; rights and, 344; treatment
        of, 23, 50, 149; women as, 231
working conditions: Church's
        responsibility and, 348; in developed
        countries, 279; rights and, 345;
        hours and, 233
workplace property, 50
World Bank, 5, 11, 152, 280:
        development and, 215, on family,
        243; on gender inequality, 234, 239;

programs for Africa, 279; social
        capital and, 215; strategies for
        wealth creation, 201
work ethic, 208, 218: cooperative, social
        capital and, 208; work ethic, in
        wealth creation, 201; work ethic,
        Protestant, 75; Puritanism
        and, 200
world church, 275
World Economic Forum. *See* WEF.
WEF, 320
World Health Organization, on women's
        health, 323
World War II, consequences of, 107
world, measuring the quality of, 245:
        religious vision of, 104
worldview, Catholic/Thomistic, 181:
        social, 38
worship, human fulfillment and, 22
worth, transformation of, 74

Yellen, 241
Ypsilanti v. General Motors, 133, 135
Yuengert, Andrew M., xvi, 9, 13, 14, 18,
        37, 181, 182, 278, 308, 343, 344; four
        constitutive goods and, 21; on
        personal initiative, 22; on
        prosperity, 64

Zamagni, Stefano, xvii, 9, 21, 63, 119,
        130, 181, 208; civil economy and, 21;
        social capital in, 201
Zamagni, Vera Negri, xvii, 9, 40, 95. 96,
        138, 213: on worker teams, 218
Zambia: debt in, 281; literacy in, 270:
        unfair debt in, 281, 282
zero sum game, 7
Zimbabwe, state power in, 277
zoning, 24
Zurich, Congress in (1908), 100